Water Lifting Devices

A handbook for users and choosers

Water Lifting Devices

A handbook for users and choosers

Peter Fraenkel and Jeremy Thake

PRACTICAL ACTION
Publishing

Food and Agriculture
Organization of
the United Nations

IT Power

Published by Food and Agriculture Organization of the United Nations
and Intermediate Technology Publications Ltd
trading as Practical Action Publishing
Schumacher Centre for Technology and Development
Bourton on Dunsmore, Rugby,
Warwickshire CV23 9QZ, UK
www.practicalactionpublishing.org

ISBN 18-5-339538-2 (Practical Action Publishing)
ISBN 92-5-105430-4 (FAO)
ISBN 978-18-5-339538-3 (Practical Action Publishing)
ISBN 978-92-5-105430-7 (FAO)

A catalogue record for this book is available from the British Library.

Since 1974, Practical Action Publishing has published and disseminated books and information in support of international development work throughout the world. Practical Action Publishing (formerly ITDG Publishing) is a trading name of Intermediate Technology Publications Ltd (Company Reg. No. 1159018), the wholly owned publishing company of Intermediate Technology Development Group Ltd (working name Practical Action). Practical Action Publishing trades only in support of its parent charity objectives and any profits are covenanted back to Practical Action (Charity Reg. No. 247257, Group VAT Registration No. 880 9924 76).

This book has been made possible through the Knowledge and Research (KaR) Programme of the Department for International Development (DFID), under the Project Research and Dissemination of Water Lifting Techniques. The views in the book are those of the authors and not necessarily of DFID.

The designations employed and the presentation of material in this publication do not imply the expression of any opinion whatsoever on the part of the Food and Agriculture Organization of the United Nations concerning the legal status of any country, territory, city or area or of its authorities, or concerning the delimitation of its frontiers or boundaries.

The designations 'developed' and 'developing' economies are intended for statistical convenience and do not necessarily express a judgement about the stage reached by a particular country, territory or area in the development process.

The views expressed herein are those of the authors and do not necessarily represent those of the Food and Agriculture Organization of the United Nations.

Index preparation: Indexing Specialists (UK) Ltd
Typeset in Trade Gothic and Stone Serif
by S.J.I. Services
Printed by Replika Press

CONTENTS

FOREWORD

Although the Earth is largely covered by water, the acute shortage of water for humans and their livelihoods is of global proportion. More than one billion people still do not have access to safe drinking water, and almost two billion people suffer from diseases arising from contaminated water due to poor sanitation. Irrigation is essential for the basic food requirements of billions of people.

The growing world population and global climate change makes the challenges of providing adequate clean water, sanitation and food ever more pressing. Images of women walking many kilometres to collect water, sick children, and advancing deserts are now common on our television screens and in newspapers. In 2000, the international community, all 191 members of the United Nations, launched The Millennium Development Goals. These set clear and ambitious targets for 2015, for example to halve the proportion of people without access to safe drinking water, and to halve the proportion of people suffering from hunger.

This book, written by my colleagues, is a comprehensive guide to pumps and water lifting devices, the essentials for water supply and irrigation. It is an expanded update of the book originally published in 1986, and released as a second edition in 1997, and part of a continuous process of updating of the first book on the subject published by the UN Food and Agriculture Organisation in 1956. Over the years, many experts and practitioners have provided inputs and reviews for the process. The UK Department for International Development have both used the earlier editions and supported the writing of this one. This book is intended for use by planners and engineers responsible for the selection and implementation of water supply systems for drinking water and irrigation.

As well as the myriad of technical information, the book provides important observations, for example: *Contrary to popular belief, human muscular energy is not cheap…the willingness of people to spend so much time water lifting does not reflect the effectiveness of human power, but rather the poverty that deprives people of alternatives.* The authors are well experienced in the realities of everyday life in the developing world.

I hope that the timely publication of this book will contribute to meeting the targets of the Millennium Development Goals quickly and efficiently.

Bernard McNelis
Managing Director
IT Power

PREFACE

It will be clear, after reading this book, that there is a wide variety of water pumping devices, a wide variety of prime movers that can be used to drive them, and an even wider variety of combinations of the two. Most users will only have a few of the options described here available to them, but it is hoped that in describing many more this book will encourage some users to try new and possibly better methods.

The other aim of the book is to help users and planners to understand the technologies, so that they can be applied effectively and efficiently. This in itself will encourage the use of simple, small-scale technology for community water supplies and for irrigation. The hope is that an ever-increasing number of people will benefit from improved and clean water supply, and from greater food security and agricultural incomes. There is still great potential for the introduction and extension of small-scale pumping in many countries.

ACKNOWLEDGEMENTS

This book could not have been produced without the help of the UK Government's Department for International Development (DFID), who supported IT Power in the research and writing, through their Knowledge and Research (KaR) facility under the project 'The Research and Dissemination of Water Lifting Techniques'. The authors would like to thank all the DFID staff involved in this project for their support and help, particularly to Michael Snell for his comprehensive review of the draft for DFID.

The authors would also like to express their thanks to a large number of people who assisted in the preparation of this book, in particular Peter Fraenkel and Jeremy Thake's colleagues at IT Power, Lara Bertarelli, who wrote the introductory chapters and Simon Taylor and Jamie O'Nians who edited and brought the manuscript together for publication.

The following people read through all or part of the draft manuscript, making corrections and suggestions, and providing much useful information: Richard Carter, Silsoe College of Cranfield Institute of Technology; David Fulford, Energy Group, Reading University; David Hall, King's College, London; Sandy Polak, Neale Consulting Engineers Ltd; Terry Thomas, Development Technology Unit, Warwick University.

Information on various aspects of water lifting was generously provided by many others: Charles Batchelor, Institute of Hydrology, Wallingford; John Burton, Energy Group, Reading University; Simon Batchelor; Glenn Creelman, DCS Technology Development, Nepal; John Chilton, British Geological Survey; Mike Duddon, Consumer Association; Carole Harper, El Porvenir; Ray Heslop, Water Aid; Allen Inversin, NRECA; Reinhold Metzler, FAKT; Brian Skinner, WEDC, Loughborough University; Paul Sherlock, Oxfam; Don Wells, Nottingham.

While this book includes much new material, it is based on previous editions of Water-pumping Devices by Peter Fraenkel, which were supported by Food and Agriculture Organization of the United Nations. The authors are indebted to FAO for commissioning the original work and for continuing to support the publication of this revised edition.

The authors and publishers would also like to acknowledge a number of people and organizations for the use of material from which the illustrations have been drawn. From the earlier editions of the book: BYS, Nepal; Grundfos; Khan, H.R. and the Institute of Civil Engineers, London; Lysen, E. and CWD, The Netherlands; National Aeronautical Laboratory, Bangalore; Smithsonian Institute; UN Economic and Social Commission for Asia and the Pacific. For this new edition: Marlec Engineering Co. Ltd.; Simon & Sue Batchelor; WEDC; Institute of Hydrology, UK; UNDP & World Bank; El Porvenir; Agricultural College, Bapatla, India; Fluxinos S.R.L.; Robert Lambert; Industrial and Allied Sales Private Limited, India; Volanta; IRRI Philippines; Water Aid; Risø National Laboratory, Denmark; CADDET. All the new illustrations for this edition were prepared by Ethan Danielson.

1

INTRODUCTION

1.1 Scope and purpose of this book

The book provides an overview of the entire spectrum of pumps and water lifting devices for small-scale applications and a basis for comparing and choosing between them. The main purpose is to provide a comprehensive single source of practical information for decision-makers concerned with the selection, sizing and procurement of water lifting systems and their power sources for both the supply of drinking water and for small-scale lift irrigation. It is hoped that the overall beneficiaries will be end-users in rural areas of developing countries gaining more accessible, cost-effective and efficient water lifting systems as a result of better planning and procurement decisions.

The book covers both technical and non-technical aspects that should be addressed when choosing methods for water lifting. Areas covered include physical and engineering principles, irrigation scheduling, operational factors, economic and financial aspects, gender roles, community involvement, health and hygiene. A thorough discussion of the non-technical aspects that are related to water lifting techniques is, however, beyond the scope of this publication as these tend to be well documented in a range of existing material, but the publication does intend to provide a basis of understanding on the main underlying non-technical issues.

The book handles references in two ways; footnotes in the text are used to acknowledge the sources of information quoted. Many of these footnotes are technical papers that are not readily available, though they can be obtained from academic libraries if required. References that are more generally useful are given at the end of the book, where the reader will find books that expand on various topics covered in the text. This is generally less academic, and more practical, and includes details of some other resources such as videos and Internet web sites.

1.2 Importance of water and water lifting devices

Water has always been a primary human need; probably the first consideration for any community has always been the need for ready access to it. Good clean water is essential for health, and water that is near at hand and available for agriculture and industry is an important basis for development. The benefits accrued from water lifting techniques are not easily quantifiable as water is an essential element to life and ready access to it is a basic requirement for development.

Fresh water is a finite resource and competition for it is fierce. More than 97% of the earth's surface water belongs to the oceans, leaving 42 million km^3 of fresh water on the earth of which only about one million km^3 is accessible for drinking water, industry and irrigation. On average, each human being needs about 40 m^3 of water per year for drinking, cooking, washing and sanitation and about 300 m^3 of water for agriculture and food processing. The world population is expected to increase by more than 1 billion people over the next 6 years, of which the large majority of people will be residing in developing countries. Already there is a scarcity of fresh water in the world; over a billion people lack access to adequate supplies of water and close to two billion people suffer from the consequences of poor sanitation related mostly to contaminated water. This shortage is predicted to worsen as the level of water demand and consumption increases. It is widely recognized that the growing scarcity of water poses a serious threat to sustainable development. It is of crucial importance to develop sustainable ways to bring this finite resource to those that have no access to it, together with enhancing water-use efficiency and improving sanitary conditions.

1.2.1 Drinking water

Drinking water is a basic requirement to all, but especially in the rural areas of developing countries its collection and transportation is usually a time-consuming, energy sapping and a health-hazardous job.

Improved drinking water supplies especially benefits the women and children of many societies who are responsible for the collection and transportation of water used in the household. Women and young girls in rural Africa spend up to 40 billion hours per year hauling water, where anything up to a five-mile walk to collect water is normal, and where this amount of time can easily double during the dry season when water is harder to find. Waiting in line at the water source is also a time consuming task adding at times up to five hours onto the journey. It can take up to an hour for one woman to fill her water container. To avoid such long waits many women and children sleep out at night or set-off before sunrise to avoid the long queues at the water source. The International Labour Office recommends a maximum load, for women, of 25 to 30 kg, but in practice this is often exceeded. Transporting heavy containers of water commonly on the head, back or hip has severe health implications. Backache and joint pains are common and in extreme cases curved spines and pelvic deformities can result, creating complications at childbirth. Pregnant women sometimes keep on carrying water until the day they give birth. Women carrying water are frequently exposed to malnutrition, anaemia and water-related diseases (Kerr, 1990 [1]). One of the most serious effects is that children who are burdened with the collection of water and other household tasks are often not able to attend school.

It soon becomes clear that the provision of more appropriate means of transport, siting water supplies within a reasonable distance and the use of efficient water lifting devices can lessen the health problems of women and children and result in a huge saving of time that can be used for family care, other work, or for increased leisure. Aids such as animals or wheelbarrows and handcarts may be introduced to decrease the muscular efforts required. But animals must be trained, fed, watered and cared for, making it impossible for many poor families to use them [1]. It is important to note that the benefits attributed to ready access to safe drinking water are not only beneficial to women and children but to the community as a whole.

For drinking purposes water should not only be readily accessible but should be potable (i.e. uncontaminated with bacteria or other pollutants). In many areas of the world, people collect water from open, dirty, infected pools, streams or rivers. In 1991 it was estimated that water-related diseases led to around 4 million child deaths in the world, and that the provision of safe water supplies and adequate sanitation could halve infant and child mortality. Water lifting devices allow water to be taken from deeper underground sources, where it is usually pure and uncontaminated.

Great strides have already been made in the provision of clean water (Table 1.1), especially under the United Nations Water Decade of the 1980s. The objective of the Water Decade was to improve clean water supplies and sanitation facilities in the world. At the beginning of the decade 2,000 million people were without safe water, but by 1991 1.3 billion people had been given access to a safe water supply, and 750 million to improved sanitation (Whittington et al. 1994 [2]).

Table 1.1 Global access to water and sanitation [2]

Sub-sectors	Percentage of population with access to safe water and adequate sanitation	
	Water supply	Sanitation
Urban	95%	95%
Marginal urban	36%	45%
Urban total	83%	65%
Rural total	67%	22%

This was made possible at least in part by the adoption of less expensive and more sustainable technologies, particularly in rural areas [2].

An estimated 1.1 billion people are today still without clean drinking water. It is the rural and marginal urban populations that still suffer the greatest service deficiencies. To supply all these people, a significantly accelerated rate of service provision is needed if full coverage is ever to become a reality [2]. WHO and UNICEF have estimated that around 10 million handpumps (or their equivalent) will be needed.

1.2.2 Water for irrigation

Irrigation of crops is a primary route to bringing more marginal or unusable land under cultivation and to increasing yields from existing farm land. Irrigation is essential for meeting the basic food needs of billions of people in the world. In the future, the irrigated sector will have to provide the extra food needed to feed the rapidly growing populations despite an increasing water scarcity and inter-sectional competition by the domestic and industrial sectors.

Agricultural water consumption, the largest consumer of fresh water, has grown approximately six-fold to 3,250 km^3 (Rabindranath, 1993 [3]) between the years 1900 and 2000 [4]. In 1961, 10.3% of the world's land under arable and permanent crops was irrigated, by 1996 this had grown to 17.4% equivalent to 263 million ha. These trends seem set to continue. Table 1.2 provides data on land placed under irrigation practices in the different regions of the world. The majority of the land brought under irrigation

Table 1.2: Irrigated areas of the world, FAOSTAT web site http://www.fao.org/faostat

Region	Irrigated area (million ha)				Irrigated as % of total arable and permanent area	
	1961	1989	1996	2003	1996	2003
AFRICA	7.8	11.2	12.3	12.9	6	6
Egypt	2.6	2.6	3.3	3.4	100	100
Sudan	1.5	2.0	2.0	1.8	15	16
ASIA	90.2	149.1	183.3	193.9	33	34
China	30.4	45.3	49.9	54.6	37	35
India	24.7	44.9	57.0	55.8	34	33
Iran	4.7	7.0	7.3	7.6	38	41
Iraq	1.3	2.6	3.5	3.5	61	58
Pakistan	10.8	16.9	17.6	18.2	81	90
Thailand	1.6	4.2	5.0	5.0	25	28
NORTH and CENTRAL AMERICA	18.0	28.6	30.1	31.4	11	12
Mexico	3.0	5.4	6.1	6.3	22	23
SOUTH AMERICA	4.5	8.4	9.8	10.5	8	9
Argentina	1.0	1.6	1.7	1.6	6	6
EUROPE	8.3	16.4	25.1	25.2	8	8
FORMER USSR	9.4	20.7	19.4	20.9	9	10
OCEANIA	1.1	2.1	2.6	2.8	5	5
Developed World	37.0	64.9	65.0	69.13	10	11
Developing World	101.7	171.2	198.3	207.9	23	23
WORLD TOTAL	138.8	236.1	263.3	276.7	17.4	17.9

since 1961 is in countries where irrigation is already generally practised. Not many countries have significant areas of irrigated land, and the two most populous countries, China and India, have about half of the entire world's irrigated land area within their borders. These two large and crowded countries will have to increase their irrigated land still further to improve their food production, while other countries facing similar population pressures on the land will have to do tomorrow what India and China do today.

It has been estimated that overall agricultural yields will have to deliver average output increases of at least 3.5% per year (Rabindranath, 1993 [5]) to achieve global food security.

The industrial approach to agriculture in developed countries, while yielding bountiful harvests, has in most cases been accompanied by damage to the environment and impoverishment of the land. Food production per capita has since the mid-1960s risen by 7% for the world as a whole, with the greatest increases experienced in Asia, where per capita food production has grown by about 40% (Pretty, 1995 [6]). However, an additional problem encountered is that these benefits have been poorly distributed. Many people have missed out, and hunger still persists in many parts of the world. The challenge facing farmers in developing countries today, therefore, is to strike a balance between boosting yields to feed expanding populations, and adopting environmentally sustainable agricultural methods that do not deplete the natural resources needed for future decades of farming. Sustainable agriculture techniques coupled with the sustainable access to and use of water for irrigation of crops is a primary route to bringing more land under cultivation and to increasing yields from existing farm land.

Intensive irrigation of small-holdings is likely to become increasingly important and widely used during the next few decades in developing countries. This is because the majority of land-holdings, particularly in Asia and Africa are quite small; typically under 2 ha. Even in South America, where there are many large farms, the most numerous type of land-holding is under 5 ha.

Studies have shown that small land-holdings are often more productive, in terms of yield per hectare, than larger units. An Indian farm management study (World Bank, 1983 [7]), indicated that small, family-run land-holdings are consistently more productive than larger units, although they are more demanding in terms of labour inputs. A similar survey in Brazil [7], also showed better land utilization on small land-holdings; however this was achieved by applying between 5 and 22 times as much labour per hectare compared to large farms.

Small land-holdings also generally achieve better energy ratios than large ones; i.e. the ratio of energy available in the crop produced, to the energy required to produce it. Energy ratios for tropical subsistence and semi-subsistence agriculture are in the range 10 to 60 (i.e. the food product has 10 to 60 times as much energy (calorific value) as the energy input to grow it) (Leech, 1975 [8]). Mechanized large-scale commercial agriculture, which usually, but not necessarily produces a better financial return, generally has energy ratios in the range from about 4 to less than 1. Therefore, in a situation where commercial fuels will get both scarcer and more expensive, there is more scope for increasing food production through improving the productivity of small labour-intensive land-holdings which have the potential capability to produce more food from a given investment in land and energy.

Small-scale irrigation has also been shown to offer positive results in alleviating poverty. For example, the introduction of irrigation can double the labour requirements per hectare of land, and hence raise the incomes not only of the farmers but also of landless labourers. The same reference gives examples from actual surveys of the average percentage increase in income for farmers who practised irrigation compared with those who did not; examples of increases obtained were 47% in Cameroon, 75% in South Korea, 90% in Malaysia, and 98% in Uttar Pradesh, India. In the Malaysian case, the increased income for landless labourers resulting from the introduction of irrigation averaged 127%.

Finally, there is probably more scope for significantly increasing yields in the small farm sector through irrigation than with large farms. For example, the average rice yield in the poorer South and South East Asian countries is typically 2 t/ha, while in Japan, with sophisticated small-scale irrigation and land management, 6 t/ha is commonly achieved. In the 1990s, the Asian Development Bank has reported that a doubling of rice production per hectare should be possible in the region within 15 years. Obviously irrigation is not the only factor necessary to achieve such improvements, but it is perhaps one of the primary needs.

1.3 Water lifting and the environment

With population growth, the demand for water has increased profoundly, placing considerable pressures on natural water resources. In 1950 about 10–15% of the estimated accessible water was being abstracted; by the 1990s, this had risen to 35–50%; if consumption levels continue to increase at this rate, existing fresh water resources will be insufficient in some 20–40 years from now. There are huge local variations in the average abstraction, and there are many places where this problem is not 30 to 50 years away but has already arrived. Global warming is also predicted to affect the availability of water supplies. Higher temperatures and decreased precipitation are likely to reduce the quality of fresh water resources, straining the already fragile balance between water supply and demand in many

---

Irrigation offers the following important benefits. It:

- Increases land area brought under cultivation,
- Allows introduction of more valuable crops,
- Improves crop yield over rain-fed agriculture three- or four-fold,
- Allows greater cropping intensity,
- Produces improved economic security for the farmer,
- Reduces drought risk, which in turn allows the:
  - . Use of high-yield seeds
  - . Control of timing for delivery to market
  - . Control of timing for labour demand.

---

countries. Rising sea levels will often cause the intrusion of salt water into aquifers near estuaries and small islands, and the flooding of low-lying coastal areas. In addition, unsustainable and unmanaged practices of water use are reducing the availability of water available for consumption. As water resources become more constrained, water table depths get greater, distances to water sources larger, the technicalities more complex, the running costs higher and the burden on women and children greater.

A lot of natural water resources are also becoming increasingly polluted as the source of water is used for more than one purpose. Industrial discharges upriver, for example, can cause profound effects to those bathing and drinking water down river. Also the lack of latrines, or inappropriate designs of latrines, leads to faecal contamination of natural water resources. Putrefied animals are also known to accumulate in many open wells. The resource should be maintained and cleaned on a regular basis. Drawing water at the edge of the well barefoot can also be a source of contamination. Appropriate design and use should be priority areas.

The general objective when planning a water supply programme is to make certain that adequate supplies of water of good quality are maintained for the entire population, while preserving the hydrological and biological functions of ecosystems, adapting human activities within the capacity limits of nature and combating vectors of water-related diseases. Innovative technologies, including the improvement of indigenous technologies, are needed to fully utilize limited water resources and to safeguard those resources against pollution.

Rational water utilization schemes for the development of surface and underground water-supply sources have to be supported by water conservation measures.

Irrigation development may have both positive and negative impacts on the environment. To be sustainable, irrigation must avoid the negative impacts. The potentially negative environmental impacts of irrigation development may occur off-site as well as on-site. The off-site effects may take place upstream of the land to be

5

developed, as where a river is dammed for the purpose of supplying irrigation water. Another set of problems may be generated downstream of the irrigated area by the disposal of irrigation run-off containing harmful concentrations of salts, organic wastes, pathogenic organisms and agrochemical residues (Hillel, 1997 [9]). The use of chemical fertilizers, pesticides and intensive irrigation methods also have environmental costs and health inputs.

Of most direct concern are the potential on-site impacts. Irrigated lands, especially in river valleys prone to high water-table conditions, typically require drainage. Overuse of water in agriculture has led directly to the rapid increase, in recent years, of land lost to water-logging and salinity. It is thought that something of the order of 1.5 million ha are lost annually. Curing the saline and waterlogged soils requires lowering the water table below the root zone of crops, followed by leaching to remove the excess salts. Although small-scale irrigation development is less likely to cause water-logging and salination than large-scale development, the danger of land degradation should not be ignored [9].

The development of major irrigation schemes (or numerous small schemes) should be supported by environmental impact assessments identifying hydrological consequences within watersheds of inter-basin transfers, and the assessment of social impacts on peoples in river valleys.

Much of the expansion of access to drinking water and irrigation can be attributed to the increased use of engine and mains-electrified pumps. However, fluctuations in real terms in the price of petroleum (and hence of electricity), such as sharp temporary rises in the 1970s, can reduce the margin to be gained by farmers from irrigation, since food prices have generally been prevented from rising in line with energy costs. Some governments attempt to mitigate this situation by subsidizing oil and rural electricity for use in agriculture, but many of these governments are the very ones that can least afford such a policy which has exacerbated balance of payments deficits by, in effect, encouraging the greater use of oil. Despite short-term fluctuations

in oil prices, and widespread problems with the distribution of oil and electricity into remoter rural areas, conventional oil-based engine-driven power sources and mains electricity are expected to continue to increase in cost in real terms and in the longer term especially in the poorer countries. There are also major problems associated with the reliable operation and maintenance of diesel engines, and especially with the logistic problems of assuring that spare parts, lubricants and other consumables are available when needed. Mains electricity is a preferable means for energizing irrigation pumps, but the costs of grid-extension are high and the demand for electricity to meet irrigation needs is extremely peaky and hence difficult to meet for many utilities in developing countries. There is therefore a considerable incentive in most of the poorer developing countries to discourage the use of mains electricity or oil for irrigation pumping, even though there is an equally strong incentive to encourage the increase of agricultural production. As a result, there is an increasing need to find methods for energizing irrigation pumps that are independent of imported oil or centralized electricity.

Also connected with the use of fossil fuels is the hazard to the environment through its combustion end products including CO_2, NO_x and SO_x, and spillage or careless disposal. Renewable energy technologies can displace considerable levels of fossil fuels that would otherwise be used and at the same time comply with the Kyoto protocol of CO_2 reductions. However, so far as the farmer is concerned, the main advantage of renewable energy technologies is that they are less dependent on the chain of supply.

1.4 Water lifting and development

Tens of million of people in the developing countries, especially women and children, spend vast amounts of their time and energy transporting water. Human muscle power or domestic animals have been used since antiquity, and still are being used in many parts of the world, to lift and distribute water, but as will be explained later, these techniques are often extremely costly in real terms due to the low productivity that is achieved. Therefore, mechanized lift irrigation techniques are becoming increasingly important to meet growing future demand.

A global effort is underway to increase accessibility to water sources and bring safe water and adequate sanitation to everyone in need. Governments, international aid agencies, community groups and the private sector are co-operating and contributing to create a safer, healthier environment in the developing world. The progress obtained through the Water Decade of the 1980s was achieved through the collaborative efforts of governments, development agencies, and the people who had the most to gain. During the Decade some 1.35 billion people gained access to potable water, however, the goal of providing drinking water to all by 1990 could not be realized. Improving access proved difficult and complex, especially amid global climates of escalating population growth and declining resources. One of the Decade's finest accomplishments was to demonstrate how community participation, especially of women, is a key factor in the success of programmes and projects. The Decade also witnessed a breakthrough in innovative, appropriate and low-cost technologies; these made facilities more affordable for users, enabled communities to install, operate and maintain them, and transferred responsibility and ownership to communities [6].

Similarly, the UNDP-World Bank Water and Sanitation Programme is committed to its threefold strategy of working with partners to support sustainable investments, to build the capacity of governments and people to develop and maintain systems, and to exchange the knowledge cultivated in so doing. The UNDP-World Bank Water and Sanitation Programme is now operational in more than 40 countries of Africa, Asia and the Pacific, Latin America and the Caribbean and the Arab region. Most of the country work has concentrated on improving water supply and sanitation services in rural areas. In September 1990, UNDP and the Indian government developed the Global Consultation on Safe Water and Sanitation for the 1990s. The outcome was the New Delhi Statement, which sets out four principles for sustainable sector development strategies during the 1990s. These principles focus on health and environment, people and institutions, community management, and finance and technology.

Despite the actions taken by a number of large intergovernmental organizations during the 1980s water accessibility is still a problem for a large number of people; an estimated total of 1.2 billion people still remain without access to good quality potable water while another 1.7 billion have no sanitary means of disposing of human waste. In the past the majority of capital expenditure for access to drinking water and irrigation in developing countries has focused on large-scale projects, in the hope of achieving quick and massive increases in production. However, in practice many such projects soon ceased to function, because, for example, of a failure of a single cog or inexpert or uncaring operation. Lack of local resources and the difficulty of obtaining replacements or expertise from abroad, exacerbated by an underpaid and indifferent workforce deprived of incentives, often combined to delay the necessary repairs and perpetuated the failure [9].

The most urgently needed actions are to build up developing countries' capacities to plan and carry out sustainable water-related programmes and projects. Institution building and training are considered steps in the right direction. It has generally been found that water and sanitation programmes can only be successful if communities themselves become more involved in all aspects of their planning, operation and maintenance.

1.5 The choice of water lifting technique

There are many different types of human and animal powered water lifting techniques, all with various advantages and disadvantages, depending on the local conditions. While the power source or prime-mover so often attracts most interest, the correct selection of water conveyance and field distribution system can often have a greater influence on the effectiveness (technically and economically) of any irrigation system than differences between pumping power sources. In fact the use of a well-optimized and efficient water distribution system is vital when considering certain renewable energy systems where the cost is closely related to the power rating, and therefore a minimum power system needs to be selected. Similar considerations can also apply with water supplies, especially if some form of reticulation (piped distribution) is provided.

Before looking for radical new water lifting techniques, there is also much scope for improving traditional and conventional pumping and water distribution methods; for example, petroleum-fuelled engines are frequently badly matched to both the pump and the piping system used for water distribution, which can waste a considerable proportion of fuel used.

The range of options for providing power for pumping water includes some traditional technologies, such as windmills, and some entirely new technologies owing their origins to comparatively recent developments in technology, such as solar photovoltaic (solar electric) powered pumps. There are also technologies which have been widely and successfully used in just one region but which remain unknown and unused elsewhere with similar physical conditions; an example is the hydro-powered turbine pump which has been used in their tens of thousands but solely in China. There are also some interesting new (and some not so new) options which are being tried in some cases on an experimental basis, some of which may become available for general use in the near future; for example, steam pumps, Stirling engine pumps, and gasifiers for running internal combustion engines. All of these can produce pumping power from agricultural residues, fuel crops or other biomass resources and may become more important as oil becomes scarcer and more expensive.

In practice, however, offering choices is not straightforward. The selection of an appropriate water lifting technique for any given combination of physical and socio-economic condition involves complex and sometimes conflicting considerations. Cost is an important factor, but it is not the only consideration, since various other social, geographical, environmental and technical factors need to be addressed. For example, where water shortage is acute, the obvious overriding need is to raise the efficiency of water utilization. Where capital is short, the major requirement might be for a water lifting device with minimal dependence on capital investment or expensive equipment. In other cases, the deciding factor may be energy requirements, labour availability or maintenance costs [9]. It is also important to realize that it is unlikely there will be just one ideal choice; there may be many alternatives, any one that might be quite appropriate. The job of the chooser is to present the options available in relation to good irrigation practice, water availability, equipment, its reliability and cost. The farmer or community can then choose the system which he or she feels is most appropriate (Kay and Hatcho, 1992 [10]).

The success or failure of a project within a community is highly dependent on its social aspects. In such situations, for example village water supplies, a technically perfect scheme will fail if the community is not interested in it. Ideally for genuine community based projects, the community should be offered a choice of solutions to their domestic water supply and sanitation needs. Whatever technology is employed, it is essential that the users understand how it works, so that they can have the know-how and confidence to maintain and repair it [9].

2

DRINKING WATER SUPPLIES

2.1 Planning for human and livestock water supplies

The planning stage of a water supply programme is usually the key to success. Experience has shown that it is not enough just to address the technicalities as it is often the non-technical aspects that render the project a success. This section deals with the main non-technical aspects of planning drinking water supply programmes.

2.1.1 Community involvement

So far as community water supplies are concerned, the experience gained during the 1980s, through major programmes like the Water Decade and the UNDP-World Bank Water and Sanitation Programme, highlighted the need to shift towards a new flexible and innovative process approach to project design. It became clear that increased investments and focus on technology alone, while important, were not enough to sustain a project. Low-cost technologies had been refined, but systems fell idle and into disrepair because not enough attention was paid to the capacities of institutions and communities that managed and paid for them. Indeed, to ensure that the system will be used properly, and maintained for years to come, generally, requires the full involvement of the local community.

Community education and participation helps to overcome any gap that may exist between people and planners as a result of their different perceptions of community needs [1]. More specifically, community participation allows for:
- Decentralization of capacity building and empowerment of the people at the grassroots level;

- Improved sustainability of the projects through increased beneficiary commitment;
- Provision of an effective learning mechanism for better project designs in the future.

Community participation should be ensured at each stage of the project development, and this is crucial at the beginning of the planning and decision making process. Communities need to be educated on the benefits accrued from access to water supply, sanitation and hygiene. The range of technical solutions should be discussed among the community together with information about the level and costs of services. This allows for the community to decide which option is best suited for them. The community should also select a water committee to oversee the day-to-day maintenance and collection of water fees where these are charged. It should be ensured that the communities and the individuals within them are not only fully aware of the relationships between water, sanitation, hygiene and health, but also that they are motivated and given the facilities and assistance to participate in all stages of improving their own living conditions [1]. When people put much of their time, effort and savings into a scheme they will be more determined to maintain it.

Obtaining genuine community consensus, however, is not a straightforward process since poor rural communities are often far from democratic and they also tend to lack knowledge of appropriate solutions to their problems. Indeed in many cases communities have been known not to realize that they have a water supply problem despite suffering numerous water-borne diseases. The solution, therefore, no doubt involves some combination of education and consultation appropriate to the local culture.

2.1.2 Village level operation and management of maintenance

At the start of the Water Decade, lots of handpumps were installed in villages by governments and large organizations; these organizations also tried to cover maintenance centrally. It soon became apparent that there were widespread problems with this approach. Many of the handpumps that had been installed were being reported as having serious functioning problems and the organizations responsible for the maintenance were unable to respond to the high repair needs. In 1992, it was estimated that at least one in four of the rural water supplies in developing countries was out of order (Franceys et al., 1992 [11]).

In some cases the failures were caused by the use of poor pump designs which lacked the capacity to survive intensive use. The kinds of problems experienced with handpumps included:

- Poor quality of pump design and manufacture. This partly resulted from manufacturers trimming the weight (and hence the strength) of key components to make their pumps more competitively priced than those of their rivals;
- Provision of iron and steel plain bearings and journals with poor fits and large clearances that required frequent lubrication (impossible to provide in rural areas of developing countries and so leading to rapid wear);
- Great variety of pump types in use lead to difficulties in finding the right spare parts;
- Frequent use of poor quality materials, especially for pump barrels and components, in which corrosion and rapid wear caused unreliability;
- Limited record keeping and feedback from the field made it difficult to analyze the reasons for failures and to introduce remedial measures;
- Limited maintenance skills and equipment made it difficult for local people to undertake even basic overhaul operations, while lack of transport and poor communications made it difficult to summon help from a central source.

Attempts were made to overcome some of the problems by either introducing a centralized system in which a maintenance team toured around repairing and maintaining a few dozen pumps in a district (which proved ineffective and expensive in practice). The other option being advocated was a 'two tier' maintenance system, in which a central agency carried out the original installation, and provided a source of spare parts, training, transport, etc., and where local people were trained to carry out the routine repairs and maintenance. It soon became apparent that involving the user community in the maintenance was essential for the success of the project. This meant that the design of the water lifting device had to be suitable for repair by a trained caretaker or area mechanic with basic tools, and that spare parts were to be affordable and readily available to the community.

Slowly, over the past decades, the concept of a Village Level Operation, Maintenance and Management (VLOM) principle evolved. VLOM stemmed from the handpump project that was initiated by UNDP and World Bank. It sought to avoid the high cost, long response time, unreliable service and other operational difficulties in the repair of handpumps through central maintenance systems (Arlosoroff et al., 1999 [12]). Originally the concept was applied only to hardware, and pumps were specifically designed to be:

- Easily maintained by a village caretaker, requiring minimal skills and few tools;
- Suitable for in-country manufacture, primarily to ensure the availability of spare parts;
- Robust and reliable under field conditions;
- Cost-effective.

VLOM principles were well received and manufacturers either moved quickly to improve their designs or lost market share. The principle of VLOM was soon extended to incorporate management of maintenance, meaning that communities would have the choice of when to service pumps, who should service pumps, and to pay directly for those services. VLOM now forms the basis of most water and sanitation projects.

2.1.3 Gender issues

The involvement of women in water supply and sanitation programmes began to emerge as an important theme in the 1980s. Women, in some respects a subordinate group, can easily be denied an active role in development processes. The self-determination of the community may then become the self-determination of men. The gender approach means that attitudes, roles and responsibilities of women and men are taken into account, that it is recognized that both sexes do not necessarily have the same access to resources and that work, benefits and impacts may be different for both groups.

It is women who are most often the users, providers and managers of domestic water and responsible for household hygiene. Thus women are not a group only to be consulted but a group that should be fully involved in both the planning and design phases of water supply and sanitation programmes. To date the role of women has been focused primarily on providing and using water at the household and community level. While important, the contributions of women are not limited exclusively to these activities. Equally important are the significant roles women play as decision-makers, planners, managers and research scientists in making sustainable water resources development and management possible. Sadly, women's current and potential contributions in these important areas have been largely ignored.

A recent workshop 'Contribution of Women to the Planning and Management of Water Resources' in Mexico City in 1998, with the objective of analysing women's current and potential role in sustainable water resources management, started the process of developing a forum for women wherein their experiences can be exchanged and practical and operational lessons can be drawn.

2.1.4 Perceived benefits

Improvements in water supply can result in a number of substantial direct and indirect health, economic and social benefits.

An improved water supply contributes to reducing the mortality rate of children and to increasing life expectancy. Moreover, it reduces the suffering and hardship caused by water-related diseases, and results in significant benefits to individuals and to society. These benefits may include:

- Savings in medical treatment, including costs of medicines;
- Reduced loss of income and workdays to sickness, both for individuals and those responsible for caring for them;
- Increased productivity and extended lifespan (Okun and Ernst, 1987 [13]).
- Savings in travel costs and time required to obtain health care;

Many of the potential health benefits from rural water supply come from an increased use of water. There is therefore good reason for designing water points so as to encourage the maximum possible water use, particularly for hygiene.

Improved water supply produces economic benefits:

- It reduces time and hard labour required to collect and transport water, primarily for women and children thus releasing more time for education, income generation, cultivation, leisure, child care;
- It improves opportunities for keeping livestock;
- Communities with adequate water supply attract small businesses, which may reduce outmigration;
- The development process for water supply may be extended to other community projects [13].

2.1.5 Economic and financial factors

For each proposed new water supply project an analysis should be carried out to evaluate whether the community to be served (a) can afford the project, and (b) is willing to pay for the proposed level of service. The cost to be borne by the community depends on the conditions of project financing (such as interest rates and the level of capital grants and subsidies) and the level of service provided [13].

11

The ability to pay depends particularly on the economic conditions of the potential users. The ability to pay has been suggested to be about 3 to 5% of family income, although this may vary considerably depending upon the nature of the economy; a subsistence economy will afford less for water. The willingness to pay, however, is most likely influenced by the actual and perceived benefits of an improved water supply. People may have too limited understanding of the benefits of safe water to be willing to pay for an improvement of water quality alone. Convenience, reliability, and quality through a higher level of service, and public education regarding the potential benefits, are likely to increase the willingness to support a new water supply system.

The evaluation of costs of various levels of service and community information and involvement are key components in the analysis of willingness to pay for and support a new or improved water supply system. Users should be informed about the approximate costs they would have to bear given local financing conditions and the benefits accrued from various service levelsn [13].

Financial planning should ensure that sufficient funds are available at all stages of the project by considering the costs and revenues of a project. The costs the community has to meet include:

- The full (or a portion of the) capital costs which the community may have to provide at the start of the project as a down payment (often 10 to 30% of the total capital costs);
- Amortization of the remaining capital cost, debt service, and operation and maintenance [13].

The organization supporting or implementing the project will usually provide the machinery and skilled labour to drill the borehole, install the pump and construct the apron and drainage. The local community may be required to provide labour or some of the materials (such as sand and cement). The village community will then have to take responsibility for the monitoring and operation of the pump and the development of an adequate revenue collection system.

Financial costs may be reduced by grants from internal or external sources that cover part of the capital costs, or by loans with interest rates below the market rates. In cases where full cost recovery is not feasible, direct or indirect subsidies of even the operation and maintenance costs may be required to keep these costs at an affordable level. Indirect subsidies may consist of logistic and maintenance support by regional institutions below actual costs [13]. In some cases government authorities will even provide a water supply at no direct cost to the local community.

2.1.6 Hygiene and health considerations

Whilst water is the source of life, it is also often the source of disease in developing countries. More than a billion people in developing countries do not have access to safe drinking water and more than 2.5 billion are without hygienic means of personal sanitation, meaning that, because there are no alternatives, villagers have to consume surface water either from rivers or rain-fed ponds. The result is a horrifying toll in death and debilitating disease that particularly affects children. Every day, around 25,000 children die as a result of dirty water in the developing world. Diarrhoea *per se* kills each year about 4 million children below the age of five and an estimated 132,000 households are faced with excess fluoride, arsenic, salinity or iron in drinking water (Chatterjee, 1997 [14]). The deaths, suffering and financial losses caused by sanitation-related diseases cry out for the urgent promotion of sanitation at all levels.

Women and children collecting water from certain environments are in most cases exposed to water-related diseases. Waterborne diseases include typhoid, cholera, hepatitis, guinea worm and schistosomiasis (bilharzia). Other diseases include those that are transmitted between people and include scabies, trachoma, dysentery, and hookworm, and those that are transmitted to humans by insects that breed in or live in water and include sleeping sickness, yellow fever and malaria. Prevention of these diseases requires a clean water supply; improved hygiene, which is made possible by the availability of water for frequent washing; the enclosure or removal of stagnant water sources; improved water points; and a good drainage system for waste water.

Heading the list of human impacts on water quality is faecal contamination. Taking Africa as a whole, only 25% of the rural population have appropriate sanitation. In urban areas less than 12% of the population is connected to a sewerage system. As a result, the quality of water resources can be adversely affected. In the Democratic Republic of the Congo for example virtually all shallow wells appear to be faecally contaminated. Contamination of the water supply point also often occurs from handling dirty containers, seepage of dirty water from the surface, rubbish falling down the well or the introduction of extraneous matter during collection and transportation. Even where handpumps are fitted over a borehole or well, contamination can seep into the water supply. Some experiments done in Africa where tracer bacteria were put around a borehole showed that they made their way into the pumped water in just 1 to 2 hours (Walling, 1984 [15]). Dirty water percolates down through the surrounding ground, but it also goes into cracks in the concrete borehole cover, and through gaps between the apron and the ground. It is very important, therefore, to fit the pump on a slightly raised piece of ground, not in a hollow, to provide a well-finished, concrete apron, and to ensure that wastewater drains away from the handpump. Ideally, aprons should be 3 m in diameter, and the run-off should be taken 6–10 m away in a concrete or cemented channel. Such measures will reduce infections, but are also found to improve the taste and the clarity of the water (Morgan, 1990 [16]). In addition a watertight seal of clay, concrete or bentonite should be fitted into the gap between the hole and the lining for at least 1 to 2 m below the ground to stop leakage into the water at the bottom. The lining should extend 150–300 mm

above the ground so that wastewater cannot drain back into it, with the apron built up around it.

It is of paramount importance that a water-supply system is able to deliver water that is safe to drink. Basic requirements have to be met to ensure the bacterial and chemical quality of the water, the quantities available, the convenience of the source, and reliability of the supply. Drinking water should be free of pathogenic bacteria and viruses as well as of protozoa and helminths (a parasitic worm). There are three main types of intervention employed to safeguard drinking-water quality:

- Protection of water sources from direct faecal contamination and from secondary pollution caused by leaching from pit latrines, septic tanks, cesspools etc. by positioning them sufficiently far from water supply points. Because water from small-community installations is often not chlorinated, source protection is the first and most important means of providing hygienic drinking water;
- Treatment of water sources prior to supply to make the water potable, for example the treatment of surface waters from rivers, canals or reservoirs by the removal of suspended matter and pathogenic organisms (for example through the use of a slow sand filter);
- Health education to guarantee proper use and maintenance of the facilities is mandatory to any water supply and sanitation programme. Consumers must be made aware of the links between water and health. The use of safe water supplies has to be explained to prevent people reverting to water of questionable micro-biological quality.

Where the existing infrastructure and resources permit, national drinking water standards should be formulated to support countrywide improvement of drinking water quality. The implementation of such standards must be accompanied by practical and feasible surveillance, and with the provisions and means to take remedial action when required. However, securing safe drinking water for small populations scattered over a large geographical area poses tremendous logical problems for which standards or guideline values can at best provide a reference point.

2.2 Water requirements for humans and livestock

2.2.1 Human water supplies

The global annual aggregate of abstractions of water from rivers, lakes and aquifers was about 1,360 km³ in 1950, 4,750 km³ in 1996, and reached 5,200 km³ per year in the year 2000. There is no sign to show that any countervailing constraint will be operating to moderate the rise of water consumption. However, growth in demand for water is in fact not a bad thing as, if water availability falls below 1,000 m³ per capita per year (water scarcity), health, economic development and human well-being can be expected to be hampered.

In order to design a community water supply, some estimation has to be made of the requirement. A WHO survey showed that the average per capita water consumption in developing countries varies widely. Villagers who have to fetch water from some distance away may use very small amounts of water at home, perhaps 5 litres per person per day. Where water is carried by hand from a village handpump to the house the demand will probably not exceed 18 litres per person per day, but once the water is piped to each house this figure will rise quickly. With a single tap the quantity may go up to 45 litres per person per day but with a fully piped system with bathroom and toilet, the quantity will almost certainly exceed 225 litres per person per day. The loss of water through faulty jointing of the pipelines and poor plumbing can easily be 25% per cent of the total demand (Mann and Williamson, 1982 [17]).

A minimum provision for a water supply system would be 10 litres per person per day (in many parts of Africa 10 litres per person per day is regarded as an acceptable and realistic quantity for rural areas), but a more realistic amount is 20–25 litres. In drought conditions many people survive near the biological minimum of just 2 litres of water per day. If only a small amount of clean water is available, the usage will be restricted to basic needs for drinking and cooking, and villagers will walk to rivers or springs to wash clothes and bathe. If more water is available, the standpipe will be used for laundry and bathing. Making allowance for all these needs, plus a small amount for livestock, the WHO has set a target of 45 litres per person per day for developing countries. Seasonal changes in per capita consumption (for both people and animals) may be about 15% either side of the mean, with the maximum being in the dry season. Extra provision needs to be made for any schools, health posts, or offices that will use the water.

For example, a continuously flowing standpipe with a standard flow of around 13.5 l/min. would serve a community of 200–300 persons (Jordan, 1996 [18]).

2.2.2 Livestock water supplies

The drinking water requirements of livestock vary according to species and the environment in which they are kept. It is estimated that the current global livestock drinking water requirement is about 60 billion litres per day and based on livestock population growth estimates, this daily requirement is predicted to increase by 0.4 billion litres per annum in the foreseeable future.

Table 2.1 shows typical per capita daily water requirements for a range of livestock. It is important to note that water supplies should be

Table 2.1: Water requirements for a range of livestock (from Meel and Smulders, 1989 [19] and others)

Animal	Daily requirement per head (litres/day)
Horses	30–50
Dairy cattle	70–100
Other cattle	20–40
Pigs	3–6
Sheep and goat	1–5
Poultry	0.1–0.3

provided near enough to fresh grazing for browsing livestock thus avoiding the long distances that most livestock have to cover to reach a water supply and a new fresh grazing patch. Small, reliable and well distributed water supplies are therefore needed to allow for efficient grazing.

WATER LIFTING FOR SMALL-SCALE IRRIGATION

3.1 Water management

Sustainability of food production increasingly depends on sound and efficient water use and conservation practices consisting primarily of irrigation development and management. Agriculture must not only provide sufficient food for growing populations, but also conserve water for other uses.

Irrigation development requires careful design, construction and management to be successful. Properly applied, a new irrigation method can raise yields while minimizing waste (by runoff, evaporation and excessive seepage), reducing drainage requirements and promoting the integration of irrigation with concurrent operations. Poor irrigation wastes precious water and energy, depletes or pollutes water

resources, fails to produce good crops and/or poses the danger of soil degradation. Irrigation methods have been well documented and for further reading the following references may be used: Kay and Hatcho, 1992 [10], Brouwer et al., 1989 [20], Hillel, 1997 [9], Snellen, 1996 [21] and Bosch et al., 1992 [22] give a more detailed treatment of this subject.

Wasteful practices of water use are in most cases caused by the unmeasured and generally excessive application of water to land. It is a universal fallacy that if a little of something is good, then more must be better. In irrigation, just enough is best, and by this it is meant a controlled quantity of water that is sufficient to meet the requirements of the crop and to prevent accumulation of salts in the soil, no less and certainly no more. The application of too little

---

Ways to improve water-use efficiency

Conservation of water

- Reduce conveyance losses by lining channels or, preferably, by the use of closed pipes or conduits.
- Reduce direct evaporation during irrigation by avoiding mid-day sprinkling. Minimize foliar interception by under-canopy, rather than by overhead sprinkling.
- Reduce runoff and percolation losses due to over-irrigation.
- Reduce evaporation from bare soil by mulching and by keeping the inter-row strips dry.
- Reduce transpiration by weeds, keeping the inter-row strips dry and applying weed control measures where needed.

Enhancement of crop growth

- Select most suitable and marketable crops for the region.

- Use optimal timing for planting and harvesting.
- Use optimal tillage (avoid excessive cultivation).
- Use appropriate insect, parasite and disease control.
- Apply manures and green manures where possible and fertilize effectively (preferably by injecting the necessary nutrients into the irrigation water).
- Practice soil conservation for long-term sustainability.
- Avoid progressive salinization by monitoring water-table elevation and early signs of salt accumulation, and by appropriate drainage.
- Irrigate at high frequency and in the exact amounts needed to prevent water deficits, taking into account of weather conditions and crop growth stage.

water is an obvious waste, as it fails to produce the desired benefit. Extensive flooding of the land is, however, likely to be still more harmful, as it tends to saturate the soil for too long, inhibit aeration, leach nutrients, induce greater evaporation and salinization, and ultimately raise the water-table to a level that suppresses normal root and microbial activity and that can only be drained and leached at great expense. Apart from wasting water, excessive irrigation contributes to its own demise by the twin scourges of water-logging and soil salinization. Instead of achieving its full potential to increase and stabilize food production, irrigation in such cases is in danger of becoming unsustainable.

3.2 Outline of principles of small-scale irrigation

A wide spectrum of High-frequency, Efficient, Low-volume, Partial-area, Farm-Unit, Low-cost (HELPFUL) irrigation options exist that are consistent with the principles of sustainable irrigation development [9].

HELPFUL irrigation methods can be divided into two broad categories: first, above-ground application methods, and second, below-ground application methods. These include a range of possibilities. At one end, systems of water conveyance, distribution and application that can be fabricated entirely locally, of a sort that even small-scale subsistence farmers can adopt them and be self-sufficient in their maintenance. At the intermediate levels are systems based in part on manufactured components, preferably of a type that can be fabricated by workshops or factories within each country or region [9].

3.2.1 Above-ground application methods

These include the steady or intermittent supply of water to a fraction of the soil surface which is usually done by delivering the water in closed conduits to specific points, located and spaced in accordance with the configuration of the crop to be grown. At these points, the water is released at a rate that, ideally, does not exceed the soils infiltrability, so the water penetrates into

---

Small-scale irrigation methods

Methods based entirely on local materials and workmanship
- Low-fired porous ceramic pots are placed on the surface or embedded in the soil within the root zone. When filled with water and dissolved fertilizers, their permeable clay receptacles ooze water and nutrients into the soil.
- Sectioned ceramic pipes constitute line sources that feed elongated beds.

Methods based on imported components*
- Manufactured drip emitters and micro-sprayer assemblies are carefully supervised and maintained.
- Ancillary equipment such as screen and media filters, metering valves, pressure regulators and fertilizer injectors are used in various combinations.

---
*These options will be justified only for cash crops in a stable market economy.

Methods based on imported materials but local fabrication
- Moulded plastic pipes or extruded plastic tubing are perforated manually and lain over the ground to stimulate drip irrigation.
- Vertical sections of plastic pipes (or even discarded plastic containers such as bottles) are embedded in the ground.
- Thin-walled plastic vessels are filled with sand or gravel to provide mechanical resistance to crushing.
- Slit plastic sleeves cover the perforated sections of the tubes to prevent root penetration into the outlet holes.
- Sand filters prevent suspended particles or algae from clogging the outlets.
- Auxiliary containers are used to dissolve and inject fertilizer into the irrigation water.
- Vertical stand pipes are used to deliver water from an underground pipe to small basins.

the root zone without any of it either ponding or flowing over the surface.

Closed-conduit (piped) irrigation distribution systems are generally capable of saving water by increasing the uniformity of application and by avoiding losses of both quantity (resulting from seepage and evaporation) and quality (resulting from contamination of water in open channels). Piped systems tend to be costly and they also require pressurization that in turn demands more pumping energy. Therefore although water is saved this is often at the expense of increased energy consumption and capital investment. Methods are needed, therefore, that minimize those capital and energy costs.

The most common methods of irrigation used on small-scale land holdings are surface, sprinkler, and trickle and drip irrigation. Table 3.1 illustrates the efficiency of these three different irrigation methods.

Surface irrigation is the most common method used on small schemes. Basin, border and furrow irrigation are all surface irrigation methods. The choice of surface method depends on crop, cultivation practices, soils and topography, and farmer preferences. Basins are flat areas of land, surrounded by low bunds that prevent water from flowing into adjacent fields. Basin irrigation is commonly used for rice grown on flat lands or in terraces on hillsides. In general the basin method is suitable for crops that are unaffected by standing in water for long periods (e.g. 12 to 24 hours).

Sprinkler irrigation involves distributing water in pipes under pressure and through a series of nozzles. Water is sprayed into the air so that it breaks up into small droplets and falls to the ground like natural rainfall. Each nozzle can water an area of several square metres. The

pressure requirements are in the order of 1 to 2 atmospheres. The disadvantages include: (a) an increased level of evaporation; and (b) because of wetting the foliage, the use of brackish water can lead to an increased incidence of fungal diseases.

Trickle irrigation or drip irrigation is the slow localized application of water, literally drop by drop at a point or grid of points on the soil surface. Water is applied at a controlled rate (ranging from 1 to 10 litres per hour per emitter) close to the plants so that only the part of the soil volume in which the roots develop is wetted. Water is delivered to the drip points via a set of plastic tubes, generally weathering-resistant. The operating water pressure is usually in the range of 0.5 to 2.5 atmospheres meaning that the energy required to operate it is less than a sprinkler irrigation system and in some cases less than basin irrigation. With drip irrigation, it is possible to use somewhat brackish water (e.g. with a salt concentration of about 1,000 to 2000 mg/l) for the irrigation of crops such as cotton, sugar beet, tomatoes or dates that are not too sensitive to salinity. The brackish irrigation water does not come into direct contact with the foliage, which is therefore not prone to salt-scorching as in sprinkle irrigation.

A more simple technology to those described above is the use of hosepipe irrigation, Fig. 3.1. This method although more labour intensive is simple, not costly and at the same time effective.

3.2.2 Below-ground application methods

With below-ground irrigation, water is applied directly to the root zone. This can be through using proprietary distribution systems, often made from plastic pipe, or it can be done using simple improvized systems based on porous or perforated receptacles that are embedded in the soil to a depth ranging from 10 to 50 cm, with their openings protruding above the soil surface. These receptacles, which are filled with water periodically or kept filled continuously, exude the water through their permeable walls into the

Table 3.1: Typical field application efficiencies for irrigation methods [10]

Irrigation method	Efficiency (%)
Surface	60%
Sprinkler	75%
Trickle and drip	90%

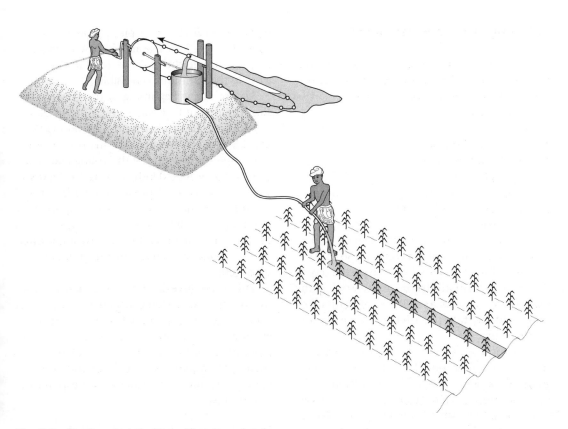

Fig. 3.1: Small-scale irrigation with a hosepipe from a rope and washer pump

surrounding soil. The moisture applied in this manner feeds the roots of the crop. The rate of infiltration and the distribution of the moisture within the root zone also depends on the properties of the soil itself. In principle, this type of irrigation can provide water steadily, as long as the receptacles contain water. The frequency with which they must be refilled depends on their capacity as well as on the rate water percolates into the soil. If the applied water contains particulate matter (suspended sediment, either mineral or organic) or if it contains perceptible chemicals (such as calcium salts), these may eventually clog the pores of the receptacles. Algal or bacterial growth may also cause clogging. The remedy is to flush out the receptacles periodically with an acidic or fungicidal solution, and to replace them after some time. The exposed openings of the soil embedded porous jars

may attract thirsty land animals as well as birds, and these may in turn damage the crop. For this reason, as well as to prevent clods of soil from falling into the jars and reducing their effective volumes, irrigators should cover the tops of the jars between watering. This can be done by simply placing a stone over each jar.

It is also possible to use perforated or porous buried pipes as an alternative method under-soil irrigation, Fig. 3.2. The porous pipe method spreads water in a continuous strip along a row of plants, so it is more suitable for closely spaced row crops grown in beds, such as vegetable crops, or for seedling trees for example. To allow water entry the pipe is bent at one end and the orifice is made to protrude above the ground . Other below ground irrigation methods include the perforated plastic sleeves, and the below-ground drip that are well documented.

3.3 Irrigation water requirements

The estimation of how much and how often water is required for irrigation depends on numerous factors, the most important being:

- nature of crop
- crop growth cycle
- climatic conditions
- type and condition of soil
- topography
- conveyance efficiency
- field application efficiency
- water quality
- effectiveness of water management.

Few of these factors remain constant, so that the quantity of water required will vary from day to day, and particularly from one season to the next. The selection of a small-scale irrigation system needs to take all of the above factors into account.

The crop takes its water from moisture held in the soil in the root zone. The soil therefore effectively acts as a water storage for the plants. The soil moisture needs replenishing before the moisture level falls to what is known as the 'Permanent Wilting Point' where irreversible damage to the crop can occur. The maximum capacity of the soil for water is when the soil is 'saturated', although certain crops do not tolerate water-logged soil and in any case this can be a wasteful use of water. In all cases there is an optimum soil moisture level at which plant growth is maximized (see Fig. 3.3). The art of efficient irrigation is to try to keep the moisture level in the soil as close to the optimum as possible.

Ideally, at the beginning of the growing season, the amount of water given per irrigation application, also called the irrigation depth, is small and given frequently. This is due to the low evapotranspiration of the young plants and their shallow root depth. During the mid-season, the irrigation depth should be larger and given less frequently due to high evapotranspiration and maximum root depth. Thus, ideally, the irrigation depth and/or the irrigation interval (or frequency) vary with the crop development [20].

The evaporative demand is a variable imposed by weather conditions, which fluctuate over time. It can be determined by monitoring relevant weather variables (e.g. temperature, wind, atmospheric humidity and solar radiation) and then applying any of several functional equations or formulae to calculate the potential evapotranspiration.

3.4 Net irrigation requirement

The estimation of irrigation water requirement starts with the water needs of the crop. First the 'Reference Crop Evapotranspiration' ET_0 is determined; this is a standardized rate of

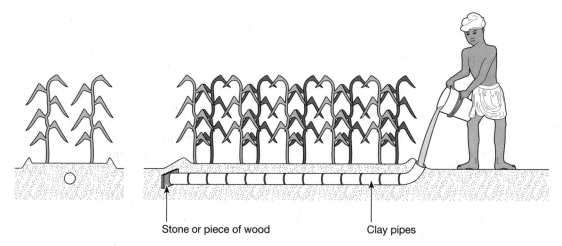

Stone or piece of wood   Clay pipes

Fig. 3.2: Sub-surface irrigation using clay pipes to avoid evaporation losses [23]

evapotranspiration (related to a reference crop of tall green grass completely shading the ground and not short of water) which provides a baseline and which depends on climatic factors including pan evaporation data and wind speed. A full description on the determination of ET_0 is presented in reference (Doorendos and Pruitt, 1977 [24]). Because ET_0 depends on climatic factors, it varies from month to month, often by a factor of 2 or more. The evapotranspiration of a particular crop (ET_{CROP}) will of course be different from that of the reference crop, and this is determined from the relationship:

$$ET_{CROP} = ET_0 \cdot K_c$$

K_c is a 'crop coefficient' which depends on the type of crop, its stage of growth, the growing season and the prevailing climatic conditions. It can vary typically from around 0.3 during initial growth to around 1.0 (or a bit over 1.0) during the mid-season maximum rate of growth period; Fig. 3.4 shows an example. Therefore the actual value of the crop water requirement, ET_{CROP}, usually varies considerably through the growing season.

The actual net irrigation requirement at any time is the crop evapotranspiration demand, minus any contributions from rainfall, groundwater or stored moisture in the soil. Since not all rainfall will reach the plant roots, because a proportion will be lost through run-off, deep percolation and evaporation, the rainfall is factored to arrive at a figure for 'effective rainfall'. Also, some crops require water for soil preparation, particularly for example, rice, and this need has to be allowed for in addition to the net irrigation requirement.

To give an idea of what these translate into in terms of actual water requirements, an approximate 'typical' net irrigation requirement under tropical conditions with a reasonably efficient irrigation system and good water management is 4,000 m³/ha per crop, but under less favourable conditions as much as 13,000 m³/ha per crop can be needed. This is equal to 400–1,300 mm of water per crop respectively. Since typical growing cycles are in the range of 100–150 days in the tropics, the average daily requirement will therefore be in the 30–130 m³/ha range (3–13 mm/day). Because the water demand varies through the growing season, the peak requirement can be more than double the average, implying that a net peak output of 50–200 m³/ha will generally be required (which gives an indication of the capacity of pumping system needed for a given area of field).

3.5 Gross irrigation requirement

The output from the pump or water lifting device has to be increased to allow for conveyance and field losses; this amount is the gross irrigation requirement. Conveyance efficiencies range from 50–60% for poorly managed surface irrigation to 80–90% for well-managed, large schemes. Typical distribution system and application efficiencies are given in Table 3.2 and Table 3.3, from which it can be seen that 'farm ditch efficiency' or field application efficiency will typically be 55–90%. Therefore, the overall irrigation system efficiency, after the discharge from the water lifting device, will be the product of these two; typically 30–80%. This implies a gross irrigation water requirement at best about 25% greater than the net requirement for the crop, and at worst 300% or more.

The previous 'typical peak net irrigation' figures of 50–200 m³/day/ha imply 'peak gross irrigation' requirements of 60–600 m³/day; a wide variation due to compounding so many variable parameters. Clearly there is often much scope for conservation of pumping energy by improving the water distribution efficiency; investment in a better conveyance and field distribution system will frequently pay back faster than investment in improved pumping capacity and will achieve the same benefits. Certainly costly pumping systems should generally only be considered in conjunction with efficient conveyance and field distribution techniques. The only real justification for extravagant water losses is where pumping costs are low and water distribution equipment is expensive.

21

Table 3.2: Average farm ditch conveyance efficiencies [24]

Irrigation method	Method of water delivery	Soil type and ditch condition	Block size (ha)	Efficiency (%)
Basin rice cultivation	Continuous	Unlined: clay to heavy clay	up to 3	90%
		Lined or piped		
Surface irrigation	Rotational or intermittent	Unlined: clay to heavy clay	<20	80%
		Lined or piped	> 20	90%
	Rotational or intermittent	Unlined: silt clay	<20	60–70%
		Lined or piped	> 20	80%
	Rotational or intermittent	Unlined: sand, loam	<20	55%
		Lined or piped	> 20	65%

Table 3.3: Average application efficiencies [24]

Irrigation method	Method of delivery	Irrigated area (ha)	Depth of application (mm)	Efficiency (%)
Basin	Continuous	Clay	>60	40–50%
Furrow	Intermittent	Light soil	>60	60%
Border	Intermittent	Light soil	>60	60%
Basin	Intermittent	All soil	>60	60%
Sprinkler	Intermittent	Sand, loam	<60	70%

Table 3.4: Average intake rates of water for different soils, and the corresponding stream size

Soil texture	Intake rate (mm/h) and range		Stream size (l/s/ha)
Sand	50	(25–250)	140
Sandy loam	25	(15–75)	70
Loam	12.5	(8–20)	35
Clay loam	8	(2.5–5)	7
Silty clay	2.5	(0.03–5)	7
Clay	5	(1–15)	14

The importance of optimizing the soil moisture content in order to obtain maximum crop growth rates is illustrated by Fig. 3.3.

3.6 Pumping requirement

It follows from all this that in order to specify a water lifting system the following basic information is needed:

• the average water demand through the growing season;
• the peak daily water demand (which generally will occur when the crop coefficient and rate of plant growth are at their peak).

Having determined the daily application required by the plants, a further consideration is the 'intake rate' as different soil types absorb water at different rates (see Table 3.4). Too rapid a rate of

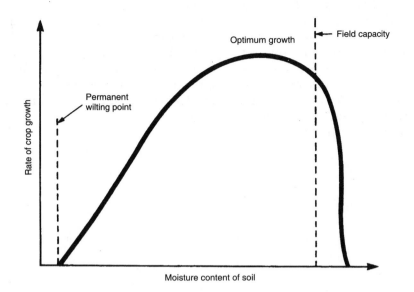

Fig. 3.3: Rate of crop growth as a function of soil moisture content

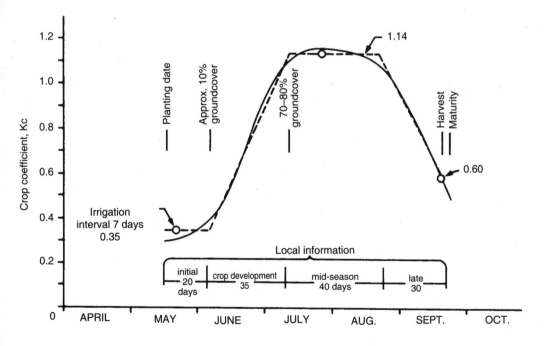

Fig. 3.4: An example of the crop coefficient curve for corn planted mid-May at Cairo, Egypt: e.g. the initial stage is 8.4 mm/d with irrigation frequency of seven days

application on some soils can cause flooding and possible loss of water through run-off. This constraint determines the maximum flow rate that can usefully be absorbed by the field distribution system. For example, some silty clay soils can only take about 7 l/s per hectare, but in contrast sandy soils do not impose a serious constraint as they can often usefully absorb over 100 l/s per hectare. Obviously lower rates than the maximum are acceptable, although the application efficiency is likely to be best at a reasonably high rate in most cases, and farmers obviously will prefer not to take longer than necessary to complete the job.

Taking account of the above constraint on flow rate, it is then possible to calculate how many hours per day the field will require irrigating, for example by using the nomogram given in Fig. 5.12.

4

WATER SOURCES

All natural fresh water originally comes from rain. Some of this runs off along the surface in streams and rivers, but the majority percolates into the ground. It seeps into the top layers, which are usually an 'overburden' made of broken, weathered rock, soil and organic matter. Underneath this overburden are layers of fractured, porous and decomposing rock, which again allow water to enter them. The water-bearing layers are called the 'aquifer'. Beneath the porous rock is everywhere an impermeable 'bedrock': this is either rock that has solidified from a molten state, or other rock that has been made impermeable by the tremendous heat and pressures within the earth. When the water meets this bedrock, it can go no further, so it collects and starts to move sideways within the aquifer. When everything settles down to equilibrium, there is a layer of completely saturated rock over the bedrock, and the level of the top of the saturated rock is called the 'water table'. Above this, the pores in the rock contain a mixture of air and water. Although vast amounts of fresh water are stored in the world's lakes and rivers, 97% of the earth's fresh water is held in this way as groundwater.

In some areas, notably on mountains, the bedrock may be at the surface, and there are no water-bearing layers. Any rain runs straight off down the mountains as streams. In other areas, the water table may reach ground level, and this gives rise to springs, rivers and lakes. In most places, the water table will be below ground. It may be just below the surface or a thousand metres or more down, but often it is within 100 m of the surface.

The following sections look at choosing a water source, checking that its quality is acceptable, and possible treatments for water that is not up to requirement. There are also brief

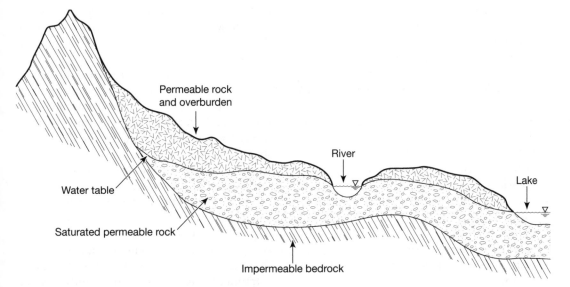

Fig. 4.1: Diagram of the water table in a typical geology

discussions of water storage (for when a supply does not match the need) and of distribution systems.

4.1 Choosing a water source

Water for irrigation may be drawn from surface water sources, such as lakes, rivers, or streams. Such sources are generally good enough for irrigation, where water quality is not too important. Obviously the water should be reasonably free of faecal pollution or harmful chemicals, but a certain amount of organic dirt or silt may actually be beneficial for the plants.

The requirements for drinking water are more stringent, as the water must be sterile and free of toxic minerals or pollutants, as well as having an acceptable taste. Fortunately, groundwater generally meets these requirements. Springs coming out of the ground, and wells and boreholes that tap into the 'aquifer', or water-bearing layer, can therefore be a supply of pure, potable water. Where it can be extracted with reasonable ease, groundwater is generally preferable to surface water for community water supply. In certain areas where groundwater is made undrinkable by contamination with iron, manganese, salt or other minerals, water from streams or lakes may have to be used.

There are a number of considerations to be taken into account when considering possible sources for a water project:

- reliability: water is a critical commodity for humans, animals, and crops, and there must be sufficient water available from the source when it is needed;
- water quality: this needs to be adequate for the required usage, unless water treatment is to be used (see Section 4.4);
- technical feasibility: how easy is it to extract the water from the source;
- transportation: how far will the water need to be taken, and what distribution system will be used;
- convenience for the users;
- costs, both of developing the source and maintaining it.

It is possible that certain sources may be useful for certain periods of the year, but other sources need to be used at other times. A spring may provide the best quality drinking water for a village, but it may dry up for many months a year, when a borehole or well may be required.

4.1.1 Surface water

Surface water is found in lakes, ponds, rivers and streams. By definition, such water is above ground, can be seen, is easy to find, and is generally accessible. The disadvantage of surface water is usually its quality, because it is open to contamination. It carries soil particles in suspension in it; this is obvious in a river that has been turned brown by a monsoon flood, but even clear-looking streams can carry a considerable sediment load. Slow-flowing waters can contain large amounts of organic matter. Both sediment and organic matter can be of positive benefit for irrigation, as they can provide useful nutrients for crops. Suspended matter is a problem for community water supply, and can make the water undrinkable as well as unsuitable for washing and cleaning. Surface water is also susceptible to more serious forms of contamination, such as from poor sanitation in upstream villages, cattle being led into the water to bath, fertilizers and pesticides being washed in off fields, and industrial effluent being discharged into streams; all these can lead to poor and sometimes dangerous water. Consequently, surface water in rural areas is normally safe for irrigation, but is not normally the first choice for drinking.

The amount of water available at any given instant can be readily measured, simply by measuring the size of the pond, or the flow in the stream (flow measurement techniques are discussed in Section 7.9.7 and in references such as Jordan, 1996 [18]. However, the flow in a stream will vary through the year. Streams will be swollen by heavy rainfall, and may dry up completely in periods of drought. The flow in a stream depends not only on the rainfall, but also on the characteristics of the area it is in. If the rainfall catchment area is rocky, then only a small amount of the rain will penetrate the ground, and the majority will flow quickly into streams and away. Streams in such areas will flood during rainstorms, but will quickly dry up afterwards. (This sort of characteristic is seen in built up areas too, where roads and concrete make the ground impermeable.) At the other extreme, areas made up of very porous ground with good water-bearing strata beneath may soak up nearly all the rain that falls. Streams in such areas will tend to be fed from groundwater at a more constant rate throughout the year, and are less affected by recent rainfall.

Not all the rain that falls on a catchment area will reach the streams within the area. Some water evaporates, some is taken up into vegetation, and some travels away underground in the aquifer. 'Run-off coefficients' are available for many places from meteorological offices, and these give the fraction of the rain falling in an area that enters the streams.

Before using a flowing stream as a water source it is important to know whether sufficient water will be available in it. For irrigation, it is particularly important to know that there will be enough water in the stream during critical irrigation months, which usually occur during the dry season when the flow is reduced. If the flow has been measured over a period of a number of years, then this data can be used to predict the

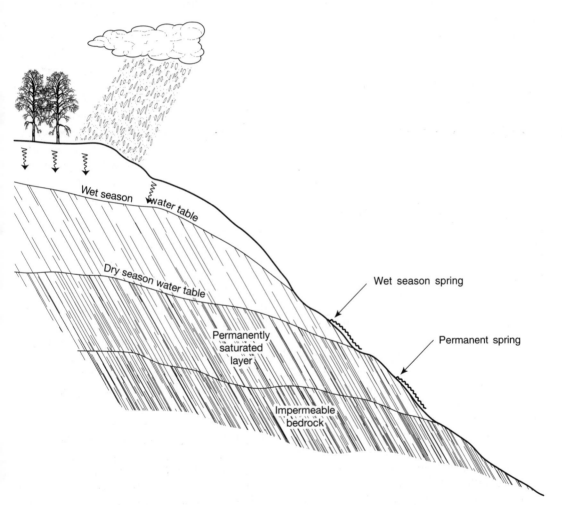

Fig. 4.2: Typical hydrology of springs

probability of exceeding the required flows in the future, but in many rural areas such data are not available. If data are available for similar catchment areas in the same region, it may be possible to estimate how the flow will vary in the area being considered. Further details are given in Section 7.9.7.

When using flowing water as a source for a water-pumping project, it is important to consider how the water will be abstracted from the stream. If the intake is temporary, it can simply be sited at a suitable point for that day's conditions. It will normally be put in where it does not pick up excessive amounts of silt or debris from the bottom. If the intake is permanent, more careful siting is needed. The pumping machinery needs to be protected from flooding, and the intake itself should not be damaged by violent monsoon flows (see WEDC, 1991 [25]).

4.1.2 Springs

Springs occur where the water table comes to the surface, as shown diagrammatically in Fig. 4.2. If the water table falls below the level of a spring at certain times of year (during the dry season) it will dry up for part of the year. If the water table never falls below the spring level, it will be a permanent water source. (Note, however, that some springs may exist because of a local variation in the water table, and may not show that the general water table for the area is at that height. For example, a local underground formation of clay or impervious rock may channel water locally to the surface, even though the true water table is lower down.)

Springs are fed by groundwater, and generally provide clean water. This is because the water is filtered as it travels through the porous rocks of the aquifer, and, if the water spends a reasonable period of time underground, the pathogens in it die from lack of nutrition. Groundwater is therefore generally sterile, though it can have high concentrations of minerals in solution, dissolved out of the rocks it has passed through. Most spring water contains a certain amount of fine sediment suspended in

the water [11] and this does not of itself prevent it being drinkable.

Local knowledge can be very helpful in the choice of a spring. Villagers will know that some springs can be drunk safely, and that some will make you ill. One should certainly be wary of using a spring the local people identify as 'bad'. Equally, if a community has been using a spring for many years without obvious health problems, it is likely to be safe, though testing the water quality is still a good idea; a local population can build up resistance to low levels of specific bacteria or toxic chemicals, and there may be better sources in the area.

Some springs emerge on steep slopes and can be simply collected and funnelled into a spout, giving a clean flow of water. Other springs appear as a pool at ground level, and these can be very unhygienic. Such springs can be improved by digging them out and building a cover over them. A brick or stone tank would be built, with a sand or gravel filter on the side that the water comes from. The other side of the wall would be backed with an impervious clay or concrete layer. Such arrangements are frequently used with a pipe running out of the tank to a standpipe or spout, with a concrete apron to keep the area clean. It is obviously possible to pump the water from such a tank, too.

Just as the water source itself needs to be protected from contamination, so does the aquifer that feeds it. There should be no latrines, livestock shelters, pools used by cattle, or other health hazards near the source. How far away they need to be depends on the local geology, but they should be at least 30 m away, and perhaps 100 m away on the uphill or upstream side. This recommendation applies to all groundwater sources: springs, wells and boreholes.

The flow in springs can vary through the year, and from year to year. The flow of a spring is determined not only by the rainfall and the runoff coefficient in the catchment area, but also by the speed at which the water flows in the aquifer, and the volume and shape of the water-bearing strata feeding it. It is very difficult to predict spring flows, and the suitability of a source can really only be judged on the basis of previous experience. Locals will know whether the stream dries up, and will be able to give some indication of its usual size.

4.1.3 Wells

Wells are holes that are dug down to a level a few metres below the water table. Some wells are shallow, being little more than enlarged springs. As with open springs, shallow, unprotected wells can get very dirty indeed. They can also be dangerous, with the risk of animals or children falling in and not being able to get out. As with all water sources, it is best to construct a proper collection area, keeping contaminated water from running into the well, and making the area safe and clean.

Wells can also be much deeper. Traditional wells, dug with picks and shovels, are often found going over 30 m deep. When looking for a water source, it is obviously easiest to use an existing well, if there is one. Local people will know whether the well dries up or not. Finding a site for a new well requires some experience and skill. First consideration should be given to making a shallow well in areas that are obviously wet: near pools and springs on slopes, near marshy patches, or near running or dry streams or rivers. If there is no obvious water around, a deeper well will need to be considered (or a borehole – see below). The best guide to suitable terrain is other wells nearby, which will give an indication of where the aquifer runs and how deep the water table is. Local water diviners can also be helpful. While it is possible to be sceptical of divining sticks and other devices, an experienced diviner will also work by looking at lie of the land, the soil type, and the local vegetation. A more scientific approach is to bring in a hydrologist. Whichever approach is taken, trial drillings on a regular pattern (typically 100 mm holes at 5–10 m spacing) are usually needed to find the best spot. If the depth is not too great this can be done with simple hand-drilling equipment.

When an apparently suitable test borehole is made, it needs to be tested for yield and quality. Yield is checked by pumping water out with a portable engine-powered pump, and checking that the borehole does not dry up at the required output. Water samples should be checked for quality as discussed in Section 4.3.

A dug well is generally about 1.2 m in diameter, so a 1.5 m hole needs to be dug if the hole is to be lined. Wells are generally dug as straight-sided holes, and care must be taken to stop the sides collapsing during construction. Support is especially important when digging into saturated soil at the bottom, and it may be necessary to insert concrete rings or build temporary supporting walls at this stage. The final linings are built from the bottom upwards, and may be of stone, brick, pre-cast concrete rings, or concrete rings cast 'in-situ'. Wells should be dug in the dry season, to allow them to go as deep into the aquifer as possible. Even then, when water is struck, the well needs to be deepened to at least 2–3 m below the water table. Water needs to be hauled out in buckets, or pumped out, to allow digging to continue. A good publication on digging and lining wells is Morgan, 1990 [16].

Instead of taking water directly from a river, it can be advantageous to make a well (or borehole) close to the river to provide an intake for a pumping system. The intervening ground then serves to filter the river water, and the intake can be more easily protected from flood damage.

Well yield can be increased by using 'collector wells', with horizontal holes drilled radially outwards from the main well into the aquifer. This technique has been used successfully in arid areas of Zimbabwe where the local aquifer had poor permeability. Wells of about 1.5–2.0 m diameter were dug 5–20 m deep, and from the bottom of these, four horizontal, 50 mm diameter holes were drilled radially outwards in a cross pattern. These laterals increase the capacity of the wells enormously.

4.1.4 Boreholes or tubewells

Dug wells have to be quite large (1 m in diameter or more) to allow people to work inside them. By using mechanical means to bore down from the surface, much smaller diameter holes can be made, producing 'boreholes' or 'tubewells'.

Being of smaller diameter, boreholes require far less earth to be removed than a well of the same depth, and they are obviously safer to make. Whereas wells cannot be dug far into the water table, because water in the hole prevents further digging, boreholes can penetrate well into the aquifer. If mechanically powered drilling rigs are used, boreholes can be sunk to considerable depths, even in hard ground. The disadvantage of boreholes over wells is that specialist drilling equipment is required to make them, which can be very costly and may not always be available.

Finding a suitable site for a borehole is similar to finding a site for a well (Section 4.1.3), and requires a consideration of local topography and geology, and possibly some test drilling.

In soft ground, boreholes can be made by 'water-jetting' or 'well-jetting', using a steel pipe with a recirculating water system. The pipe is driven into the ground, and at the same time water is pumped down it to wash out the spoil. This is sometimes known as the 'palm and sludger' method. A simple variant of well-jetting that has been used in the Prey Cla area of Cambodia to make over 7,000 boreholes is shown in

Fig. 4.3 (Batchelor and Goodchild, 1994 [26]). Initially the pumping was done with a handpump, as shown in the illustration, but it is now usually done with a petrol-driven pump.

Driven tube wells are made by driving a specially made 'well-point' into the ground. The well point consists of a perforated or slotted pipe with a pointed end. Commercially made well points are expensive, but galvanized-iron well points can be made locally. The well point itself is hammered or driven into the ground first, and then extra sections of pipe are fixed to it and driven down to attain greater depths. Hand driven tube wells can be used to make boreholes of up to 10–15 m depth in soft ground, but pile driving machinery can also be used.

Probably the most common way of making boreholes is to drill them using an auger, which cuts a hole for itself as it is twisted and pushed into the ground. Various designs of augers are available for different ground conditions. Hand-driven boring rigs can be used for shallower boreholes, as shown in Fig. 4.4. A procedure for doing this is described in detail in Morgan, 1990 [16]. Using a hand-powered auger, boreholes can be made to depths of around 40 m.

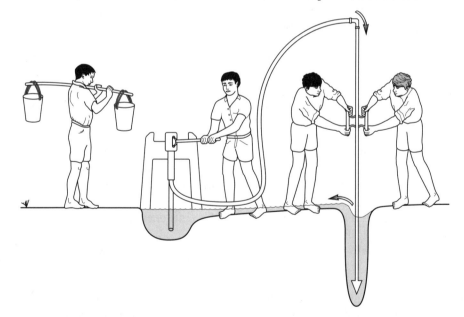

Fig. 4.3: Using a metal pipe to excavate a borehole in sandy soil, with recirculating water to bring waste material out of the hole

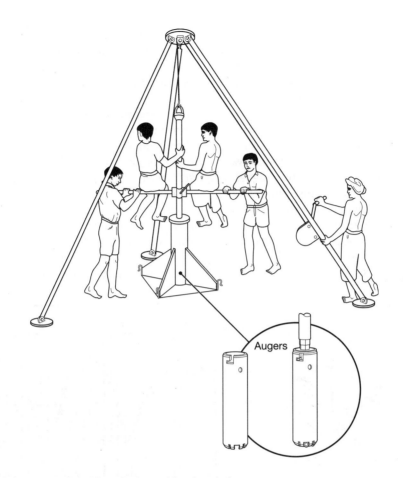

Fig. 4.4: A hand-operated drilling rig for making boreholes

All the above methods for making boreholes can be mechanized. Drilling rigs are commonly mounted on trucks so that they can easily be moved between sites. Such equipment is expensive, but it can make a hole quickly, so the cost per borehole can be reasonable. Mechanical drilling is essential to produce very deep boreholes.

When complete, a borehole will have a pipe or 'well-casing' fitted into it. This stabilizes the sides of the hole, and prevents earth from falling in, dirtying the water, and blocking the pump. The pipe is sometimes made of steel, but is usually made of PVC, and has a filter or 'screen' section at the bottom with holes or slots in it to allow water to flow in. It is also possible to use local materials to make screens, and a bamboo screen is described in WEDC, 1991 [25]. When water is first drawn from a borehole, it will contain a lot of fine sediment as this is washed out of the ground surrounding the screen. There is a period of 'well development' while the soil around the screen settles in place, which should leave a permeable layer of larger soil particles against the screen.

4.2 Draw-down and seasonal variations of water level

Groundwater and river water levels vary, both seasonally and in some cases, near to a well or borehole, due to the rate of pumping. Such changes in head can significantly influence the power requirements, and hence the running costs. However, changes in head can also influence the efficiency with which the system works, and thereby can compound any extra running

31

costs caused by a head increase. More serious problems can arise, resulting in total system failure, if for example a surface mounted suction pump is in use, and the supply water level falls sufficiently to make the suction lift exceed the practical suction lift limits discussed in Section 5.1.

Figure 4.5 illustrates various effects on the water level of a well in a confined aquifer. The figure shows that there is a natural ground water level (the water table), which is often higher on either side of a river or pond since ground water must flow slightly downhill into the open water area. The water table tends to develop a greater slope in impermeable soils (due to higher resistance to flow and greater capillary effects), and is fairly level in porous soil or sand.

If a well is bored to below the water table and water is extracted, the level in the well tends to drop until the inflow of water flowing 'downhill' from the surrounding water table balances the rate at which water is being extracted. This forms a 'cone of depression' of the water table surrounding the well. The greater the rate of extraction, the greater the drop in level. The actual drop in level in a given well depends on a number of factors, including soil permeability and type, and the wetted surface area of well below the water table (the greater the internal surface of the well the greater the inflow rate that is possible). Extra inflow can be gained either by increasing the well diameter (in the case of a hand-dug well), by deepening it (the best

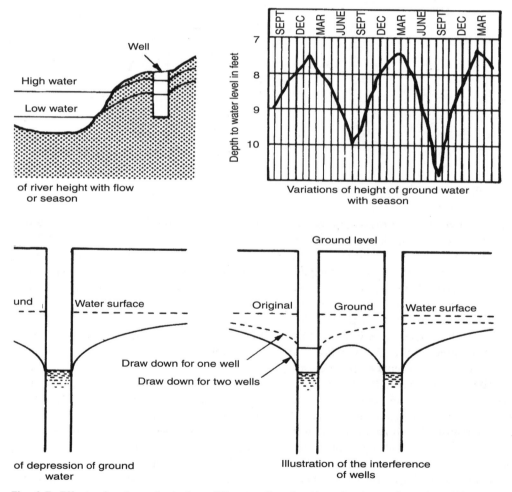

Fig. 4.5: Effects of various physical conditions on the elevation of water surfaces in wells

possibility being with a borehole), or by drilling laterals (see Section 4.1.3).

Draw-down usually will increase in proportion to extraction rate. A danger therefore if large and powerful pumps are used on small wells or boreholes is to draw the water down to the pump intake level, at which stage the pump goes on 'snore' (to use a common descriptive term). In other words, it draws a mixture of air and water, which in many cases causes it to lose its prime and cease to deliver. A 'snoring' pump can soon be damaged. But not only the pump is at risk; excessive extraction rates on boreholes can damage the internal surface below the water table and cause voids to be formed which then leads to eventual collapse of the bore. Even when a fully lined and screened borehole is used, excessive extraction rates can pull a lot of silt and other fine material out with the water and block the screen and the natural voids in the surrounding sub-soil, thereby increasing the draw-down further and putting an increasing strain on the lowermost part of the bore. Alternatively, with certain sub-soils, the screen slots can be eroded by particles suspended in the water, when the extraction rate is too high, allowing larger particles to enter the bore and eventually causing a possible collapse of the screen.

Neighbouring wells or boreholes can influence each other if they are close enough for their respective cones of depression to overlap, as indicated in Fig. 4.5. Similarly, the level of rivers and lakes will often vary seasonally, particularly in most tropical countries having distinct monsoon type seasons with most rain in just a few months of the year. The water table level will also be influenced by seasonal rainfall, particularly in proximity to rivers or lakes with varying levels (as indicated in Fig. 4.5).

Therefore, when using boreholes, the pump intake is best located safely below the lowest likely water level, allowing for seasonal changes and draw-down, but above the screen in order to avoid producing high water velocities at the screen.

When specifying a mechanized pumping system, it is therefore most important to be certain of the minimum and maximum levels if a surface water source is to be used, or when using a well or borehole, the draw-down to be expected at the proposed extraction rate. A pumping test is necessary to determine the draw-down in wells and boreholes; this is normally done by extracting water with a portable engine-pump, and measuring the drop in level at various pumping rates after the level has stabilized. In many countries, boreholes are normally pumped as a matter of routine to test their draw-down and the information from the pumping test is commonly logged and filed in the official records and can be referred to later by potential users. Drawdown data for nearby boreholes or wells provide useful pointers to likely yield when planning new boreholes.

4.3   Water quality

4.3.1   Water quality for community water supply

Water quality is of primary importance for community water supply. Many endemic illnesses in developing countries are caused by bacteria, protozoa, viruses or intestinal parasites that are transmitted through water. Bacterial and viral diarrhoeas and epidemics of cholera and typhoid are transmitted primarily via drinking water, thus making water quality a crucial factor in maintaining good health. Improved sanitation and the promotion of personal and domestic hygiene also play a major role in the elimination of such diseases, but it is much easier to improve the health of a community if the basic water supply does not contain infection.

The water quality of a potential source should be checked at an early stage in the project. It is a very expensive mistake to find that the water is undrinkable after a borehole has been completed. Samples of the water should be analysed for disease-causing organisms and for mineral content.

A quick and easy first check is to put a sample of water into a clear container. This will show if the water is clear or turbid, and whether there is suspended matter in it that settles out. Microbes will, of course, not be visible, but slightly larger parasites, animal and plant life may be seen. If there is a high iron concentration, red iron oxide may precipitate out. The taste will also quickly indicate high mineral content.

Full water quality testing is a job for a skilled laboratory. Samples should be collected in clean plastic or glass bottles with close-fitting, watertight stoppers or screw-on caps. It is important that the water is not contaminated by the bottles, as this will give false results. For chemical tests, the bottle simply needs to be clean, with no smell of its previous contents. For bacteriological tests, the bottles need to be sterile too. When filling the bottle, care should be taken not to catch debris from the bottom or sides of the stream or borehole. The bottles should be labelled with date, time, and location, and the samples should be tested as soon as possible after collection. Simple descriptions of field sampling techniques and tests are described in WEDC, 1991 [25], with more detail in Mann and Williamson, 1982 [17].

The most common problem with drinking water is faecal pollution. The WHO gives guidelines for acceptable bacteria levels in WHO, 1993 [27], but these are stringent and thought by many to be unrealistic for many rural situations. Guidelines given by the IRC are that there should be less than 2.5 faecal *E. coli* per 100 ml sample, and less than 10 coliforms of any type per 100 ml sample. Different countries and organizations all have different limits, which stems from the fact that there is no level below which water can be guaranteed not to cause infection; even a single coliform can cause disease. The various standards should be regarded as guidelines to help identify water that may be potentially harmful. Another way of approaching this, for a source that is already being used, is to investigate the general health of the local people.

Some minerals found in water are harmless but unpleasant, but there is a maximum safe concentration for all minerals. World Health Organisation recommended limits for various chemicals are given in Table 4.4. Any source should be checked first for salinity. If the salt levels are too high, people will not drink it. A village's tolerance of salty water depends to some extent on the salinity of their existing water sources. The salinity of a new source can be compared (by measuring the conductivity) with the water currently drunk, though whether the level is acceptable will ultimately be decided by whether the villagers will drink it or not. Iron is another contaminant that can give a bad taste, usually occurring as ferrous sulphate or ferrous bicarbonate. Water with more than 5 mg/l of iron is not often used for drinking. In addition, high iron levels can stain clothing, and villagers may neglect a water pump because of this. Iron can come from the aquifer, but in boreholes it can also come from corrosion of steel rising mains and pump components. Corrosion can lead to high iron content in handpumps for the first 1–2 hours pumping.

Some naturally occurring chemical contaminants are harmful. Toxic minerals, such as arsenic, lead, and fluoride are occasionally found in deep boreholes. Arsenic, a poison in larger doses, gives skin problems at lower levels. Lead and some other heavy metals are highly toxic. While a moderate level of fluoride is often added to water supplies in the West, excessive amounts lead to dental and skeletal flourosis. Surface waters in the Rift Valley, and groundwater in Morocco, Senegal and the Rift Valley naturally have a high fluoride content which gives rise to widespread health problems. Other chemicals may be introduced to water supplies by man. Toxic organic substances such as phenols and pesticides enter the water from agricultural use. Nitrates can come from fertilizers, but also from manure heaps, latrines or livestock yards, and they are toxic to small babies. An example of nitrate pollution was found in the Mitidja Plain, south of Algiers, where 35 per cent of wells have been found to contain more than 50 mg/l nitrate [28]. Toxic industrial waste is not usually present in rural areas, but must be avoided if it is. Major potential polluters include textile mills, sugar cane factories, breweries, pulp and paper mills and gold, copper, aluminium and phosphate mines. Such mines and factories often lack appropriate wastewater treatment facilities and so pollute waters downstream.

Other properties of water do not directly influence health, but have other effects. The acidity or alkalinity is measured by pH values, which

Table 4.4: WHO recommended limits for acidity and impurity levels in drinking water [27]

Measure	Acceptable level
pH	pH 6.5–9.5

Chemicals Affecting Health	(mg/l)
Antimony (Sb)	0.005
Arsenic (As)	0.01
Barium (Ba)	0.7
Boron (B)	0.3
Cadmium (Cd)	0.003
Chromium (Cr)	0.05
Copper (Cu)	2
Cyanide (CN⁻)	0.07
Fluoride (F)	1.5
Lead (Pb)	0.01
Manganese (Mn)	0.5
Mercury (Hg)	0.001
Molybdenum (Mo)	0.07
Nickel (Ni)	0.02
Nitrate (NO_3^-)	50
Nitrite (N)	3
Selenium (Se)	0.01
Uranium (U)	0.014

Chemicals Affecting Acceptability	(mg/l)
Aluminium (Al)	0.2
Ammonia (NH_4^+)	1.5
Calcium carbonate ($CaCO_3$)	500
Chlorine (Cl)	250
Hydrogen sulphide (H_2S)	0.05
Iron (Fe)	0.3
Manganese (Mn)	0.1
Sodium (Na)	200
Sulphate (SO_4^{2-})	250
Zinc (Zn)	4
Total dissolved solids	1,200

can easily be tested by the colour change of pH papers. Neutral water has a pH of 7; values less than 7 mean the water is acidic, and values greater than 7 mean it is alkaline. WHO limits the pH to the range 6.5–9.5, but other references recommend 6.8–7.6, while stating that 6.5–8.2 can be acceptable [17]. Values below 6.5 indicate a corrosive water requiring treatment with limestone. Values above 9.5 require treatment outside the scope of small rural projects and should be rejected if possible. Calcium carbonate in water, which determines its 'hardness', does not affect health, but does affect taste, and influences the pH of the water. Soft water, with low calcium carbonate levels, tends to be acidic and leads to corrosion in pipes and pumps. Conversely, hard water, with high pH levels, can cause limescale to form inside pipes. The turbidity of water from suspended matter in the water may not be injurious to health, but is a nuisance in community water supply, and is always better removed if possible. Many rivers have very high suspended solids at the beginning of the rainy season. Treatment methods are discussed in Section 4.4.

4.3.2 Water quality for irrigation

Water quality is important for irrigation in two different ways. Firstly, the whole point of irrigation is to allow the production of crops, and the water must not be contaminated in ways that adversely affects the growth of the crops it is applied to. Salinity, for example, can kill plants, as well as making the land useless for crops in the future. Secondly, crops grown by irrigation are consumed by people, and the water must not contain pathogens or toxic chemicals that can contaminate the crops and cause health problems for those eating the food.

Salinity is a major problem for many irrigation schemes. Over-pumping from the ground in coastal areas can lead to salt water entering the aquifer from the sea, as has been found in Bangladesh. Some inland areas, such as parts of the Maghreb, Ethiopia and the Rift Valley, also have a high salt content in their groundwater. The effects of salinity on plants are similar to the symptoms caused by drought: early wilting, leaf burning, a bluish-green colour in some plants, reduced growth, and small leaves. Crop sensitivity to salinity varies for different plant species and for different soil types, so generalized salinity limits for irrigation are hard to give. Dougherty and Hall, 1995 [29] tabulate various guidelines for the restriction of irrigation for water with varying levels of salinity.

The extent to which bacteria and viruses are transmitted from polluted irrigation water to humans via crops is something of a grey area. Direct fertilization with night soil is traditional in a number of cultures, and untreated sewage water is widely used for irrigation in India and other countries. Tests in Israel showed that the irrigation of certain crops with untreated sewage had no effect on the bacteria and virus count on the vegetables produced (Rybczynki et al., 1982 [30]). Using mildly polluted water for irrigation would seem to present few health dangers via the food itself, and, indeed, in many countries irrigation is practised with whatever water is available, without regard to its quality. The problems seem to arise from the contact between people working on the land and the infectious water. In developed countries, legislation usually requires that farmers use clean water for irrigation. The WHO has produced guidelines on the use of wastewater for irrigation [31], which should be consulted before using a contaminated source for irrigation.

Chemical pollution is more rare, but can be very serious when present. Some chemicals can contaminate the soil; metals of particular concern are aluminium, arsenic, beryllium, chromium, cadmium, mercury, nickel, antimony and tin. Other chemicals are plant nutrients, but can be damaging if present in excessive quantities, such as boron, cobalt, copper, iron, manganese, molybdenum and zinc. High levels of pesticides, herbicides or fertilizer in the water should also be avoided. Chemicals can not only harm crops, but can be toxic to the people and animals who consume them, and can cause lasting damage to the ecosystem. This is a specialist subject, and if it is suspected that toxic chemicals may be present in a water source, expert advice should be sought.

4.4 Water treatment

If a water source of adequate quality cannot be found, then it may be necessary to use a contaminated source and treat the water before it is used. It should be stressed that treatment is not an easy option, and every effort should be made to find a clean source before resorting to a treatment system. Water treatment is really only of concern

for community water supplies; the large volumes of water needed for irrigation make treatment impractical and uneconomic, and in any case the water-quality requirements for irrigation are nothing like as stringent as for drinking water.

The problem with all treatment methods is that they require regular attention. Sedimentation tanks and filters need to be cleaned, and chemical methods need to have the chemicals replaced. This places a burden on the community, who need to both organize the maintenance, and be able to afford whatever inputs are required. Ideally, the system should use only locally available materials, and the costs must be within the economic means of the community.

The treatment of water for small communities can be considered under five headings:
• storage and settlement;
• filtration;
• disinfecting or sterilization;
• removal of minerals;
• correction of acidity.

The first three of these can be seen as three possible stages in a treatment system, each producing cleaner water, though there are situations where they can be used individually. Storage helps to sediment out the suspended solids, and storage in a dark, closed tank can also improve the bacteriological quality of the water. Filtration is used primarily to remove pathogens from the water, while also helping to remove suspended matter and some dissolved chemicals; settlement is usually required before filtration to protect the filter medium against premature blockage. Disinfecting is used to ensure both that pathogens are destroyed, and that further re-infection of the water cannot take place; disinfecting works best if most of the organic matter has been removed from the water, which generally means having a filter prior to it. Mineral removal and the correction of acidity are treatments that may be needed for specific water sources.

4.4.1 Storage and settlement

The simplest method of treating water is to store it in a covered tank. Most water-supply installations include some form of primary storage tank or pond, and these can be given the dual purpose of being settling tanks for the system too. Settlement cleans the water of suspended solids and colour, even if it does not remove many of the harmful organisms from polluted water. However, if the water remains in a tank for two weeks, the bacteria populations can be reduced by 50–90%, depending on the severity of the pollution.

Sedimentation can be improved or speeded-up by flocculation: using chemicals to coagulate the suspended matter so that it settles out of the water. Suitable coagulants are aluminium sulphate, sodium aluminate, ferrous sulphate plus lime, and ferric chloride. Aluminium suphate, also called alumina, alum and aluminoferric, is the most common, and is often the only flocculant available; ferrous sulphate is often used in conjunction with aluminium sulphate. It has been reported that the powdered seed of *Moringa oleifera* plants have been used successfully on a small-scale in Indonesia [1], and other naturally-occuring plants may be known locally that fulfil the same function. Laboratory tests need to be carried out on the raw water to determine which coagulant to use, and in what quantity. To give an idea of the amount that might be used, dosage typically varies between 5 and 100 mg/l. Coagulant solution can be added continuously to the tank provided a uniform flow rate can be maintained. Some simple 'doser' units are given in Mann and Williamson, 1982 [17]. The sediment will settle out to the bottom of the tank, and periodically needs to be flushed, drained, or pumped out. Sedimentation tanks are usually made with baffles to ensure that water cannot flow directly from the inlet to the outlet. The cross-sectional area of the flow path of the water must be large enough to give slow flow, sufficient for most of the particles to have time to fall to the bottom. Designs for sedimentation tanks are given in Mann and Williamson, 1982 [17] and Franceys et al., 1992 [11].

4.4.2 Filtration

There are two main types of filter used for water supply, gravel filters and sand filters. Gravel filters provide coarse filtration that can be used to remove sediment as an alternative, or in addition, to settlement tanks. Sand filters give finer filtration, but also remove pathogens from the water, making it biologically clean and drinkable.

Sand filters can be constructed with a number of different layouts. The type most commonly recommended for community water supply is the 'slow sand filter'. Slow sand filters have the advantages of simplicity, and of requiring less critical attention than other types. The cleaning action of the sand in a slow filter is complex, but remarkably effective. Mineral and organic particles are trapped as they pass through the small gaps between the sand, are chemically and electrically attracted to the surface of the sand grains, and are sedimented out of the water in the open spaces between the grains. Algae, protozoa, and other micro-organisms take up residence in the sand, and feed on bacteria in the water. These organisms are concentrated in a skin on the surface of the sand, sometimes known as the 'schmutzdecke'. As the water passes deeper into the filter, little nutrient matter remains, and pathogens, unable to compete with the specialist organisms, die off. As stated before, sand filters become clogged by sediment in the water, and if water needs filtration it will usually need to be pre-treated in sedimentation tanks or gravel filters.

One design of slow sand filter is shown in Fig. 4.6. It consists of a leakproof tank-like structure, which may either be dug into the ground, or built up from cement or masonry. In the middle of its base it has an underdrainage arrangement that leads the purified water out of the filter. This may be constructed from a network of perforated or porous pipes, or from a layer of bricks, tiles, or stones. Over this underdrainage are placed graded layers of gravel, with the largest diameter gravel at the bottom, to a depth of about 300 mm. The box is then filled with sand of 0.2–0.5 mm particle size. Note that the gravel is kept away from the walls of the box, so that water which seeps between the sand levels and the walls cannot go directly into the gravel. The sand bed needs to be about

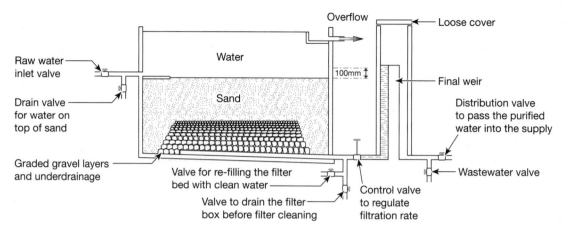

Fig. 4.6: A slow sand filter

1–1.2 m deep, with a water depth above it of 0.5–1.0 m. The rate of filtration will be around 0.1 m³/hour per square metre of plan area of the filter [25]. Thus a tank which is 10 m by 7 m will have an output per day of:

$$0.1 \times 10 \times 7 = 7m^3 / h$$

Designs for sand filters are given in Mann and Williamson, 1982 [17], Morgan, 1990 [16] and WEDC, 1991 [25]. Over time, the build up of organic matter and residue from the organisms will accumulate at the surface and block the pores and passages in the sand, and the throughput will be noticeably reduced. After several weeks or months of operation (depending on the quality of the feed water) filters will require periodic cleaning, which is done by draining down the water, scraping off 25–50 mm of the top layer, and replacing it with fresh sand. A cleaned filter requires a few days to re-establish the skin of organisms on its surface, and so filters should either be built in pairs or divided in two so that one side can run while the other is being cleaned and re-started.

Slow sand filters do have a number of disadvantages. Firstly, they are much larger than other types for a given throughput; a slow sand filter may require 40–50 times the area of a rapid sand filter. Secondly, unlike rapid sand filters described below, they cannot be cleaned by reverse flushing, and layers of the sand have to be removed

manually as described above. Nevertheless, they are still probably the most appropriate design of filter for small rural communities.

A variation of the slow sand filter, the horizontal sand filter, is described in Mann and Williamson, 1982 [17]. This uses a large bed of sand contained in a lined pit with a bottom that slopes down at about 1 : 20 from the inlet to the outlet. Water is introduced into a small hole in the sand at one end, and removed from another hole at the other end. The filter is sized to retain the water for about 36 hours. The flow rate at the inlet is high enough to stop the formation of a schmutzdecke, and the biological digestion of bacteria and organic matter occurs within the body of the sand. This means that, provided silt does not block the inlet, a horizontal sand filter does not need regular cleaning. The volume required for a horizontal sand filter can be estimated assuming that 40% of the volume of sand is composed of voids that can be filled with water, and that the water should take 36 hours to pass through:

$$V = Q \times 36 \times 0.4 = 14.4Q$$

V – volume of horizontal sand filter (m³)
Q – water flow (m³/h)

Slow sand filters can be adapted to handpumps by making small units (around 300 mm in diameter and 800 mm tall) which fit under the handpump outlets. These filters will readily

38

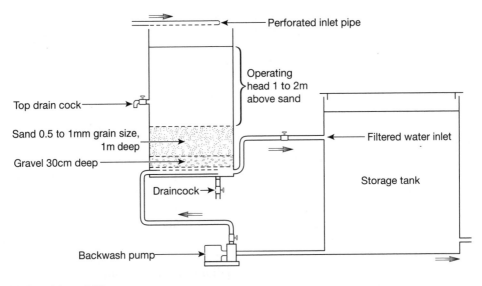

Fig. 4.7: A rapid sand filter

handle pump flows of 0.25–0.3 l/min, but give a delay between the pumping and the water being available, which is not very convenient. Such filters will improve the bacterial quality of the water from a polluted source, and also help to remove iron from boreholes (see Section 4.4.4).

Rapid sand filters (Fig. 4.7) are similar in layout to slow sand filters, but have higher head of water over the sand, typically 1.5–2 m. Throughput can be as much as 2.4–7.2 m³/m²/h [17]. The filtering action of a rapid filter is entirely mechanical; the higher flow-rate prevents the build up of colonies of micro-organisms. Rapid sand filters require frequent cleaning, but this can be done by flushing them with filtered water, which is pumped back through the sand while agitating the sand bed mechanically (or with compressed air in commercial installations). Rapid sand filters need to be checked frequently, and the backwashing requires trained staff. Thus, while they make compact and efficient filters with a high throughput, they are difficult to operate and maintain reliably for community water supply systems.

Upwards flow sand filters are typically made on a smaller scale, and might supply a school, a health post, or a group of houses. A simple filter that can be made in an old 200 litre oil drum is shown in Fig. 4.8. Raw water, under pressure, is

introduced into a space at the base of the filter made by resting a plate with holes in it (which can be made from the top of the drum) on a number of stones. The water then flows up through a 250–300 mm layer of 3–4 mm diameter sand. The action of this type of filter is primarily mechanical, but some cleansing by micro-organisms does take place. The flow rate has to be restricted to prevent the sand from lifting off, but upwards sand filters can achieve rates of 100–1,500 l/h/m², depending on water quality. This type of filter needs regular cleaning, every day or so, but the cleaning method is very simple: the inlet is stopped, the drain plug is removed,

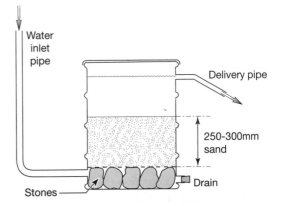

Fig. 4.8: An upwards flow sand filter

and the filtered water is allowed to drain quickly out of the filter, flushing out debris with it. A simple upwards flow filter promoted by UNICEF that is suitable for up to 10 people is described in Kerr, 1990 [1].

4.4.3 Disinfecting and sterilization

Another way of ensuring that water is bacteriologically safe is to disinfect or sterilize the water. This is usually done chemically, by adding chlorine to the water. Chlorination involves mixing controlled doses of one of a number of chlorine-bearing compounds with the water. The chlorine combines with the hydrogen in the water, liberating the oxygen, which then rapidly oxidizes bacteria and other organic matter. Since the chlorine acts on both the pathogens and other organic matter, the dosage required can be reduced considerably if the water is de-sedimented and filtered first.

The dosage of chlorine required is determined by experiment. The cheapest form of chlorine is bleaching powder or chloride of lime, though this degrades if it is not stored properly; alternatives are sodium hypochlorite or HTH (High Test Hypochlorite). Testing is done by adding a measured amount of a standard solution of chlorine to a known quantity of raw water. This is allowed to stand for 30 minutes, and then tested for the residual chlorine content using a standard kit (those sold for swimming pools are adequate). The results can be used to calculate the required dosage for water treatment, which should give a residual chlorine level, or free chlorine residual, of 0.3 ppm (0.3 mg/l). For water with a high pathogen level, or containing resistant organisms such as *Bilharzia cercaria*, this level should be raised to 0.5 ppm. When the chlorine is added to the raw water in the actual community water supply, the dosing should be done at a point that allows the chlorine to remain in the water for at least 30 minutes before it is distributed. This is often done by adding the chlorine to a storage tank.

A chlorination programme will only be effective if it is managed and monitored properly. The chlorine will need to be purchased, and those responsible for dosing and testing the water will require training. Whilst some rural water supplies have successfully used chlorination, it is not a method that is applicable to all situations.

Chlorination can be used as a short-term measure during periods of high risk, such as epidemics of water-borne diseases. An example is the chlorination of village wells by temporarily hanging a pot containing a mixture of coarse sand and bleaching powder below the water level [11].

Ultra violet light can be used to sterilize water. Low-power electrical UV sterilization units are commercially available, and these can be powered from the mains or, for example, solar PV units. Care has to be taken that the water supply to the units is stopped if there is a power failure, otherwise contaminated water passes straight through them. Such systems are necessarily rather complex, and will not be suitable from most rural situations. Sunlight also kills off bacteria. If reasonably clear water is left in a clear glass or plastic container for a period of 4 hours, then most of the bacteria in it will be made harmless [16].

A common method of sterilization that ought to be mentioned is boiling. Simply bringing water to a 'rolling boil' and letting it cool naturally kills off most of the pathogens, though extended boiling (the usual recommendation is 10 minutes) may be needed for some viruses such as hepatitis. Boiling requires a large amount of energy, and is only suitable for processing drinking water in small quantities.

4.4.4 Removal of minerals

Iron and manganese compounds can be removed from water by slow sand filters. Aeration also causes these compounds to precipitate out of the water as fine, dark sediment, provided the pH of the water is 7.0 or greater. Aeration is achieved automatically in many systems when the water falls into a storage tank or pond, but can be forced by dripping the water through a bed of coarse gravel.

Most other mineral solutions are difficult to treat at a village level. Excessive levels of fluoride can be removed by adding alum (aluminium sulphate) to the water and settling out the sediment formed. Salt, nitrates, and heavy metals are not practically treatable for community water supplies, and sources containing unacceptable levels of them should be avoided.

4.4.5 Correction of acidity

Where waters are excessively acidic (i.e. with low pH values), treatment can be made by adding lime slurry directly to the water. The amount of lime added needs to be carefully controlled, making this a difficult system for community water supply.

A simple method of correcting acidity is to incorporate layers of crushed limestone (calcium carbonate) into an upwards sand filter, and to pass the water through it [17]. The water naturally emerges with a pH of 7.5, and the system requires no careful control or dosing. The limestone is used up by the process, but only very slowly. The crushed limestone method works well provided the water does not contain high concentration of sulphates, which will react with the limestone.

Alkalinity is often associated with turbidity, and flocculation with alum corrects both conditions. Direct control of alkalinity by adding acidic mineral salts is possible, but needs careful administration and testing; as with many other treatment methods, it is not realistic for a community water supply.

4.5 Water storage

Storage is needed to ensure that water is available when it is required. Storage tanks can also maintain uniform pressure in the distribution system.

For community water supply, it is essential that the water does not run out, and a storage tank or reservoir maintains continuity of supply. Irrigation systems often need a flow that is larger than the associated water source can provide, and a pond will allow water to be stored so that it can be released as required.

Pumped systems, in particular, commonly require storage. Intermittent systems, such as PV-powered pumps and windpumps, may suffer from extended periods when they have insufficient output to meet the demand. Other pumping systems, like ram pumps, may operate continuously at low output, and storage will be required to make the water available in greater quantities when it is needed. For other types of pump, storage will allow smaller, and therefore cheaper, pumps to be used than would otherwise be the case.

Storage can take place at different levels. Large-scale storage in ponds, reservoirs or tanks can supply a whole irrigation or community water system. Medium-sized tanks may serve groups of houses or buildings such as schools, hospitals, or offices. Small tanks can be built for individual houses, and containers within houses are often used to store water for immediate needs.

Stored water can become contaminated, and it is important to ensure that drinking water storage is protected. Open tanks can easily become infected, so it is generally best to use covered tanks for community water supply storage. Open tanks and pools can also become breeding grounds for malaria-carrying mosquitoes, which is another reason for using closed tanks in many areas. Infestation can be reduced in open ponds by keeping the sides clear of weeds, by paving or using concrete around the edges.

Storage is expensive to construct, especially if large concrete or steel structures are used. The cost can be reduced by using locally available materials. Ponds can be made with small earth dams or bunds, and it is often possible to use masonry, rip-rap or bricks to make walls and facings instead of using concrete. Small household tanks can be made of corrugated iron, blocks, bricks or masonry, and lined with cement, ferro-cement on chicken-wire or steel mesh, soil cement, or pre-cast concrete rings or panels (see, for example, WEDC, 1991 [25] and Jordan, 1980 [18]. In many areas cheap plastic tanks are available.

FUNDAMENTAL PHYSICAL PRINCIPLES OF WATER LIFTING

5.1 Suction lift: the atmospheric limit

Certain types of pump are capable of sucking water from a source. These pumps can be located above the water level and pull water up a pipe by creating a vacuum at the top, allowing atmospheric pressure outside to push the water up the pipe. Drawing water by suction depends on the difference between the atmospheric pressure on the free surface of the water and the reduced pressure in the suction pipe developed by the pump. The greater the difference in pressure, the higher the water will rise in the pipe. However, the maximum pressure difference that can be created is between sea level atmospheric pressure on the free surface and a pure vacuum, which theoretically will cause a difference of level of water of 10.3 m (or 34 ft). However, before a drop in pressure even approaching a pure vacuum can be produced, the water will start gassing due to release of air held in solution (just like soda water gasses when released from a pressurized container); if the pressure is reduced further, the water can boil at ambient temperature. As soon as this happens, the pump loses its prime and the discharge will cease (due to loss of prime) or at least be severely reduced. In addition, boiling and gassing within the pump (known as cavitation) can cause damage if allowed to continue for any length of time.

Thus, although atmospheric pressure can theoretically support a 10.3 m column of water, the true physical limit is less than this because of the vapour pressure of the water. Even this physical limit is not achievable in practice, because of the need to accelerate the water into the pump. The water in the source is usually stationary, but the water passes into the pump with a certain velocity. The head required to accelerate the water to this velocity acts against the suction, reducing the allowable head even further. Centrifugal pumps are particularly prone to cavitation because of the high accelerations of the water as it enters the fast-moving impeller, and are generally limited to a suction lift of 4.5 m, even at sea level with a short suction pipe. Reciprocating pumps generally impose lower velocities on the water and can therefore pull a higher suction lift, but again, for practical applications, this should never normally exceed about 6.5 m. Some small pumps can readily work on heads of up to 7.5 m (for example, the rower pump and the treadle pump).

At higher altitudes, or if the water is warmer than normal, the suction lift will be reduced further. For example, at an altitude of 3,000 m above sea level, due to reduced atmospheric pressure, the practical suction lift will be reduced by about 3 m compared with sea level, (and proportionately for intermediate altitudes, so that 1,500 m above sea level will reduce suction lift by about 1.5 m). Higher water temperatures also cause a reduction in practical suction head, because a lower pressure drop is needed to cause boiling to occur; for example, if the water is at, say, 30°C, (or 86°F) the reduction in suction head compared with water at a more normal 20°C will be about 7%.

Extending the length of the suction pipe also reduces the suction head that is permissible, because pipe friction adds to the suction required; this effect depends on the pipe diameter, but typically a suction pipe of say 80 m length will only function satisfactorily on half the above suction head.

5.2 Definitions of energy, work, power and efficiency

Energy is required, by definition, to do work; the rate at which it is used is defined as power. A specific amount of work can be done quickly using a lot of power, or slowly using less power, but in the end the identical amount of energy is required.

The cost of pumping or lifting water, whether in cash or kind, is closely related to the rate at which power is used (i.e. the energy requirement in a given period). There is often confusion on the meaning of the words 'power' and 'energy'; in fact they are often wrongly assumed to mean much the same thing. Therefore, it is worth clarifying that energy consists of the product of power and time; for example, a power of say, 5 kW expended over a period of say, 6 h (hours), represents an energy consumption of 30 kWh (kilowatt-hours). Power is the rate at which energy is applied. The watt (W), and kilowatt (kW) are the recommended international units of power, but units such as horsepower (hp) and even foot-pounds per second (ft.lb/s) are still in use in some places. The joule (J) is the internationally recommended unit of energy; however it is largely a unit used within the scientific community and not well known in the 'real world'. Moreover, the joule is a very small unit, being equivalent to only 1 W.s (watt-second). For practical purposes it is common to use MJ (megajoules or millions of joules), or in the world outside scientific laboratories, kWh (kilowatt-hours). 1 kWh (which is one kilowatt for one hour or about the power of two horses being worked quite hard for one hour) is equal to 3.6 MJ. Fuels of various kinds have their potency measured in energy terms; for example petroleum fuels such as kerosene or diesel oil have a gross energy value of about 36 MJ/l, which is 10 kWh/l. Engines can only make effective use of a fraction of this energy, but the power of an engine will even so be related to the rate at which fuel (i.e. the supplied energy) is consumed.

The hydraulic power required to lift or pump water is proportional to both the apparent vertical height lifted and the flow rate at which water is lifted:

$$P_{hydraulic} = pressure \times flow = H \cdot \rho \cdot g \times Q$$

$P_{hydraulic}$	–	hydraulic power
ρ	–	density of water
g	–	acceleration due to gravity
H	–	vertical height lifted
Q	–	flow rate

In other words, power needs are related *pro rata* to the head (height water is lifted) and the flow rate. In reality, the actual pumping head imposed on a pump, or 'gross working head', will be somewhat greater than the actual vertical distance, or 'static head', water has to be raised, because of friction losses. Figure 5.1 indicates a typical pump installation, and it can be seen that the gross pumping head (which determines the actual power need) consists of the sum of the friction head, the velocity head and the actual static head (or lift) on both the suction side of the pump (in the case of a pump that sucks water) and on the delivery side.

The friction head consists of a resistance to flow caused by viscosity of the water, turbulence in the pump or pipes, etc. It can be a considerable source of inefficiency in badly implemented water distribution systems, as it is a function which is highly sensitive to flow rate, and particularly to pipe diameter, etc. This is discussed in more detail in Section 5.4.2.

The velocity head is the apparent resistance to flow caused by accelerating the water from rest to a given velocity through the system; any object or material with mass resists any attempt to change its state of motion so that a force is needed to accelerate it from rest to its travelling velocity. This force is 'felt' by the pump or lifting device as extra resistance or head. Obviously, the higher the velocity at which water is propelled through the system, the greater the acceleration required and the greater the velocity head. The velocity head is proportional to the square of the velocity of the water. Therefore, if the water is pumped out of the system as a jet, with high velocity (such as is needed for

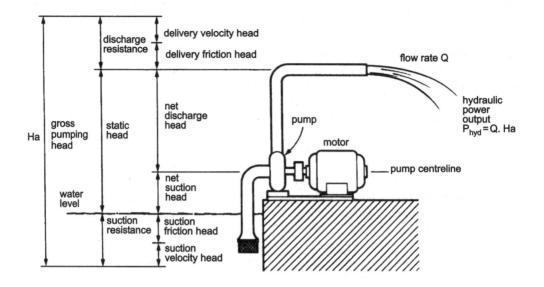

Fig. 5.1: A typical pump installation

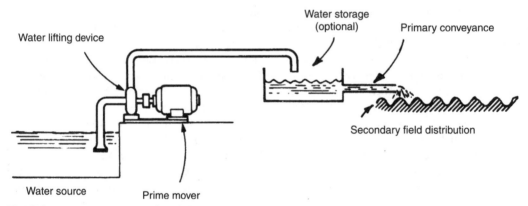

Fig. 5.2: Key components of an irrigation system

sprinkler irrigation systems), then the velocity head can represent a sizeable proportion of the power need and hence of the running costs. But in most cases where water emerges from a pipe at low velocity, the velocity head is relatively small.

5.3 System losses

This book focuses on the water-lifting mechanism, its prime mover and energy supply, but this represents only part of a water system. There must also be some means of taking in the water from the source, and a conveyancing system to deliver the water to where it is needed. Figure 5.2 indicates in outline the various possible components of an irrigation system; a particular system may have some of all of these. Almost all the other components of a system affect the pump, in that they introduce losses that the pump has to overcome.

Figure 5.1 showed how the total or gross pumping head is built up from the static head

44

plus the various losses. The suction and delivery friction heads shown are due to losses occurring when water flows through pipes. It is important to appreciate that these losses are there even if the pipes are horizontal. They are due to friction between the water and the pipe internal surfaces and to turbulence within the water itself. Useful energy is lost by friction heating up the water, though the change in temperature is hardly noticeable. These losses are obviously affected by the length and sizes of the pipes, and long, small pipes will have more losses than large diameter, short pipes; this is discussed in more detail below in Section 5.4.2. There are also friction losses associated with pushing water through restrictions such as valves, bends, junctions or changes in pipe cross-section. Energy is also wasted in accelerating water into the pump (the suction velocity head), and in the excess velocity the water has as it leaves pipes, taps, nozzles or sprinklers.

It may not be quite so obvious that losses occur when the water has to be lifted higher than the final use point. Drinking water is often pumped up into a tank so that it can be fed by gravity to taps. This has to be done to provide storage capacity (so the pump does not have to be operated continuously) and to give even pressure at the taps, but the height of the tank above the taps represents wasted energy. Irrigation systems also dissipate energy in channels and field distribution systems. Although water will flow freely by gravity down an open channel, the input end of the channel needs to be high enough above the field to provide the necessary slope or hydraulic gradient to cause the water to flow at a sufficient rate. So the outlet from the pump to the channel needs to be slightly higher than the field level, thus requiring an increased static head and therefore an increased power demand. It is important not to make the slope too steep, to minimize this loss.

The hydraulic power a pump needs to produce is proportional not only to the head, but also to the flow. This means that wasted or lost water also increases the power demanded from the pump, and represents a further source of inefficiency. Leakage in a drinking water system

may be through bad joints in the pipework or cracked tanks. Irrigation systems also loose water through seepage from channels into the earth, through evaporation, and through the percolation of water into the soil away from the crop roots.

The pumping power is therefore determined not only by the height of the outlet above the source and the flow required, but also by the losses in the various parts of the system. Each part of the system may add to the losses either by adding to the actual pumping head, or by decreasing the effective flow rate of the water (or by doing both).

Most components have an optimum efficiency. In the case of passive items like pipes or distribution systems this might be redefined as 'cost-effectiveness' rather than mechanical efficiency. All components need to be chosen so as to be optimized close to the planned operating condition of the system if the most economical and efficient system is to be derived.

As an example of the 'cost-effectiveness' in this context, consider the choice between earth channels and aluminium irrigation pipes as a conveyance for an irrigation system. Channels are usually cheap to build, but they require regular maintenance, offer more resistance to flow and, depending on the soil conditions, are prone to lose water by both percolation and evaporation. Aluminium pipe is expensive, but usually needs little or no maintenance, and involves little or no loss of water. Which is chosen depends on the running costs of the channel maintenance and the 'cost' of the lost water versus the extra capital cost of the pipes. This trade-off between capital cost and running costs is dealt with more fully in Chapter 8.

Small pumping systems are often designed without any calculation or consideration of losses, and consequently may be very inefficient. For drinking water systems the volumes pumped are usually quite low, and people do not notice the small amount of wasted power, especially as drinking water supply is often viewed as a necessity, to be paid for whatever the cost. Nevertheless, a considerable amount of energy can be wasted over the lifetime of a poorly designed, inefficient system, and this represents money 'down the drain'. In irrigation systems losses are usually more costly, because the volumes pumped are many times greater. The economics of irrigation are a balance between the cost of providing the water, and the value of the crop, and lost energy can represent a substantial increase in the cost of operating the scheme. Even so, because purchase costs are obvious and running costs (and what causes them) are less clear, there is a tendency for small farmers to err on the side of minimizing capital costs. They also do this as they so often lack finance to invest in a better system. This frequently results in poor irrigation system efficiencies, and financial returns that are lower than with a more capital-intensive but better optimized systems.

5.4 Flow through channels and pipes

The proper design of water conveyance systems is complex, and numerous text-books deal with this topic in detail [18, 32]. It is therefore only proposed to provide an outline of the basic principles so far as they are important to the correct choice and selection of water lifting system.

5.4.1 Channels

When water is at rest, the water level will always be horizontal; however, if water flows down an open channel or canal, the water level will slope downwards in the direction of flow. This slope is called the 'hydraulic gradient'; the greater the frictional resistance to flow the steeper it will be. Hydraulic gradient is usually measured as the ratio of the vertical drop per given length of channel, e.g. 1 m per 100 m is expressed as 1/100 or 0.01. The rate of flow (Q) that will flow down a channel depends on the cross sectional area of flow (A) and the mean velocity (v). The relationship between these factors is:

$$Q = v \cdot A$$

Q –   flow (m³/s)
v –   mean velocity across A (m/s)
A –   cross-sectional area of the flow (m²)

For example, if the cross sectional area is 0.5 m², and the mean velocity is 1 m/s, then the rate of flow will be:

$$1 \times 0.5 = 0.5 \quad m^3/s$$

The flow in a channel can be found from Manning's equation:

$$Q = A \cdot \frac{r^{2/3} \cdot s^{1/2}}{n}$$

Q –   flow (m³/s)
A –   cross-sectional area of the flow (m²)
r –   hydraulic radius (m)
s –   hydraulic gradient, the height dropped divided by the horizontal distance (unitless)
n –   coefficient of roughness for the channel material (s/m^{1/3})

The hydraulic radius is the area of cross-section of submerged channel divided by its wetted submerged perimeter. The roughness coefficient is related to the surface roughness of the material used for the channel walls, and typical values are given for common materials in Table 5.1. Note that some books use another roughness coefficient, often denoted 'k', which has quite different values from 'n' and is used in a different formula. It is important to use the correct roughness coefficient for the equation being used.

Table 5.1 is also of interest in that it indicates the recommended side slopes and maximum flow velocities for a selection of commonly used types of channels, ranging from earth ditches to concrete, metal or wooden flumes.

A channel of a given cross-section could obviously be wide and shallow or narrow and deep. It can be shown that the optimum shape is one that allows a semi-circle to sit inside the water cross-section, touching both sides and the bottom, as shown in Fig. 5.3. This gives the maximum flow for the minimum amount of excavation. Note that channels should not run brim full, as they will overflow, but should be made with a certain freeboard allowance. (As a

46

Table 5.1: Typical coefficients of roughness, seepage coefficients, and suggested maximum flow velocities and side slopes for lined and unlined ditches and flumes

Type of surface	Maximum flow velocities		Coeffic. of roughness n	Side slopes or shape (vert./horiz.)	Seepage coefficient c (10^{-6} m^3/s per m^2)
	(m/s)	(ft/s)			
UNLINED DITCHES					
Sand	0.3–0.7	1.0–2.5	0.030–0.040	3:1	8+
Sandy loam	0.5–0.7	1.7–2.5	0.030–0.035	2:1 to 22:1	6–8
Clay loam	0.6–0.9	2.0–3.0	0.030	1½:1 to 2:1	1.5–6
Clays	0.9–1.5	3.0–5.0	0.025–0.030	1:1 to 2:1	0.5–1.5
Gravel	0.9–1.5	3.0–5.0	0.030–0.035	1:1 to 1½:1	10–20+
Rock	1.2–1.8	4.0–6.0	0.030–0.040	41:1 to 1:1	0
LINED DITCHES					
Concrete					
Cast-in-place	1.5–2.5	5.0–7.5	0.014	1:1 to l½:1	
Pre-cast	1.5–2.0	5.0–7.0	0.018–0.022	l½:1	
Bricks	1.2–1.8	4.0–6.0	0.018–0.022	l½:1	
Asphalt					
Concrete	1.2–1.8	4.0–6.0	0.015	1:1 to l½:1	
Exposed membrane	0.9–1.5	3.0–5.0	0.015	l½:1 to 1:1	
Buried membrane	0.7–1.0	2.5–3.5	0.025–0.030	2:1	
Plastic					
Buried membrane	0.6–0.9	2.0–3.0	0.025–0.030	2½:1	
FLUMES					
Concrete	1.5–2.0	5.0–7.0	0.0125		
Metal					
Smooth	1.5–2.0	5.0–7.0	0.015		
Corrugated	1.2–1.8	4.0–6.0	0.021		
Wood	0.9–1.5	3.0–5.0	0.014		

rule-of-thumb, the freeboard should be about 30% of the water depth.)

To obtain a greater flow rate, either the channel needs to be large in cross section (and hence expensive in terms of materials, construction costs and land utilisation) or it needs to have a greater slope. Therefore irrigation channel design always introduces the classic problem of determining the best trade-off between capital cost or first cost (i.e. construction cost) and running cost in terms of the extra energy requirement if flow is obtained by increasing the hydraulic gradient rather than the cross sectional area. The nature of the terrain also comes into consideration, as channels normally need to follow the natural slope of the ground if extensive re-grading or supporting structures are to be avoided. Obviously in reality, the design of a system is complicated by bends, junctions, changes in section, slope or surface, etc.

A further point to be considered with channels is the likely loss of water between the point of entry to the channel and the point of discharge caused by seepage through the channel walls and also by evaporation from the open surface. Any such losses need to be made up by

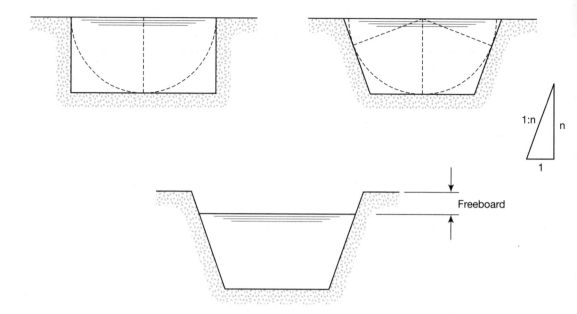

Fig. 5.3: Construction for finding the optimum shape of a channel with a given side slope

extra inputs of water, which in turn require extra pumping power (and energy) in proportion. Seepage losses are of course most significant where the channel is unlined or has fissures which can lose water, while evaporation only becomes a problem for small and medium scale irrigation schemes with channels having a large surface area to depth ratio and low flow rates, particularly under hot and dry conditions; the greatest losses of this kind occur generally within the field distribution system rather than in conveying water to the field. The main factors affecting the seepage rate from a channel or canal are:

- soil characteristics;
- depth of water in the channel in relation to the wetted area and the depth of the groundwater;
- sediment in water in relation to flow velocity and length of time channel has been in use.

This latter point is important as any channel will leak much more when it has been allowed to dry out and then refill. Seepage decreases steadily through the season due to sediment filling the pores and cracks in the soil. Therefore, it is desirable to avoid letting channels dry out

completely to reduce water losses when irrigating on a cyclic basis.

Typical conveyance efficiencies for channels range at best from about 90% (or more) with a heavy clay surface, or a lined channel in continuous use on small to medium land holdings, down to 60–80% in the same situation, but with intermittent use of the channel. In less favourable conditions, such as on a sandy or loamy soil, also with intermittent use, the conveyance efficiency may typically be 50–60% or less (i.e. almost half the water entering the channel failing to arrive at the other end).

Methods for calculating conveyance losses have been derived and are discussed in detail in specialist references (Kraatz, 1977 [33]). One simple method for calculating conveyance losses uses a seepage coefficient, c, as given in Table 5.1. The seepage loss is then calculated from the area of the channel sides and bottom in contact with the water (Harvey et al., 1993 [34]):

$$Q_{loss} = c \cdot L \cdot P$$

Q_{loss} –   conveyance loss (m³/s)

48

c – coefficient depending on nature of soil (m³/s per m²) equivalent to (m/s) (see Table 5.1)

L – length (m)

P (m) – wetted perimeter of cross section

5.4.2 Pipes

A pipe can operate like a channel with a roof on it, i.e. it can be un-pressurized, often with water not filling it. The advantage of a pipe, however,

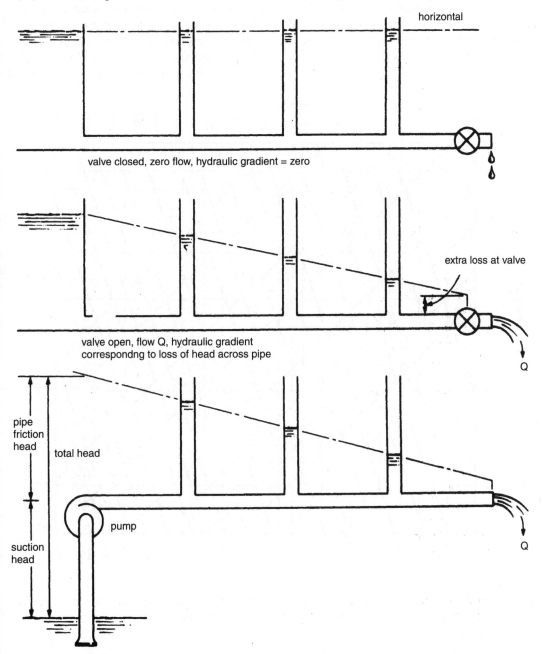

horizontal

valve closed, zero flow, hydraulic gradient = zero

extra loss at valve

valve open, flow Q, hydraulic gradient correspondng to loss of head across pipe

Q

pipe friction head

total head

pump

suction head

Q

Fig. 5.4: The concept of a hydraulic gradient

49

is that it need not follow the hydraulic gradient like a channel, since water cannot overflow from it if it dips below the natural level. In other words, although pipes are more expensive than channels in relation to their carrying capacity, they generally do not require accurate levelling and grading and are therefore more cheaply and simply installed. They are of course essential to convey water to a higher level or across uneven terrain.

As with a channel, a pipe also is subject to a hydraulic gradient which also necessarily becomes steeper if the flow is increased; in other words a higher head or higher pressure is needed to overcome the increased resistance to a higher flow. This can be clarified by imagining a pipeline with vertical tappings on it (as in Fig. 5.4). When no flow takes place due to the outlet valve being closed, the water pressure along the pipe will be uniform and the levels in the vertical

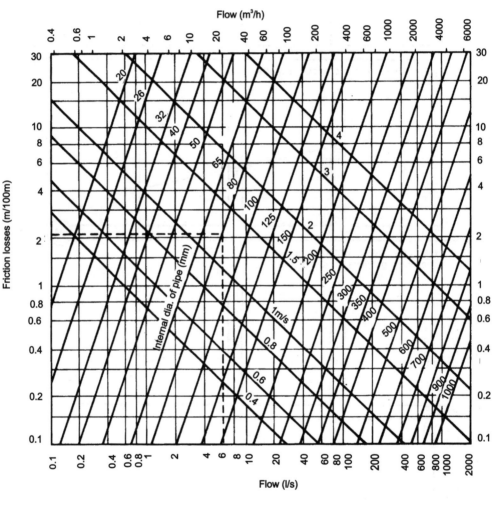

Fig. 5.5: Friction losses in metres head per 100 m of length for a new, straight, cast iron pipe. For other types of pipe multiply the friction loss by the following factors:

New rolled steel	0.8
New plastic	0.8
Old rusty cast iron	1.25
Pipes with encrustation	1.7

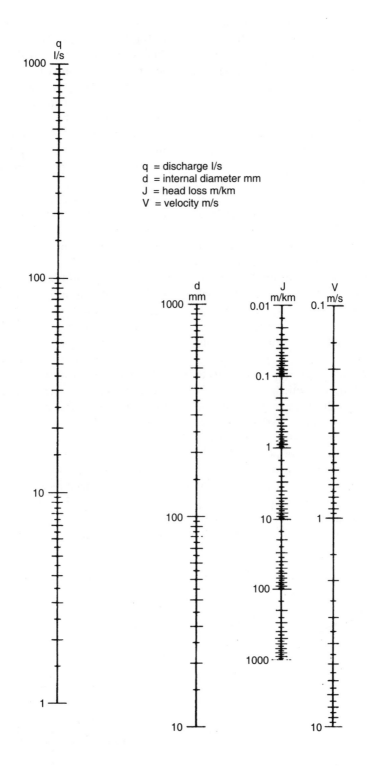

q = discharge l/s
d = internal diameter mm
J = head loss m/km
V = velocity m/s

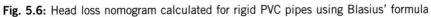

Fig. 5.6: Head loss nomogram calculated for rigid PVC pipes using Blasius' formula

tappings will correspond to the head of the supply reservoir. If the valve is opened so that water starts to flow, then a hydraulic gradient will be introduced, as illustrated in the second diagram, and the levels in the vertical tappings will relate to the hydraulic gradient, in becoming progressively lower further along the pipe. The same applies if a pump is used to push water along a pipe as in the lowest diagram in the figure. Here the pump needs to overcome a resistance equal to the static head of the reservoir indicated in the two upper diagrams, which is the pipe friction head. In low lift applications, as indicated, the pipe friction head can in some cases be as large or larger then the static head (which in the example is all suction head since the pump is mounted at the same level as the discharge). The power demand, and hence the energy costs will generally be directly related to total head for a given flow rate, so that in the example, friction losses in the pipe could be responsible for about half the energy costs.

The easiest way to estimate pipe friction is to use charts, such as Fig. 5.5, which are commonly published both in the literature of pipe and pipe fitting manufacturers and in hydraulics textbooks. For example (see the dashed line in Fig. 5.5), a flow of 6 l/s through a pipe of 80 mm diameter results in a loss of head per 100 m of pipe of just over 2 m (and the flow velocity is around 1.2 m/s). As an alternative method, Fig. 5.6 gives a nomogram for obtaining the head loss, given in this case as m/km, for rigid PVC

pipe. These results must be modified, depending on the type of pipe, by multiplying the result obtained from the chart by the roughness coefficient of the pipe relative to the material for which the chart or nomogram was derived; for example, if Fig. 5.5 is to be used for PVC pipe, the result must be multiplied by the factor 0.8 (as indicated at the foot of the figure). This is because PVC is smoother than iron and typically therefore imposes only 80% as much friction head.

Account must also be taken of the effects of changes of cross section, bends, valves or junctions, which all tend to create turbulence that in effect raises the effective friction head. Ageing of pipes due to growth of either organic matter or corrosion, or both, also increases the friction head per unit length because it increases the frictional resistance and it also decreases the available cross section of flow. This is a complex subject and various formulae are given in textbooks to allow this effect to be estimated when calculating head losses in pipes.

Hydraulic gradient must be considered when designing pipelines for water collection or for distribution systems. If the profile of the proposed pipeline is drawn from map and survey data, then a Hydraulic Gradient Line, or HGL, can be drawn on top of it, as in Fig. 5.7. The vertical scale is normally exaggerated in such diagrams to make it more clear. The slope of the HGL for a particular length of pipe is found from the friction loss in the pipe for the flow being considered. If the frictional head loss factor for a

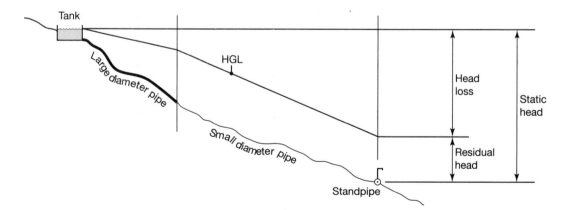

Fig. 5.7: Designing a distribution pipeline to a standpipe using a Hydraulic Gradient Line

given pipe is, say, 2.5 m per 100 m (sometimes written as 2.5%), and there is a length of 800 m of pipe on the profile, then the head loss over the pipe will be 800/100 × 2.5 = 20 m, and this can be plotted as a vertical drop in the HGL on the profile. Figure 5.7 shows a tank feeding a length of large diameter pipe followed by a length of small diameter pipe down to a standpipe. The slope of the HGL for the small pipe is greater than the slope of the large pipe, because the losses are higher. Some pressure is left at the standpipe, giving a 'residual head' which makes the water come out of the tap. The general rule for pipelines is that the HGL must always be *above* the actual pipe by a certain amount, usually 10 m, in order to maintain positive pressure. If the HGL falls below the pipe at any point, this means that there will be negative pressure in the pipeline, and this can result in air or polluted water being sucked in through leaky joints. Large negative pressures can cause air to come out of solution from the water and create pockets of air at high points, which may block the pipe.

It should be noted carefully that the HGL is drawn for one particular flow. If the flow changes, the slopes of the lines will also change. For a complex system, particularly one with a number of branches in it, the HGL may need to be drawn for a number of different flow conditions to find the worst case. If there is no flow, the HGL is horizontal, and the residual head is the static head. The pipes and the standpipe tap must be able to withstand the static head. If the drop from the tank to the standpipe is greater than the pressure rating of the pipe, additional 'break-pressure' tanks need to be incorporated in the line to reduce the pressure. The ideal residual head for a standpipe is 15 m; this is not always achievable, but a reasonable range is between 10 and 50 m, or at the outside, 7–56 m.

The head loss, h_f, due to friction in a pipeline is approximately related to the mean velocity and hence the flow rate squared:

$$h_f = K \cdot Q^2$$

If the water emerges from the outlet with a significant velocity, this too represents wasted energy, and a loss of head. The 'velocity head' of the water at the outlet is proportional to the square of its velocity:

$$h_v = \frac{V^2}{2g}$$

The total head, H_t, felt by a pump will be the sum of the static head, the friction head, and the velocity head at the outlet:

total head = static head + friction head + velocity head

or:

$$H_t = h_s + K \cdot Q^2 + \frac{V^2}{2g}$$

Since the velocity of flow is proportional to the flow rate, Q, the above equation can be re-written:

$$H_t = h_s + K' \cdot Q^2$$

where: $\quad K' = K + \dfrac{1}{2g \cdot A^2}$

Figure 5.8 illustrates the relationship between the total head and the flow rate for a pumped pipeline, and the pipeline efficiency, η_{pipe}, which can be expressed in energy terms as:

$$\eta_{pipe} = \frac{h_s - K' \cdot Q^2}{h_s}$$

5.5 Efficiency of components: the importance of matching

The general principle that:

power = pressure × flow

and

energy = head × weight of water lifted

53

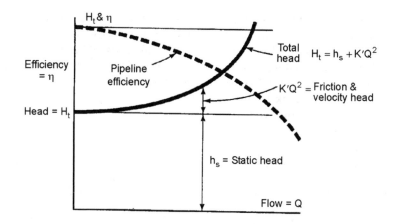

Fig. 5.8: How total head and efficiency vary with flow

apply to any water lifting technique, whether it is a centrifugal pump, or a rope with a bucket on it. The actual power and energy needs are always greater than the hydraulic energy need, because losses inevitably occur when producing and transmitting power or energy, due to friction. The smaller the friction losses, the higher the quality of a system. The quality of a system in terms of minimizing losses is defined as its 'efficiency', η

where:
$$\eta = \frac{hydraulic\ energy\ output}{actual\ energy\ input}$$

Using energy values in the equation gives the longer-term efficiency, while power values could be used to define the instantaneous efficiency.

A truly frictionless pumping system would in theory be 100% efficient, i.e. all the energy applied to it could reappear as hydraulic energy output. However, in the real world there are always friction losses associated with every mechanical and hydraulic process. Each component of a pumping system has an efficiency (or by implication, an energy loss) associated with it; the system efficiency or total efficiency is the product of multiplying together the efficiencies of all the components. For example, a small electrically driven centrifugal pump consists of an electric motor, (efficiency typically 85%), a mechanical transmission (efficiency if direct drive of say 98%), the pump itself (optimum efficiency say 70%) and the suction and delivery pipe

system (say 80% efficient). The overall system efficiency will be the product of all these component efficiencies.

In other words, the hydraulic power output, given by (static pressure) × (flow) will in this case be 47% of the gross power output from the pump, derived as follows:

$$0.85 \times 0.98 \times 0.7 \times 0.8 = 0.47$$

This means that only 47% of the gross hydraulic power output of the pump ends up as useful hydraulic power.

The efficiencies of the various components are not generally constant. There is usually an operating condition under which the efficiency is maximized or the losses are minimized as a fraction of the energy throughput; for example a centrifugal pump always has a certain speed at a given flow rate and head at which its efficiency is a maximum. Similarly, a person or draft animal also has a natural speed of operation at which the losses are minimized and pumping is easiest in relation to output.

Therefore, to obtain a pumping system which has a high overall efficiency depends very much on combining a chain of components, such as a prime mover, transmission, pump and pipes, so that at the planned operating flow rate and static head, the components are all operating close to their optimum efficiencies – i.e. they are 'well matched'. A most important point to consider is that it is common for irrigation systems to perform badly even when all the components considered individually are potentially efficient, simply because one or more of them sometimes are forced to operate well away from their optimum condition for a particular application due to being wrongly matched or sized in relation to the rest of the system or in relation to the flow rate required.

5.6   Practical power requirements

Calculating the power requirement for water lifting is fundamental to determining the type and size of equipment that should be used, so it is worth detailing the principles for calculating it. In general the maximum power required will simply be:

$$\frac{maximum\ mass\ flow\ delivered \times static\ head\ \times g}{total\ system\ efficiency\ at\ maximum\ flow}$$

where the mass flow is measured in kg/s of water. 1 kg of water is equal to 1 litre in volume, so it is numerically equal to the flow in litres per second; g is the acceleration due to gravity of 9.81 m/s². Therefore, for example, 5 l/s pumped through 10 m head in a system having an overall efficiency of 10% requires:

$$\frac{5[kg/s] \times 10[m] \times 9.8.1[m/s^2]}{0.10[efficiency]} = 4,905\ W$$

The daily energy requirement will similarly be:

$$\frac{mass\ of\ delivered\ per\ day \times head \times g}{average\ system\ efficiency}$$

e.g. for 60 m³/d lifted through 6 m with an average efficiency of 5%:

$$\frac{60,000 \times 6 \times 9.81}{0.05} = 70.6\ MJ/day$$

(million Joules per day)

Note: 60 m³ = 60,000 litres which in turn has a mass of 60,000 kg (= 60 tonne). Also, since 1 kWh = 3.6 MJ, we can express the above result in kWh simply by dividing by 3.6, so:

$$70.6\ MJ/day = 19.6\ kWh/day$$

It follows from these relationships that a simple formula can be derived for converting an hydraulic energy requirement into kWh, as follows:

$$E_{hyd} = \frac{Q \cdot H}{367}$$

E_{hyd} – hydraulic energy (kWh)
Q – volume of water lifted (m³)
H – head through which water is lifted (m)

Another unit used for measuring hydraulic energy is m³.m (sometimes m⁴), which is the energy required to lift 1 m³ of water through 1 m. Although m³.m may seem an unusual method of expressing energy, it is useful because it can readily be converted to a daily output of water at any particular pumping head. Re-arranging the above equation and putting Q and H as 1, it can be seen that:

$$1000\ [W.h] = 1\ [kW.h] = 367\ [m^3 \cdot m]$$

What this means is that 1 kWh of hydraulic energy delivered corresponds to 36.7 m³ of water lifted through 10 m, or 3.67 m³ lifted through 100 m, etc. (Note that m³.m does not truly have the units of energy, and the above conversion implies both the standard density of water of 1,000 kg/m³ and an acceleration due to gravity of 9.8 m/s²; both of these assumptions are reasonably accurate anywhere on the earth's surfaces.)

Irrigation water requirements are often given in millimetres. This means that the area being considered should have sufficient water put onto it to cover it to that depth in millimetres; such depth requirements are usually given per day. A rectangular plot of land 20 m by 30 m irrigated with 12 mm of water, would require, in a 24 hours period:

$$20 \times 30 \times \frac{12}{1,000} = 6\ m^3/day$$

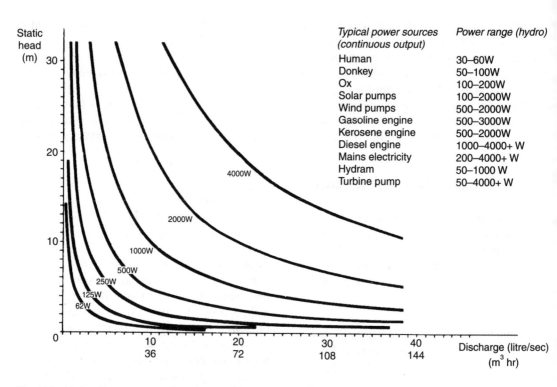

Fig. 5.9: Hydraulic power requirements to lift water

Irrigation areas are often given in hectares, where 1 ha is 10,000 m². So, for example, 9 mm on 0.3 hectares is equivalent to

$$0.3 \times 10,000 \times \frac{9}{1,000} = 27 \text{m}^3 / \text{day}$$

Figure 5.9 illustrates the hydraulic power requirement to lift water at a range of pumping rates appropriate to the small to medium sized land-holdings this publication relates to. These figures are the hydraulic output power and need to be divided by the pumping system efficiency to arrive at the input power requirement. For example, if a pump of 50% efficiency is used, then a shaft power of twice the hydraulic power requirement is needed; (pump efficiencies are discussed in more detail in Chapter 6). The small table on Fig. 5.9 indicates the typical hydraulic power output of various prime movers when working with a 50% efficient water lifting device; i.e. it shows about half the 'shaft power'

capability. The ranges as indicated are meant to show 'typical' applications; obviously there are wide variations possible in practice.

These power curves, which are hyperbolas, make it difficult to show the entire power range of possible interest in connection with land-holdings from less than 1 ha to 25 ha, even though they cover the flow, head and power range of most general interest. Figure 5.10 is a log-log graph of head versus flow, which in effect straightens out the power curves and allows easier estimation of the hydraulic power requirement for flows up to 100 l/s and hydraulic powers of up to 16 kW.

Figure 5.11 is perhaps more generally useful, being a similar log-log graph, but of daily hydraulic energy requirement to deliver different volumes of water through a range of heads of up to 32 m. The area of land that can be covered, as an example to 8 mm depth, using a given hydraulic energy output over the range of heads is also given.

56

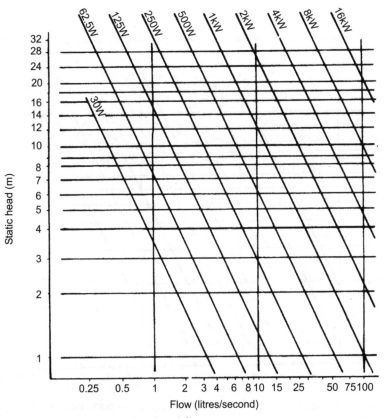

Fig. 5.10: Relationship between power, head and flow

Finally, Fig. 5.12 is a nomograph which allows the entire procedure of calculating power needs for a given irrigation requirement to be reduced to ruling a few lines so as to arrive at an answer. An example helps to illustrate the procedure: starting with the area to be irrigated (in the example 3 ha is used), rule a line vertically upwards until it intersects the diagonal. This point of intersection gives the required depth of irrigation; 8 mm is used in the example but field and distribution losses are not accounted for in this nomograph, so the irrigation demand used must be the gross and not the net requirement. Rule horizontally from the point of intersection, across the vertical axis (which indicates the daily water requirement in cubic metres per day – 240 in the example) until the line intersects the diagonal relating to the pumping head; 10 m head is used in the example. Dropping a vertical line from the point of intersection gives the hydraulic energy requirement (6.5 kWh [hyd.]/d). This is converted to a shaft energy requirement by continuing the line downwards to the diagonal which corresponds with the expected pumping efficiency; 50% efficiency is assumed for the example (the actual figure depends on the type of pumping system) and this gives a shaft power requirement of 13 kWh/d when a line is ruled horizontally through the shaft power axis. The final decision is the time per day which is to be spent pumping the required quantity of water; 5 h is used as the example. Hence, ruling a line vertically from the point of intersection to the average power axis (which coincides with the starting axis), shows that a mean power requirement (shaft power) of about 2.6 kW is necessary for the duty chosen in the example. It should be noted that this is mean shaft power; a significantly higher peak power or rated power may be necessary to achieve this mean power for the number of hours necessary (as discussed later in relation to different power sources).

This nomograph readily allows the reader to explore the implications of varying these

57

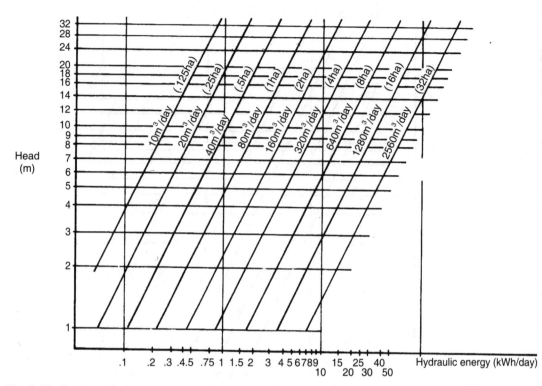

Fig. 5.11: Relationship between energy, head, and daily output; the areas that can be irrigated to a depth of 8 mm with the outputs are shown in parentheses

parameters; in the example it is perhaps interesting to explore the implications of completing the pumping in say 3 h rather than 5 h and it is clear that the mean power requirement then goes up to about 4.25 kW.

In some cases it may be useful to work backwards around the nomograph to see what a power unit of a certain size is capable of doing in terms of areas and depths of irrigation.

The nomograph has been drawn to cover the range from 0–10 ha, which makes it difficult to see clearly what the answers are for very small land-holdings of under 1 ha. However, the nomograph also works if you divide the area scale by 10, in which case it is also necessary to divide the answer in terms of power needed by 10. In the example, if we were interested in 0.3 ha instead of 3 ha, and if the same assumptions are used on depth of irrigation, pumping head, pump efficiency and hours per day for pumping, the result will be 0.26 kW (or 260 W)

instead of 2.6 kW as indicated. Obviously the daily water requirement from the top axis will also need to be divided by ten, and in the example will be 24 m³/d. Similarly, it is possible to scale the nomograph up by a factor of ten to look at the requirements for 10 to 100 ha in exactly the same way. Note that in most real cases, if the scale is changed, factors like the pump efficiency ought to be changed too. An efficiency of 50% used in the example is a poor efficiency for a pump large enough to deliver 240 m³/d, but it is rather a high efficiency for a pump capable of only one tenth of this daily discharge.

5.7 Review of a complete pumping system

Figure 5.13 summarizes the discussion of system power and losses in the above sections. It is drawn for an irrigation system, but the principles are the same for a drinking water supply

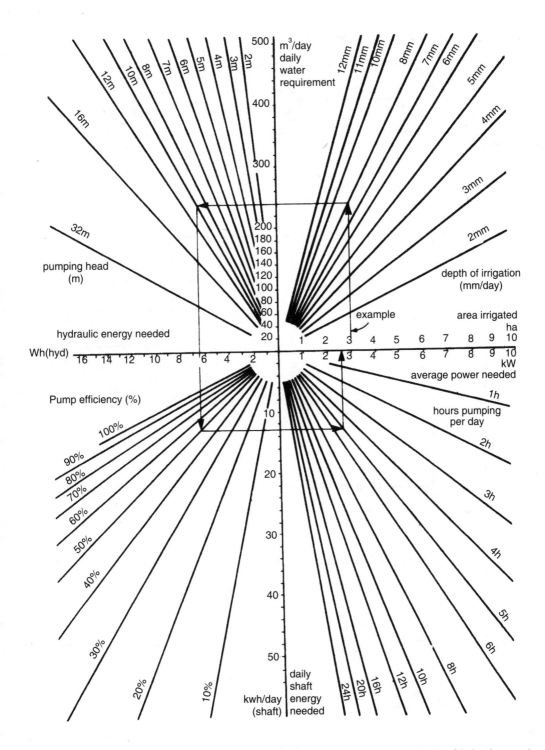

Fig. 5.12: Nomogram for calculating power needs for irrigating a given area, depth of irrigation, and head

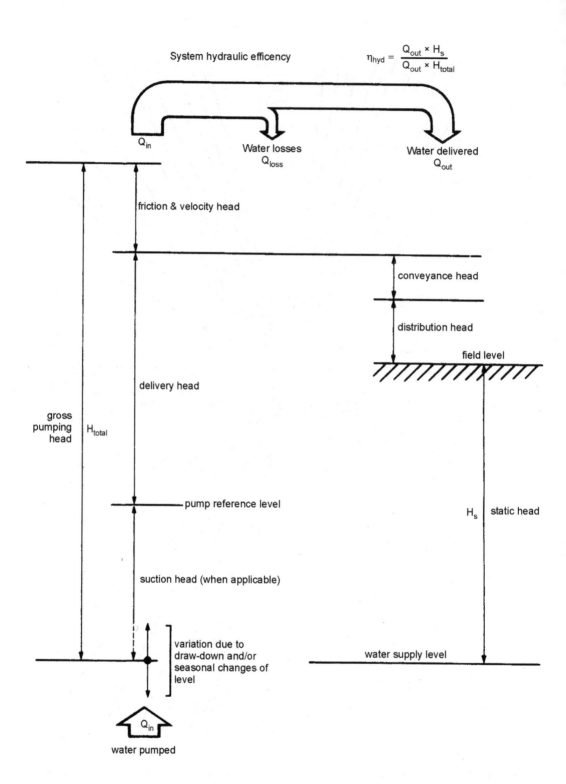

System hydraulic efficency

$$\eta_{hyd} = \frac{Q_{out} \times H_s}{Q_{out} \times H_{total}}$$

Q_{in}

Water losses
Q_{loss}

Water delivered
Q_{out}

friction & velocity head

conveyance head

distribution head

field level

delivery head

gross
pumping
head

H_{total}

pump reference level

H_s static head

suction head (when applicable)

variation due to
draw-down and/or
seasonal changes of
level

water supply level

Q_{in}

water pumped

Fig. 5.13: Factors affecting system hydraulic efficiency of an irrigation system

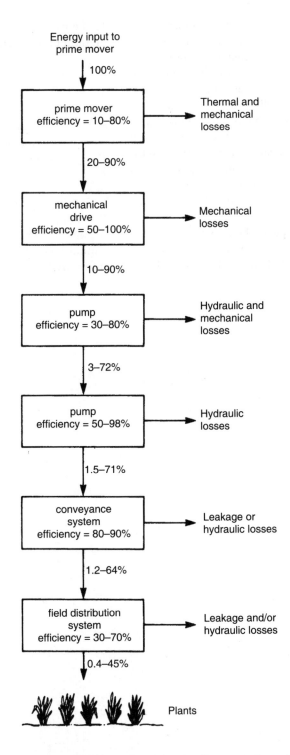

Fig. 5.14: Energy flow through a typical irrigation system, showing the percentage of the original energy that is transmitted from each component to the next

system. The figure shows in diagrammatic form the way the hydraulic output power from a pump is used in an irrigation scheme. The useful output power – the reason for having the pump in the first place – is the product of the static head, H_{static}, and the water delivered, Q_{out}. All the rest of the power is wasted. Some power is absorbed by friction and velocity head losses ($H_{friction}$ and $H_{velocity}$), some is dissipated in the slopes needed to take the water by gravity down pipes or channels to where it is needed ($H_{conveyance}$ and $H_{distribution}$), and some power is lost in water that leaks away (Q_{loss}).

The system hydraulic efficiency can be defined as the ratio of hydraulic energy to raise the water delivered to the field through the static head, to the hydraulic energy actually needed for the amount of water drawn by the pump:

$$\eta_{system} = \frac{E_{static}}{E_{gross}}$$

η_{system}	–	system hydraulic efficiency (fraction)
E_{static}	–	hydraulic energy output
E_{gross}	–	hydraulic energy actually applied

Finally, Fig. 5.14 indicates the energy flow through a typical complete irrigation water lifting and distribution systems and highlights the various losses that occur and which need to be minimized.

REVIEW OF PUMPS AND WATER LIFTING TECHNIQUES

6.1 Principles for lifting and moving water

Water may he moved by the application of any one (or any combination) of six different mechanical principles, which are largely independent. These are:

- *Direct lift*
  This involves physically lifting water in a container.
- *Displacement*
  This involves utilizing the fact that water is (effectively) incompressible and can therefore be 'pushed' or displaced.
- *Creating a velocity head*
  When water is propelled to a high speed, the momentum can be used either to create a flow or to create a pressure.
- *Using the buoyancy of a gas*
  Air (or other gas) bubbled through water will lift a proportion of the water.
- *Gravity*
  Water flows downward under the influence of gravity.

6.2 Classification of water lifts and pumps

Families of pumps and lifting/propelling devices may be classified according to which of the above principles they depend on. Table 6.1 is an attempt to classify pumps under the categories given above. It will be seen that most categories subdivide into the further classifications 'reciprocating/cyclic' or 'rotary'. The first of these relates to devices that are cycled through a water-lifting

operation (for example a bucket on a rope is lowered into the water, dipped to make it fill, lifted, emptied and then the cycle is repeated); in such cases the water output is usually intermittent, or at best pulsating rather than continuous. Rotary devices were generally developed to allow a greater throughput of water, and they also are easier to couple to engines or other types of mechanical drive. Therefore, by definition, a rotary pump will generally operate without any reversal or cessation of flow, although in some cases the output may appear in spurts or pulsations.

Before considering the differences between the diverse options available for lifting water, it is worth briefly noting the factors they all have in common. Virtually all water lifting devices can best be characterized for practical purposes by measuring their output at different heads and speeds. Normally the performance of a pump is presented on a graph of head versus flow (an H-Q graph, as in Fig. 6.1) and in most cases curves can be defined for the relationship between H and Q at different speeds of operation. Invariably there is a certain head, flow and speed of operation that represents the optimum efficiency of the device, i.e. where the output is maximized in relation to the power input. Some devices and pumps are more sensitive to variations in these factors than others; i.e. some only function well close to a certain design condition of speed, flow and head, while others can tolerate a wide range of operating conditions with little loss of efficiency. For example, the centrifugal pump characteristic given in Fig. 6.1 shows an optimum efficiency exceeding 80% is only possible for speeds of about 2,000 rpm.

Table 6.1: Taxonomy of pumps and water lifts

Category and name	Manufacturer	Head range (m)	Power range	Output	Efficiency	Cost	Suction Lift?	Use for irrigation	Use for drinking water	Availability
I. DIRECT LIFT DEVICES										
Reciprocating/cyclic										
Watering can	1	<3	★	★	★	★	×	✓	×	✓
Scoops and bailers	1	<1	★	★★	★	★	×	✓	×	×
Swing basket	1	<1	★	★★	★	★	×	✓	×	×
Pivoting gutters or dhones	2	1–1.5	★	★★	★★	★★	×	✓	×	×
Counterpoise lift or Shadoof	2	1–4	★	★★	★★	★★	×	✓	×	×
Rope, bucket and windlass	1	5–50	★	★	★	★	×	?	✓	✓
Self-emptying bucket or mohte	2	3–8	★★	★★★	★	★★	×	✓	×	×
Rotary/continuous										
Continuous bucket pump	2	5–50	★★	★★	★★★	★★	×	✓	×	×
Persian wheel or tablia	2	3–10	★★	★★★	★★★	★★	×	✓	×	×
Improved Persian wheel or zawaffa	2	3–15	★★★	★★★★	★★★★★	★★★★	×	✓	×	×
Scoop wheels or sakia	2	<2	★★	★★★★	★★★★★	★★★★★	×	✓	×	×
Water wheels or noria	2	<5	★	★★	★★	★★	×	✓	×	×
II. DISPLACEMENT PUMPS										
Reciprocating/cyclic										
Piston/bucket pumps	2 and 3	2–200	★★★	★★★	★★★★★	★★★★★★	✓	✓	✓	✓
Plunger pumps	3	100–500	★★★	★★	★★★★★	★★★★★★	✓	?	?	×
Diaphragm pumps	3	5–10	★★	★★★	★★★★	★★★	✓	✓	×	✓
Gas or vapour displacement	3	5–10	★★★★	★★★★	★★★	★★★	✓ or ×	?	×	×
Rotary/continuous										
Flexible vane	3	10–20	★★	★★★	★★★★	★★★★★	✓	×	×	×
Progressing cavity or Mono	3	10–200	★★★	★★★	★★★★	★★★★★	×	?	✓	✓
Archimedes' screw	3	<2	★★	★★★	★★★	★★★	×	✓	×	×

	Manufacture	Head range (m)							Suction lift	Usage		General availability
Open screw	3	<6	★★★★	★★★★★	★★★★	★★★★	★★★★★	×	✓	×	×	×
Coil and spiral	2	<6	★★	★★★	★★★★	★★★	★★★	×	✓	×	×	×
Flash wheels and treadmills	2 and 3	<2	★★★★	★★	★★★★	★★	★★★★★	×	✓	×	×	×
Water ladders	2	<2	★★★	★★★	★★★★	★★★	★★	×	✓	×	×	×
Chain/rope and washer	2 and 3	3–80	★★★	★★★	★★★	★★★	★★★★	×	✓	✓	✓	✓
III. VELOCITY PUMPS												
Reciprocating/cyclic inertia												
Inertia and joggle	2 and 3	2–4	★	★★	★★	★★	★★	×	✓	×	×	×
Resonating joggle	2	2–10	★★	★★★★	★★★★★	★★★	★★★	×	✓	×	×	×
Rotary/continuous												
Axial-flow/propeller	3	3–5	★★★★	★★★★★	★★★★★	★★★★★	★★★★★	×	✓	×	×	✓*
Mixed-flow	3	2–10	★★★★★	★★★★★★	★★★★★★	★★★★	★★★	×	✓	✓	✓	✓
Centrifugal	3	3–20+	★★★★★★	★★★★★★	★★★★★	★★★★	★★★★	✓	✓	✓	✓	✓
Regenerative	3	10–30	★★★	★★★	★★★★	★★★★	★★★★	✓	'	?	?	✓
Jet (water/air/steam)	3	2–20	★★★	★★★	★★★	★★★	★★★	×	'	×	×	✓
IV. BUOYANCY PUMPS												
Air-lift	3	5–50	★★	★★★	★★★	★★★	★★★★★	×	?	×	×	×
V. IMPULSE PUMPS												
Hydraulic ram or hydram	3	10–100	★★	★★★	★★★★	★★★	★★★	×	✓	✓	✓	✓
VI. GRAVITY DEVICES												
Siphons	1, 2 and 3	1–(–10)	★★★★★	★★★★★	–	★★	–	✓	–	×	×	×
Qanats or foggara	2	–	★★	★★★★★	★★★★	–	★★★★★	–	?	–	✓	✓

Key to Table 6.1:

Manufacture: 1 – basic, 2– traditional, 3 – industrial;

Ratings: ★ – very low, ★★ – low-medium, ★★★ – medium, ★★★★ – medium–high, ★★★★★ – high;

Suction lift: ✓ – yes, × – no;

Usage: ✓ – yes, ? – possible, ' – unlikely;

General Availability: ✓ – widely available, × – only available in certain areas, ✓* – only large pumps widely available.

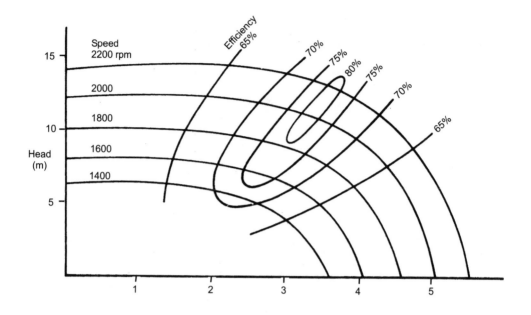

Fig. 6.1: Typical centrifugal pump curves showing the relationship between head, flow, speed and efficiency

The remainder of this section describes in some detail each of the devices given in Table 6.1, the taxonomy of pumps and water lifts

6.3 Reciprocating and cyclic direct lift devices

6.3.1 Watering cans, buckets, scoops, bailers and the swing-basket

These are all variations on the theme of the bucket. They are hand-held and represent the earliest artificial methods for lifting and carrying water. The watering can is effectively a bucket with a built-in sprinkler and represents an efficient but labour-intensive method for irrigating very small land-holdings. Artisan-made watering cans are quite widely used in Thailand and many other countries. Buckets can be carried more easily if a pair of them are fitted to a yoke, and this is often done when the water needs to be carried some distance.

Scoops (Fig. 6.2), bailers, and the swing-basket (Fig. 6.3) represent methods of speeding up the process of filling, lifting and emptying a bucket; the latter also uses two people rather than one and thereby increases the mass of water that can be scooped in each swing. These are more fully described in Section 7.2 in the context of using human muscle power, since they have evolved in such a way as to fit the human prime mover but to be unsuitable for any kind of mechanization. They are rather inefficient, since water is lifted over 1 m and allowed to fall back to 0.3–0.5 m, which is the approximate operating head for devices of this kind.

6.3.2 Suspended scoop, see-sawing gutters (dhones or doons) and the counterpoise-lift (shadoof)

The next stage of technical advance is to support the mass of water being lifted by mounting the scoop or bucket on a suspended pivoted lever to produce a swinging scoop

Fig. 6.2: The scoop used as a simple hand tool

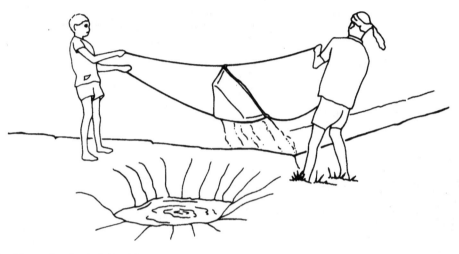

Fig. 6.3: The swing basket in use

(Fig. 6.4). An alternative is to pivot a channel or gutter. An Indian version of this is shown in Fig. 6.5.

A variant of this from Bangladesh is the see-sawing gutter, which is called a 'dhone' or 'doon' (Fig. 6.6). These still can only operate through low lifts (0.5–1 m) at relatively high speed.

The water container can be balanced with a weight to make a counterpoise lift, or a water-crane, as shown in Fig. 6.7. These simple 'shadoofs' (or 'shadufs') date back to around 2,500 BC in ancient Egypt, and are still used today in the Middle East. The output of a shadoof depends on the strength of the operator, but it can lift around 2.5 m³/h from up to 4 m depth (Bielenberg and Allen, 1995 [35]).

If the terrain permits, such as on a sloping river bank, a series of these types of lifts can be used to raise water in stages through a greater height than is possible with one.

6.3.3 Bucket hoists, windlasses, mohtes and water skips

To increase the lift it becomes necessary to introduce a rope to pull the container of water from the source to a level where it can be tipped into a suitable container, or into a conveyance channel. There is therefore a family of devices for pulling up a container of water on a rope. The simplest form for this is a rope and bucket, which in an improved form has a simple windlass, i.e. a hand operated winch, to increase the leverage and hence the size of bucket that can be lifted. A typical installation is shown in Fig. 6.8. Some winches have a ratchet mechanism to prevent

Fig. 6.4: Scoop with rope support

Fig. 6.5: An Indian pivoting-gutter lift

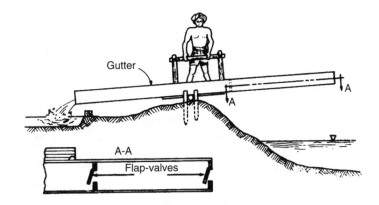

Fig. 6.6: A dhone as used in Bangladesh

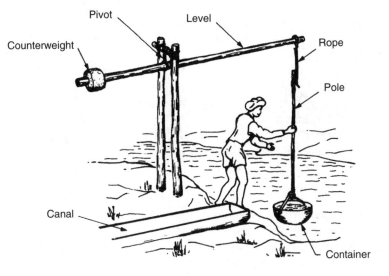

Fig. 6.7: Counterpoise lift or shadoof

the drum from running backwards, in case the operator looses grip of the handle.

The 'Bucket Pump' developed in Zimbabwe is a variant of the simple bucket-and-windlass design that has been developed to look more like a pump (Fig. 6.9). The bucket is a long, narrow piece of pipe with a valve at the bottom. The bucket is winched down a pipe into the water, where it fills through the valve, and is then winched up again. The user's water container is placed under a 'discharge unit' on one of the side posts. When the full bucket is brought out of the downpipe it is placed in this unit, which opens the valve and discharges the water. The idea of this is to keep physical contact with the bucket to a minimum to reduce the chance of contamination. The Bucket Pump does produce water that is of substantially better bacteriological quality than a standard well. It is used up to a depth of 15 m, and can produce 5–10 litres per minute.

Winched bucket systems tend to be used for domestic or livestock water supply, because the output is low, but by powering the device with animals, usually oxen, sufficient water can be lifted to irrigate, even through heads as great as 5–10 m. This encouraged the evolution of the

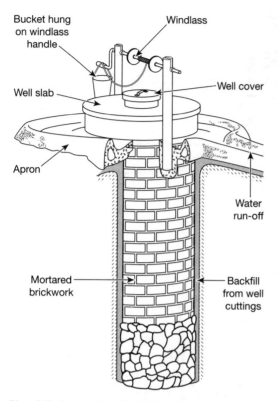

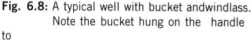

Fig. 6.8: A typical well with bucket andwindlass. Note the bucket hung on the handle to keep it clean

'self-emptying bucket', known in India as a 'mohte', (Fig. 6.10 and Fig. 7.18). These usually have a bucket made of leather or rubber, with a hole in its bottom which is sealed by a flap pulled tight by a second rope harnessed to the animals. It was estimated that around a million were in use some years ago, though their numbers have probably declined since. Mohtes are discussed in more detail under Section 7.3 dealing with animal power as a prime mover.

6.4 Rotary direct lift devices

It generally improves efficiency, and hence productivity, if the water lifting machine rotates continuously rather than moving back and forwards. If the machinery moves in a circle it can build up momentum, and the energy input can be

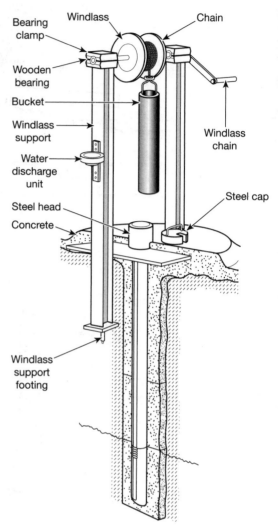

Fig. 6.9: The Bucket Pump. Note the use of the discharge unit to empty the bucket

continuous. Cyclic machines require energy to accelerate and reverse the movement of their components, and energy can usually only be put in at certain points in the cycle. In general, cyclic/reciprocating devices tend to be less efficient than rotary devices. (This is not a firm rule however, as some reciprocating devices include means to store energy through the non-productive part of the cycle while some rotary devices are less efficient for other reasons.)

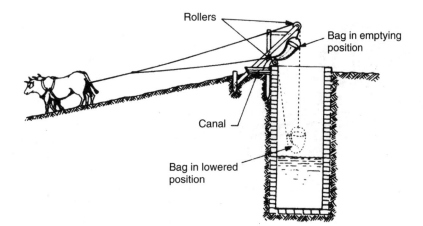

Fig. 6.10: Self-emptying mohte with inclined towpath

6.4.1 Bucket elevators: Persian wheels and norias

An obvious improvement to the simple rope and bucket is to fit numerous small buckets around the periphery of an endless belt to form a continuous bucket elevator. The original version of this, which is ancient in origin but still widely used, was known as a 'Persian wheel' (Fig. 6.11, Fig. 7.19 and Fig. 7.20); the earliest forms consisted of earthenware pots roped in a chain which is hung over a drive wheel. The water powered 'noria' (Fig. 6.12, Fig. 7.76 and Fig. 7.77), a water wheel with pots, buckets or hollow bamboo containers set around its rim, is similar in principle except the containers are physically attached to the drive wheel circumference rather than to an endless belt suspended from it.

The flow with any of these devices is a function of the volume of each bucket and the speed at which the buckets pass across the top of the wheel and tip their contents into a trough set inside the wheel to catch the output from the buckets. Therefore, for a given power source and speed of operation roughly the same number of containers are needed regardless of head. In other words, a higher head Persian wheel requires the buckets to be proportionately more spaced out; double the head and you more or less need to double the spacing.

Fig. 6.11: A Persian wheel

The Persian wheel has been, and still is, widely used particularly in the north of the Indian subcontinent and is discussed in more detail under Section 7.3 on Animal Power, while the noria was widely used in China, S. E. Asia and to some extent in the Middle East, and being normally water powered, is discussed in more detail in Section 7.8.4. Both devices are generally being replaced by more modern mechanical water lifting techniques as they are old-fashioned and low

71

Fig. 6.12: A noria

in output. It should be noted that the term 'Persian wheel' is sometimes used to describe other types of animal powered rotary pumps.

Although Persian wheels and norias are mechanically quite efficient, there are some inherent losses. There is spillage from the buckets, and the wheel is obliged to lift the water past the top of the wheel before discharging it, which can significantly increase the pumping head, particularly in the case of low lifts. There is also a certain amount of drag caused when the buckets scoop up water, which again reduces efficiency. Some performance figures for animal powered Persian wheels are given in Table 6.2.

Depending on the assumptions used for the power of the animals in the above examples, the implication is that the efficiency is in the order of 50% at medium lifts such as 6 m; it is slightly better at higher lifts, but worse at lower lifts.

Table 6.2: Performance figures for animal-powered Persian wheels (Molenaar, 1956 [36])

Height lifted (m)	Discharge (m³/h)
9	8–10
6	10–12
3	15–17
1.5	20–22

A traditional wooden Persian wheel needs to be of large diameter to accommodate a collection trough big-enough to catch most of the water spilling from the pots; this in turn requires a large diameter well, which further increases the cost.

The water-powered noria uses the same principle as the Persian wheel, and therefore also needs to be of larger diameter than the pumping head, which either limits it to very low lift pumping or requires very large, cumbersome and expensive construction. Small, low-lift, inexpensive norias, were traditionally used in Thailand and China, while much larger norias were used in Vietnam and Syria. Some of the largest in Syria exceeded 10 m in diameter, but in relation to their size they tend to be unproductive compared with more modern pumping systems. A fuller description of Vietnamese and other norias is given in Section 7.8.4.

6.4.2 Improved Persian wheel: zawaffa or jhallar

Traditional wooden Persian wheels were fitted with earthenware water containers, but a variety of all-metal improved Persian wheels have been built, some as commercial products, in China, India, Pakistan and Egypt. Metal Persian wheels can be made smaller in diameter, which reduces the extra height the water needs to be lifted before it is tipped out of the containers, and also reduces the well diameter that is necessary.

A modified version of the Persian wheel used in Syria and also in Egypt (where it is called the 'zawaffa' or 'jhallar') includes internal buckets within the drive wheel which catch the water and direct it through holes in the side plate near the hub into a collection trough; Fig. 6.13. This reduces both splashing and spillage losses and also reduced the height above the collection channel at which the water is tipped. A modernized metal Persian wheel, is reported as giving an output of 153 m³/h over a 0.75 m lift (Roberts and Singh, 1951 [37]). This implies that efficiencies as high as 75% for modernized devices are possible.

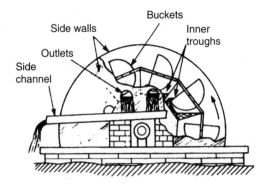

Fig. 6.13: Zawaffa-type Persian wheel (side wall shown partially removed)

6.4.3 Scoop-wheels: drum-wheel, tympanum, sakia, or tablia

The scoop-wheel shown in Fig. 6.14 has some factors in common with the noria. This type of wheel is also called a 'drum-wheel', or 'tympanum' (from the Greek word for drum), but are called 'sakia' in Egypt, where they originated. Although hundreds of thousands have been used in the Nile valley and the delta region of Egypt, it has failed to become popular anywhere else. It is however an efficient and effective device.

It consists of a large hollow wheel divided into a number of compartments. Each compartment is shaped to form a scoop on the periphery of the wheel. In the simplest designs, all the compartments discharge into a single annulus near the centre of one side. A more complex design, known generically as the 'tablia', has each compartment discharging into individual inner chambers which have separate discharge holes. This design prevents water in one compartment from running back into the compartment adjacent to it. The tablia design also discharges a few centimetres above the centre shaft, instead of just below it, thereby increasing the useful head. In tests conducted by the Hydraulic Research and Experimental Station (HRES) in Egypt, it was found that the tablia gave better performance than the simpler design. The shape of the internal walls between the compartments was also significant. Overall, the best designs had outputs 50% better than the worst. Another important conclusion was that for wheels operated in the 2–15 rpm range, 6–8 compartments provide the optimum discharge.

Sakias range from about 2–5 m in diameter, but the lift is only about half this since water discharges at hub level. The rule of thumb used in Egypt is that a sakia will lift water through a head of half its diameter less 0.7 m, to allow for the depth of submergence of the rim in order to scoop up water effectively. Therefore sakias of

Fig. 6.14: A sakia or tympanum (electrically powered in this case)

diameters from 2–5 m will lift water from 0.3–1.8 m respectively. Tablias do rather better: typically a 3 m tablia will lift water 1.5 m compared with 0.90 m for a centre-discharge sakia.

Most sakias are animal powered, but they are increasingly being driven by either mains electric motors or small engines, via suitable reduction gearing. The normal operating speed is 2–4 rpm for animal-driven sakias, and 8–15 rpm for motorized or engine-powered units. Sakias are now normally made from galvanized sheet steel. Second-hand vehicle roller bearings are commonly used to support the substantial weight of a sakia and its water contents.

Typical outputs of traditional sakias (not the improved tablia) are given in Table 6.3. Comparison of these outputs with those from the Persian wheel in Table 6.2 indicate that the sakia is somewhat more efficient, although of course it cannot lift water as high as is possible with a Persian wheel.

6.4.4 Coil and spiral pumps

These pumps are similar to the Archimedes' screw, but they run horizontally while the Archimedes' screw is tilted at about 30°. The coil and spiral pump family, if fitted with a suitable rotating seal, can deliver water to a height of, typically, 5–10 m above their discharge opening. Fig. 6.15A shows a spiral pump, and Fig. 6.15B shows a coil pump.

Both these pumps work on the same principle, involving either a spiral or a coiled passage (in the latter case a coiled hosepipe serves the purpose) rotating on a horizontal axis. One end of the passage is open at the periphery and dips into

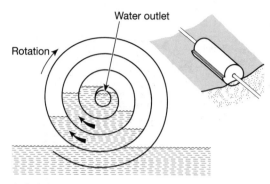

A Spiral pump

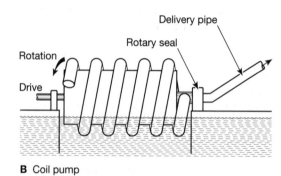

B Coil pump

Fig. 6.15: Hydrostatic pressure pumps

the water once per revolution, scooping up a pool of water each time. Due to the shape of the spiral or the coil, sufficient water is picked up to fill completely the lower part of one turn, thereby trapping air in the next turn. The pools of water move progressively along the base of the coil (or spiral) as the pump turns, similarly to an Archimedes' screw in principle. However, when acting against a positive head, the back-pressure forces the pools of water slightly back from the lowest position in each coil as they get nearer to the discharge; so they progressively take up positions further around the coil from the lowest point. The maximum discharge head of either type of pump is governed by the need to avoid water near the discharge from being forced back over the top of a coil by the back pressure, so this is still a low head device.

Table 6.3: Typical performance of traditional sakias[36]

Diameter of Sakia (m)	Head lifted (m)	Output (m³/h)
5	1.8	36
4	1.3	51
3	0.9	75
5	0.3	114

The spiral pump has to be designed so that the smaller circumferences of the inner loops are compensated for by an increased radial cross-section, so it would normally be fabricated from sheet metal; the coil pump is of course much easier to build.

This type of pump was originally described in the literature as long ago as 1806, and attracted fresh interest during the 1980s (Collett, 1981 [38]). Although historically the coil pump was used as a ship's bilge pump, it has also been tried for river-current-powered irrigation pumps. Section 7.9.12 deals with some of the practical applications of this device.

The advantage of these devices is their inherent mechanical simplicity combined with the fact that, unlike an Archimedes' screw, they can deliver into a pipe to a head of up to about 8–10 m, making them more versatile. The only difficult mechanical component is a rotary seal to join a fixed delivery pipe to the rotating output from the coil. They are ideal for water wheel applications due to the low speed and high torque needed.

Their main disadvantage is that their output is small unless rather large diameter hose is used, being proportional to the capacity of the lower part of one turn of hose per revolution. A simple calculation indicates that a significant and not inexpensive length of hose is needed to produce an adequate coil pump, (e.g. just 20 coils of only 1.5 m diameter needs nearly 100 m of hose). Supporters of this concept argue that its simplicity, suitability for local improvization and reliability should compensate for these high costs, but this type of pump has so far not been popularized successfully for general use and it does not exist as a commercial product.

6.5 Reciprocating positive displacement pumps

Positive displacement pumps are those in which the water is displaced from one sealed compartment to another. Reciprocating pumps are those in which the pumping action is cyclic. Most common reciprocating pumps have a piston moving backwards and forwards in a tube, where an arrangement of seals and valves make the water move in the correct direction through the pump. The most widely used type of reciprocating pump is the village handpump, like the one shown in Fig. 6.16.

Reciprocating pumps were used in Roman times for fire fighting and as ships' bilge pumps. A precursor of modern handpumps, a wooden pump with metal flap valves and a leather seal, was designed by the German scientist Georgius Agricola (1494–1555) in Saxony in the 16th century. From this period onwards, reciprocating pumps spread over Europe, initially made of wood, then of lead, then almost universally of cast iron. With the advent of the Industrial Revolution, cast iron pumps were made in large numbers. These pumps became standard in backyards and village squares throughout Europe and North America in the 19th century, supplying water in both rural areas and towns. They were replaced as piped water supplies became more common, though many handpumps remained in use into the twentieth century.

Reciprocating pumps are still widely used in many areas of the world. A major impetus in the installation of such pumps was the International Drinking Water Supply and Sanitation Decade, from 1981–1990. During this Water Decade a huge effort was made by governments and development organizations around the world to provide clean drinking water supplies to both urban and rural populations. There was an extensive programme of handpump development, led by UNDP and the World Bank. Indigenous production of handpumps was encouraged in many countries, and millions of handpumps were installed.

Reciprocating pumps come in numerous forms. While the most common type is the handpump, some are worked by foot, or even by jumping up and down on them (see the Kangaroo pump, Section 7.2.4). The pumping action itself is reciprocating, but by using a linkage to connect the piston to a wheel, the pump can be driven by a rotating input. This allows electric motors and internal combustion engines to be used as the source of power, and some village water pumps are driven by large diameter hand

75

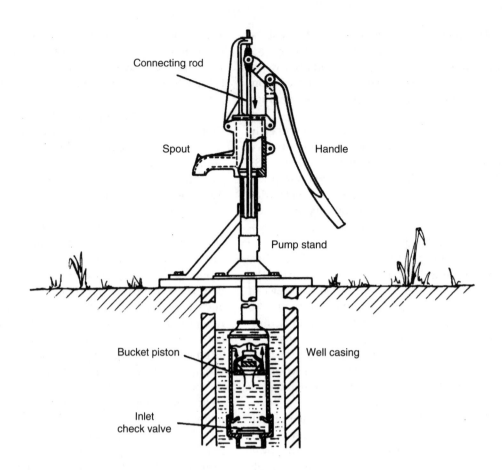

Fig. 6.16: A typical reciprocating handpump (a No. 6 handpump)

wheels. The following section describes various generic types of reciprocating pump, and the physical principles behind their operation. Subsequent sections describe examples of actual pumps.

6.5.1 Basic principles

Reciprocating pumps are based on three main principles: direct lift, suction and displacement. These are illustrated in Fig. 6.17. Direct lift is shown in A, where the water above the piston is being raised with it. All this needs is a seal between the piston and the cylinder to prevent the water leaking back down to the bottom. Suction is illustrated in B, where water is sucked in as the piston is raised. It is more accurate to say that the

atmospheric pressure outside pushes water up into the low pressure space created by moving the piston up. Suction pumping requires a seal between the piston and the cylinder to prevent air leaking down onto the water side, and sufficient pressure on the body of water to push the water up the cylinder. Displacement is shown in C, where the piston is lowered into the water so that the level rises, causing it to overflow from the spout. This is equivalent to a person climbing into a bath that is too full! Note that no seal is required between the piston and the cylinder.

The handpump in Fig. 6.16 shows one way in which valves and pistons can be arranged to use the first two pumping methods. This pump has one valve in the piston and another at the base of the cylinder. The piston valve closes as the

76

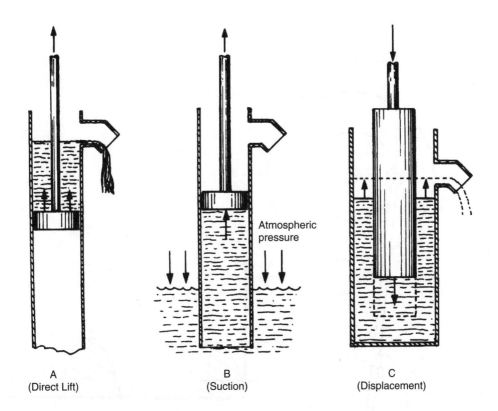

Fig. 6.17: Basic principles of reciprocating pumps

piston travels upwards, so that the water above it is lifted directly, while the water below is sucked upwards through the open lower valve. When the piston goes down (the situation shown in the figure) the foot valve closes, and the piston valve opens; no water is pumped during this stroke.

A property of water that makes it particularly suitable for reciprocating pumps is that it is virtually incompressible. So when a piston is moved, it pumps a volume of water equal to the volume through which it sweeps. When pumping a compressible fluid, such as air, the piston would compress or expand the fluid, making the action spongy, and pumping a smaller volume.

Discharge, volumetric efficiency and slippage
It is quite straightforward to calculate the theoretical discharge of a reciprocating pump. It is found from the swept volume of the piston, which is the area swept multiplied by the stroke. The swept area is simply the area of the piston for a displacement pump (Fig. 6.17C), but is the cross-sectional area of the cylinder (i.e. the piston plus the seal) for suction and direct lift pumps (Fig. 6.17A and B).

$$V = A \cdot S = \frac{\pi D^2}{4} \cdot S$$

V – swept volume (m³)
A – swept area of the piston (m²)
S – stroke (m)
D – effective piston diameter (piston + seal, or cylinder diameter) (m)

The discharge will be somewhat less than this due to leakage and other losses. This loss is expresses as the volumetric efficiency, usually as a

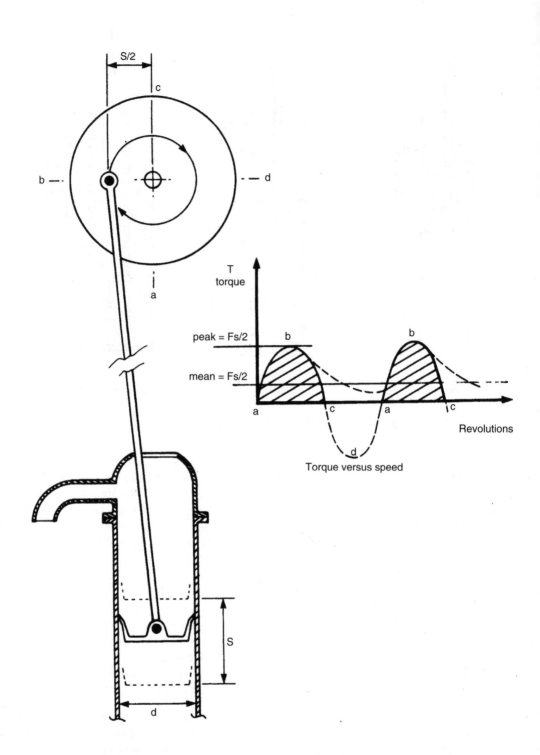

Fig. 6.18: Crank-operated piston pump (valve details not shown)

percentage (e.g. η_{vol} = 90%). The discharge per stroke is the displaced volume decreased by the volumetric efficiency:

$$q = \frac{\eta_{vol}}{100} \cdot V$$

q – discharge per stroke (m³)
η_{vol} – volumetric efficiency of the pump (%)

The pumping rate is given by this discharge per stroke multiplied by the stroke rate. The stroke rate is typically measured in strokes per minute (or the rpm if the input is rotary), whereas the output is normally given in cubic metres per hour, so a factor of 60 (minutes per hour) needs to be included:

$$Q = 60 n \cdot q = 60 n \cdot \frac{\eta_{vol}}{100} \cdot S \cdot \frac{\pi D^2}{4}$$

Q – pumping rate (m³/h)
n – number of strokes per minute (min⁻¹)

To convert this to the other commonly-used units, litres per minute, the result should be multiplied by 16.67 (1,000 l/m³ ÷ 60 min/h). To find the flow in l/s, multiply the output of the equation by 0.2778.

Volumetric efficiency may be expressed as a decimal fraction and is sometimes called 'Coefficient of Discharge' (so η_{vol} = 90% is equivalent to C_D = 0.9). Another commonly used and related term is 'Slippage' (X), which is the difference between the swept volume per stroke and the output per stroke, expressed as a fraction of the swept volume:

$$X = \frac{V - q}{V}$$

X – slippage (fraction)
V – swept volume per stroke (m³ or same as q)
q – discharge per stroke (m³ or same as V)

As stated above, slippage arises partly because of leakage round the seals, but a number of other factors also contribute. Valves controlling the flow through the pump take time to close. A valve that opens as the piston travels downwards may not have fully closed by the time the piston starts going back up, giving rise to more leakage. The valves themselves may also leak, even when shut. Slippage is therefore normally less than unity, typically 0.1 or 0.2. It tends to be worse for short-stroke pumps, and for high heads.

Under certain circumstances, the slippage can be negative, i.e. the discharge is greater than the swept volume. This apparent impossibility arises because of the inertia of the water. When the flow rate is high at low heads, the momentum of the water can keep it moving even after the piston has reversed its direction of travel. For the pump in Fig. 6.16, at the end of the up-stroke the water may keep moving upwards even when the piston has started travelling back down. Both the piston and the foot valve remain open for a while, and the pump may deliver more than the swept volume. In extreme cases the slippage can add half as much flow again to the theoretical discharge, giving an equivalent volumetric efficiency in the region of 150%.

Forces
A simple calculation of the force required to operate a pump can be done by just considering the weight of the piston and rod assembly, and the weight of the water moved:

$$F = W_p + \rho \cdot g \cdot H$$

F – force required to move piston (N)
W_p – weight of piston and pump rod (N)
A – cross-sectional area of the cylinder (m²)
ρ – density of water (1,000 kg/m³)
g – acceleration due to gravity (9.8 m/s²)
H – head (m)

There are actually other forces involved: friction between the seal and the surface it moves against; buoyancy from the water on any parts of the piston and rod assembly that are submerged; forces associated with flow losses in the water; dynamic forces arising from the acceleration of both the pump components and the water during the pumping cycle. The equation above ignores all these forces, which is often a reasonable first approximation. There are, however, cases when the water acceleration forces, in particular, can be very large, and this is dealt with below in the sub-section 'Seals'.

If the pump rod is connected to a lever, as in a hand pump (see Fig. 6.16), then the downward force required to lift the pump rod will be reduced by the ratio of the leverage (the mechanical advantage), however, the distance the hand of the operator will have to move, compared with the stroke, will be proportionately increased (by the velocity ratio of the lever).

The higher the forces on a handpump, obviously, the stronger it must be. Some of the weak points are the lever and fulcrum mechanism and the pump column itself; these can crack through metal fatigue or due to the use of poor quality castings. The pump in Fig. 6.16 is good in having a bracing strut to support the pump body, but it is bad in having the pivot bolt for the handle passing through the middle of the most highly stressed part of the pump lever. A better method of pivoting the hand lever is to have the pivot bearing passing through a lug below the lever arm to avoid weakening the arm at that point, as in Fig. 6.27.

The pump rod can also be connected to a flywheel via a crank (as in Fig. 6.18 and Fig. 7.10); this is the conventional way of mechanizing a reciprocating piston pump. The torque (or rotational couple) needed to make the crank or flywheel turn will vary depending on the position of the crank. When the piston is at the bottom of its travel (bottom dead centre or b.d.c.), marked as 'a' on the figure, the torque will be zero. In this position the pump rod pull is acting at right angles to the direction of movement of the crank and the rod simply hangs on the crank. As the wheel rotates to the horizontal position marked 'b' the torque will increase sinusoidally to a maximum value of $F \times S/2$ (force F times the leverage, which is $S/2$). Beyond point 'b' the resisting force

will decrease sinusoidally to zero at top dead centre (t.d.c.), marked 'c'. After t.d.c. the weight of the pump rod and piston will actually help to pull the crank around and while the piston is moving down the water imposes no significant force on it other than friction. If, for convenience, we assume the weight of the piston and pump rod is more or less cancelled out by friction and dynamic effects, the torque is effectively zero for the half cycle from t.d.c. at 'c' through 'd' to 'a' at b.d.c. where the cycle restarts. The small graph alongside the sketch in Fig. 6.18 illustrates the variation of torque with crank position through two complete revolutions; anyone who has turned a direct driven hand pump via a crank and hand wheel will have experienced how the load builds up in this way for a quarter cycle and falls back to (near) zero for the next quarter cycle.

If the crank has a flywheel attached to it, as it normally will, then the momentum of the flywheel will smooth out these cyclic fluctuations by slowing down very slightly (too little to be noticeable) during the 'a b c' part of the cycle and speeding up during the 'c d a' part, as illustrated by the broken line following the first revolution in the graph in Fig. 6.18. If the flywheel is large, then it will smooth the fluctuations in cyclic torque to an almost steady level approximating to the mean value of the notched curve in the figure. It can be shown mathematically that the mean value of half a sine wave, to which this curve approximates, is the peak value divided by π (where $\pi = 3.142...$). Therefore, since the peak torque felt by a crank drive is:

$$T_{peak} = \frac{F \cdot S}{2}$$

T_{peak} – peak torque (Nm)
F – force (N)
S – stroke (m)

The mean torque with a large flywheel will be:

$$T_{mean} = \frac{F \cdot S}{2\pi}$$

Therefore, the torque necessary to turn a crank through its first revolution will be about π times (approximately three times) greater than the mean torque that is needed to maintain steady running. This is important because many prime movers cannot readily produce three times the torque needed for running in order to start a pump, and even with those that can there is usually a price to pay to achieve this requirement. This is one reason why centrifugal pumps rather than piston pumps are more commonly used with engines and electric motors, as they actually need less torque to start them than to run them. The ratio of the peak to the mean torque can be reduced to π/2 by adding counterweights or springs on the crank to counterbalance the piston force, but this adds complication, and is not always possible.

The power can be calculated as the product of speed and torque:

$$P = T_{mean} \cdot \frac{2\pi n}{60} = F \cdot S \cdot \frac{n}{60}$$

P – input power (W)
n – rotational speed (rpm)

Seals
Traditional piston seals were leather, and this is still widely used. Suitable grades of cow or buffalo leather, commonly impregnated with 'neatsfoot oil' boiled from the hooves of cattle, will function for surprisingly long periods (several years) in smooth drawn brass cylinders, or in smooth uPVC (plastic). Leather cup seals are tolerant of variations in cylinder diameter, so that they can be used with locally made pipes without any finishing machining. Leather seals can tolerate fine abrasive particles, but are worn quickly by coarse sand. The Tara handpump shown in Fig. 6.25 uses a leather cup seal in a standard uPVC tube.

Leather has been replaced by nitrile rubber in some pumps. These seals can give good, long-term service, but require a close-tolerance fit, with a good surface finish on the inside of the

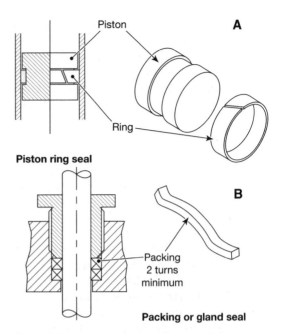

Fig. 6.19: A. A piston ring seal. B. Stuffing box or packing/gland seal on a piston rod

cylinder. The Afridev pump in Fig. 6.28 uses a nitrile rubber seal in a brass liner.

Pistons can also be sealed with piston rings. These are flexible rings with a split in them, usually made of hard plastic (see Fig. 6.19A). There is always some leakage past a piston ring seal, but with a carefully chosen fit the leakage can be quite acceptable at low heads. Piston rings generally have low friction, which makes operating the pump easier.

Packing or gland seals are common on piston rod seals, and are occasionally used on pistons. Packings are several turns of a suitable material 'packed' into a groove and compressed to make them expand sideways into the gap between the rod and the housing (see Fig. 6.19B). In this example, the nut or gland is screwed down to compress the seal. If the compression is too great, the sealing will be excellent but it will be hard to move the rod. If the compression is too small, the rod will slip easily, but there will be a lot of leakage. The gland has to be adjusted to reach a compromise between these extremes, and the seals need re-adjusting regularly. Access to the piston

81

inside a pump is usually difficult, and for this reason packing seals are not really suitable as piston seals. The packing material was traditionally graphited asbestos, but graphited PTFE (polytetrafluoroethylene) is now becoming available and offers superior sealing and wear characteristics.

Valves

All reciprocating pumps (and some rotary pumps) depend on check valves or non-return valves that, as their name suggests, allow water to flow one way but not the other. There are basically three categories of check valve:

- Flexible valves that normally lie in a closed position, but open by being bent or deformed when pressure is applied;
- Hinged valves that open like a door;
- Straight lift valves in which a ball, plate or a shaped 'poppet' rise vertically and evenly from their seats.

Figure 6.20 shows a typical check valve design of the kind that may be used in a reciprocating pump. Valves are invariably opened by the difference in water pressure across them created by piston movement, but they may be closed again either by their own weight usually in combination with the weight of water trying to flow backwards. In some cases closing is assisted by a light spring (as shown in the figure). Valve springs are usually made of bronze to avoid corrosion problems, but alternatively, valves may be made from an elastic material like rubber.

The main requirements of valves are a good seal when closed combined with lack of resistance to flow when they are open, and rapid opening and closing while achieving good durability. Usually rubber or alternatively precision ground metal mating surfaces are necessary to ensure there are no leakage gaps when the valve is closed. Effective sealing is particularly important with foot valves to prevent the rising main from emptying. To offer little resistance to flow when open (and to be capable of opening and closing quickly) demands large port areas with as few changes of flow direction as possible. Sharp edges that can cause turbulence also need to be minimized. An old rule of thumb sometimes used is that the suction valve should have a port area of at least two-thirds of the piston area, while the discharge valve (or piston valve) should have an area of at least half the piston area.

Rapid opening and closing (to minimize back leakage) depends on light weight for the valve, combined with a short travel; light weight can demand a trade off with robustness and durability, while short travel conflicts to some extent with the need for a good unobstructed passage for water when the valve is open. Therefore all valves are a compromise in achieving conflicting requirements.

Finally, valves are the main mechanical components of a pump and so are subject to wear and tear. It is therefore desirable to use pumps in which the valves and their seats can readily (and inexpensively) be replaced when necessary.

Most pumps have two valves, one for the inlet and one for the outlet. On a borehole handpump such as the India Mk. II (Fig. 6.27), the inlet valve is at the base, and is called a 'foot valve' or a 'suction valve'. The outlet or 'discharge' valve is in the piston itself. The same seal arrangement may be used on both valves, reducing the number of spare components that need to be held in stock for repairs. The Afridev handpump (Fig. 6.28), for example, uses the same seal in both locations.

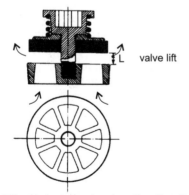

Fig. 6.20: Typical check valve: the direction of flow is shown with arrows

The effect of reciprocating pumps on pipelines

A reciprocating pump moves water in a non-continuous manner, so the water is constantly accelerated and decelerated. Large forces can be created if a long pipeline is directly connected to a reciprocating pump. This is because every cycle the pump piston tries to accelerate the large mass of water in the pipe from rest to full speed. Since water is incompressible, the whole pipe full tries to move as one mass, and since force is proportional to the mass, a large amount of water produces a large reaction force on the piston. For this reason, reciprocating pumps need to be isolated from water in long pipelines by methods described shortly, in order to cushion the water in the pipeline from the motion of the piston.

To gain an appreciation of the damage that can happen, and the consequent importance of isolating reciprocating pumps from long pipelines, it is worth running through some simple calculations to quantify the forces concerned. Figure 6.21 illustrates a simple piston pump with a long length of delivery pipeline. Newton's Laws of Motion state that a force is necessary to accelerate a mass from one velocity to another (or from rest); this force is numerically equal to the product of the mass and the acceleration at any moment in time. If we assume the pump piston is driven sinusoidally, (as it would be if driven by a steadily revolving crank, having a long connecting rod in relation to the stroke), then the maximum acceleration of the piston (and hence of water being propelled by it) will be:

$$a_{max} = \omega^2 \cdot \frac{S}{2}$$

a_{max} – maximum piston acceleration (m/s²)
ω – angular speed of the driving crank (rad/s) (2π radians = 1 revolution or 360°)

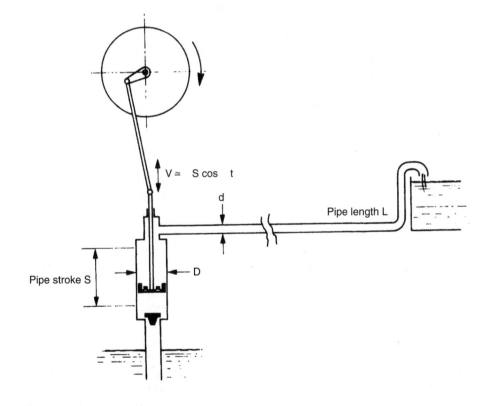

Fig. 6.21: A piston pump connected to a pipeline

The acceleration of the water in the pump is magnified for the water in the pipe, since, if the pipe cross sectional area is smaller than that of the pump, a higher velocity will be needed to pass the same flow of water, and hence a proportionately higher acceleration to reach the higher velocity. The magnification will be proportional to the ratio of pump cross sectional area to pipe cross sectional area, which in turn is proportional to the ratio of their diameters squared; hence the acceleration of water in the pipeline will be:

$$a_{pipe} = \left(\frac{D}{d}\right)^2 \cdot a_{piston}$$

a_{pipe} –   acceleration of the water in the pipe line (m/s²)

a_{piston} –   acceleration of the piston (m/s²)

D –   piston diameter (m)

d –   pipeline bore (m)

The force necessary to achieve this acceleration for the water in the pipeline will be equal to the mass of water flowing multiplied by its acceleration. The mass is the volume of water in the pipe (i.e. $(p.d^2/4).L$) times its density; hence the accelerating force is:

$$F = \left(\frac{\pi d^2}{4}\right) \cdot L \cdot \rho \cdot \left(\frac{D}{d}\right)^2 \cdot a_{piston}$$

F –   force required to accelerate the water in the pipeline (N)

L –   length of the pipeline (m)

ρ –   density of water (1,000 kg/m³)

The maximum force will occur at the moment of maximum acceleration. So, assuming sinusoidal motion of the piston and the flow:

$$F_{max} = \left(\frac{\pi d^2}{4}\right) \cdot L \cdot \rho \cdot \left(\frac{D}{d}\right)^2 \cdot \omega^2 \cdot \left(\frac{S}{2}\right)$$

For example: suppose we consider a pump of 100 mm diameter, connected to a pipeline of 50 mm (0.05 m) diameter, density of water 1,000 kg/m³, a crank speed of 60 rpm (which is 1 rev/s or (1 × 2π) rad/s) and a stroke of 300 mm (0.3 m), then:

$$F_{max} = \frac{\pi}{4} \cdot 0.05^2 \cdot L \cdot 1000 \cdot \left(\frac{0.1}{0.5}\right)^2 \cdot (2\pi)^2 \cdot \left(\frac{0.3}{2}\right)$$

$$= 46.5L$$

This result says that it would, in theory, take a peak force of 46.5 N per metre of pipe to move the water at the maximum acceleration of the piston, once every cycle (at position 'b' in Fig. 6.18). A 100 m pipeline will therefore, with conditions as specified, need a peak force of 4,650 N (0.45 tonnes or 1,000 lbs) to accelerate it while a 1 km pipeline will experience 46,500 N (4.5 tonnes or 10,000 lb). The piston needs to generate this force, putting immense strain on the mechanism. In practice, it will not be able to do it, and will slow down but the forces can still be crippling.

Since this force is proportional to the square of the pump speed, doubling the pump speed to 120 strokes per minute will impose four times the acceleration and hence four times the force. Even such modest pump speeds (by rotary pump standards) as say a few hundred rpm will therefore impose impossible accelerating forces on the water in the pipe line unless it is isolated or cushioned from the motion of the pump piston.

In reality the situation is not quite as bad, as even steel pipes are flexible and will expand slightly to take the shocks. But in some respects it can also be worse, because when valves slam shut against a moving flow, very brief but large shock accelerations can be applied to the water; these are known as 'water-hammer' because of the hammering noise when this happens. Water-hammer shocks can damage both a pump, and its prime mover, as well as even causing burst pipes.

Acceleration problems can occur in suction lines as well as delivery lines, except with a suction line the sudden *drop* of pressure caused by high acceleration can cause 'cavitation' where large bubbles of low-pressure water vapour and

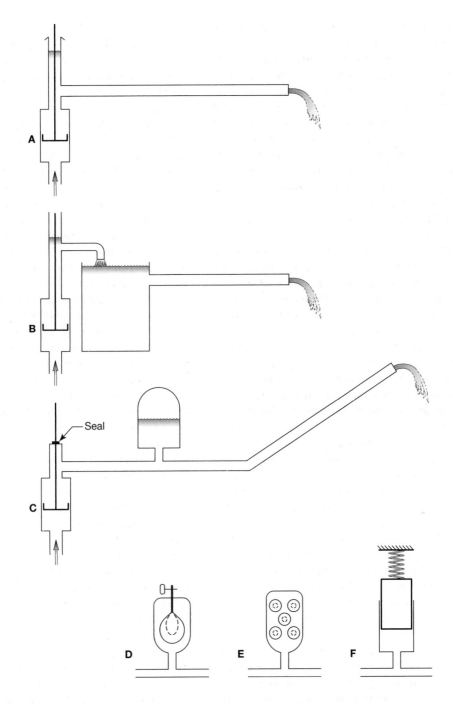

Fig. 6.22: Methods for isolating reciprocating pumps from pipelines: A. Open riser (also avoids the need for a pump rod seal); only suitable where the riser can be taken above the pipeline discharge level. B. Gravity pipeline from small tank near pump. C. Air chamber; necessary when discharge is significantly higher than the pump. D. Air chamber detail with air in flexible sealed bag. E. Chamber with compressible rubber balls. F. Spring loaded piston in a cylinder.

dissolved air suddenly form. When the pressure increases again slightly, the bubbles collapse, imploding violently and causing water-hammer.

When the pump outlet is set close to or above the pipeline discharge level, there is no great problem because the pipeline can be de-coupled from the pump by feeding into a small tank which can then gravity feed the pipeline steadily; see Fig. 6.22B. Alternatively, a riser open to the atmosphere in the pipeline near to or over the pump can achieve the same effect (as in Fig. 6.22A); because the pump rod can go down the riser it neatly avoids the need for a seal or stuffing box.

Where the pump delivers into a pipeline which discharges at a significantly higher level, it is usually impractical to have a riser open to the atmosphere at or near the pump, since it obviously would have to extend to a height above the level of the discharge. The solution generally applied in all such cases where more then a few metres of suction or delivery line are connected to a reciprocating pump is to place an air chamber or other form of hydraulic shock absorber between the pump and the pipeline (Fig. 6.22C) and always as close to the pump as possible to minimize the mass of water that is forced to follow the accelerations of the piston. Then when water from the pump seeks to travel faster than the water in the pipeline it will by preference flow into the air chamber and compress the air inside it. When the piston slows so that the water in the pipeline is travelling faster than that from the pump, the extra water can flow out of the air chamber due to a slight drop in pressure in the pipeline and 'fill the gap'. In other words, an air chamber serves to smooth the flow by absorbing 'peaks' in a reciprocating output and then filling the 'troughs' that follow the peaks.

Air chambers are generally vital on long or on large capacity pipelines when using a reciprocating pump (e.g. Fig. 7.33), but they are also well worth their extra cost not only in reducing wear and tear, but also the peak velocity of water in the pipeline will be reduced which in turn reduces pipe friction; this reduces the power requirement, improves overall energy efficiency and saves pumping energy. Air chambers can also be used on the inlet to pumps, where their smoothing of the flow in the pipes can also give significant improvement in efficiency, as has been demonstrated in the development of the rower pump, discussed in Section 7.2.3.

A special problem with air chambers on delivery lines is that the air in the chamber can gradually dissolve in the water and be carried away until there is no air left and water-hammer then occurs. Therefore simple air chambers usually require regular draining to replenish their air by opening a drain plug and an air bleed screw simultaneously. This, of course, is done when pumping is not taking place. Suction line air chambers are usually replenished by air coming out of solution from the water, although when air-free groundwater is being drawn, a small air 'snifting' valve may be needed to deliberately leak in a minute flow of air and prevent the chamber losing its air volume. There is a further discussion of snifter valves in relation to ram pumps in Section 6.10. A typical size for an air chamber will be around twice the swept volume of the pump, however it will need to be larger to cater for more severe flow irregularities or long delivery lines generally. There are other ways around the problem of replenishing air, which may be needed if regular attention cannot be guaranteed. Industrial air chambers can be purchased which have the air in a sealed rubber bag, which will retain it indefinitely (Fig. 6.22D). Alternatively a spring-loaded piston in a cylinder can also be used (Fig. 6.22F). Both of these solutions add complexity and are rather expensive. A cheaper option is to fill the chamber with closed-cell foam elements that compress under pressure (Fig. 6.22E). In some instances, small air chambers have successfully been filled with bubble-wrap (the sheets of packaging material consisting of air bubbles trapped between layers of polythene). Another useful alternative is to pump into a flexible pipe (e.g. rubber) which is less prone to water-hammer than a steel pipeline. In contrast, care must be taken with rigid plastic pipelines as they can easily be broken by water-hammer, especially in cold weather when they tend to be more brittle.

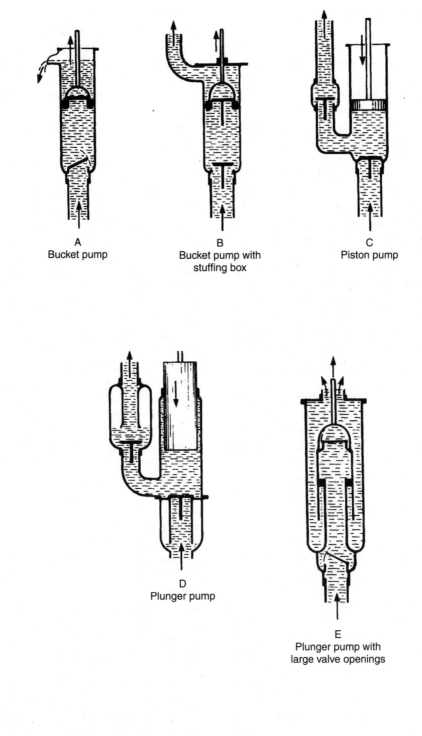

Fig. 6.23: Different types of single-acting reciprocating pumps

A
Bucket pump

B
Bucket pump with
stuffing box

C
Piston pump

D
Plunger pump

E
Plunger pump with
large valve openings

6.5.2 Single-acting piston pumps

A reciprocating pump is 'single-acting' if it only pumps as the piston moves in one direction. ('Double-acting' pumps deliver water as the piston moves in both directions, and are dealt with in Section 6.5.3.) Most reciprocating pumps are actually single acting, as are most handpumps used for community water supplies. Various single acting pumps are shown in Fig. 6.23.

Single-acting pumps work by applying both the displacement principles A and B in Fig. 6.20. Using the simple bucket pump shown in Fig. 6.23A as an example, on the up-stroke water is sucked into the body through the check valve at the base, while the piston valve is held closed by the weight of water above it (as in Fig. 6.17B). Simultaneously, the water above the piston is lifted out of the pump (as in Fig. 6.17A). On the down-stroke, the lower check valve is held closed by both its weight and water pressure, while the valve in the piston is forced open as the trapped water is displaced through the piston ready for the next up stroke.

The pump shown in Fig. 6.23B is similar to the first pump but has a closed top with a seal around the piston rod. This allows water to be delivered higher than the top of the pump. Sealing is usually achieved by fitting a packing seal in a 'stuffing box' where the rod passes through the lid of the pump. There also needs to be a gasket or other seal between the cover and the top of the cylinder.

Figure 6.23C shows a piston pump in which the piston carries no valve. Instead of the piston lifting the water, as in A and B, it displaces the water from the cylinder, forcing it through the discharge valve and up into the outlet pipe. This pump still uses suction to fill the cylinder on the up-stroke. Even though the outlet is higher than the pump it does not need a piston rod seal. It has the disadvantage that the discharge stroke requires the piston to be pushed rather than pulled, which needs a much stiffer pump rod in order to avoid buckling. There can also be problems with this kind of pump because the direction of motion of the water in the main cylinder is reversed every half cycle. This action can only be performed slowly, especially at low heads with large volumes of water per stroke, or the sudden stopping and starting of the mass of the water will cause 'water-hammer' (much as when a tap or valve is suddenly closed and causes a 'bang' in the pipes). Pumps of this kind are therefore unusual today.

Figure 6.23D is a similar pump to C, except it is a plunger pump rather than a piston pump. Here a solid plunger, sealed with a large diameter stuffing box or gland packing displaces the water. The plunger works on the displacement principle on the downstroke (as Fig. 6.17C), and the suction principle on the up-stroke. This is a more robust pump than the one shown in Fig. 6.23C. The main justification for using plunger pumps is that the piston or plunger seals are less prone to wear through abrasive solids in the water, and also, where very high pressures and low flow rates are needed, a smaller plunger or closed piston is possible because a through valve is not needed through its centre. Therefore the main use today for pumps of this kind is for pumping small volumes of water up to very high pressures or heads, such as for reverse osmosis desalination plants, where pressures of the order of 300 m head of water are required. The plunger pump also suffers from the flow reversal problem of pump C, but this is less serious where small flow rates at high heads are involved. However the diagram shows a pump with an air chamber below the inlet valve and above the delivery valve which is necessary to cushion the shocks caused by sudden reversal of flow direction, as explained in more detail in the sub-section 'The effect of reciprocating pumps on pipelines' above. Plunger pumps offered a manufacturing advantage in the past, in that it was sometimes easier to produce a good external finish on a plunger than inside a cylinder, but modern pump production techniques have reduced this advantage. This type of pump is rarely seen nowadays.

One problem with the standard designs of single-acting pumps, A and B, is that the size of the valve in the piston is restricted. In low-head pumps where high flow-rates are required this can lead to high hydraulic losses as a lot of water is forced through the small opening. One of

Table 6.4: Handpump types and typical pumping depths

Type of handpump	Maximum head
Suction	7 m
Direct Action	15 m
Deepwell	45 m typical
	100 m maximum

several methods of obtaining larger valve openings is shown in Fig. 6.23E. Here the piston is external to a seal rather than internal to a cylinder; another way of looking at it is that a cylinder is being pulled up and down over a fixed piston. Such pumps are rarely used anymore.

The majority of common reciprocating water pumps are types **A** and **B**. Type E is rarely used. Types C and D, with their reversing flow directions, are hardly ever seen. They are included for the sake of completeness, and might just prove useful in some specialist application. In most cases, the simplicity of types **A** and **B** make them the best choice. These two types still appear in numerous guises, and various practical applications are discussed in the following sub-sections. These begin with the three main categories of pump used for community water supply: suction, direct action and deepwell. These categories describe the way in which the pumps operate, but are also related to the depth at which the pumps can work (see Table 6.4).

Suction handpumps/bucket pumps
Some single-acting pumps are commonly called 'suction pumps' because they rely primarily on the suction principle to lift the water. They are also known as 'pitcher pumps' and 'bucket pumps' (the latter name not to be confused with the so-called Bucket Pump shown in Fig. 6.9). An example is the No. 6 handpump shown in Fig. 6.24. These pumps work on the principle of Fig. 6.23A. The piston is in the pump body, above the ground level, and the pump 'sucks' the water out of the ground. These pumps rely on atmospheric pressure to achieve the lift, and so can only be used for heads of up to around 7 m (at sea level). They

are widely used around the world, and are by far the most common sort of handpump. The Bangladesh No. 6 handpump (or MOSTI, Manually Operated Shallow Tubewell for Irrigation, handpump) is a design that dates back to the 1920s, although an improved version was developed by UNICEF in 1974 as the New No. 6; there are around a million or so installed in the country. China has several million suction pumps in use. Most suction pumps are of a lightweight construction and are used as family pumps. They are not generally robust enough for general village use.

A disadvantage of the suction pump is that it needs priming before it works. For simple, robust pumps it is not possible to make a totally leak proof valve, and after use, water in the pump leaks away through the foot valve, leaving the piston in air. The piston will not seal adequately against air, so water has to be poured into the top of the pump before it will develop enough suction to work. If dirty or contaminated water is used for this priming, the first water that comes out of the pump will also be contaminated, and the water source itself can become contaminated.

Variations on the suction pump are the Rower pump, which is shown in Fig. 7.13, and the Treadle pump, shown in Fig. 7.14.

Direct action handpumps
'Direct-acting' handpumps are those in which the user pulls directly on the pump rod, without any intervening mechanism. The pump itself is similar in principle to Fig. 6.23B. A widely used practical design, the Tara handpump, is shown in Fig. 6.25. The simple design makes these pumps cheaper than lever-operated pumps, and more reliable. However, the lack of any mechanical leverage means that they can only draw water up from around 15 m depth.

The Tara handpump uses a large diameter, lightweight plastic pump rod, sealed at both ends so that it stays full of air. When the rising main is full of water, the pump rod then has a good deal of buoyancy, which balances the weight of the rod material and the water being lifted, and makes the pumping action easier. The Tara pump rod is

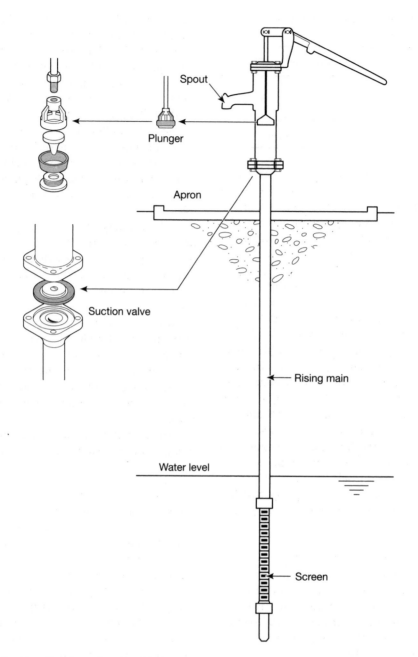

Fig. 6.24: The New No. 6 suction handpump

cemented together in one long piece, but is flexible enough to be brought out of the whole in a long curve without being dismantled. It is recommended that it is supported on a nearby tree or on a temporary pole to make sure it does not get bent (Fig. 6.26).

A novel feature of some designs of the Tara pump are that the rising main serves as the well-casing for the borehole. This obviously saves on cost, but makes it very difficult to repair a leaking rising main or damaged cylinder; fortunately, such faults are found to be rare.

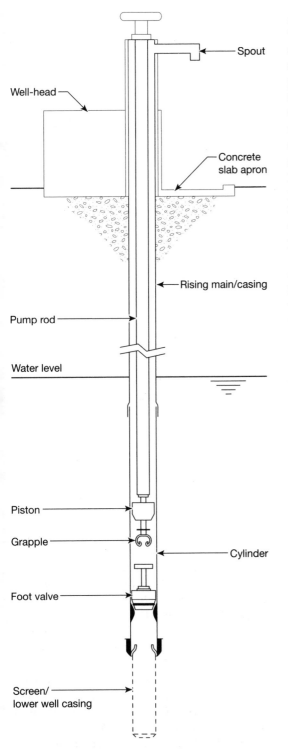

Spout

Well-head

Concrete
slab apron

Rising main/casing

Pump rod

Water level

Piston

Grapple

Cylinder

Foot valve

Screen/
lower well casing

Fig. 6.25: The Tara direct action handpump

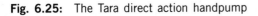

Deepwell handpumps

'Deepwell' handpumps, or indirect-action pumps, are similar to direct-action pumps, but have some sort of mechanism between the operator and the pump rod: the Afridev pump (Fig. 6.28) has a simple lever coupled directly to the pump rod; the India Mk. II (Fig. 6.27) has a chain link between the lever and the rod; a few designs (such as that shown in Fig. 6.29) have a crank wheel and link so that the input is rotary. Levers and handwheels allow a far greater force to be applied to the pump, so deepwell pumps are often rated for depths of up to 45 m, with a few capable of pumping from 100 m, albeit with small outputs.

Though most deepwell handpumps are operated by a lever, there are many advantages to a rotary input. If a reasonably large handwheel is used, as shown in Fig. 6.29, this will have a significant flywheel effect. Instead of requiring a large effort to push a lever down, and hardly any effort to lift it, the effort is smoothed out, and a steady force on the handle is all that is required. This makes it quite comfortable to operate, and means even children and small adults can achieve high outputs (or pump against high heads). The crank mechanism also controls the stroke of the pump, so that there is no potentially damaging banging against end stops at the top and bottom of the stroke as there is with lever-operated pumps.

The drawing of the Afridev handpump in Fig. 6.28 shows the common components of a pump installation. The assembly is fitted to a borehole, which has a lining or 'well casing' in it, usually made of PVC. The lower sections of the casing are slotted to allow water to flow in. The 'cylinder' in which the piston runs is at the bottom of the borehole. At the base of the cylinder is the 'foot valve', and below this most designs cater for a strainer element to prevent larger particles from entering the pump. In practice, many pumps do not have strainers fitted to them. The cylinder is connected to the surface with a pipe or 'rising main'. Most designs have supports between the rising main and the casing to hold it central, and similar supports on the pump rod to keep it in place within the rising main.

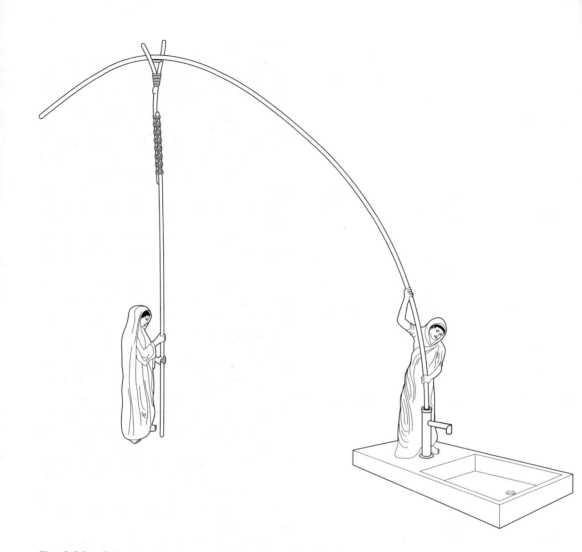

Fig. 6.26: Removing the pump rod tube from a Tara handpump

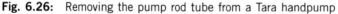

Boreholes are expensive to drill, and get more expensive as the diameter increases, so for this reason alone it is important to keep the diameter down. Most boreholes are drilled for well casings with outside diameters between 75 and 150 mm (3"–6"). The pump cylinder must obviously fit within the casing, and so there is a need to keep the piston diameter small. However, the smaller the diameter of the piston, the less water it moves for a given stroke. To some extent this can be overcome by increasing the stroke, but there is a limit to the stroke that can be achieved on a handpump. To increase the stroke, either the handle has to move further, or the leverage

has to be changed, which increases the force. Handle movement is limited by the amount it is comfortable to move the arms, and force is limited by the strength of the arms. So, piston diameters are rarely smaller than 50 mm (2"), or larger than 75 mm (3"). An advantage of the small-bore, long-stroke design is that the forces in the pump rod and bearings are smaller than with an equivalent displacement large-bore, short-stroke design.

Older designs of pumps tend to have a rising main that is smaller than the pump cylinder (as in the India Mk. II in Fig. 6.27). This kept the cost of the rising main down, particularly for deep boreholes. However, it also means that the whole

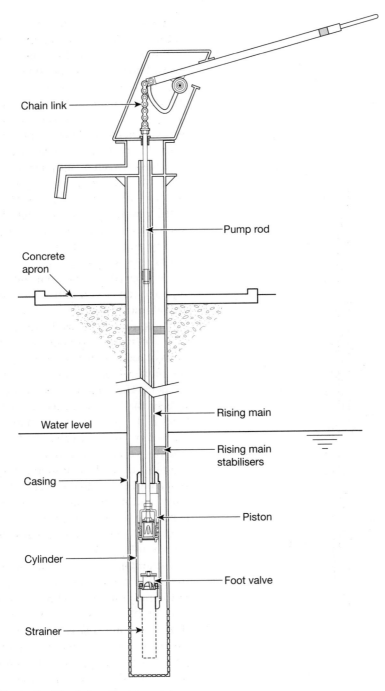

Chain link

Pump rod

Concrete
apron

Rising main

Water level

Rising main
stabilisers

Casing

Piston

Cylinder

Foot valve

Strainer

Fig. 6.27: The India Mk. II handpump

rising main and cylinder assembly has to be brought out of the borehole in order to service any of the piston or foot valve components – a difficult and lengthy procedure. Modern designs are 'extractable', with a 'full bore' or 'open-topped' rising main the same size as the cylinder (or slightly larger) so that the piston assembly and foot valve can be drawn out up the main (as

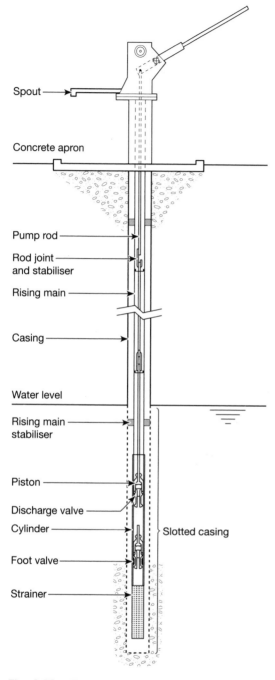

Spout

Concrete apron

Pump rod

Rod joint
and stabiliser

Rising main

Casing

Water level

Rising main
stabiliser

Piston

Discharge valve

Cylinder — Slotted casing

Foot valve

Strainer

Fig. 6.28: The Afridev deepwell handpump

in Fig. 6.28 and Fig. 6.25). Open topped designs tend to use small bore rising mains (typically 50–65 mm) to keep the cost of the pipe down. It

should be noted that there is an updated version of the India Mk. II with an open-topped design.

It is very common for groundwater to be corrosive, and this affects the choice of material used in pumps. Some years ago, rising mains were almost always made of galvanized steel, but uPVC tubing is now common. Plastic pipe does not corrode, though making adequate joints between lengths of pipe can be a challenge. Screwed connections between plastic pipes tend to crack from stress concentrations in the threads, and glued connections are very dependent on the quality of the joint (they need thorough cleaning before applying the adhesive, which must be of good-quality and not past its shelf-life). Steel rising mains are stronger and more rigid, and can easily be screwed together, but they do corrode in time and can be very difficult to dismantle after a period underground.

Pump rods are generally made of steel rod or tube. There are two main ways of joining sections of rod together: screwed connectors (as on the India Mk. II), or hooks and eyes (as on the Afridev). There has been some use of fibreglass rods in the USA, and this may extend to other areas if the price becomes competitive. Homemade rods made of galvanized steel pipe, or a suitable wood (close-grained, knot-free and rot-resistant) are used, but it should be borne in mind that a broken pump rod is at best difficult to recover, and at worst can mean the total loss of an expensive borehole. Some simple devices for extracting broken rising mains and pump rods are shown in Fig. 6.30.

On an Open-Topped Cylinder (OTC) pump, the piston can be hauled out by pulling up the piston rod. Since the rod is in sections, each section can be disconnected as it comes out of the rising main and placed on one side. There are two main methods of removing foot valves. Some pumps have a grapple or screw arrangement on the piston, which is dropped down to pick up the foot valve before the piston is withdrawn; the piston and foot valve then come up together. The Tara pump has a loop on the foot valve and a hook on the piston. On other pumps the piston is removed, and then a 'fishing tool' – a hook,

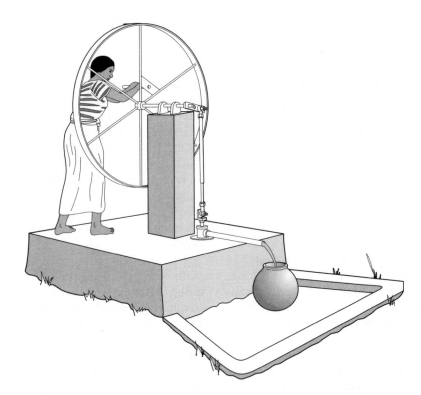

Fig. 6.29: A handpump with a rotary input

Broken rising main extraction tool   Broken pump rod extraction tool

Fig. 6.30: Simple extraction tools for broken rising mains and pump rods

latch or screw arrangement on a piece of line – is used to fish out the foot valve.

Maintenance on a pump with a cylinder unit that is bigger than the rising main is much more difficult. A block and tackle or crane needs to be positioned over the borehole so that the entire rising main can be lifted out. The procedure is to lift a complete section (usually 6 m, 20') clear of the hole, clamp the next section to stop it dropping down, and then remove the exposed section. In South Africa, the rising main is sometimes removed without using a block and tackle with a 'lift-and-grab' mechanism: the main is lifted a short distance with a lever, and then clamped to hold it in place while the levers are positioned for the next lift. Whichever method is used, pulling up a rising main is a long, expensive process, requiring a range of specialized tools and equipment, and it is generally beyond the capability of villagers to do for themselves.

As discussed before in Section 2.1.2, maintenance of handpumps is crucial. The Village Level Operation and Management of maintenance, VLOM, concept of the World Bank/UNDP handpump project has emphasized the need for pumps to be simple and robust, and that regular maintenance should be within the capabilities of local people, using a limited number of simple tools and a small stock of spare parts. Pumps for communal use do need to be very strong. While a backyard pump serving just one or two families will be quite lightly used, and can be watched over by the adults of the house, a village pump may be both very heavily worked, and heavily misused; with a large numbers of adults and children operating it, some people will apply excessive force to the end stops, try to bend the handle, rattle and bang it if it does not work, and quickly find any weaknesses. The pump must withstand all these 'attacks' without breaking down, as well as operating for, on average, around 2,000 hours operation per year. There are now a good number of designs that have proved themselves around the world, and there is probably little need to consider designing completely new pumps now. The existing pumps still have some problems, but these are being overcome by development programmes and relatively small modifications.

Mechanically driven borehole pumps

The discussion above has centred on hand-operated pumps, because of their wide use for Community Water Supply systems, but single-acting reciprocating pumps can also be driven by other means. The standard farm wind-pump, and many diesel-powered systems use reciprocating pumps. Most of what is written in the above sections on handpumps also applies to these mechanically driven pumps, but there are some additional considerations because of the increased power and depth.

The main attraction of using reciprocating pumps driven by tensile pump rods in boreholes is that they are essentially simple, and the better commercial products have become highly reliable in operation. Typically, pump rods in tension need to be safe to pull up to a ton or more, thereby allowing the use of this type of system on boreholes as deep as 300 m. As discussed above, forces can be kept down by increasing the stroke and using smaller bores. Mechanically driven pumps can in theory be moved faster than handpumps, but a limit is imposed by the need for gravity to make the pump rod and piston fall back on the down-stroke. For this reason the speed of operation of borehole pumps is usually restricted to about 30 strokes a minute, although a few operate at up to 50 strokes per minute. Higher pumping speeds tend to buckle the long train of pump rods by trying to push the piston and rods back down the hole. It is obviously most important to avoid compressing the pump rods by pushing them back down the borehole faster than they can naturally fall, or they may buckle and jam against the sides of the rising main, causing serious damage. Even if the rods do not buckle, rapid reversal of the loads on the joints and bearings causes the parts to hammer against each other as the clearances are taken up, leading to much faster wear than normal.

Hydraulically activated borehole pumps

A common problem with boreholes is that they are often not truly vertical and may be curved,

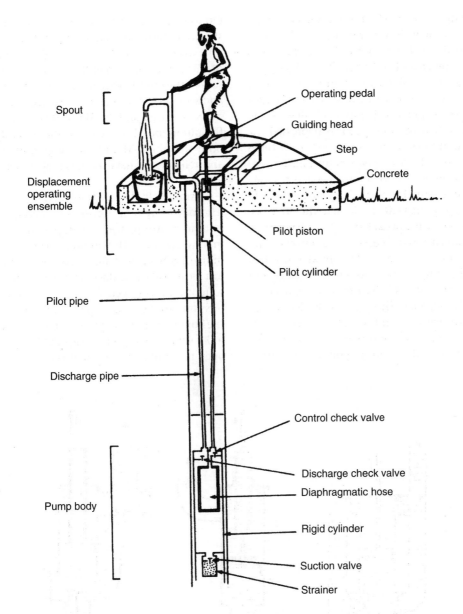

Fig. 6.31: The Vergnet hydraulic footpump

making the pump rods scrape the rising main and eventually wear a hole in it. Sometimes boreholes start off straight and earth movement causes subsequent distortion of the bore. Also, as explained, extracting a pump driven by a train of pump rods is a lengthy process. Therefore there has been a strong incentive to find methods of driving borehole pumps other than by pump rods.

An alternative is to use a hydraulic transmission. Here water under pressure is used to push more water to the surface.

An example is the Vergnet Hydro-pump, illustrated in Fig. 6.31, which has been successfully used for small water supplies, particularly in the West African Sahel regions. It works by a foot pedal which operates a drive piston to force water down a polyethylene hose. The stainless steel pump cylinder, which is located below water level in the well or borehole, has a conventional suction valve or foot valve and strainer, a pump chamber, and at the top of the chamber, a discharge check valve with another plastic pipe leading up to the surface. Instead of a piston there is an elastic bladder which expands like a small balloon. When the foot pedal is depressed the drive piston forces water down one of the tubes to inflate the bladder, which in turn pushes water up the other pipe. When the pedal is released the natural elasticity of the bladder causes it to contract, pushing water back up to the drive piston and raising the pedal to the starting position. There is an enclosed volume of water in the bladder/drive piston circuit; in early models this had to be topped up by hand to replace leakage, but later models have a small priming valve near the top of the bladder. The pump cylinder can be withdrawn easily from the hole by disconnecting the pump stand and withdrawing the two flexible hoses and the pump cylinder as one unit.

On some designs there are two separate hoses, as shown in the figure, and on others there is a small pipe inside a larger one. There are also versions of the pump with a handle replacing the pedal, so that the pump looks like a direct-acting pump, and with a lever arrangement (there is a Vergnet model like this, and the Abi-ASM pump), making the pump look like a conventional handpump. Both the Abi-ASM and the Vergnet are reasonably reliable, but have outputs that are somewhat low.

A similar hydraulic transmission called the 'Hidromite' system, for driving a reciprocating borehole pump, was developed in Australia mainly for use with windmills. Here the windmill, (or other prime mover), drives a master piston located at the surface. This is a double-acting water pump connected by two hydraulic transmission pipes to a slave piston at the bottom of the borehole, directly connected by a short pump rod to the actual pump piston below it, which operates in the conventional way.

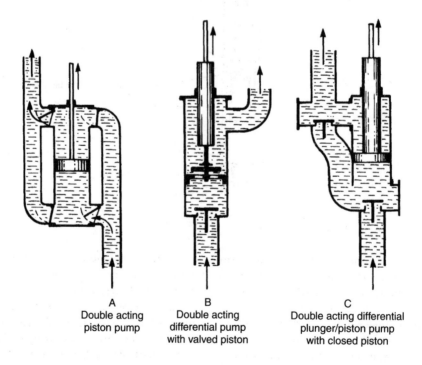

A
Double acting
piston pump

B
Double acting
differential pump
with valved piston

C
Double acting differential
plunger/piston pump
with closed piston

Fig. 6.32: Different types of double-acting reciprocating pumps

Although hydraulic transmission units are quite attractive in some respects compared with pump rods, they are significantly more complicated and expensive. Their efficiency is also likely to be lower due to the extra pipe friction involved in moving the water needed to power the submerged pump.

6.5.3 Double-acting piston pumps and plunger pumps

A single acting pump only discharges water when the piston moves in one direction, and the return stroke is utilized simply to displace more water into the working space ready for the next stroke. However, it is possible (and often advantageous) to arrange things so that while one side of the piston displaces water to discharge it, the other side induces more water. In this case discharge takes place on both strokes. Such pumps are known as 'double-acting' pumps and are significantly more productive for their size than single acting ones.
- Figure 6.32A shows a pump that is similar in principle to that in Fig. 6.23C, but double-acting. Here when the piston is on the up-stroke it induces water into the lower chamber and discharges from the upper, while on the down-stroke water is induced into the upper chamber and discharged from the lower.
- The pump in Fig. 6.32B is known as a differential pump, with a pump rod of a large diameter where it enters the upper chamber. If this rod is sized so that its cross sectional area is exactly half the cross sectional area of the chamber, it will displace half the volume of the chamber on the down-stroke (the principle being as for plunger pump Fig. 6.23D), and half the volume on the up-stroke (the principle being as for the bucket pump Fig. 6.23B).
- The pump in Fig. 6.32C applies a similar differential double-acting principle to the pump in Fig. 6.32B but uses a closed piston, without a valve. Apart from being a more complicated arrangement, it is more prone to water-hammer due to the flow reversal involved in both chambers.

Although more complicated than single acting pumps, double-acting pumps have considerably smoother outputs, and a smoother torque requirement. They were therefore widely used in conjunction with reciprocating steam engines, but as steam engines have been replaced with electric motors and high speed diesel engines, they have become rare, mainly because they have the following disadvantages:
- they are larger and more complicated, and hence more expensive;
- they usually involve flow reversal which can cause water-hammer, so some need to be run quite slowly or to incorporate air chambers (except for the type in Fig. 6.32B);
- the drive requires that the pump rod is pushed as well as pulled (at least with the configurations shown), so there must be no back-lash or free travel in the transmission (or hammering and wear and tear will result); also the pump rods must be capable of taking the compressive load on the down-stroke without buckling.

All this involves heavier more precisely engineered components in the drive train, which generally adds to the cost. Therefore, the trend in recent years has been to restrict the use of piston pumps to simple single acting bucket pumps where their essential simplicity and low cost provide the justification for choosing them. When capital cost or first cost is less critical, the trend has been to use motor-driven centrifugal pumps.

6.5.4 Diaphragm pumps

An alternative to the use of a piston in a cylinder for pumping is to fit one wall of a pump chamber with a flexible diaphragm which, when moved in and out, displaces water (see Fig. 6.33). Here the left hand valve is analogous to the foot valve of a piston pump and the right hand one is the delivery valve.

In general, the advantages of a diaphragm pump are:
- perfect sealing (except for any shortcomings of the two check valves);

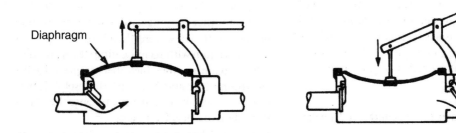

Fig. 6.33: Cross-section of a diaphragm pump

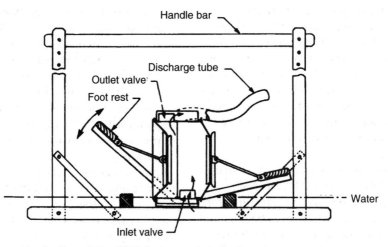

Fig. 6.34: Schematic drawing of the IRRI foot-operated diaphragm pump

- high mechanical efficiency, since flexing a diaphragm involves much less friction than sliding a piston with seals up and down a cylinder;
- no seal is needed at the pump rod, which also reduces friction losses still further compared with piston pumps;
- they are self-priming, hold their prime very well and can often handle a higher than average suction head;
- they often function well with gritty or muddy water which could damage a piston pump.

There are also disadvantages:

- diaphragms need to be high quality rubber if they are to last, and are therefore expensive;
- diaphragm pumps are often dependent on specialized spare parts that cannot easily be improvised in the field;

- a diaphragm pump is similar to a large diameter piston pump with a short stroke; so the pump rod forces are high in relation to the head and swept volume. This imposes a high load on transmission components and on the point of attachment of the pump rod to the diaphragm;
- diaphragm pumps are generally less capable of handling high pressures than piston pumps and they also do not readily fit down narrow boreholes, so they tend to be used for low head applications (usually of less than 10 m), and especially those involving suction lift from an open water source.

Figure 6.34 shows a foot-operated, double-acting diaphragm pump developed by IRRI (the International Rice Research Institute in the Philippines) specifically for irrigation purposes.

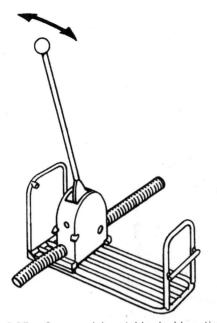

Fig. 6.35: Commercial portable double-acting diaphragm pump

Unlike traditional devices such as dhones or shadoofs, this pump is portable (by two men) and can therefore be moved along an irrigation canal in order to flood one paddy after another. However, it is less efficient than the better traditional water lifters.

Figure 6.35 shows a commercially manufactured, double-acting diaphragm pump that is mostly used for purposes such as de-watering building sites; it has the advantage of being portable, reasonably efficient and well-suited to low heads. It can deliver quite high outputs, so it, or similar designs, could equally be used for irrigating small land holdings. A pump of this kind was well liked by Ethiopian farmers irrigating small plots from the Omo River in a training project (Fraenkel, 1976 [39]).

One type of diaphragm pump that can be improvized, and which reportedly works reasonably well at low heads, is a design based on the use of an old car tyre as the flexible member (Fig. 6.36). Worn car tyres are of course widely available. The principle of this pump is to make a chamber by fitting end-plates into the openings of the tyre so that one is anchored and the other can be forced up and down. If suitable check valves are provided, this can make an adequate diaphragm pump. The prospective user should not underestimate the constructional requirements to make an adequately reliable device of this kind. For example a typical car tyre of 400 mm overall diameter will have an effective area of 0.126 m^2; this requires a force of 1,230 N per metre head; i.e. even only 3 m lift requires nearly 3,700 N pull to displace any water (this is the equivalent of 376 kg force or 830 lb). Surprisingly robust fixings and connections are therefore needed to prevent such a pump coming apart, even at quite low heads. The tyre works as a diaphragm, but only for low suction lifts (up to 1.2 m) and at low pumping rates (up to 20 pumping strokes per minute). Greater suction causes the internal structure of the tyre to separate from the outer rubber casing after a number of cycles, and too high a rate makes the tyre distort and collapse. Tyre pumps could make a useful high-volume low-head pump however, providing they are skilfully constructed, to be powered perhaps by two people working a suitably strong lever, and providing they operate submerged or with limited suction lift.

6.5.5 Gas displacement pumps

Water can be displaced by a gas or vapour as readily as by a solid. A number of air and vapour displacement pumps were manufactured at the beginning of this century. The former rely on air delivered by an engine-driven compressor, while the latter generally used steam to displace water directly, rather than through the intermediary of a steam engine and pump. The Humphrey pump is an analogous device which uses the gases generated in an internal combustion engine cycle to displace water directly in much the same way. Both compressed air and steam displacement pumps suffer from being inherently inefficient, as well as being massive (and hence expensive) in relation to their pumping capacity, but in contrast the Humphrey pump is actually more efficient than most comparably sized conventional internal combustion engine pumping systems, although it is also quite large.

101

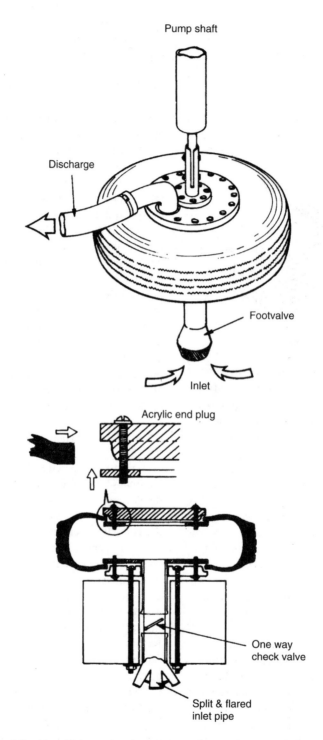

Pump shaft

Discharge

Footvalve

Inlet

Acrylic end plug

One way
check valve

Split & flared
inlet pipe

Fig. 6.36: Detail of the New Alchemy Institute (USA) tyre pump

Figure 6.37 shows the principle of the Humphrey pump, which consists in effect of a conventional four-stroke internal combustion engine cylinder-head mounted on top of a pipe. This pipe is fed with water through a series of inlet check valves around the main cylinder, and runs along a long horizontal section before rising to the discharge level. A bubble of gas/air mixture is trapped above the water in the cylinder head. When the mixture is ignited it expands and forces the water along the pipe. Momentum keeps the water travelling after the combustion expansion has finished, and draws water in through the check valves. When the momentum is dissipated, the water moves back under gravity, and the exhaust valve is opened to expel the exhaust gases. The exhaust valve is then shut, and the water column 'bounces' on the small volume of gas left at the top of the cylinder. As it goes down again, fresh gas/air mixture is sucked in through the intake valve. Finally, the water column returns again to compress the mixture before the spark starts the next expansion stroke. The pump therefore works with a series of oscillations of the water in the pipe, and the main flow occurs at the end of the combustion stroke (though there can be some through flow during the rebound stroke). The cycle is sequenced by a pressure sensor that controls a simple linkage to open and close the valves on the cylinder head at the correct times. The original engines also had a scavenger air valve which let a certain amount of fresh air into the cylinder right at the end of the combustion stroke to help clean out the exhaust gases. The Humphrey pump cycle is similar to a standard four-stroke piston engine except that instead of the engine having a metal piston driving a crank shaft, the water in the working space acts as a piston. All the Humphrey pumps so far built could only run on gaseous fuels such as coal gas or natural gas because of difficulties with vaporizing liquid petroleum fuels successfully under the cool cylinder conditions that occur when cold water acts as a piston.

The Humphrey pump was invented by Herbert A. Humphrey, and the first units installed were at Chingford for the London Water Supply Company in 1913, where they were used for pumping water into a reservoir. Similar units were installed for an irrigation project of over 4,000 ha at Cobdogla in Australia. These units were huge: 1.67 m in diameter, pumping 6,500 m³/h through a head of 10.4 m. The Chingford units were in use until the 1950s, and the Cobdogla units until 1965 (though one has since been restored to working order for an irrigation museum). Humphrey pumps were used also used for irrigation projects in the USA in the early part of the twentieth century, with some success, and the University of Reading in England developed a modern small-scale prototype in the 1970s intended for irrigation pumping with biomass fuels.

The very large Humphrey pumps had gas to water efficiencies of around 20%, while the smaller Reading University units reached around 10%. These figures, while appearing low, should be compared with the total efficiency of a prime mover, pump and pipework for comparison with other systems, and are actually rather good. The other main advantage of the Humphrey pump is its great mechanical simplicity. It therefore can readily handle muddy or sandy water and has the potential for extreme reliability, yet requires very little maintenance. The main negative features are the need for gaseous fuels and it can only readily operate from water sources where the water level does not change much. It is also rather large in relation to its pumping capacity compared with a modern small engine driven pump. Thus, while the Humphrey pump has given reliable operation for many years in some applications, it has only been used in a few places, and has not been taken up widely.

6.6 Rotary positive displacement pumps

The previous sections dealt with reciprocating positive displacement pumps. Reciprocating pumps, for all their simplicity, are not ideal for all applications. Almost all mechanical power sources – motors, engines and suchlike – are rotary, and it is best to have a rotary pump to couple to them. Also, there are losses involved in

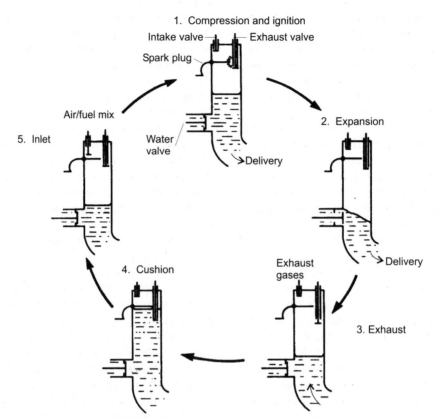

1. Compression and ignition

Intake valve —— —— Exhaust valve

Spark plug

Air/fuel mix

5. Inlet

Water valve

Delivery

2. Expansion

Delivery

Exhaust gases

4. Cushion

3. Exhaust

Principle of operation of a 4-stroke Humphrey pump

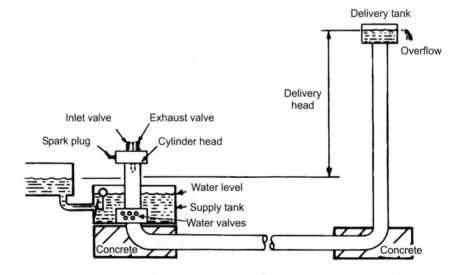

Delivery tank

Overflow

Delivery head

Inlet valve   Exhaust valve

Spark plug   Cylinder head

Water level

Supply tank

Water valves

Concrete

Concrete

Fig. 6.37: The Humphrey pump: a liquid piston internal combustion engine and pump combined

accelerating and stopping the components of a reciprocating mechanism.

There is a group of pumps which utilize the displacement principle for lifting or moving water, but which achieve this by using a rotating mechanism. These generally produce a continuous, or slightly pulsed, water output. These can readily be driven by engines or electric motors, often at quite high speeds. The faster a device can be operated the larger the output in relation to its size, and the better its productivity and cost-effectiveness. Steady discharge flows also avoid problems such as water-hammer and cavitation that can affect reciprocating pumps.

Centrifugal pumps, which are described later, are rotodynamic pumps using a completely different principle. They have in fact become the most general mechanized form of pump precisely because they can be directly driven from internal combustion engines or from electric motors. But rotary positive displacement pumps have unique advantages over centrifugal pumps in certain specialized situations, particularly in being able to operate with a much wider range of speeds or heads.

Some types of rotary positive displacement pump have their origins among the earliest forms of technology (e.g. the Archimedes' Screw – see Section 6.6.2), and even today lend themselves to local improvization. In the past, industrially manufactured rotary displacement pumps were less successful than centrifugal ones, possibly because they suffered from a number of constructional and materials problems. Modern, tougher, more durable plastics and synthetic rubbers have encouraged the manufacture of a number of new types of rotary positive displacement pumps which could be advantageous in some situations, as will be described.

6.6.1 Paddle-wheels, treadmills and flash-wheels

These devices are, in effect, rotary versions of a simple scoop; however instead of one scoop being moved back and forth, a number are set around the periphery of a wheel, (Fig. 6.41). Like the scoop, a paddle wheel is only useful for very low lift pumping, such as flooding paddy fields at no more than about 0.5 m height above the water source.

The simplest version is the paddle-wheel in which an operator walks directly on the rim, turning it so that it continuously and steadily scoops up water and deposits it over a low bund (as in the figure). In its basic form the paddle wheel is not very efficient since a lot of the water lifted flows back around its edges. Therefore an improved version involves encasing the wheel in a closely fitting box which not only reduces the back-leakage of water but also slightly increases the head through which the device can operate. Paddle wheels are simple to make, and can readily be made locally. Their major limitation is the small lift that can be achieved, because they can only lift to a fraction of their own diameter. Higher heads would require enormous wheels, which are impractical.

Paddle wheels have been mechanized in the past, although they are uncommon as water lifting devices today. Many of the windmills formerly used in the Netherlands to de-water large parts of the country drove large paddle wheels, which when mechanized and refined, were known as 'flash-wheels'. Flash-wheels functioned best with raked back blades, and the best had measured efficiencies in the range 40–70%. Small straight-bladed paddle-wheels are probably only 10 or 20% efficient, but have the virtue of being simple to build and install in situations were a lot of water needs to be lifted through a small head. They are occasionally used on traditional windpumps, as shown in Fig. 7.37.

6.6.2 Archimedes' screw and open screw pumps

The Archimedes', or Archimedean, screw consists of a helix enclosed in a tube (see Fig. 6.38). Water is first scooped into the helix as its end dips below the surface, and then a quantity of water is trapped between the lower two turns of the helix and the outside tube. As the whole assembly continues to rotate, so the water is passed up the helix, with each pool of water flowing by gravity into the corners formed between the helix and the casing. At the top, the water discharges from the open end.

The Archimedes' screw was supposedly invented by the Greek mathematician and inventor Archimedes (287–212 BC). Figure 6.38 illustrates a typical traditional hand-operated Archimedes' screw pump made up of a helix of square cross-section wooden strips threaded onto a metal shaft and encased in a tube of wooden staves, bound like a barrel with metal bands (an animal powered version is shown in Fig. 7.22). This sort of pump is still used in Egypt, and records exist of it being used for irrigation there 2,000 years ago.

The Archimedes' screw can only operate through low heads, since it is mounted with its axis inclined so its lower end picks up water from the water source and the upper end discharges into a channel. Each design has an optimum angle of inclination, usually in the region of 30° to 40°, depending on the pitch and the diameter of the internal helix. If it is inclined at too steep an angle the water all drains back down the helix to the bottom, and it does not work. Traditional wooden Archimedes' screws of the kind just described have been tested and found to have efficiencies in the region of 30%, though it should be possible to improve this considerably with modern materials and construction methods.

The modern version of the Archimedes' screw is the 'screw pump', Fig. 6.39. This consists of a helical steel screw welded around a steel tubular shaft. However, unlike an Archimedes' screw,

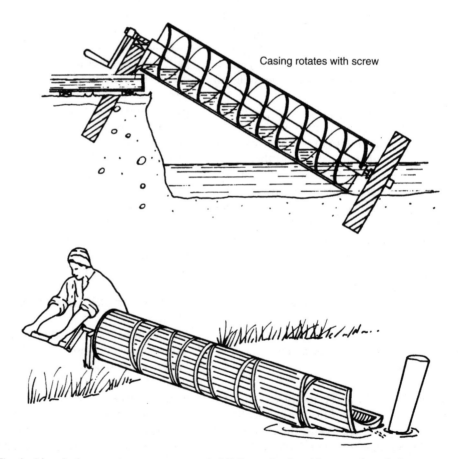

Fig. 6.38: The Archimedes' screw; two men are needed if the water head is more than 0.6 m

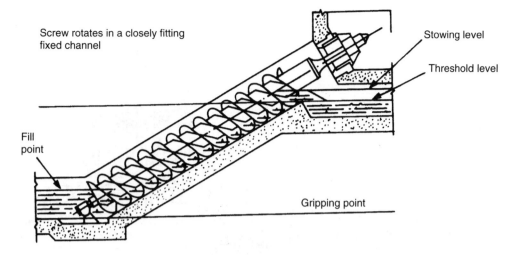

Fig. 6.39: Cross-section through an open-screw pump

there is no casing fixed to the screw, but it is mounted instead in a close fitting, but not quite touching semi-circular cross-section inclined channel. The screw pump is like a rotary version of the water ladder described above. The channel is usually formed accurately in screeded concrete. Because of the small clearance between the screw and its channel, some back-leakage is inevitable, but the total flow rate produced by a screw pump is so large that the backflow is but a small percentage. Therefore modern screw pumps can achieve high efficiencies in the region of 60–70%.

Their primary advantage is that the installation and civil workings are relatively simple, compared with those for large axial flow pumps necessary to produce the same volume of output (which would need a concrete sump and elaborate large diameter pipework as in Fig. 6.61). Also, the screw can easily handle muddy or sandy water and any floating debris, which is readily pulled up with the water.

Probably the main disadvantage of screw pumps is that an elaborate transmission system is needed to gear down an electric motor or diesel engine drive unit from typically 1,500 rpm to the 20–40 rpm which is normally needed. Mechanical transmissions for such a large reduction in speed are expensive and tend to be no more than 60–70% efficient, thereby reducing the total efficiency of the screw pump, including its transmission to about 50–60%. The maximum head that can be handled will be limited to around 6 m in most cases, and may be no more than 4 or 5 m for smaller screw pumps.

6.6.3 Water ladders and dragon-spine pumps

A water ladder consists of an angled flume or channel with a series of paddles that are pulled up through it. The paddles are a close fit in the channel, and divide it into a series of compartments. The paddles are connected together by pivoting links to make an endless chain, which runs around a freewheeling sprocket at the lower end of the channel, and is turned by a sprocket at the upper end (Fig. 6.40). The lower end of the channel is submerged, and as the chain is driven the paddles trap water between them and carry it up to be discharged at the top. There is always some back-leakage, but with a well-built unit this is but a small fraction of the high flow that is established.

The water ladder is still used on small farms in S. E. Asia for flood irrigation of fields and paddies from open streams and canals. They are also used for pumping sea water into evaporation pans to produce sea salt. In China this device is known

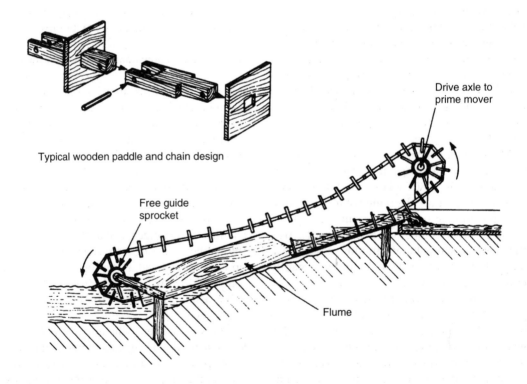

Typical wooden paddle and chain design

Drive axle to
prime mover

Free guide
sprocket

Flume

Fig. 6.40: The water ladder or Chinese dragon spine

as a 'dragon spine' or 'dragon wheel' and in Thailand as 'rahad'. In most cases it is made mainly of wood, and can consequently easily be repaired on-farm. It is one of the most successful traditional, high-flow, low-lift water pumping devices and is particularly applicable to rice production, where large volumes of water are needed at very low heads.

On traditional Chinese water ladders, the upper sprocket is normally driven by a long horizontal shaft that is pedalled by from two to eight people working simultaneously, as shown in the figure. The treadles are spaced around the drive shaft so that one or more of the operators is applying full foot pressure at any moment, which helps to smooth the torque output and keep the chain of boards tensioned and running smoothly. Versions of it have been mechanized by using windmills, as in Fig. 7.38 (in Thailand as well as China), or a buffalo sweep (China), or with small petrol engines.

Water ladders range in length from 3 to 8 m, and in width from 150 to 250 mm; lifts seldom exceed 1.0 to 1.2 m, but two or more ladders are sometimes used where higher lifts are required. A rough test made in China [36] with a water ladder powered by two teams of four men (one team working and one resting) showed an average capacity of 23 m³/h through a lift of 0.9 m. Further details of Chinese water ladders are given in Table 6.5.

Tests on a traditional wooden water ladder powered by a 2–3 hp engine were carried out in Thailand in 1961 [38]. The trough was 190 mm deep by 190 mm wide and the paddles were 180 mm high by 150 mm wide and spaced 200 mm apart; note that the clearance was quite large, being 20 mm each side. The principle findings of this study were:

- the flow rate is maximized when the submergence of the lower end of the flume is 100%;
- a paddle spacing to paddle depth ratio of approximately 1.0–1.1 minimizes losses and maximizes output;
- the sprocket speed has to be kept to less than 80 rpm to avoid excessive wear and frequent breakage;
- the average efficiency of the device was 40%.

It is possible that if a smaller clearance had been used between the paddle edges and the trough, a higher efficiency may have resulted; no doubt the optimum spacing is quite critical. If it were too small, friction would become excessive and possibly cause frequent breakage of the links, while if too large, back-leakage becomes excessive and reduces the overall efficiency.

Table 6.5: Specifications of Chinese Dragon Spine water lifts: Chengqiao Water Lift and Agricultural Tool Plant, Hangjiang Commune, Putian County. Output is estimated from typical figures.

Type	Length of trough (m)	Dimensions of intake height × width (m)	Weight of water lifted (kg)	Volume of timber used (m³)	Typical output (m³/h)
One man, hand turned	1.5	0.18 × 0.14	18	0.2	11
	1.8	0.18 × 0.14	20	0.2	9
	2.0	0.18 × 0.14	22	0.2	8
	2.3	0.18 × 0.14	24	0.3	6
	3.0	0.18 × 0.14	30	0.3	5
	3.5	0.18 × 0.14	35	0.3	4
Two men, treadling	2.3	0.25 × 0.20	50	0.3	19
	3.0	0.25 × 0.20	55	0.4	13
Four men, treadling	3.5	0.25 × 0.19	70	0.5	23
	4.1	0.25 × 0.19	75	0.5	19
	4.7	0.25 × 0.19	85	0.6	16

Fig. 6.41: Paddle-wheel or treadmill

6.6.4 Rope and washer, rope and rag, chain and washer, or paternoster pumps

The origins of this type of pump go back over 2,000 years. The pumping principle is similar to that of the water ladder described in Section 6.4.6, except that instead of pulling a series of linked paddles through an open inclined flume or trough, a series of linked discs or plugs are pulled through a closed pipe (Fig. 6.42, Fig. 7.4 and Fig.

7.21). They are sometimes called 'paternoster' pumps, because of their resemblance to a beaded prayer chain ('Pater noster' being Latin for 'Our Father' from the Christian prayer). As with the ladder pump, they lend themselves to human, animal or mechanical prime movers and are most commonly powered by either a team of two to four people or by a traditional windmill. There are numerous designs using many different materials. The plugs may be made of wood, leather, plastic, or bits of old tyres, and can be in the shape of flat disks, cups, or balls. The plugs can be strung on chain or rope, or fixed together on pivoting links. A common plug design is to have a metal washer with a slightly larger disk of leather on top of it. It is even possible to make a low-head pump work with rags tied on at intervals to a piece of rope. Rag pumps were used centuries ago in wells and on board ships (for pumping seawater in the latter case).

As discussed in more detail in the next chapter covering the use of human and animal power, a major advantage of this kind of pump is that it requires a steady rotary power input which suits the use of a crank drive with a flywheel, which is a mechanically efficient as well as a comfortable way of applying muscle power. It also readily matches with engines and other mechanical prime movers. The way in which the pump primes itself also leads to a gentle start-up, particularly at higher heads. The plugs do not seal in the tube, so water leaks back down it when the pump is idle. At start-up, there is no water in the riser, and the handle turns easily. This allows the operator to build up momentum while the column of water is rising up the pipe, so that the pump is working at full speed by the time it pumps at full head.

Another advantage of the rope and washer pump is that it can be used over a wide range of pumping heads; in this respect it is as versatile as the commonly-used reciprocating handpump. It can readily be used for heads from 1 m up to about 20 m, and it can be used at significantly higher heads. For low lifts, loose fitting washers are good enough to lift water efficiently through the pipe, since back-flow will remain a small and acceptable fraction of total flow. At higher lifts, however, tighter fitting plugs rather than washers are necessary to minimize back-leakage. Most pumps have a bell mouth at the base of the riser pipe to guide the washers smoothly into the pipe. With higher lift units where a tighter fit is needed, a tight clearance is only necessary near the lower end of the riser pipe; therefore the riser pipe usually widens to a larger diameter for the upper sections to minimize friction (see Fig. 6.42). They are generally installed vertically, and are said to be more efficient operating like this, but they can be worked with the tube at an angle (for example, the do-it-yourself rope and washer pump in Lambert, 1990 [40]. Some designs have been made that can be fitted down a standard 150 mm (6") borehole, making them competitive with standard handpumps (as in Fig. 6.43).

The capacity of a chain and washer pump is a function of the diameter of the riser pipe and of the upward speed of the chain. The greater the capacity, the greater the power input required, so for example, four men are necessary to power a unit with 6 m lift and a 100 mm riser tube [36]. Table 6.6 indicates that the chain and washer pump is not only versatile, but also rather more efficient than most pumps.

Chain and washer pumps have been in widespread use in China, where industrially manufactured pumps of this kind were often known as 'liberation wheels'. They represented a major improvement over more traditional and primitive water lifting techniques and offered an extremely effective interim step to modernization using powered centrifugal pumps. Two to three million Liberation pumps were used in China at the peak of their use in the 1960s (Watt, 1977 [41]). Table 6.6 shows the performance characteristics of typical chain and washer pumps used in China.

Rope and washer pumps have been used extensively in Nicaragua, where they are often installed in preference to a conventional reciprocating handpump. The Nicaraguan design, called a rope pump or 'bomba de mecate', was developed in the 1980s, and uses a specially moulded plastic cup for the plugs, fixed on to a knotted nylon rope – see Fig. 6.43. The part that guides the cups into the bottom of the pipe is made of glazed pottery to reduce friction and wear. These pumps are reported to pumps around 2–3 m³/h,

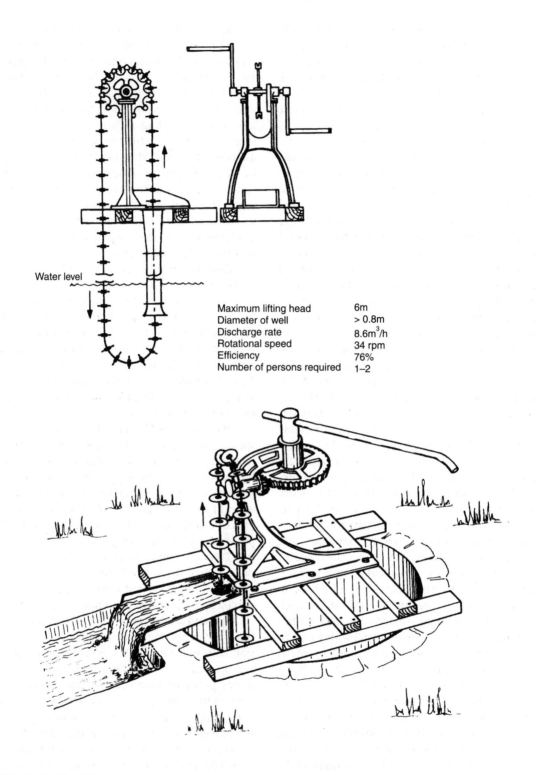

Maximum lifting head	6m
Diameter of well	> 0.8m
Discharge rate	$8.6m^3/h$
Rotational speed	34 rpm
Efficiency	76%
Number of persons required	1–2

Water level

Fig. 6.42: The Chinese 'liberation wheel' chain and washer pump

Table 6.6: Performance characteristics of typical Chinese chain-and-washer pumps

Motive power	Pumping head	Discharge rate	Efficiency (pump only)
2 men	6 m	5–8 m³/h	76%
donkey	12 m	7 m³/h	68%
3 kW electric motor	15 m	40 m³/h	65%

Fig. 6.43: A Nicaraguan rope pump

even when operated by children. They are normally used at heads of up to 30 m, but are said to be able to pump at heads of up to 85 m, though it is hard work at this depth. There are around 3,500 such pumps installed in the country.

Rope and washer pumps are quite widely used, but would seem to merit even greater adoption. They are relatively cheap and simple to make, and can be maintained with a minimum of skill and tools. Even crude chain and washer pumps achieve efficiencies of 50–70%, which compares very well with other designs. They are therefore especially appropriate for human and animal-powered applications, where the power available is obviously limited, and the efficiency is more important.

6.6.5 Progressive cavity, helical rotor or mono pumps

'Progressive cavity' (or 'progressing cavity') pumps consist of a single helix rotor inserted in a double-helix stator, as shown in Fig. 6.44; a handpump installation using this type of pump is shown in Fig. 7.11. The cross-section of the rotor is always circular, but this circle spirals around the axis, a bit like a spiral staircase. The stator has a cavity in it like two of the rotors, 180° apart, forming two intertwined helixes. When the rotor is fitted into the stator, there are spaces trapped between the helixes, and as the rotor is turned these spaces are screwed along the axis of rotation. If the assembly is placed in water, discrete volumes of water are trapped in the spaces, moved upwards, and discharged into the rising main. The rotor is actually held laterally by the stator at the sections AA, so that the rotor axis moves around the stator axis in a small circle. The drive to the rotor has to allow for this eccentric motion, and this is usually achieved by a long, thin, flexible driveshaft.

This pump was invented by the French engineer Moineaux, which leads to its common commercial names 'Mono' and 'Moyno'. Because it is naturally a long, thin cylindrical shape it can readily be fitted inside a borehole, and this makes it somewhat unique among commercially-available rotary positive displacement pumps. Using

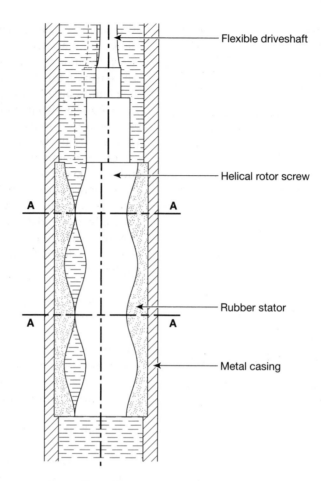

Fig. 6.44: Detail of a progressive cavity or Mono pump

a positive-displacement pump can be advantageous in situations where the water level may change significantly with the seasons or due to drawdown, or even where the drawdown is uncertain, because the flow varies very little with head (see Fig. 6.45), and so the output will not change. Progressive cavity pumps have a reputation for reliability, particularly with corrosive or abrasive impurities in the water. The reasons for this relate to good construction materials combined with a mechanically simple mode of operation.

Pumps of this kind are usually driven at speeds of typically 1,000 rpm or more, and when installed down a borehole they require a long drive shaft which is guided in the rising main by water lubricated 'spider bearings' usually made of rubber. Hand pump versions of the Mono pump can pump from depths of up to 90 m. Although friction forces exist between the rotor and stator, they are reduced by the lubricating effect of the flow of water, and they act at a small radius so that they do not cause much loss of efficiency. Progressive cavity pumps therefore have been shown to be at least as efficient as, and in some cases better than, the best multi-stage centrifugal pumps. Combined Mono-pump/electric-motor units can achieve electric to water efficiencies of 70–75% when new, which is very good. The main disadvantage of Mono pumps is their need for specialized components, which cannot be improvised, and their high initial cost; however, high cost is unfortunately a feature common to all types of good quality borehole pump and is

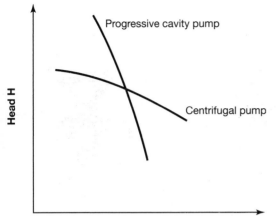

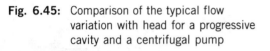

Fig. 6.45: Comparison of the typical flow variation with head for a progressive cavity and a centrifugal pump

usually justified by the need to minimize the frequency of the expensive procedure of removing and overhauling any pump from a deep borehole.

The progressive cavity pump can be 'sticky' to start, i.e. it sometimes needs more starting torque than running torque (similarly to a piston pump) to unstick the rotor from the stator and get the water that lubricates the rotor flowing. This can cause start up problems when electric motors or engines are used, but certain improved versions of this kind of pump include features which reduce or overcome this problem.

6.6.6 Vane pumps, gear pumps, lobe pumps and peristaltic pumps

There are many other types of rotary positive displacement pumps, but few of them are suitable for drinking water or irrigation pumping. Gear pumps, lobe pumps, and vane pumps (Fig. 6.46A, B, C, and D) are widely used in industry for pumping many different liquids. The advantages of these pumps are that they are self-priming, can handle air bubbles without problems, and can produce high heads. They also have minimal leakage, and can be used for metering or measuring flow. Their disadvantage is that they all have sliding components in them, and rely on good

surface finishes and close tolerances in order to work. This means that they are intolerant of dirt or abrasive particles within the liquid. Depending on the materials they are made from, they may only be able to handle liquids that have suitable lubricating properties, such as oils. It is, however, possible to make variants of these standard pumps using rubber and plastic components that can handle water without needing special filtration or added lubricants. They are not widely used for the sorts of applications described in this book, but they may be found suitable for special applications. Another special sort of pump is the peristaltic pump, E, which works by squeezing liquid along a flexible tube; the action is similar to the way in which food is moved along the human gut. A flexible plastic pipe is seated in a block with a circular depression, and a wheel with rollers presses down on it. As the wheel turns the rollers trap a portion of liquid between them and squeeze it along the pipe. This is a very simple type of pump that can be readily improvised. It has no seals, and can produce reasonable head, but it is a small, low speed, low output device.

An example of a rotary positive displacement pump designed for water pumping is shown in Fig. 6.46F. This is a flexible vane pump, and has a vaned rotor rotating in a cylindrical casing. This is a very simple concept, like a revolving door. Water is carried round between the vanes or teeth from the inlet to the outlet. These pumps are widely used for draining water out of building basements. The durability of these pumps depends on the quality of manufacture and the material used. They are rather more complicated and expensive than centrifugal pumps, and need special spare parts to repair them.

6.7 Reciprocating inertia pumps

This range of pumps depend on accelerating a mass of water and then using the momentum it has gained to make it travel upwards. It is a little like throwing a ball up in the air: your arm accelerates the ball from stationary to a given speed, and when it is let go it continues on up by itself.

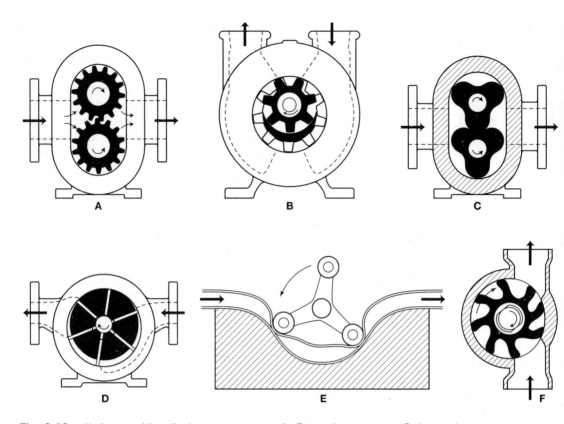

Fig. 6.46: Various positive displacement pumps: A. External gear pump. B. Internal gear pump. C. Lobe pump. D. Sliding vane pump. E. Peristaltic pump F. Flexible vane pump.

6.7.1 Flap valve pump

This is an extremely simple type of pump that can readily be improvised (see Fig. 6.47). Versions have been made from materials such as bamboo. The dimensions are not critical, so that little precision is needed in building it.

The entire pump and riser pipe is joggled up and down by a hand lever. On the up-stroke the valve is sucked closed and the column of water is accelerated with the pipe. At the top of the stroke, the pump body comes to a halt, but the momentum of the water keeps it moving upwards. The valve opens and the water flows into the splash chamber and out of the spout, while more water is sucked up into the base of the pipe. This flow continues on the down-stroke, being augmented by the downward motion which forces more water into the base of the riser pipe. Towards the bottom of the stroke the momentum is dissipated

and the motion is no longer sufficient to push water up the riser; the valve shuts, and the pump is ready for the next cycle. The joggle pump obviously has to be cycled at a reasonable speed to generate enough momentum to make it work; if it is only moved slowly, it does nothing at all. Joggle pumps are self-priming, though it can take a little while to draw water up to the top if the pipe is empty to begin with.

The maximum lift is limited by the atmospheric pressure. If the weight and the inertia of the column of water on the up-stroke create a pressure greater than atmospheric then there will be cavitation at the top of the riser, and the pump will not draw. For this reason, a joggle pump will only work up to around 5–6 m head. The riser and the valve must obviously be reasonably airtight, because if air can leak in the suction will be lost. If cavitation is found to be a problem on longer risers, it can be overcome by putting the

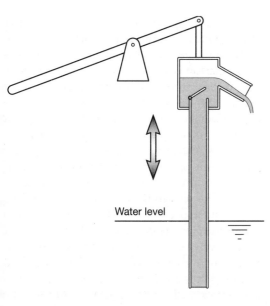

Fig. 6.47: A flap-valve or joggle pump

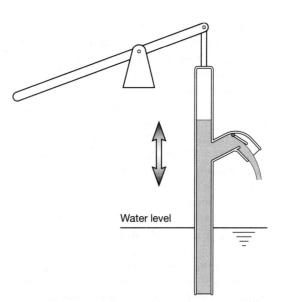

Fig. 6.48: A resonant joggle pump

valve lower down the pump (usually at the bottom), or by having two valves – one at the top and one at the bottom. The lower valve pushes the water above it upwards on the up-stroke, rather than relying on suction to pull the water up. Another limitation on pumping head is the weight of the pump and the water column. A 6 m long pump assembly full of water has a considerable weight and inertia, making them hard to move, and pumps are typically kept much smaller, lifting perhaps 1–2 m.

Joggle pumps can achieve very good outputs. They rely on having negative slippage (see the sub-section 'Discharge, volumetric efficiency and slippage' in Section 6.5.1), and can have outputs well in excess of the swept volume. Their high output makes them more suitable than most handpumps for small-holding irrigation under low heads. They are not so suitable for drinking water pumps because it is difficult to seal the connection between the pump and a well or borehole, so contamination can leak back into the water source.

6.7.2 Resonant joggle pump

Figure 6.48 shows an improved version of the flap-valve pump. Here there is an enclosed air space at the top of the pump which interacts with the column of water by acting as a spring, to absorb energy and then use it to expel water for a greater part of the stroke than is possible with a simple flap-valve pump. This uses exactly the same principle as a damping air chamber (see the sub-section 'The effect of reciprocating pumps on pipelines' in Section 6.5.1).

This type of joggle pump depends on being worked at the correct speed to make it resonate. An example of a resonant device is a weight hanging from a spring, which will bounce up and down with a natural frequency determined by the stiffness of the spring and the magnitude of the weight. The heavier the weight in relation to the spring stiffness, the slower the natural frequency and vice-versa. If the spring is tweaked regularly, with a frequency close to its natural frequency, then a small regular pull applied once per bounce can produce a large movement quite easily, which is an example of resonance (in much the same way as pushing a child on a swing demands a quick push at the right moment to get a good movement from the swing). In exactly the same way, each stroke of a resonant joggle pump makes a column of water of a certain mass bounce on the cushion of air at the top of the column. Depending on the size of the air

117

chamber and the mass of the water, this combination will tend to bounce at a certain resonant frequency. Once it has been started, a pump of this kind needs just a regular 'tweak' of the handle at the right frequency to keep the water bouncing. This effect not only improves the overall efficiency but also makes it relatively effortless to use. Dunn, 1978 [42] reports performance figures of 60 to 100 l/min lifted through 1.5 to 6 m at a frequency of 80 strokes per minute. The feel of the pump tends to force the operator into working at the resonant rate.

It is worth noting that the performance of some reciprocating piston pumps fitted with air chambers (as in Fig. 6.25C) can be similarly enhanced if the speed of the pump is adjusted to match the resonant frequency of the water in the pipeline and the 'stiffness' of the trapped air in the air-chamber. The rower pump (Section 7.2.3) uses this principle. Resonance is only feasible with short pipelines at fairly low heads, as otherwise the natural frequency in most practical cases is far too low to match any reasonable pump speed. If resonance is achieved in such situations the pump will often achieve *volumetric* efficiencies in the region of 150 to 200%, i.e. as much as twice the swept volume of the pump can be delivered at each stroke. This is because the water continues to travel by inertial effects even when the pump body is moving against the direction of flow, (the valves of course must remain open). As a result, water gets delivered for part of the down-stroke as well as on the up- stroke. Well-engineered reciprocating systems taking advantage of resonance can achieve high speeds and high efficiencies. Conversely, care may be needed in some situations (such as pumps where there is a reversal of the direction of flow) to avoid resonance effects, as although they can improve the output, they can also impose excessive loads on the pump or on its drive mechanism.

6.7.3 Pulsa pump

A novel variant on the resonant joggle pump is the Pulsa pump, illustrated in Fig. 6.49. The pump has a piston in a cylinder above ground connected by a polythene pipe to another chamber at the bottom of the well or borehole. This lower chamber has a standard strainer element and foot valve, but instead of a piston it contains a number of elastomer balls. In the rest position (Fig. 6.49A) the piston sits against a seal in the upper piston, and the foot valve is closed. When the handle is depressed the piston pushes water down the hose to compress the balls (B). When the handle is released the balls expand, pushing water up the pipe and raising the piston. The inertia of the moving water causes the piston to lift beyond the seal, to flood the upper part of the piston and to overflow from the outlet (C). It also lowers the pressure in the lower chamber so that the foot valve opens and water flows in from the well. When gravity overcomes the inertia and stops the flow, the foot valve closes and the piston settles back to the original position. The pump has a natural frequency at which it works best, and operators quickly discover this and settle down to pumping at the appropriate speed. The pump is very easy to install, and to remove for servicing. Like the Vergnet diaphragm pump (see the sub-section 'Hydraulically activated borehole pumps' in Section 6.5.2) the Pulsa can be used in curved boreholes. The simplicity of the mechanism, particularly for the below ground components, makes it reasonably reliable, but the output is somewhat low. Pulsa pumps used by women and children in Benin were found to give only 50–70% of the output of India Mk. II pumps used by nearby communities.

6.8   Rotodynamic pumps

6.8.1   Basic principles

The whole family of what are called 'rotodynamic pumps' have some sort of impeller or rotor spinning inside a casing to move the water. The impeller has blades or vanes on it which catch the water and accelerate it, so that it leaves the impeller at a much higher speed than it entered.

The earliest practical rotodynamic pumps were developed in the 18th and early 19th centuries. Three different types are shown in Fig. 6.50. In type **A** the handle is used to turn the

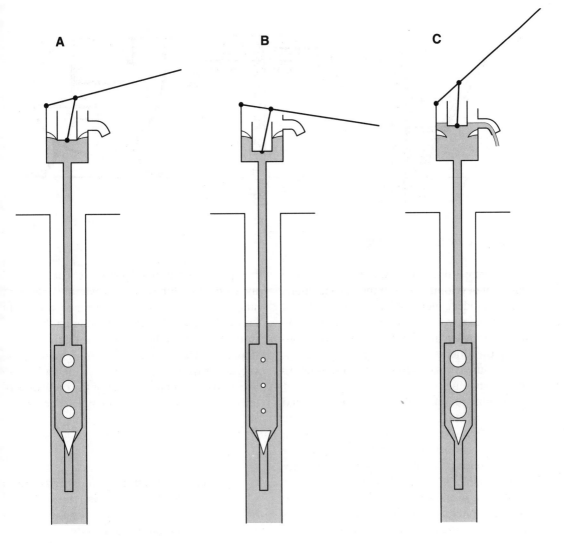

Fig. 6.49: The Pulsa handpump

structure, which whirls the angled tube around. Centrifugal force acts on the water in the pipe, throwing it out the top and sucking more water in at the bottom. Type **B** is similar, but the centrifugal action occurs in a circular chamber at the top. Water is flung out around the edge of this to be caught in a stationary casing surrounding it. This is actually a suction pump, and needs priming in order to initiate pumping; a foot valve is provided to prevent the loss of the priming water when the pump stops. Pump C, the Massachusetts pump of 1818, had a casing built around a horizontal shaft so that the high speed water leaving the impeller could be directed up the discharge pipe, which could carry it to some height. In many respects this last pump is the forerunner of the modern centrifugal pump, which today is by far the most commonly used mechanically driven type of pump.

Both pumps **A** and **B** are extremely inefficient as the water leaves the impeller with a high velocity, which is simply dissipated as lost energy. Pump C does a little better in utilizing the exit velocity, but it is rather crude and much of the

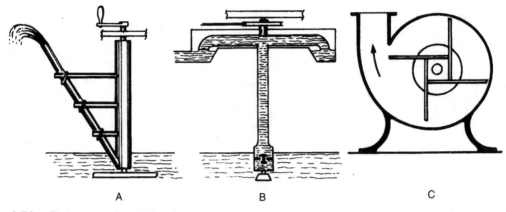

Fig. 6.50: Early types of centrifugal pump

outlet energy is dissipated in friction losses. The important development from the Massachusetts pump to produce modern pumps was the design of casings that would slow down the water leaving the impeller in a controlled fashion, converting the kinetic energy into pressure energy. This pressure is then used to push the water up the delivery pipe.

The principle that velocity can be converted into pressure, and vice versa, is illustrated in more detail in Fig. 6.51, which shows water passing through a contraction and a diffuser. Consider first the contraction. Because water is virtually incompressible, if a given flow is forced into a smaller pipe it can only do so by flowing faster. This faster moving water has more kinetic energy than the original slower-moving water, but energy has to be conserved, and there has been no input of energy to the water. The additional kinetic energy comes from the pressure energy. Another way of looking at this is to say that pressure is used up in accelerating the water, so a pressure drop is seen across the constriction. Thus the velocity increases, but the pressure drops. Conversely, in the diffuser, if a flow expands into a larger cross-section, it slows down (to avoid creating a vacuum) and the energy in the flow is converted to increased pressure.

The pressure drop across a contraction is known intuitively by most people. The nozzle on the end of a hosepipe is a contraction, and there has to be a reasonable pressure in the hosepipe to produce a jet from it. The pressure increase over a diffuser is less obvious. These pressure changes are an application of the well-known hydraulic law called Bernoulli's theorem, from which it can be shown that (ignoring frictional effects) if water flows through a duct of varying cross-sectional area then the change in the head of water (a measure of the pressure difference) is related to the velocity change by:

$$v_{out}^2 - v_{in}^2 = \sqrt{2g \cdot H}$$

v_{out} – velocity of water leaving the transition
v_{in} – velocity of water entering the transition
H – head change across the transition
g – acceleration due to gravity

Modern rotodynamic pumps use this principle in two main ways. In centrifugal pumps, the high-velocity water coming out of the impeller is taken through a gently expanding passage so that it slows down and its pressure increases. In propeller pumps, the impeller imparts swirl to the water, and this swirl is then gently removed to increase the pressure. Many pumps make use of a mixture of these effects, changing both the cross-sectional area and the swirl to retrieve the velocity energy from the impeller flow.

Propeller pumps make use of another fluid effect to achieve pumping, that of lift. This is the same effect that allows aircraft to fly. An aircraft

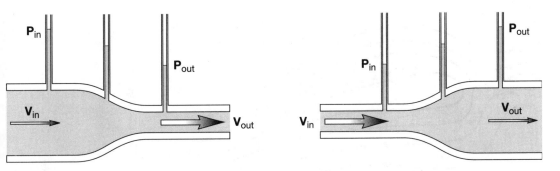

Fig. 6.51: The relationship between pressure and velocity through both a contraction and a diffuser

wing and a pump blade are shown in Fig. 6.52 to illustrate the principle. Air flowing over the aerofoil section of an aircraft wing (Fig. 6.52A) travels faster over the convex upper surface than over the concave underside. The Bernoulli effect discussed above means that the faster air will be at lower pressure than the slower air, so that the pressure on top of the wing is somewhat lower than the pressure below. The net pressure force on the wing is therefore upwards, and the aircraft stays in the air. The upward force on the wing implies that there is a downward force on the air. The blade in a pump is usually the other way up (Fig. 6.52B), but it works in a similar way. The blade moves forward through the water, and the pressure above the blade will be somewhat higher than the pressure below – so the water is being pumped. Another way of looking at this is to say the 'lift force' pushes the blade downwards, but it is fixed on its shaft. The resultant force on the water is upwards, pumping it past the propeller.

6.8.2 The various type of rotodynamic pump

One way of classifying rotodynamic pumps is by the direction of movement of the water through them. If the movement is radial, from the centre to the outside of the impeller, then the pump is known as a centrifugal pump, as in Fig. 6.53A. Axial pumps have the water moving through a tubular arrangement parallel with the axis, as in Fig. 6.53B. Mixed flow pumps are those where the movement is neither purely radial nor axial, but somewhere between the two; Fig. 6.53C.

By far the most common type of centrifugal pump is the volute-casing pump, an example of which is illustrated in Fig. 6.54A. They are similar to the Massachusetts pump in Fig. 6.50 C, in that the water enters axially at the centre of the impeller, and leaves tangentially from the outside edge of the impeller. The difference is that the impeller does not fill the casing, and there is space around the perimeter. In Fig. 6.54A it can be seen that this gap is quite narrow just behind the outlet pipe, and that it increases progressively clockwise around the casing, in the direction of the impeller rotation. The water coming out of the impeller flows around this passage, where the cross-sectional area gradually increases as it goes round to the outlet. This smoothly slows the flow down, and converts the velocity energy into pressure. This sort of spiral casing looks like a snail's shell, and is called a 'volute' casing.

The other common type of centrifugal pump is the turbine pump shown in Fig. 6.54B. This has a ring of diffuser vanes which create a number of smoothly expanding passages between the impeller and the outer casing (there are six such vanes shown in Fig. 6.54B). At the inside edge these vanes are angled so as to be in line with the water coming out of the impeller, and they turn the flow as they slow it so that it leaves the diffuser nearly radially, thus removing as much of the velocity energy from it as possible. The number of impeller and diffuser blades is usually different to avoid resonant vibrations.

In passing, it should be mentioned that there is another type of pump which is also sometimes referred to as a 'turbine pump', but which is

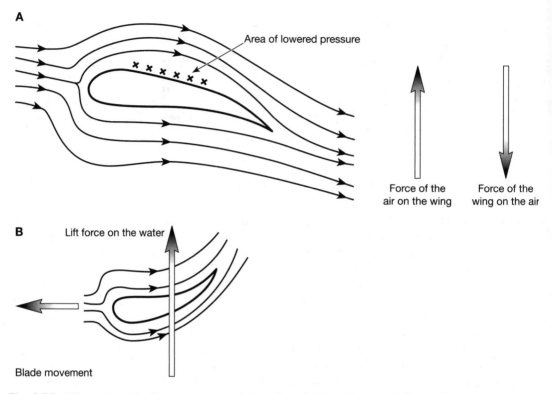

A

Area of lowered pressure

Force of the
air on the wing

Force of the
wing on the air

B

Lift force on the water

Blade movement

Fig. 6.52: Lift produced by flow over an aerofoil section. A. Aircraft wing. B. Pump blade

completely different from the centrifugal turbine pump just described. This is variously known as the regenerative, regenerative-turbine, peripheral, or side-chamber pump. A regenerative-turbine pump is shown in Fig. 6.55. It has a narrow impeller disk, with vanes around the outside, which turns inside a rectangular-section annular passage in the casing. The water inlets at one point on the circumference, and travels nearly all the way round before being taken out again. The vanes create strong vortices on either side of the impeller as they move through the water, so that the water travels around the annulus in a corkscrew movement, going in and out of the impeller. Each time it passes through the impeller it is accelerated, so that by the time it leaves the annulus it has received considerable energy. When the water leaves it passes through a diffuser which converts its velocity back into pressure. The main advantage of this sort of pump is that it generates a very high head. Because

regenerative pumps require close internal clearances to work they are very vulnerable to grit or dirt, and so are not generally suitable for the pumping applications described in this book. They are occasionally used for pumping clean water, for example on board ships. The use of the term 'turbine pump' for regenerative pumps is very confusing, and the reader should be aware that this difficulty exists. However, for most irrigation and drinking water uses the term 'turbine pump' will almost certainly refer to the centrifugal turbine pump described above.

Axial-flow pumps are like tubes with a propeller inside. A typical axial-flow is shown in Fig. 6.56. As discussed in the previous section, axial-flow pumps work by a combination of two effects. Firstly, there is aerodynamic lift that pushes the water past the propeller. Secondly, the impeller imparts a spin to the water, sending it corkscrewing around the direction of flow. This spin is then straightened out, usually by an

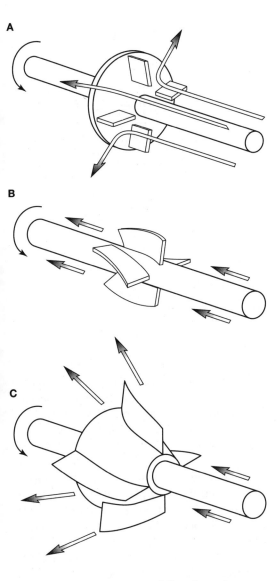

A

B

C

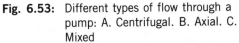

Fig. 6.53: Different types of flow through a pump: A. Centrifugal. B. Axial. C. Mixed

arrangement of fixed guide vanes, slowing the overall speed and increasing the pressure. In most axial flow pumps lift is the dominant pumping effect. Axial flow pumps are also called propeller pumps, because they are like boat propellers in a tube. Axial flow turbines tend to run fast, and have a high output, but they generate less head than an equivalent size of centrifugal pump.

Mixed-flow pumps are somewhere between axial and centrifugal pumps. The water travels both axially and radially as it passes through the impeller. A typical mixed flow pump is shown in Fig. 6.57. The pumping occurs by a mixture of the effects described above. The blades may have a lift effect due to their section, the impeller will impart swirl to the flow, and the impeller throws the water radially by centrifugal force. Different configurations will have different proportions of these effects. Mixed-flow pumps may or may not have diffuser vanes around the impeller to slow and redirect the flow; the pump shown in Fig. 6.57 has vanes at the top of the bulb-shaped casing.

Mixed-flow pumps can have characteristics anywhere between centrifugal and axial-flow pumps, and this is their great merit. By adjusting the geometry, and the mixture of radial and axial flow, the pump can be tuned to work best at a given head, flow and speed.

6.8.3 Rotodynamic pump characteristics and impeller types

It is not intended to deal with this complex topic in depth, but it is worth running through some of the main points relating to pump design to appreciate why pumps are generally quite sensitive to their operating conditions.

All rotodynamic pumps have a characteristic of the kind illustrated in Fig. 6.1, which gives them a limited range of speeds, flows and heads in which good efficiency can be achieved. Although most pumps will operate over a wider range, if you move far enough from their peak efficiency with any of these parameters, then both the efficiency and output will eventually fall to zero. For example, Fig. 6.1 shows that if you drive the pump in question with a motor having a maximum speed of say 2,000 rpm, there is a maximum flow which can be achieved even at zero head, and similarly there is a head beyond which no flow will occur. The design point is usually at the centre of the area of maximum efficiency.

Since any single rotodynamic pump is quite limited in its operating conditions, manufactur-

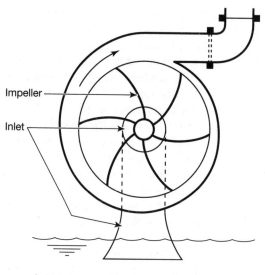

A Volute centrifugal pump

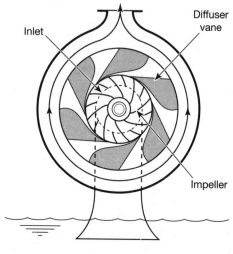

B Turbine centrifugal pump

Fig. 6.54: Two types of centrifugal pump: A. Volute-casing centrifugal pump. B. Turbine centrifugal pump

ers produce a range of pumps, usually incorporating many common components, to cover a wide range of heads and flows. Because of the limited range of heads and flows any given impeller can handle, a range of sub-sets of different types of impellers has evolved, and it will be shown later there are then variations within each sub-set which can fine tune a pump for different duty requirements. The main sub-sets are shown in Fig. 6.58, which shows a half-section through the impellers concerned to give an idea of their appearance.

In the previous section it was shown how pump impellers can impose radial or axial flow on the water, or some combination of both. For high heads and low flows a centrifugal (radial flow) impeller is needed with a large ratio between its inlet diameter and its outlet diameter, as in Type A to the left of Fig. 6.58. Conversely, where high flows at low heads are required (which is common with irrigation pumps), the most efficient impeller is an axial flow one, shown as Type E at the extreme right of Fig. 6.58. In between these two extremes are centrifugal pumps with smaller ratios of discharge to inlet diameter for their impellers (D_2/D_1), Types B and C, and mixed-flow pumps, Type D.

The graph in Fig. 6.58 shows the efficiency versus the 'specific speed' of the various impeller sub-sets. In some ways, the concept of specific speed is an unnecessary complication, and it is quite possible to choose and use pumps without referring to it. It is dealt with here because textbooks on pumps frequently refer to it, and because it does give some insight into the comparison between different pump designs. The basic idea is that different designs of pump impeller could, in theory, be scaled up or down in size so that they gave the same output and pumping head. To do this, they would have to run at different speeds, and this is the specific speed for that runner.

Specific speed is defined as the speed in revolutions per minute at which an impeller would run if reduced in size to deliver 1 m³/s to a head of 1 m. It provides a means for comparing and selecting pump impellers, and it can be calculated as follows:

$$N_s = n \cdot \frac{\sqrt{Q}}{H^{3/4}}$$

N_s – specific speed

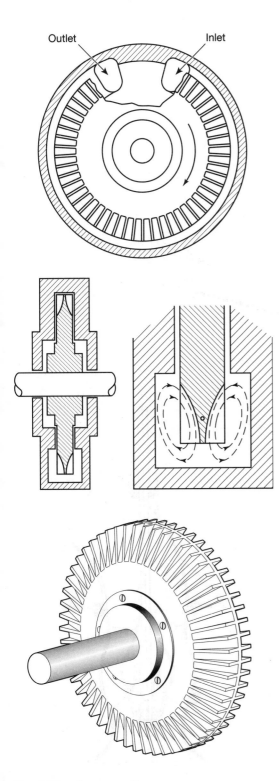

Fig. 6.55: A regenerative pump

n – nominal rotational speed (rpm)
Q – optimum pump discharge (m³/s)
H – optimum head (m)

Figure 6.58 shows approximate specific speeds that can be expected for different types of impeller. Centrifugal impellers fall roughly between 12 and 70 rpm; impellers with greater outlet/inlet diameter ratios have the lower specific speeds. Mixed-flow impellers occupy the middle region between about 35 and 160 rpm, and axial-flow impellers continue from 160 to 400 rpm and possibly even higher. Typical operating head figures are given, and the graph shows the sort of flow ranges and efficiencies that can be expected from the different types of impeller. To give an example, a centrifugal pump with a ratio D_2/D_1 of 1.75 will have a specific speed of about 30 rpm; running with a flow of 6 l/s its impeller efficiency will be around 65%, and at the largest normal flow of 630 l/s it would be about 88% efficient. It can be seen that axial-flow pumps tend to be high flow, low head pumps, whereas centrifugal pumps produce much higher heads at lower flow. Mixed-flow pumps occupy the middle ground. Using the figure it can be seen that the choice of impeller is not only a function of head and flow but of pump size too; smaller, low-powered pumps of any of these configurations tend to be less efficient and they also operate best at lower heads than geometrically similar larger versions. Note that the graph and figures are not definitive – it is possible to operate pumps away from the typical figures and ranges given – but they show typical good operating points.

Specific speed can be converted back to actual speed at any given head and flow as follows:

$$n = \frac{N_s H^{3/4}}{\sqrt{Q}}$$

N_s can be read from Fig. 6.58 to use in this equation. Note that the units of flow for calculating specific speed, and in this equation, are m³/s, not l/s.

It should be noted that while specific speed is quoted in rpm, its units are actually rather messy

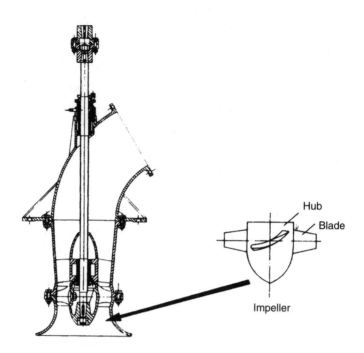

Hub

Blade

Impeller

Fig. 6.56: An axial flow pump

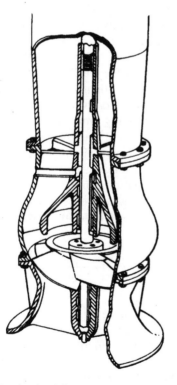

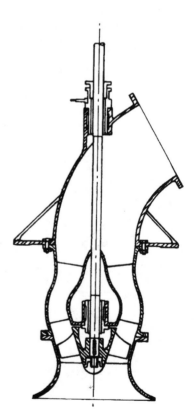

Fig. 6.57: A mixed flow pump

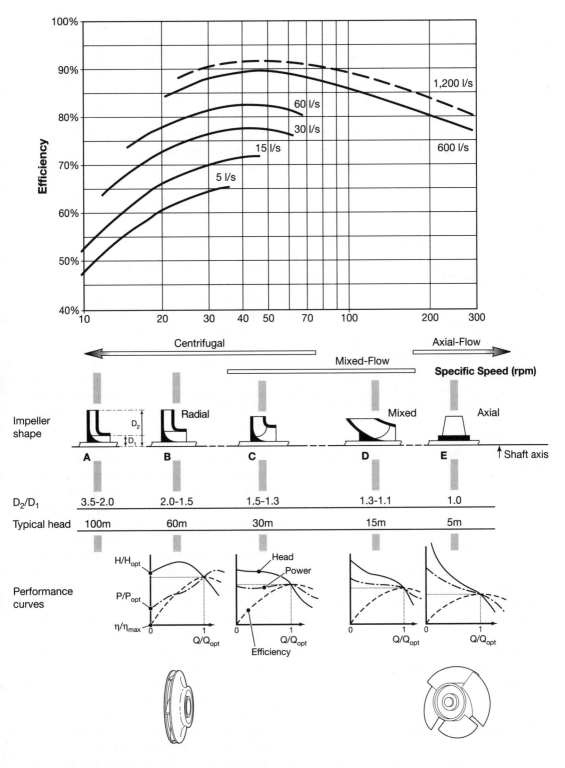

Fig. 6.58: Typical rotodynamic pump characteristics

(rpm.m$^{3/4}$.s$^{-1/2}$), and the value changes if different units are used. The definition used here is the common metric usage, but books also use other units; in the British system, using rpm, Imperial gallons/minute and feet, the specific speed is 47.13 times the metric value; in American units, using rpm, U.S. gpm, and ft, the specific speed is 51.64 times the metric value. There is also a definition of specific speed given by the German standard DIN 24620 which does have the units rpm, and this has the same numerical value as the metric specific speed.

Further information is given in Fig. 6.58 in the small graphs below the different impeller types. These indicate the effect on power requirements and efficiency of varying the key parameter of head away from the design point. In the case of an axial-flow pump, Type E, increasing the head increases the power demand, while in the case of a centrifugal pump increasing the head reduces the power demand. This latter result is somewhat surprising, but the reason is that decreasing the head (by, say, 10%, or a factor of 0.9) can increase the flow by a much greater amount (25%, or a factor of 1.25). The efficiency may also decrease by 10%, and since the power requirement is head times flow divided by efficiency (η), the new power demand will change from:

$$\frac{H \cdot Q}{\eta} \text{ to}$$

$$\frac{0.9 \times H \times 1.25 \times Q}{0.9 \times \eta} = 1.25 \frac{H \cdot Q}{\eta}$$

The ratio of these is 1 : 1.25, so the power demand will be increased by 25% in this case. This illustrates that varying the conditions under which a pump operates away from the design point can have an unexpected and sometimes drastic effect. The use of pumps off their design point is a common cause of gross inefficiency and wasted fuel.

6.8.4 Centrifugal pumps

Centrifugal pumps are by far the most commonly used pumps for small- and medium-scale water pumping. Small centrifugal pumps are used in their millions for pumping water up into domestic water storage tanks in buildings around the world. Many more centrifugal pumps are used for small-scale irrigation. Small centrifugal pumps are not very efficient, but they are simple to mass-produce, and can consequently be very cheap. For the smallest applications, those of a few hundred watts power, working at medium to high heads, other types of pump are often superior to centrifugal pumps, but the low price, general availability, and convenience of centrifugal units mean they that they are commonly used anyway.

Horizontal shaft centrifugal pump construction
The most common arrangement of centrifugal pump for small- to medium-sized electric or engine-powered water pumping applications is the horizontal shaft pump. Figure 6.59 shows a typical mass-produced volute-centrifugal pump in cross-section. In this type of pump the casing and frame are usually cast iron or cast steel, while the impeller may be bronze or steel. Critical parts of the pump are the edges of the entry and exit to the impeller as a major source of loss is back-leakage from the spiral casing back into the inlet. To prevent this, good quality pumps, including the one in the diagram, have a closely fitting wear ring fitted into the casing around the front rim of the impeller. If this is subject to some wear by grit or particulate matter in the water it can be replaced when the clearance becomes large enough to cause significant loss of performance. However, many farmers probably do not recognize wear of this component as being serious and simply compensate by either driving the pump faster or for longer each day, both of which waste fuel or electricity. Another wearing part is a stuffing box packing where the drive shaft emerges from the back of the impeller casing. This needs to be periodically tightened to minimize leakage, although excessive tightening increases wear of the packing. The packing is usually graphited asbestos, although graphited PTFE is more effective if available. The back of the pump consists of a bearing pedestal and housing enclosing two deep-groove ball-bearings. This

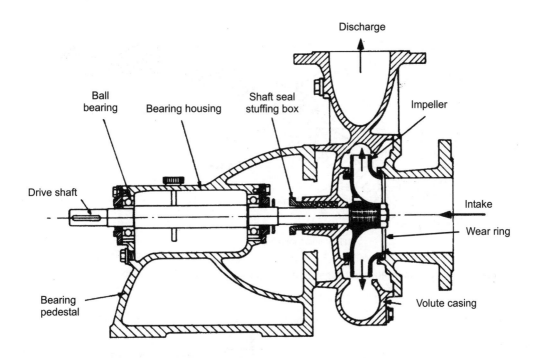

Fig. 6.59: A typical surface-mounted pedestal centrifugal pump

particular pump is oil lubricated, and has a filler, dip-stick and drain plug. Routine maintenance involves occasional changes of oil, plus more frequent checks on the oil level. Failure to replenish lost oil leads to bearing failure, which if neglected for any time can allow the shaft to whirl and damage the impeller edges.

Centrifugal pump installations
Figure 6.60 and Fig. 6.61 show two alternative typical low lift centrifugal pump installations; the simplest is the suction installation of Fig. 6.60. As mentioned earlier in Section 5.1 Suction Lift, centrifugal pumps are limited to a maximum in practice of about 4–5 m suction lift at sea level (reducing to around 2 m suction lift at an altitude of 2,000 m, and further reduced if a significant length of suction pipe is involved). If the suction limit is exceeded, problems are almost certain to be experienced in priming the pump, retaining its prime, etc. A foot valve is a vital part of any such installation, as otherwise the moment the pump stops, or slows down, all the water in the pipeline will run back through the pump, making it impossible to restart the pump unless the

pipeline is first refilled. Also, if water flows back through the pump, it can drive it backwards and possibly damage the electrical system.

If the delivery pipeline is long, it is also important to have another check valve (non-return valve) at the pump outlet. This is to protect the pump from the effect of water-hammer if it stops suddenly. What happens is that when the pump cuts out, the flow in the delivery pipeline continues under its own momentum and causes the pressure to drop inside it. If the pipe is long enough, the pressure drop will be sufficient to cause cavitation bubbles to form. When the momentum of the water is exhausted these bubbles will implode, and the water will quickly be accelerated back the wrong way down the pipe. When the bubbles have collapsed the column of water becomes incompressible, and the flow is suddenly slowed down, causing a water-hammer pressure spike. There is a further spike when the reversed flow goes through the pump and causes the foot valve to slam shut. The impact of such events has been known to burst a centrifugal pump's casing. The discharge check valve therefore protects the pump from any such back surge

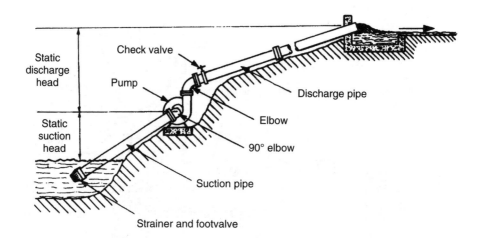

Fig. 6.60: A surface-mounted centrifugal pump installation

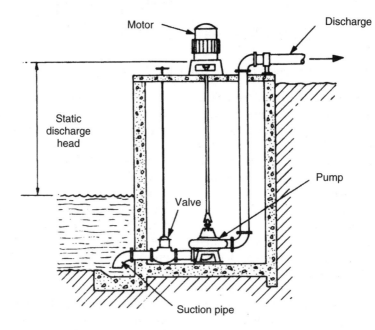

Fig. 6.61: A centrifugal pump installed below the water level in a sump

down the pipeline (though it does not protect the pipeline, which must either be able to withstand the shock, or have an alternative form of protection).

In many cases there is no surface mounting position low enough to permit suction pumping. In such cases centrifugal pumps are often placed in a sump or pit where the suction head will be small, or even as in Fig. 6.61 where the pump is located below the water level. In the situation illustrated a long shaft is used to drive the pump from a surface mounted electric motor (to keep the motor and electrical equipment above any possible flood level).

Centrifugal pump impeller variations

The component that more than anything else dictates a centrifugal pump's characteristics is its impeller. Figure 6.62 shows some typical forms of impeller construction. Although the shape of an impeller is important, the ratio of impeller exit area to impeller eye area is also critical (i.e. the change of cross-section for the flow through the impeller), and so is the ratio of the exit diameter to the inlet diameter. A and B in the figure are both open impellers, while C and D are shrouded impellers. Open impellers are less efficient than shrouded ones (because there is more scope for back leakage, and there is also more friction and turbulence caused by the motion of the open blades close to the fixed casing), but they are less prone to clogging by mud or weeds. Shrouded impellers are considerably more robust, and less inclined to be damaged by stones or other foreign bodies passing through. Arguably, open impellers are less expensive to manufacture, so they tend to be used on cheaper and less efficient pumps; shrouded impellers are generally superior where efficiency and good performance are important. It should be noted that centrifugal pumps can pass quite large pieces of debris, basically up to the size of the galleries through the impeller and diffuser; for example, some portable submersible pumps can handle solids up to 30 mm in diameter. Impellers with fewer blades are less likely to block than those with many blades: for pumping slurry, single-blade impellers can be used with are almost uncloggable, but better efficiency is obtained with more blades, and up to 10 may be used.

Also in Fig. 6.62, A and C are impellers for a single-suction pump, while B and D are for a double-suction pump in which water is drawn in symmetrically from both sides of the impeller. The main advantage of a double-suction arrangement is that there is little or no end thrust on the pump shaft, but double suction pumps are more complicated and expensive, and are uncommon in small and medium pump sizes.

The shape of the impeller blades is also of importance. Some factors tend to flatten the H–Q curve for a given speed of rotation, while others steepen it. Figure 6.63 shows the effect of backward raked, radial and forward raked blade tips; the flattest curve is obtained with the first type, while the last type actually produces a maximum head at the design point. Generally the flatter the H–Q curve, the higher the efficiency, but the faster the impeller has to be driven to achieve a given head. Therefore impellers producing the most humped characteristics tend to be used when a high head is needed for a given speed, but at some cost in reduced efficiency.

Series and parallel operation of centrifugal pumps

Where a higher head is needed than can be achieved with a single pump, two can be connected in series as in Fig. 6.64A, and similarly, if a greater output is needed, two centrifugal pumps may be connected in parallel as in Fig. 6.64B. The effects of these arrangements on the pump characteristics are illustrated in Fig. 6.65. The horizontal axis shows the discharge as a fraction of the optimum discharge of a single pump. The vertical axis shows the efficiency as a fraction of the maximum efficiency, and the head as a fraction of the nominal head of a single pump (which is the head at the most efficient discharge). The graph shows that series connection of pumps has no effect on efficiency or discharge but doubles the effective head. In theory, parallel operation will double the discharge without affecting the head or the efficiency, as shown in the graph, but this is only the case if the pipework size is increased so that friction losses stay the same. If the pipework losses are higher, then the flow will be somewhat less than double that of a single pump.

To run pumps in series the pumps need to be matched. If not, one pump can be trying to pass too much on to the next pump, leading to overpressure in the pipe between them. Pressure relief or balancing valves can be used to guard against this, as can small bleed pipes which bypass the pumps.

6.8.5 Axial-flow or propeller pumps

As already explained, an axial-flow (or 'propeller') pump propels water primarily by the reaction to lift forces produced by rotating its blades.

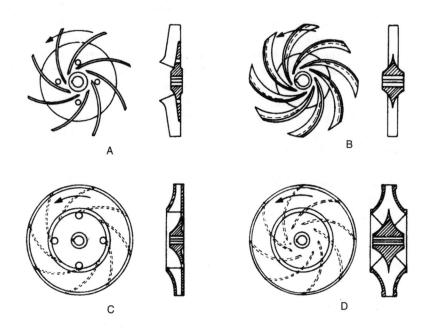

Fig. 6.62: Various types of centrifugal pump impellers

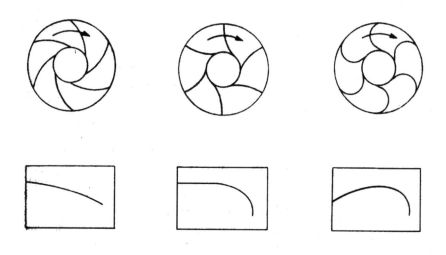

Fig. 6.63: The effect of the of curvature of impeller vanes on the head-flow characteristic of centrifugal pumps

The rotor also imparts spin to the water, which if left uncorrected would represent wasted energy, since it will increase the friction and turbulence without helping the flow of water down the pipe. Axial flow pumps therefore usually have fixed guide vanes, which are shaped so as to straighten the flow and convert the spin component of velocity into extra pressure, in much the same way as with a diffuser in a centrifugal pump. Figure 6.56 shows a typical axial flow pump of this kind, in which the guide vanes, just above the impeller, also serve a second structural purpose of housing a large plain bearing, which positions the shaft centrally. This bearing is usually water lubricated and has features in common with the stern gear of an inboard-engined motor boat.

Axial flow pumps are generally manufactured to handle flows in the range 150 to 1,500 m^3/h for vertically mounted applications, usually with heads in the range 1.5–3.0 m. By adding additional stages (i.e. two or more impellers on the same shaft) extra lift up to 10 m or so can be engineered.

Most axial flow pumps are large-scale devices, which involve significant civil works in their installation, and which would generally only be applicable on the largest land-holdings addressed by this publication. They are mainly used in canal irrigation schemes where large volumes of water must be lifted 2–3 m, typically from a main canal to a feeder canal.

Small-scale propeller pumps may quite easily be improvized but are not usually manufactured; ordinary boat propellers mounted on a long shaft have been used for flooding rice paddies in parts of Southeast Asia. The International Rice Research Institute (IRRI) has developed this concept into a properly engineered, portable high volume pumping system, shown in Fig. 6.66. It is designed to be manufactured in small machine shops and is claimed to deliver up to 180 m^3/h at heads in the range 1–4 m. This pump requires a 5 hp (3 kW) engine or electric motor capable of driving its shaft at 3,000 rpm; its length is 3.7 m, the discharge tube is 150 mm in diameter and the overall mass, without the prime mover fitted, is only 45 kg.

6.8.6 Mixed-flow pumps

As discussed above, and as its name suggests, the mixed-flow pump involves something of both axial and centrifugal pumps. Mixed-flow pumps tend to be used for medium flow rates and medium heads, and as such are generally more suited to irrigation uses than for small-scale drinking-water supply. They avoid the limited lift of an axial flow pump, but still achieve higher efficiency and larger flow rates than a centrifugal volute pump. Also, mixed flow pumps can, like centrifugal pumps, be used as suction pumps, whereas axial-flow pumps cannot. Figure 6.67 shows a surface mounted, suction mixed-flow pump and its installation. Here the swirl imparted by the rotation of the impeller is recovered by delivering the water into a snail-shell volute or diffuser, identical in principle to that of a centrifugal volute pump.

An alternative arrangement more akin to an axial flow pump is shown in Fig. 6.57. Here what is often called a 'bowl' casing is used, so that the flow spreads radially through the impeller, and then converges axially through fixed guide vanes that remove the swirl and thereby, exactly as with axial flow pumps, add to the efficiency. Pumps of this kind are installed submerged, which avoids the priming problems that can afflict large surface suction rotodynamic pumps such as in Fig. 6.67. The 'bowl' mixed-flow pump is sometimes called a 'turbine' pump, and it is in fact analogous to the centrifugal turbine pump described earlier; the passage through the rotor reduces in cross-section and serves to accelerate the water and impart energy to it, while the fixed guide vanes are designed as a diffuser to convert speed into pressure and thereby increase both the pumping head and the efficiency. A number of bowl pumps can be stacked on the same shaft to make a multi-stage turbine pump, and these are quite commonly used as borehole pumps due to their long narrow configuration. Mixed-flow bowl pumps typically operate with flows from 200–12,000 m^3/h over heads from 2–10 m. Multiple stage versions are often used at heads of up to about 40 m.

133

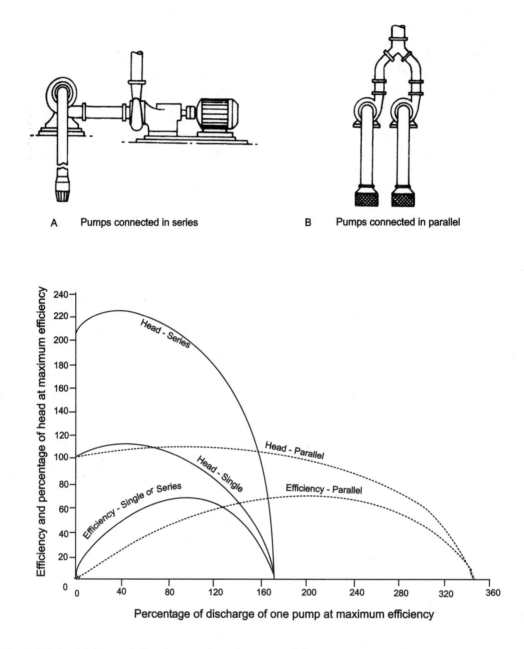

| A | Pumps connected in series | B | Pumps connected in parallel |

Fig. 6.64: Combining centrifugal pumps in series or parallel

6.8.7 Multi-stage and borehole rotodynamic pumps

Where high heads are needed, the primary means to achieve this with a single impeller centrifugal pump are either to drive the impeller faster or to increase its diameter. In the end there are practical limits to what can be done in this way, particularly for borehole pumps where the diameter of the impeller is limited by the size of the

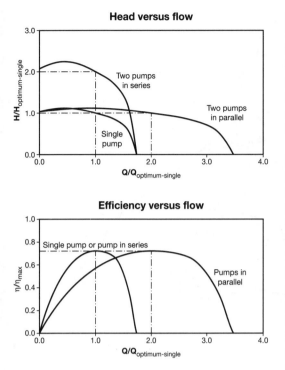

Fig. 6.65: The characteristics of two similar centrifugal pumps connected in series or parallel

borehole. One solution is to connect pumps in series, as discussed in the sub-section 'Series and parallel operation of centrifugal pumps' above. A neater solution is to use a multiple impeller pump in which the output from one impeller feeds directly, through suitable passages in the casing, to the next, mounted on the same shaft. Figure 6.68 shows such a pump, in this case a 5-stage borehole pump. Figure 7.73B shows a three-stage centrifugal pump, coupled to a turbine as a prime mover, as another example of multi-staging.

Surface-mounted multi-stage pumps are probably only likely to be of relevance to irrigation in mountainous areas since there are few situations elsewhere where surface water needs to be pumped through a high head. More important from the irrigation point of view is the vertical shaft multi-stage submersible borehole pump which has an integral submerged electric motor and directly coupled to it, as in below the pump, as in the example of Fig. 6.68. However, it is

possible to get so-called 'bare-shaft' multi-stage borehole pumps in which the pump is driven from the surface via a long drive shaft supported by spider bearings at regular intervals down the rising main (see Fig. 7.64B), or arrangements similar to that shown in Fig. 6.61 with a vertically-mounted multi-stage pump instead of a centrifugal pump down either a sump or a well.

In recent years numerous, reliable, submersible electric pumps of the type shown in Fig. 6.68 have evolved. Section 7.6 discusses in more detail the electrical implications and design features of this kind of unit. Extra pump stages can be fitted quite easily to produce a range of pumps to cover a wide spectrum of operating conditions. The pump in Fig. 6.68 is a 5-stage mixed-flow type, and the same figure also shows how, simply by adding extra stages (with increasingly powerful motors) a whole family of pumps can be created capable, in the example illustrated, of lifting water from around 40 m with the smallest unit to around 245 m with the most powerful; the efficiency and flow will be similar for all of these options. Only the head and the power rating will vary in proportion to the number of stages fitted.

Finally, Fig. 6.69 and Fig. 7.64A show typical borehole installations with submersible electric pumps. The pump in Fig. 6.69 has level sensing electrodes clipped to the rising main, which can automatically switch it off if the level in the borehole falls too low.

6.8.8 Self-priming rotodynamic pumps

Rotodynamic pumps, of any kind, will only start to pump if their impellers are flooded with water prior to start-up. Obviously the one certain way to avoid any problem is to submerge the pump in the water source, but this is not always practical or convenient. This applies especially to portable pump sets, which are often important for irrigation, but which obviously need to be drained and re-primed every time they are moved to a new site.

If sufficient water is present in the pump casing, then even if the suction pipe is empty, suction will be created and water can be lifted. A

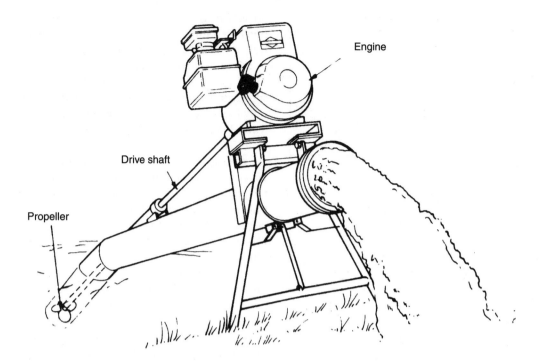

Fig. 6.66: A portable axial-flow pump developed by the International Rice Research Institute in the Philippines

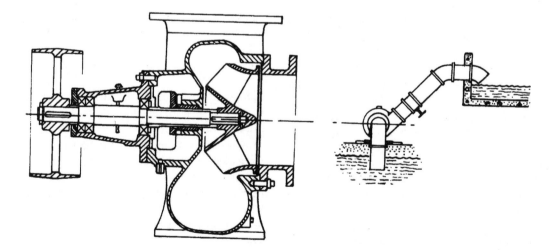

Fig. 6.67: A surface mounted mixed-flow pump

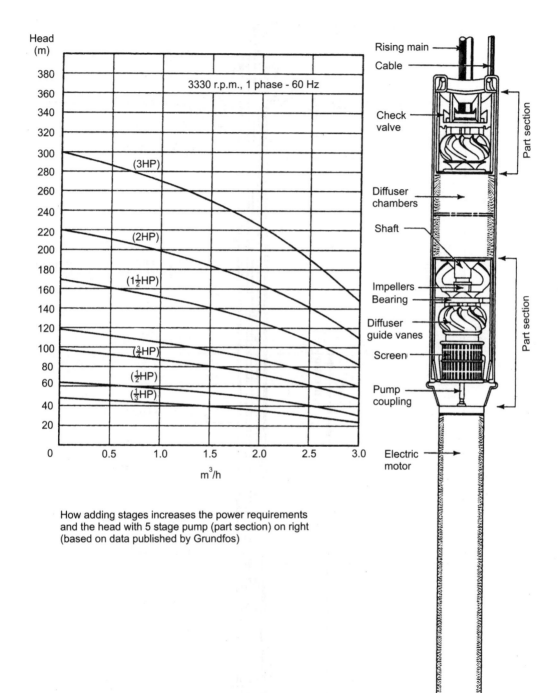

How adding stages increases the power requirements
and the head with 5 stage pump (part section) on right
(based on data published by Grundfos)

Fig. 6.68: A multi-stage submersible electric borehole pump

137

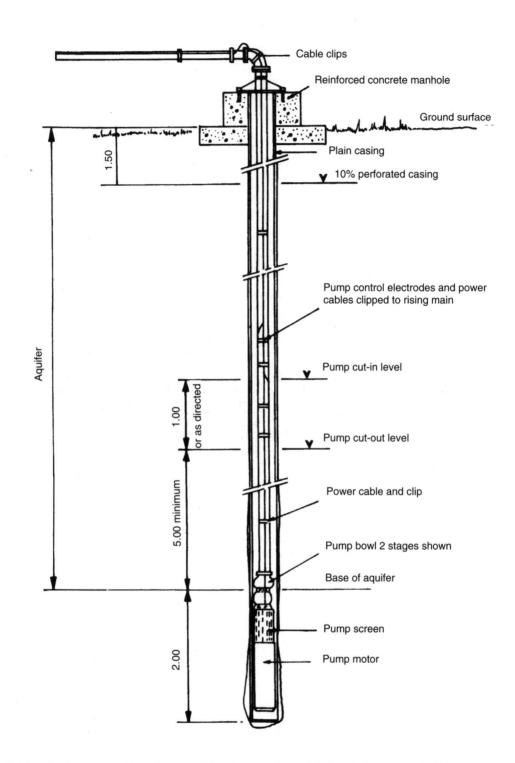

Fig. 6.69: A schematic section of a complete electric submersible borehole pump installation

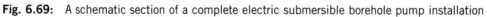

variety of methods are used to fill rotodynamic pumps when they are mounted above the water level. It is, however, most important to note that if the suction line is empty but the delivery line is full, it may be necessary to drain the delivery line in order to remove the back pressure on the pump, to enable it to start. Otherwise it will be difficult, if not impossible, to flush out the air in the system. Another method is to fit a branch near the pump outlet with a hand valve on it, which can allow the pump to be 'bled' by providing an easy exit for the air in the system.

The most basic method of priming is to rely on the foot valve to keep water in the system. The system has to be filled initially by pouring water into the pipes from a bucket; after that it is hoped that the foot valve will keep water in the system even if the pump is not used for some time. In many cases this is a vain hope, as foot valves quite often leak, especially if mud or grit is present in the water and settles between the valve and its seat when it attempts to close. Apart from the nuisance value when a pump loses its prime, many pumps suffer serious damage if run for any length of time while dry, as the internal seals and rubbing faces depend on water lubrication. Also, a pump running dry will tend to overheat; this will melt the grease in the bearings and cause it to leak out, and can also destroy seals, plastic components or other items with low temperature tolerance.

A common method for priming surface-mounted, engine driven suction centrifugal pumps is with a small hand pump on the delivery line. The pump in Fig. 6.70 has a diaphragm priming pump, which has particularly good suction capabilities.

Several alternative methods of priming surface suction pumps may be improvized. For example, a large container of water may be mounted above the pump level so water can be transferred between the pump and the tank via a branch from the delivery line with a valve in it. Then when the pump has to be restarted after the pipeline has drained, the valve can be opened to drain the tank into the pump and suction line. Even the worst foot valves leak slowly enough to enable the system to be started, after which the tank can

be refilled by the pump so as to be ready for the next start. Alternatively, as shown in Fig. 6.71, a large sealed container can be included in the suction line, mounted above the level of the pump, which will always trap enough water in it to start the pump. When the pump is not in use the water in the tank may drop to the level of the suction pipe shown by the dotted line, but enough water is left in the tank that will allow the pump to produce sufficient vacuum to draw water up the suction pipe again. Care is needed in designing an installation of this kind, to avoid introducing air-locks in the suction line.

Yet another simple method to use, but only if the delivery line is long enough to carry a sufficient supply of water, is to fit a hand-valve immediately after the pump discharge (instead of a non-return valve) so that when the pump is turned off, the valve can be manually closed. Then the opening of this valve will refill the pump from the delivery line to ensure it is flooded on re-starting.

Sometimes the most reliable arrangement is to use a special 'self-priming' centrifugal pump (Fig. 6.72). Here, the pump has an enlarged upper casing with a baffle in it. When the pump and suction line are empty, the pump casing has to be filled with water from a bucket through the filler plug visible on top. Then when the pump is started, the water in the casing is thrown up towards the discharge and an eye is formed at the hub of the impeller which is at low pressure; until water is drawn up the suction pipe the water discharged from the top of the pump tends to fall back around the baffle and some of the entrained air carries on up the empty discharge pipe. The air which is discharged is replaced by water drawn up the suction pipe, until eventually the suction pipe fills completely and the air bubble in the eye of the impeller is blown out of the discharge pipe. Once all the air has been expelled, water ceases to circulate within the pump and both channels act as discharge channels. A check valve is fitted to the inlet of the pump so that when the pump is stopped it remains full of water. Then even if the foot valve on the suction line leaks and the suction line empties, the water trapped in the casing of the pump will allow the

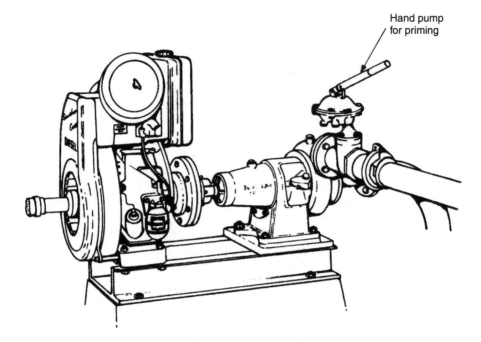

Fig. 6.70: A direct-coupled air-cooled diesel engine and pump installation with a hand-operated diaphragm pump for priming

same self-priming function as described earlier to suck water up the suction line. Hence, pumps of this kind only need to be manually filled with water when first starting up after the entire system has been drained.

6.8.9 Self-priming jet pumps

An alternative type of self-priming centrifugal pump uses the fact that if water is speeded up through a jet, it causes a drop in pressure (see Section 6.8.1). Here the pump is fitted into a secondary casing which contains water at discharge pressure, as illustrated in Fig. 6.73. A proportion of the water from this chamber is bled back to a nozzle fitted into the suction end of the pump casing and directed into the eye of the impeller. Once the pump has been used once (having been manually primed initially) it remains full of water so that on start up the pump circulates water from the discharge through the jet and back into the suction side. As before, air is sucked through

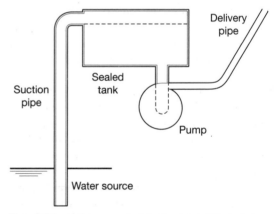

Fig. 6.71: Using a sealed tank above the pump in the suction line to prime a pump

and bubbles out of the discharge, while (until the pump primes) the water falls back and recirculates. The jet causes low pressure in the suction line and entrains air that goes through the impeller and is discharged, hence water is gradually drawn up the suction line. As soon as all the air is expelled from the system, most of the

Fig. 6.72: A self-priming centrifugal pump

discharge goes up the discharge line, but a proportion is fed back to the nozzle and increases the suction considerably compared with the effect of a centrifugal impeller on its own. Therefore, this kind of pump not only pulls a higher suction lift than normal, but the pump can reliably run on 'snore' (i.e. sucking a mixture of air and water without losing its prime). This makes it useful in situations where shallow water is being suction pumped and it is difficult to obtain sufficient submergence of the foot valve, or where a water source may occasionally be pumped dry.

This jet pump principle can also be applied to boreholes as indicated in Fig. 6.74. An arrangement like this allows a surface-mounted pump and motor to 'suck' water from depths of around 10–20 m; the diffuser after the jet serves to raise the pressure in the rising main and prevent cavitation. Although the jet circuit commonly needs 1.5–2 times the flow being delivered, and is consequently a source of significant power loss, pumps like this are sometimes useful for lifting sandy or muddy water as they are not so easily clogged as a submerged pump. In such cases a settling tank is provided on the surface between the pump suction and the jet pump discharge to allow the pump to draw clearer water.

The disadvantages of jet pumps are first greater complexity and therefore cost, and second, reduced efficiency since power is used in pumping water through the jet (although some of this power is recovered by the pumping effect of the

jet). Obviously it is better to use a conventional centrifugal pump in a situation with little or no suction lift, but where suction pumping is essential, then a self-priming pump of this kind can offer a practical solution.

6.9 Air-lift pumps

The primary virtue of air-lift pumps is that they are extremely simple. A rising main, which is submerged in water so that it goes well below the water level, has compressed air blown into it at its lowest point (see Fig. 6.75). The compressed air produces a froth of air and water, which has a lower density than water and consequently rises to the surface. The compressed air is usually produced by an engine-driven air compressor, but windmill powered air compressors are also used. To make an air-lift pump work, the rising main needs to extend below the water for at least 70% of the distance it lifts above it, though this can be reduced to 40% for lifts of 6 m or more. The greater the ratio of the submergence of the rising main to the static head, the more froth will be discharged for a given supply of air and hence the more efficient an air-lift pump will be.

An air-lift pump has no mechanical belowground components to wear out, so it is essentially simple, reliable, virtually maintenance-free, and can easily handle sandy or gritty water. The disadvantages are rather severe; first, it is inefficient as a pump, probably no better, at best, than

141

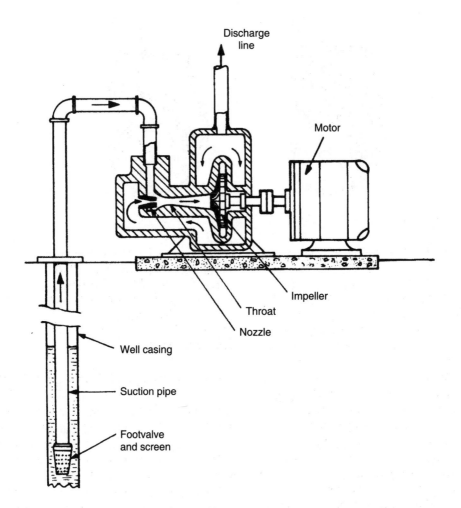

Fig. 6.73: A schematic diagram of a surface suction jet pump

20–30% in terms of compressed air energy to hydraulic output energy, and this is compounded by the fact that air compressors are also generally inefficient. Therefore the running costs of an air-lift pump will be very high in energy terms. Second, it requires a borehole to be drilled considerably deeper than otherwise would be necessary in order to obtain enough submergence, and this is generally a costly exercise. This problem is obviously less serious for low head applications where the extra depth required would be small, or where a borehole needs to be drilled to a considerable depth below the static water level anyway to obtain sufficient inflow of water. If the submergence can be achieved, air-lift pumps can lift water to a surprising height, to 100 m and more. Lastly, air compressors are costly, and need regular maintenance.

6.10 Water-hammer or impulse devices: the hydraulic ram pump or hydram

These devices apply the energy of falling water to lift a fraction of the flow to a higher level than the source. They work by letting the water from

142

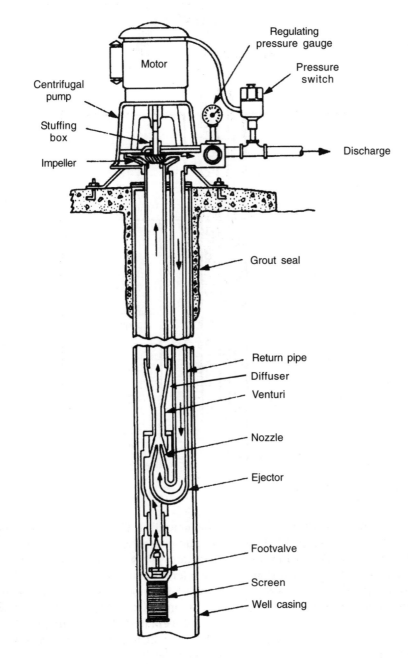

Fig. 6.74: A borehole jet pump installation

143

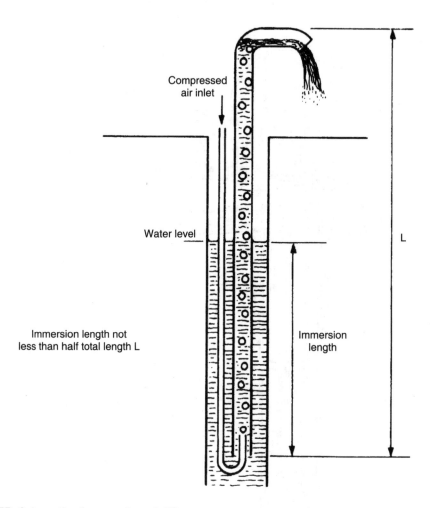

Compressed
air inlet

Water level

Immersion length not
less than half total length L

Immersion
length

L

Fig. 6.75: Schematic diagram of an air-lift pump

the source flow down a pipe and then creating sudden pressure rises by intermittently letting a valve in the pipe slam shut. This causes 'water-hammer' which results in a sudden sharp rise in water pressure sufficient to carry a small proportion of the supply to a considerably higher level.

6.10.1 Basic principles

The hydraulic ram pump, or hydram, concept was first developed by the Montgolfier brothers, better remembered for their pioneering work with hot-air balloons, in France in 1796. A diagram of a rampump is shown schematically in Fig. 6.76. Ram pumps have a cyclic pumping action consisting of four phases: acceleration, compression, delivery and recoil. The power for the pump comes from the 'drive' or 'feed' water on the input, and its output is to the 'delivery' or 'supply' side. The input head is thus known as the drive or feed head, and the output head (measured from the impulse valve level) as the delivery or supply head.

Acceleration. Initially the impulse valve (or waste valve) 1 is open and water flows down the drive pipe 2 from the collection tank 3, through pump body 5 and out through this valve. The strainer element 4 is to prevent debris entering the hydram.

144

Resistance to the flow as the water goes around the impulse valve causes a pressure build up behind it which tries to close it. As the flow accelerates, this hydraulic pressure increases until the force on it overcomes its weight and starts to close it. As soon as it starts to close, and the aperture decreases, the water pressure in the valve body builds up rapidly and slams the valve shut.

Compression. The moving column of water in the drive pipe is no longer able to exit via the waste valve so its velocity must suddenly decrease; the kinetic energy in the water is converted to pressure, and there is a very rapid and considerable rise in pressure – 'water-hammer', which travels noisily up the drive pipe.

Delivery. This pressure is higher than the delivery head, and forces open the one-way delivery valve 6. Water flows through the valve, which stays open until the pressure in the pump body has fallen back below the delivery pressure, by which time the water in the drive pipe has come to an almost complete standstill. The function of the air-chamber 7 is to protect the drive pipe by absorbing the shock of the water-hammer pressure; the initial surge compresses the air in the tank, which then expands more slowly to push the water up the delivery pipe.

Recoil. There will still be a small amount of momentum left in the drive pipe when the delivery valve closes, and this causes the water to recoil or bounce in the dead-ended pipe. The flow momentarily reverses its direction, creating low pressure in the pump body. This is sufficient to re-open the impulse valve (aided by the weight of the valve), and to suck air in through the small 'snifter' non-return valve 9. This air sits under the delivery valve until the next cycle when it is pumped into the air chamber, ensuring that the chamber stays full of air. When the recoil energy is dissipated, water starts to flow out of the impulse valve again, beginning a new cycle.

A ram pump typically runs at between 40 and 120 cycles per minute. The mean delivery flow is much less than the drive flow. A ram pump only pumps a small fraction of the water used, the rest being discharged from the impulse valve as 'waste' water. It is quite common for people to

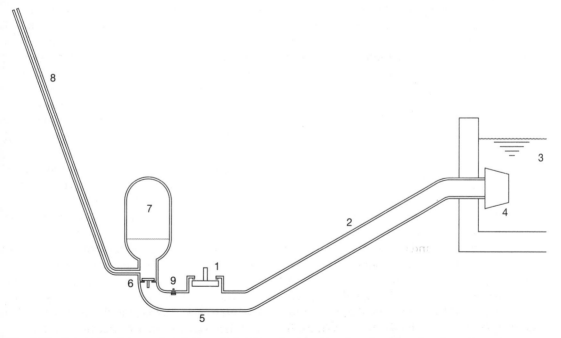

Fig. 6.76: Schematic diagram of an hydram installation; 1 - impulse valve; 2 - drive pipe; 3 - water source; 4 - strainer; 5 - ram pump body; 6 - delivery valve; 7 - air chamber; 8 - delivery pipe; 9 - snifter valve

view ram pumps as magic, or as some form of perpetual motion machine, since from a small drop they manage to pump water to a great height. Disappointingly, the laws of physics are obeyed, and the power output is less than the input. The efficiency of a ram pump is defined as the output power divided by the input power, and can be calculated as:

$$\eta = \frac{P_{output}}{P_{input}} = \frac{h \cdot \rho \cdot g \cdot q}{H \cdot \rho \cdot g \cdot Q} = \frac{h \cdot q}{H \cdot Q}$$

η – efficiency (fraction)
Q – drive (input) flow (l/s or the same units as q)
H – drive head (m)
q – delivery (output) flow (l/s or the same units as Q)
h – delivery head (m)
ρ – density of water
g – acceleration due to gravity

Efficiency is typically 50–70%, and may be as high as 80%. Efficiencies of 60–70% are obtained for well-tuned ram pumps with drive heads of 4 m or more. Ram pumps running off drive heads of more than 7 m will usually have lower efficiencies, say 40–60%. If the ram pump has a very long drive pipe, or a very high delivery head compared with the drive head ($h/H > 25$), then the efficiency may fall to less than 40%. The equation above may be used to estimate the delivery flow for an installation where the input flow is known:

$$q = Q \cdot \frac{H \cdot \eta}{h}$$

Note that this equation works whatever units are chosen for head and flow, provided the same units are used for the drive and delivery values. To give an example of the calculation, suppose a site has a drive head of 7 m, the water is to be lifted 55 m (this latter is the vertical lift from the impulse valve outlet, **not** from the collecting tank) and the available drive flow is 80 litres per minute. If an efficiency of 60% is assumed, then the output flow can be expected to be:

$$q = 80 \cdot \frac{7}{55} \cdot 0.6 = 6.1 \ 1/min$$

The effective slope of the drive pipe affects how fast the drive water accelerates, and the length of the drive pipe and the delivery head affect the length of time the pump pushes water through the delivery valve. Each site will have a different combination of flow available, drive and delivery head, and drive pipe length. The impulse valve will generally need to be adjusted to achieve the best drive flow. This is done either by adding or removing weights, by adjusting a pre-tensioned spring, or by setting stops to limit the maximum opening. The impulse valve will close when the water velocity through the pump body reaches a critical speed. If the impulse valve shuts too early, when the water speed is low, the water-hammer pressure will be reduced, and only a small delivery head will be reached. If the valve shuts too late the proportion of the water that is pumped becomes a small fraction of the total water used. Tuning a ram pump to obtain the best output is a skilled job, and ram pumps in the field are often set up badly. For this reason, some work has been done on making simple pumps without adjustment for areas where there are no skilled mechanics to install or service the pumps. It is worth noting that the best operating flow may not be when the ram pump is at its most efficient: it is often desirable to tune the pump so that it takes virtually the whole flow in the stream, because this will increase the delivery flow even though the ram pump works at a lower efficiency.

The air chamber improves the efficiency of the pump by storing energy so that water flows up the delivery pipe continuously, not just during the brief instant when the delivery valve is open. It also cushions the delivery pipe from the shock of the water-hammer pressure, and gives some protection to the pump body and drive pipe from the full force of the pressure spike. As a general rule, the working air volume needs to be a minimum of twice the volume of water delivered each cycle. The air chamber must stay full of air. If not replenished, over time the air will slowly dissolve in the water, and the output flow will be reduced. Eventually, if the air dissolves away completely, the whole assembly will feel the full shock of the water-hammer, which can result in the fracture of the pipework, the pump body, or the air chamber itself. Some basic designs of ram pump have no snifter valve, and the air chamber needs to be manually drained periodically. In most ram pumps, as in Fig. 6.76, a snifter valve is used to replenish the air, and it is important to inspect this regularly to ensure that it does not become clogged with dirt. The snifter valve design has another important advantage in that it allows a smaller air chamber to be used, for the following reason. Before the ram pump is filled with water, the air chamber is obviously full of air. When the pump is started, it begins to pump water up the delivery pipe, and the pressure of this head starts to compress the air in the chamber. When the delivery pipe is full, the air is at the pressure of the delivery head, and will occupy only a fraction of the total chamber. The ram pump will operate somewhat below peak efficiency – and rather noisily – because of the reduced amount of air. However, because the snifter valve puts a small quantity of air into the chamber each cycle, over the first few hours of operation the chamber will fill with air again. Without a snifter valve this replenishment of the air cannot happen, and consequently the chamber has to be much larger. Simple gas laws can be used to calculate the initial air volume required to produce the required working air volume:

$$\frac{V_{initial}}{V_{working}} = \frac{p_{delivery}}{p_{atmosphere}} = \frac{(h \cdot r \cdot g + p_{atmosphere})}{p_{atmosphere}}$$

$$\approx \frac{h}{10} + 1$$

$V_{initial}$ – total volume of the air chamber (units same as $V_{working}$)

$V_{working}$ – required working air volume (units same a $V_{initial}$)

$p_{delivery}$ – delivery pressure (absolute) (N/m²)

$p_{atmosphere}$ – atmospheric pressure (absolute) (1.01×10^5 N/m² at sea level, 0.89×10^5 N/m² at 1000 m above sea level)

h – delivery head (m)

ρ – density of water (1000 kg/m³)

So for a delivery head of 60 m, the volume of the air initially has to be 6.8 times the required working volume, if there is no snifter valve to replenish the air. This is a significant disadvantage of not having a snifter arrangement.

Instead of a conventional air chamber, it is possible to use a diaphragm or foam-element air chambers (as described in the sub-section 'The effect of reciprocating pumps on pipelines' in Section 6.5.1). These are more-or-less maintenance free, but have the disadvantage discussed above: their volume has to be significantly larger than the required working volume. An unexpected advantage of doing away with a snifter is that the pump can be run submerged.

6.10.2 Construction

Traditional hydram designs, such as that shown in Fig. 6.77, were developed a century ago in Europe and are extremely robust. They tend to be made from heavy castings and have been known to function reliably for 50 years or more. A number of such designs are still manufactured in Europe and the USA in small numbers.

Lighter designs, fabricated using a welded sheet steel construction (Fig. 6.78) were developed first in Japan and are now in production in other parts of S. E. Asia including Taiwan and Thailand. This type of ram pump differs from the schematic diagram of Fig. 6.76 in having its waste valve on the same side as the drive pipe, but its principle of operation is identical. They are cheaper, but only likely to last a decade or so as they are made from thinner material which eventually corrodes; nevertheless they offer good value for money and are likely to perform reliably for a respectably long time. Some simple designs that can be improvised from pipe fittings have also been developed by aid agencies (such as shown in Fig. 6.79), and some interesting versions have been crudely improvised using scrap materials. Needless to say, such devices are very low in cost; the pipes in the end cost considerably more than the hydram. They are never as

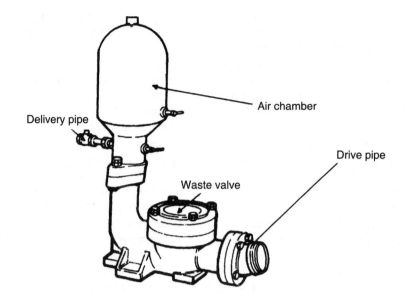

Fig. 6.77: A traditional European ram pump design (Blake's)

reliable as traditional designs, but are easy to repair when they fail.

At first sight, plastic looks an ideal material for ram pumps, being cheap, easy to work with, and corrosion resistant, but it has two main problems. The pressure generated by water-hammer in a pipe is strongly affected by the stiffness of the material. A stiff material such as steel produces a high pressure, but in plastic the same flow stoppage will give a much reduced pressure. A ram pump with a steel drive pipe can produce a delivery head about three times that of the same pump with a plastic drive pipe. Secondly, a ram pump in continuous use may experience between 15 and 100 million cycles per year. To obtain adequate life with plastics, which do not have a fatigue limit, the stresses have to be kept very low indeed. Some pumps have been made from PVC, ABS and HDPE, but they are either limited to very low heads, or have steel reinforcement, or both.

6.10.3 Ram pump operation

It is important to appreciate that the water a hydram pumps is the same as the water it is fed with. Therefore, if the water is to be pumped for drinking, the source must be clean (or the water will need treating). For drinking water systems this is one disadvantage of ram pumps, that a large, clean source is required to provide a small clean supply. Ram pumps do, nevertheless, have a role in supplying drinking water to settlements on ridges and hilltops from mountain streams located at a lower level. In the past, 'indirect' ram pumps have been developed which deliver water from a different source than the drive supply, but few sites have the right combination of a clean water source and a suitable drive flow, and these pumps tend to be rather complicated, expensive, and less reliable.

For irrigation the water quality is not so important, but the output of a ram pump is generally somewhat low for most applications. Pump output is typically 1–3 l/s, and so for irrigation, ram pumps are best suited for small-holdings or single-terrace fields, seedlings in nurseries, etc. Low output of individual units can sometimes be overcome by running a number of ram pumps in parallel, with all of them operating off the same channel or stream. Such an arrangement gives greater reliability, too, since some of the pumps will be working even if one of them breaks down or needs servicing. An advantage of ram pumps

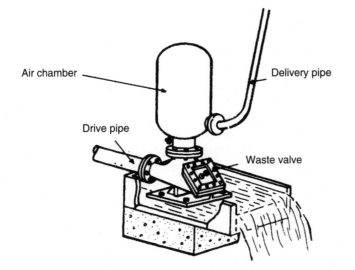

Fig. 6.78: A South-East Asian ram pump

over other pumping methods is that they can readily be run continuously, day and night. If this is done, they compare rather more favourably with other methods that may only be used for a few hours a day. For example, a ram pump producing 3 l/min for 24 hours a day is equivalent to a 25–35 l/min petrol-driven pump that can only be driven for 2–3 hours a day when it can be attended. Because of the low flow, a storage tank is usually included at the top of the delivery pipe to allow water to be drawn in the variable amounts needed. When comparing a ram pump with other pumps the cost of the delivery pipe can be a significant point in the ram pump's favour. The lower flow of a 24-hour ram pump can be delivered through a relatively small delivery pipe. A different pump delivering at a higher flow for only a few hours will require a larger – and much more expensive – delivery pipe, and the extra cost of this pipe alone can make the ram pump the most economic option.

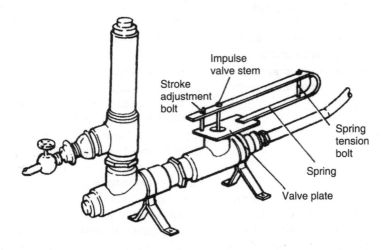

Fig. 6.79: A low cost ram pump design using standard pipe fittings (from Jeffrey et al., 1992 [43])

149

Noise can be a problem with ram pumps. A steel ram pump with a metal-seated valve produces a thump or a loud clacking noise around once a second, and this can be irritating for those who live within earshot. If there are dwellings nearby, it may not be acceptable to run the pump during the night. The noise can be reduced by using rubber impulse valves (as in the Blake's pump shown in Fig. 6.77), by using plastic pumps and plastic drive pipes, by running the pump submerged, or by burying the drive pipe.

Installing a pump with the body underwater has both advantages and disadvantages. As discussed above, submerged pumps cannot use snifter valves to keep their air chamber full. They may also suck silt and debris in, resulting in clogging. They are more difficult to tune and service, and more prone to flood damage. Their advantages are that they make the maximum use of the available drive head – which is important if the head is small – and they run more quietly.

In summary, ram pumps are simple, reliable water pumps. Their low output makes them most appropriate for drinking water applications, but they can be used for micro irrigation. Potential users are often put off by the perceived difficulty of choosing and installing a ram pump. Some technical expertise is required to find a suitable site, to calculate what is required, and for the site installation and adjustment, but there is simple literature available to explain what is required (e.g. Jeffrey et al., 1992 [43]). Some good ram pump designs have been made for local manufacture, and there are a number of quite simple, cheap ram pumps commercially available.

There is some additional information on ram pumps in the discussion on water power in the next chapter, Section 7.9.10.

6.11 Gravity devices

6.11.1 Siphons

Strictly speaking siphons are not water-lifting devices, since, after flowing through a siphon, water finishes at a lower level than it started. However siphons can lift water over obstructions at a higher level than the source and they are

therefore potentially useful in irrigation. But they also have a reputation for being troublesome, and their principles are often not well understood, so it is worth giving them a brief review.

Figure 6.80A to C shows various siphon arrangements. Siphons are limited to lifts of about 5 m at sea level for exactly the same reasons relating to suction lift for pumps. The main problem with siphons is that due to the low pressure at the uppermost point, air can come out of solution and form a bubble, which initially causes an obstruction and reduces the flow of water, and which can grow sufficiently to form an airlock that eventually stops the flow. Therefore, the siphon pipe, which is entirely at a sub-atmospheric pressure, must be completely air-tight. Also, in general, the faster the flow, the lower the lift and the more perfect the joints, the less trouble there is likely to be with air locks.

Starting a siphon can also present problems. The simplest siphons can be short lengths of flexible plastic hose which may typically be used to irrigate a plot by carrying water from a conveyance channel over a low bund; it is well known that all that needs to be done is to fill the length of hose completely by submerging it in the channel and then one end can be covered, usually by a hand, and lifted over the bund to allow siphoning to start. Obviously, with bigger siphons, which are often needed when there is an obstruction which cannot easily be bored through or removed, or where there is a risk of leakage from a dam or earth bund if a pipe is buried in it, simple techniques like this cannot be used.

In Fig. 6.80A, a non-return valve or foot-valve is provided on the intake side of the siphon, and an ordinary gate valve or other hand-valve at the discharge end. There is a tapping at the highest point of the siphon that can be isolated, again with a small hand valve. If the discharge hand valve is closed and the top valve opened, it is possible to fill the siphon completely with water; the filler valve is then closed, the discharge valve opened and siphoning will commence.

Figure 6.80B is similar to A except that instead of filling the siphon with water to remove the air, a vacuum pump is provided which will draw out the air. Obviously this is done with the discharge valve closed. The vacuum pump can be a hand pump, or it could be a small industrial vacuum pump. Once the air is removed, the discharge valve can be opened to initiate siphoning.

Figure 6.80C shows a so-called 'reverse' siphon, used for example where a raised irrigation channel needs to cross a road. Reverse siphons operate at higher than atmospheric pressure and there is no theoretical limit to how deep they can go, other than that the pipes must withstand the hydrostatic pressure and that the outflow must be sufficiently lower than the inflow to produce the necessary hydraulic gradient to ensure gravity flow.

6.11.2 Qanats and foggara

'Qanats', as they are known in Farsi, or 'foggara' in Arabic, are 'man-made springs' which bring water out to the surface above the local water table, but by using gravity. Like siphons they are not strictly water lifting devices, but they do offer an option in lieu of lifting water from a well or borehole in order to provide irrigation. They have been used successfully for 2,000 years or more in Iran, and for many centuries in Afghanistan, much of the Middle East and parts of North Africa.

Figure 6.81 shows a cross-section through a qanat; it can be seen that the principle used exploits the fact that the water table commonly rises under higher ground. Therefore, it is possible to excavate a slightly upward-sloping tunnel until it intercepts the water table under higher ground, possibly at some distance from the area to be irrigated. It is exactly as if you could take a conventional tube well and gradually tip it over until the mouth was below the level of the water table, when, clearly water would flow out of it continuously and without any need for pumping. Qanats can be anything from one to as much as 50 kilometres long (some of the longest are in Iran near Isfahan). They are excavated by hand, sinking wells every 50 to 100 m and then digging horizontally to join the bases of the wells, starting from the outflow point. Traditional techniques are used, involving the use of simple hand tools, combined with sophisticated surveying and

tunnelling skills. Many decades are sometimes needed to construct a long qanat, but once completed they can supply water at little cost for centuries. The surface appearance of a qanat is distinctive, consisting of a row of low crater-like earth bunds (or sometimes a low brick wall) surrounding each well opening; this is to prevent flash floods from pouring down the well and washing the sides away. The outflow from a qanat usually runs into a network of irrigation channels in a cultivated oasis in the desert, resulting from the endless supply of water.

Efforts have been made in Iran to mechanize qanat construction, but without great success, although in some cases qanats are combined with engine powered lift pumps in that the qanat carries water more or less horizontally from under a nearby hill possessing a raised water table to a point on level ground above the local water table but below the surface, where a cistern is formed in the ground. A diesel pump is then positioned on a ledge above the cistern to lift the water to the surface.

6.12 Materials for water-lifting devices

This is a complex technical subject if discussed fully, but it is worth briefly setting out some of the advantages and disadvantages of different materials that are commonly used, as an aid to appraising the specification of different equipment.

Four main considerations apply for construction materials used for pumping water:

- strength: stressed components need to be able to function over a long period of time without either failing through overload or, more likely, through fatigue;
- corrosion resistance and general ability for different materials to coexist under wet conditions;
- resistance to wear and abrasion is important for components that rub or slide or parts which are in contact with flowing water if any particulate matter is likely to be suspended in the water;
- cost.

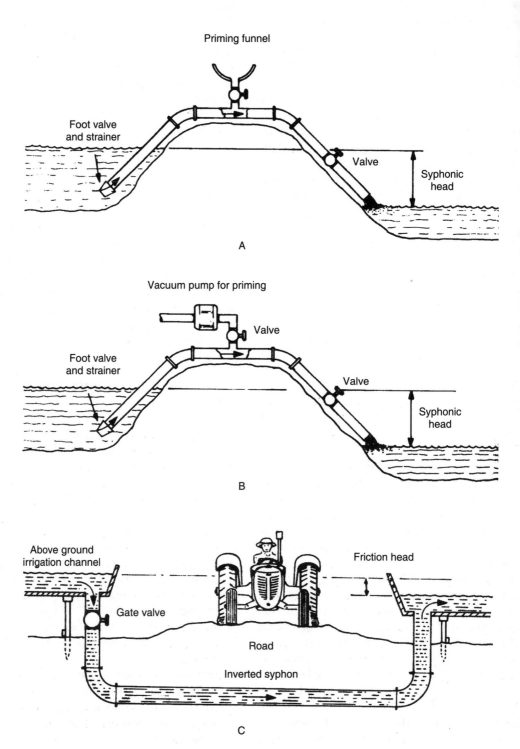

Fig. 6.80: Siphon arrangements

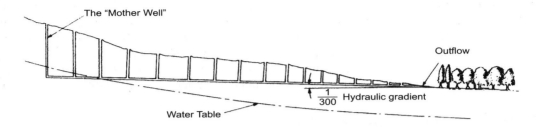

Fig. 78 Cross-section through a qanat

Fig. 6.81: Cross-section through a qanat

As in most branches of engineering, nature has not been kind enough to offer materials that simultaneously satisfy all these requirements completely; invariably compromises are necessary. The important point is to be aware of these and to judge whether they are the right compromises for the application of interest.

It is worth reviewing briefly the pros and cons of various different materials which feature frequently in pumps and water lifts; these are also summarized in Table 6.7.

6.12.1 Ferrous metals

Most ferrous, or iron-based materials are subject to corrosion problems, but to compensate, they are perhaps the most familiar low-cost 'strong material' that is widely available. Generally speaking iron and steel are best suited for use in structural components where strength is important but a surface coating of rust will not cause serious problems.

Ordinary mild steel is one of the materials most susceptible to corrosion. Iron and steel castings, except where they have been machined, are partially protected by black iron oxide that forms when the casting is still hot. There are several methods to protect steels from corrosion, including conventional paints, various modern corrosion inhibitors that chemically bond with the surface of the metal, and various forms of plating and metallic coatings such as zinc (galvanizing) and nickel.

Various chromium and nickel-based steel alloys, the so-called 'stainless steels', are also resistant to oxidation and corrosion. There has been a trend in recent years for stainless steel to be use more and more extensively in commercial rotodynamic pumps. Good quality submersible pumps will often be largely made of various grades of stainless steel. Stainless steels are used both for the casings, pipework and fittings as well as for the working parts such as shafts, impellers and diffusers. The disadvantages of stainless steel are that it is expensive, and is much harder to cast, work with, and machine than the other corrosion resistant metals, brass or bronze. For this reason, pump manufacturers in less-developed countries still often use non-ferrous metals instead of stainless steel. One important application for stainless steel is as nuts and bolts in situations where mild steel nuts and bolts readily corrode; stainless steel nuts and bolts are expensive compared with mild steel ones, but cheap in terms of time saved in the field on items that need to be dismantled. Taking apart a handpump after a few years in service when all the bolts have corroded solid is a long and difficult job, where stainless bolts will come apart even after years of being untouched.

A primary mechanism for corrosion of steel, and other metals, in wet conditions is electrolytic corrosion. This occurs when the dissimilar metals are used together in water. If there is an electrical link between them, a 'galvanic couple' is formed which will cause small currents to flow

153

between them, and this will lead to corrosion of the more reactive metal at a far quicker rate than would normally be seen. So, for example, if steel is used in conjunction with a more base or noble metal, such as copper, the steel will corrode at a rapid rate. The effect is more pronounced if the water has a significant mineral content that increases its conductivity.

Stainless steel excepted, ferrous components need to be well protected from corrosion, and are generally best suited as structural items not having any 'high quality' surfaces in contact with water. An example of a bad use for iron, where it sometimes is applied, is as cast iron cylinders for piston pumps. Here the internal surface will often keep in quite good condition so long as the

Table 6.7: Comparison of different pump materials

Material	Strength	Corrosion resistance in water	Abrasion resistance	Cost	Typical applications
Mild steel	high	very poor	moderate to good	low	• shafts • pump rods • nuts and bolts • structural items
Cast iron	moderate	moderate	moderate to good	low	• pump casings
Stainless steel	high	very good	good	high	• impellers • shafts • wet rubbing surfaces • valve components • nuts and bolts
Brass	moderate	good	moderate to good	high	• impellers • pump cylinders • wet rubbing surfaces
Bronze/gun-metal	high to moderate	very good	moderate to good	high	• impellers • pump pistons • wet bearing and rubbing surfaces • valve parts
Phosphor bronze/lead bronze	moderate	good	good	high	• plain bearings • thrust washers
Aluminium and light alloys	high to moderate	moderate to good	poor	moderate to high	• pump casings • irrigation pipes
Thermoset plastic	moderate	good	moderate	moderate to high	• impellers and diffusers • pump casings and components • bearings
Thermoplastic: PVC, polythene, etc.	moderate to low	very good	moderate to good	moderate	• valves • components • pipes
Hardwood	moderate to good	moderate	moderate to good	moderate to high	• structures • bearings
Softwood	poor	poor	poor	low	• lightly loaded structural items
Bamboo	moderate	moderate	poor	low	• moderately loaded structures

pump is worked, but in any lengthy period during which it is stopped a certain amount of oxidation will occur; even a microscopic outgrowth of iron oxide (rust) forming will quickly wear out piston seals once the pump is started again. However, cast steel centrifugal pump casings are often quite satisfactory, although parts requiring critical clearances such as wear rings are usually inserts made of a more appropriate corrosion resistant metal. Similarly, cast mild steel centrifugal pump impellers are sometimes used; they are not as good as stainless or non-ferrous ones, but are obviously a lot cheaper. Pumps with mild steel impellers usually cannot have close clearances and machined surface finishes, so their efficiencies are likely to be lower.

Various treatments can be applied to irons and steels to modify their properties. Various methods of heat treatment and case-hardening have been common means of improving the wear resistance of steels, and chrome, zinc or nickel-plating are well-known methods of combating corrosion. There are now also a growing number of modern treatments that can be used on a variety of metals. These use plasma sprays or chemical deposition to implant thin layers of other elements into the surface of components, and they can dramatically alter the properties of the base metals. For example, such treatments can put a very hard, wear-resistant material that would normally be too brittle to use by itself on a strong ductile base material. Such processes can overcome many of the compromises that were previously unavoidable in the choice of materials. The treatments are expensive and rather sophisticated, but can be of value for critical components, and are likely to become increasingly common.

6.12.2 Non-ferrous metals

The main non-ferrous materials used for pumps are the brasses and bronze, which are copper-based alloys. The term 'brass' is usually used if the primary alloying element is zinc and 'bronze' if another element is used. Other metals may be added in small quantities to modify the properties.

Brass is a good general-purpose metal with moderate corrosion and wear resistance. It has good wear resistance in 'rubbing' situations against rubber and leather seals, but it is not a particularly strong metal structurally, especially in tension. So called 'Admiralty brass' includes a few per cent of tin, which greatly improves its corrosion resistance, though it can be a little weak.

The bronzes and gun-metals are a large family of copper based alloys, which are generally expensive but effective in a wet environment. They have all the advantages of brass, are structurally stronger, but are even more expensive. Bronzes can contain copper alloyed with tin, plus some chromium or nickel in various grades and traces of other metals including manganese, iron and lead. So-called leaded bronzes replace some of the tin with lead to reduce costs, which still leaves them as a useful material for pump components. The inclusion of antimony, zinc and lead in various proportions produces the form of bronze known as gun-metal, which is a useful material for corrosion resistant stressed components. A bronze containing a trace of phosphorus, known as phosphor bronze, is widely used for plain bearings and thrust washers, and works well if run with an oil film against a well-finished ferrous surface such as a machined shaft. Lead bronze is an even better bearing material, which works well in water. Aluminium bronze, which is cheaper but less corrosion resistant, replaces much or all of the scarce and expensive tin with aluminium.

Most brasses and bronzes can be readily cast and easily machined. Both are used for precision components that run in water, such as pistons, valves, and impellers. Bronzes tend to be used when higher strength is required or other special properties. Bronzes such as phosphor bronze, and particularly lead bronze, are good plain bearing materials, and run well with water lubrication against stainless steel. Brass tubes used to be used as a lining for reciprocating pump cylinders, inside a steel casing, though now plastic and stainless steel tend to be preferred. Brass and bronze lends itself to low-technology manufacture, and is often used in cheaper products where stainless steel or plastic might be used in more sophisticated products.

Other materials, such as aluminium and the light alloys are generally not hard or wear-resistant enough for hydraulic duties, although by virtue of being very light they are sometimes used to make portable irrigation pipes; even then they are not cheap as pipe material and can only be justified where the need to be able easily to move pipelines justifies the cost.

6.12.3 Plastics

There is a large and growing family of plastics, which broadly divided into three main categories:

- Thermoplastics, which soften with heat, and which can therefore readily be heated and worked, or extruded. These materials tend to be the softer, less wear resistant, and somewhat weaker than thermoset plastics. Examples include polyamide (nylon), polyethylene (polythene), acetal, acrylic, PVC (PolyVinyl Chloride), polycarbonate, polystyrene, and ABS (Acrylo-nitrile-Butadiene-Styrene).
- Thermoset plastics, which undergo an irreversible chemical change during processing to become hard solids. Examples include epoxy, phenolics, silicones and formaldehydes.
- Elastomers, which are flexible, rubber-like materials. Examples are the various synthetic rubbers, such as the many variants of nitrile rubber.

These basic plastics can be modified by adding various fillers (such as china clay) or reinforcing material (such as glass fibres in epoxy to make fibreglass).

There has been a tremendous increase in the use of plastics in pumps in recent years. Whereas plastics used to be thought of as too weak and soft for structural and working parts, plastic is now frequently replacing metal components. The rising main and most of the down-the-hole components of many handpumps are now made of plastic, plastic impellers and diffusers are commonly used in borehole pumps, and many small pump units have some or all of their casings made out of plastic. Plastics have the big advantage that they can be moulded to complicated shapes very accurately. The moulds and production equipment are expensive, but if the components are mass-produced the unit cost can be very competitive. Plastic may not be appropriate for small-scale, local manufacture because the tooling costs make small volume production very expensive. It may, however, be possible to machine or form components from stock material, and an increasing number of standard components are becoming available in plastic; HDPE and PVC pipe is now available almost universally at reasonable rates.

Thermoplastics based on polymerized petrochemicals are generally the cheapest plastics; those commonly used in water supply and irrigation applications include:

- PVC (PolyVinyl Chloride) is commonly used for extruded pipes. It can be flexible PVC or rigid (which is unplasticized PVC, uPVC or UPVC). It is important to note that only certain grades of PVC (and other plastics) are suitable for pipes to convey drinking water for people or livestock, since traces of toxic plasticizer can be present in the water passed through some grades. PVC is relatively cheap and durable, but it is subject to attack by the UV (ultra-violet) wavelengths in sunlight and should therefore either be buried to protect it from the sun, or painted with a suitable finish to prevent surface penetration by UV radiation. PVC is also a thermoplastic and therefore softens significantly if heated above about 80°C; however this is not normally a problem in 'wet' applications, but it is if pipes are left empty of water in hot conditions.
- High Density PolyEthylene, HDPE, or 'polythene' is cheaper and less brittle than PVC (especially at low temperatures) and is commonly used to make black flexible hose of use for irrigation. It is structurally much weaker than PVC, and though this is not a disadvantage for surface water conveyance at low pressure, PVC is better for pressurized pipes. Polythene has lower friction with seals than

PVC, but is softer and more easily abraded. Another polythene variant used for pipes is MDPE, Medium Density PolyEthylene, MDPE.

- Polypropylene is in the same family as polythene, but is intermediate in some respects in its properties between polythene and PVC. Polypropylene is less liable to fracture or to be sub-standard due to bad management of the extrusion equipment, than is PVC; which is to say that quality control is less stringent, so it can be more consistently reliable than poorly produced PVC.

None of the above plastics are generally applicable for manufacturing pump components for which strength and durability are important; these require more expensive and specialized plastics, such as:

- Polycarbonate is a hard, wear resistant thermoset plastic that is commonly used for impellers and diffusers in submersible borehole pumps, and for structurally demanding applications in other pumps. It is unfortunately also rather expensive, and not so easy to mould.
- Acetal, or polyacetal, is a mouldable thermoplastic that is reasonably hard and strong. It is readily moulded or machined. It is used for many handpump components.
- Nylons (polyamides) are a range of plastics that are readily moulded and which can have a variety of fillers added to them to vary their properties, such as glass strands for strength, or molybdenum disulphide for low friction. They are used for handpump components.
- Nitrile rubber (NBR or acryloNitrile-Butadiene Rubber) is an elastomer that comes in many different forms. It is a very common material for moulded seals and O-rings. Rubber can also be used to deflect grit, so that rubber-coated components may survive abrasive particles in water where hardened metal components wear away (just as rubber gloves will protect hands in a sand-blasting machine used for abrading metal).
- PTFE (polytetrafluoroethylene) is an expensive plastic of great value for bearings and rubbing surfaces on account of its low friction and good wear resistance. Certain water-lubricated bearings rely on a thin layer of PTFE

for their rubbing surfaces. PTFE is also used for seals, and is more heat-resistant than most plastics.

Most 'pure' plastics are inclined to creep if permanently loaded. This means that they gradually deform over a long period of time, though this can be avoided, and considerable extra strength can be gained, through the use of composite materials where glass fibre mat (for example) is moulded into a plastic. Various polyesters and epoxies are commonly used to make glass-reinforced plastics (GRP or 'fibreglass'); these are used to make small tough components or, in some cases, to make large tanks. Another example of composite plastics is the phenolic composites where cloth made of natural or synthetic fibres and phenolic resin are combined to make a very tough and wear resistant, but readily machinable material which makes an excellent (but expensive) water lubricated bearing, with trade names such as Tufnol, Railco, Orkot and Luytex.

6.12.4 Timber and bamboo

Natural materials such as timber and bamboo are attractive for locally made water pumping components because they are often readily available and they are easily worked. Timber is a natural choice for simple water lifting devices such as dhones, shadoofs or water ladders. Timber can be used for water channels and low-pressure pipes, and bamboo has been used for low-cost screens in tubewells. Hardwoods can be used for bearings (the handle bearing in the Blair pump is made of wood).

Timbers exist in a very wide variety of types; their densities can range from around 500 kg/m³ (or less) up to 1,300 kg/m³. They also offer a very large variation in mechanical properties, workability, wear resistance and behaviour in wet conditions. Timber is of course also susceptible to damage by rot, insects, fungus or fire.

The most durable timbers are generally tropical hardwoods such as Greenheart, Iroko, Jarrah, Opepe, Teak and Wallaba. The durability of many timbers can be improved by treating them with various types of preservative; the most effective

Table 6.8: Review of pumps and water lifts

Category and name	Head range (m)	Input power (kW)	Flow range (m³/h)	Efficiency (%)
I. DIRECT LIFT DEVICES				
Reciprocating/cyclic				
Watering can	1–5	0.02	0.5	5–15
Scoops and bailers	< 1	0.04	8	40–60
Swing basket	0.6	0.06	5	10–15
Pivoting gutters or dhones	0.3–1	0.04	5–10	20–50
Counterpoise lift or shadoof	1–3	0.02–0.08	2–4	30–60
Rope, bucket and windlass	5–50	0.04–0.08	1	10–40
Self-emptying bucket or mohte	5–10	0.5–0.6	5–15	10–20
Rotary/continuous				
Continuous bucket pump	5–20	0.2–2	10–100	60–80
Persian wheel or tablia	1.5–10	0.2–0.6	5–25	40–70
Improved Persian wheel or zawaffa	0.75–10	0.2–1	10–140	60–80
Scoop wheels or sakia	0.2–2	0.2–1	15–160	60–80
Water wheels or noria	0.5–8	0.2–1	5–50	20–30
II. DISPLACEMENT PUMPS				
Reciprocating/cyclic				
Piston/bucket pumps	5–200+	0.3–50+	2–100+	40–85
Plunger pumps	40–400	0.5–50+	2–50+	60–85
Diaphragm pumps	1–2	0.03–5	2–20	20–60
Gas or vapour displacement	5–20	1–50+	40–400+	n/a
Rotary/continuous				
Flexible vane	5–10	0.05–0.5	2–20	25–50
Progressing cavity or Mono	10–100	0.5–10	2–100+	30–70
Archimedes' screw	0.2–1	0.04	15–30	30–70
Open screw	2–6	1–50+	40–400+	60–80
Coil and spiral	2–10	0.03–0.3	2–10	60–70
Flash wheels and treadmills	0.2–1	0.02–20	5–400+	20–50
Water ladders	5–1	0.02–1	5–20	50–70
Chain/rope and washer	5–20	0.02–1	5–30	50–80
III.	VELOCITY PUMPS			
Reciprocating/cyclic inertia				
Inertia and joggle	2–6	0.03	1–3	20
Resonating joggle	2–6	0.03	2–4	50
Rotary/continuous				
Axial-flow/propeller	3–5	10–500+	100–500+	50–90
Mixed-flow	2–10	150–500+	10–500+	50–90
Centrifugal	4–60	0.1–500	1–500+	30–85
Multistage mixed flow	6–20	50–500+	10–100	50–80
Multistage centrifugal	10–300	5–500+	1–100	30–80
Jet	10–30	5–500+	50–500	20–60
IV. BUOYANCY PUMPS				
Air-lift	5–20+	1–5	2–10+	5–10
V. IMPULSE PUMPS				
Hydraulic ram or hydram	10–100	0.1–1	0.3–6	50–70
VI. GRAVITY DEVICES				
Siphons, qanats/foggara	1–6			

treatments involve pressure impregnation with either tar or water-based preservatives. *Lignum vitae* works well as a bearing with water lubrication because of the natural lubricating oils within it, but other hardwoods impregnated with oil can work reasonably well.

One of the main factors affecting the strength of a wooden member is whether knots are present at or near places of high stress. Where wood is used for stressed components, such as pump rods for windpumps or handpumps, it is important that it is fine-grained and knot-free to reduce the risk of failures. Good quality hardwoods like this are not easily obtained in some countries and, where available, they are usually expensive. Cheap wood is limited in its usefulness and must be used for non-critical components. Certain woods like *lignum vitae* have also been used in the past as an excellent plain bearing material when oil lubricated running against a steel shaft, although various synthetic bearing materials are now more readily available and less expensive.

Wood is available processed into plywood and chipboards; with these a major consideration is the nature of the resins or adhesives used to bond the wood. Most are bonded with urea-based adhesives that are not adequately water resistant and are not suitable for outside use, but those bonded with phenolic resins may be suitable if applied correctly and adequately protected from water with paints. Therefore, for any irrigation device it is essential that nothing but 'marine' quality plies and chipboards are used.

6.13 Summary review of water lifting devices

Table 6.1, at the beginning of this chapter, is sorted into categories of pump types based on their working principles, but it is difficult to see any pattern when looking through it. Therefore, Table 6.8, which concludes this chapter, attempts to quantify the characteristics of all pumps and water lifts in terms of their operating heads, power requirements, output and efficiency. Finally, Fig. 6.82 (A, B and C) indicates the different categories of pump and water lift demarcated on a log-log head-discharge graph (similar to that of Fig. 5.10). Obviously there are no hard and fast boundaries which dictate the choice of pump, but the figure gives a graphic indication of which pumps fit where in terms of head and flow, and hence of power. Note that Table 6.8 shows input power requirements, whereas Fig. 6.82 gives the hydraulic power produced, which will be a lesser figure by the factor of the pump efficiency. Due to the use of the log-log scales, the smaller devices appear to occupy a larger area than they would if linear scales had been chosen, however in this case, had a linear scale been applied, it would not have been possible to fit sufficient detail in to the corner where the multiplicity of low-powered, low-head and low-flow devices fit.

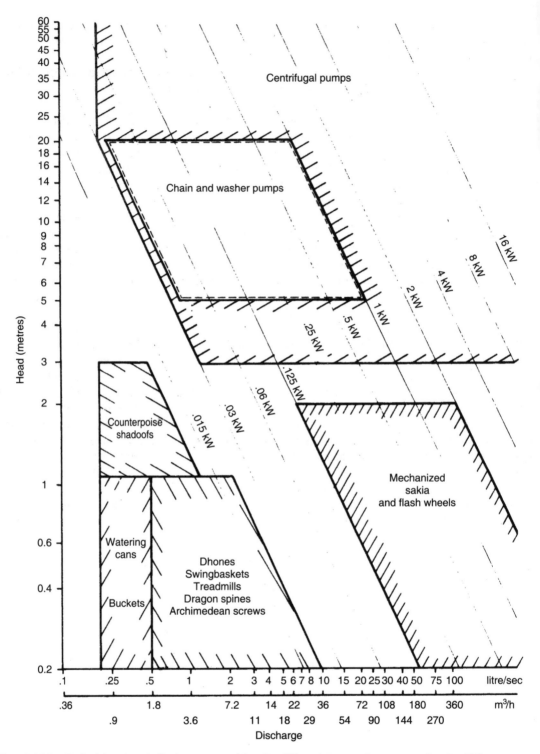

Fig. 6.82A: Typical head and discharge capacities for different types of pumps and water-lifting devices

(on a log-log scale)

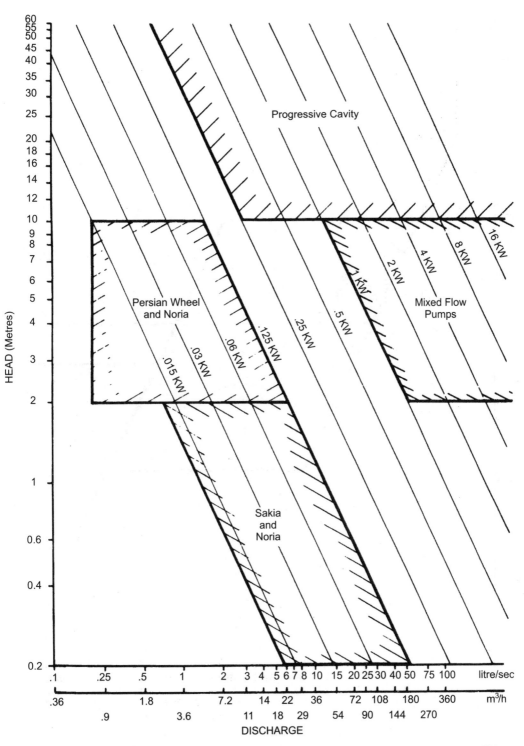

Fig. 6.82B: Typical head and discharge capacities for different types of pumps and water-lifting devices (on a log-log scale)

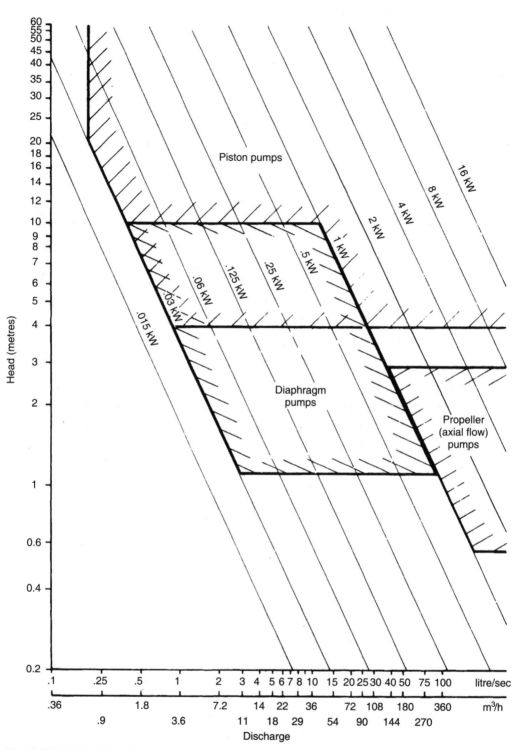

Fig. 6.82C: Typical head and discharge capacities for different types of pumps and water-lifting devices (on a log-log scale)

162

7

POWER FOR PUMPING

Figure 7.1 indicates the most feasible linkages between different energy resources and prime movers (a prime mover is a power source that can convert an energy resource into shaft power or electricity). It shows how all energy sources of relevance to small or medium scale water pumping originate from either renewable energy resources or from fossil fuels; the arrows then show all the routes that can apply to take energy from a resource and apply it to produce pumped water. In some cases similar components can be used within systems energized in completely different ways; for example electric motors are necessary either with a solar photovoltaic pumping system or with a mains electrical system, so the motor-pump sub-systems of both types of system can have a lot in common.

The details of the components in Fig. 7.1 are discussed through the following section, but it is first worth reviewing a few generalities relating to the combination of prime movers and pumps.

7.1 Prime movers as part of a pumping system

7.1.1 Importance of 'cost-effectiveness'

Small-scale irrigation and water-supply systems are often found to be highly inefficient and uneconomic. This can stem from a lack of understanding, but it also reflects the priorities of local communities and individuals in less-developed areas. There is a general tendency to purchase cheaper systems regardless of the running costs; the choice of pumping system is, clearly, not made on purely economic grounds.

An economic analysis is an important part of making a choice, but a true measure of the 'cost-effectiveness' of a system must include such factors as the convenience, ease of use, and the risks involved – as seen by the users. When institutions are involved, choices tend to be made after an analysis of the specific technical, market and financial conditions that prevail, often with little weight given to social factors, which are harder to measure. When local people make decisions, the reverse is often true, and the economics are ignored, except in as much as whether the initial capital can be raised. In both cases, the full cost effectiveness in the broader sense is not being considered.

The economics of choosing a pumping system involves compromises, or trade-offs, between the capital (or first) cost of the system and the running (or recurrent) costs. So, for example, renewable energy resources such as solar energy or wind power are free, making the running costs of such systems low, but the capital costs are high because the equipment required to harness them tends to be larger and therefore more expensive to buy and install than fossil fuel engines. In the end, successful selection depends on the choice of the best trade-off between the availability of finance, the capability of maintaining and financing the recurrent costs of the system, and the performance or productivity that is required. Table 7.1 compares the costs and benefits of different pumping prime movers in general terms. Costs are divided into first costs and running costs, and the benefits are analyzed as the productivity and the opportunity cost. The opportunity cost is loosely defined in the economic sense of the usefulness of the energy supply if it were used for something else other than water pumping. Solar, wind and hydro power are generally simply dissipated if they are not harnessed for a useful application: the sun shines

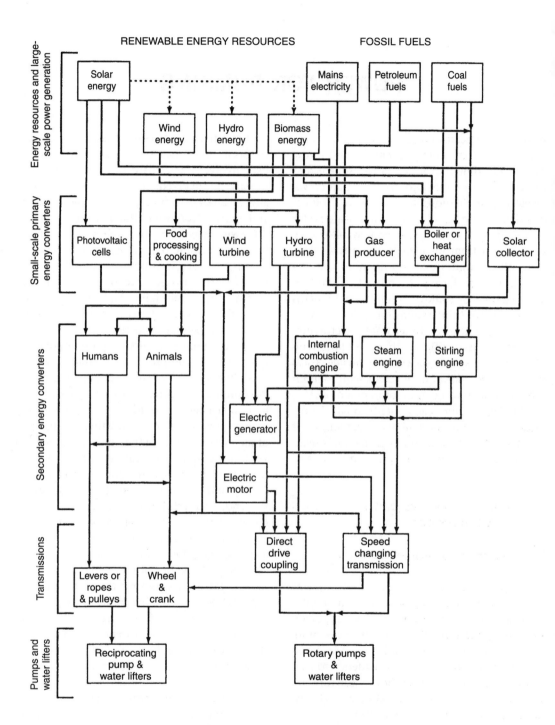

Fig. 7.1: Linkages between energy resources

Table 7.1: Cost and benefit comparison of various prime movers

Prime mover:	Human	Animal	Solar	Wind	Hydro	Biomass engines	Mains electricity	Diesel/petrol engines
First costs								
Capital	★	★★	★★★★★	★★★★	★★★★	★★★★	★ or ★★★★★	★★
Shipping	★	★	★★★	★★★★	★★★	★★★★	★★	★★
Installation	★	★★	★	★★★	★★★	★★★	★ or ★★★★★	★★
Running costs								
Fuel	★★★★★	★★★	Nil	Nil	Nil	★★	★★★	★★★
Spares	★	★	★	★	★	★★★★	★	★★★★
Maintenance	★	★	★	★	★	★★★★	★★	★★★★
Attendance	★★★★★	★★★★	★	★	★	★★★	★	★★★
Productivity	★	★★	★★	★★ to ★★★	★★★	★★★	★★★★	★★★★
Opportunity cost	★★★★★	★★★	★	★	★	★★	★★★	★★★★

Ratings: ★ - low, ★★ - low to moderate, ★★★ - moderate, ★★★★ - moderate to high, ★★★★★ - high.
Notes: 1 – Electricity can vary from high to low depending on whether a mains connection is already available or not.
2 – 'Attendance' quantifies the level of human intervention required

on the ground, the wind blows past, and the streams flow by. Human beings, however, can be doing a large variety of productive tasks if they are not pumping water, electricity can power lights and radios, and diesel can be used in lorries. It is clear from this table that no single prime mover offers both low first costs and low recurrent costs and the highest productivity (if it did it would be used universally, and the other options would be of little interest).

In reality, the selection decision is often limited to what is known to be available and affordable and yet is capable of fulfilling the required pumping duty. People avoid systems with high capital costs both because they lack the money, and because large capital investments are seen as being inherently more risky than regular running costs (even though these latter may, in time, mount up to a considerably greater sum). One function of development agencies and governments working in irrigation or drinking water provision can be to provide suitable credit arrangements and financial inducement to encourage the use of more efficient and cost-effective systems.

Many water supply and irrigation systems are not implemented on a commercial basis at all. Community water supply systems are frequently installed by governments or aid organizations, and the communities do not have to bear the capital costs at all. Though the implementing agencies are concerned with the cost, the choice of technology will be based on other factors, such as long-term sustainability, environmental impact, or the social effects. While the underlying cost-effectiveness of such schemes may be hidden, it is important to appreciate the full costs to know if the technology is appropriate and can be sustained independently if the financial aid is withdrawn.

It is often the case that useful systems are not considered simply because they are unfamiliar, so that potential users either have not heard about them, or know too little to commit themselves. It is hoped that publications such as this may encourage attempts to try new methods, preferably by institutions or individuals with the resources to underwrite the risks inherent in experimenting with new or unfamiliar technologies.

Cost-effectiveness and efficiency

Generally, a cost-effective system needs to be technically efficient; i.e. a relatively high output is needed in relation to the energy input. This is just as true for renewable energy powered systems as for fossil fuelled systems. In the former case, the energy resource, if it is solar energy, wind or water power is notionally cost-free, but the capital cost of the system is closely linked to the efficiency. This is because for a given pumping requirement, if you halve the efficiency of the system you must double the 'cross section' of the energy resource to be intercepted; you need twice the area of solar collector or twice the rotor area of a windmill, or a turbine capable of passing twice the flow rate of water. This tends to require a system that is twice as large and therefore roughly twice as expensive.

In all cases there is an ultimate technical efficiency that can be approached but never quite achieved. The principle is illustrated in Fig. 7.2A. Pursuing the cause of better efficiency is usually worthwhile up to a point, but thereafter it brings diminishing returns as increasing complication, sophistication and cost is required to achieve small further gains in efficiency. However it usually requires a mature technology to be at the level where further improvements in efficiency are counter-productive, and in any case, new manufacturing processes and materials or increases in recurrent costs (due to inflation) sometimes allow improvements to become cost-effective in the future which were not justifiable in the past.

The influence of efficiency on costs is illustrated in Fig. 7.2B, which shows how low efficiency commonly causes high costs and that there is an optimum range of efficiency for most technologies where reasonably low costs are achieved, but above which diminishing returns set in. In the case of renewable energy systems these costs will be largely attributable to the capital cost and hence to financing the investment, while in the case of fossil-fuelled devices a large proportion of the costs will relate to running and maintaining the system

Combining system components with differing efficiencies

Virtually all pumping system components achieve an optimum efficiency at a certain speed

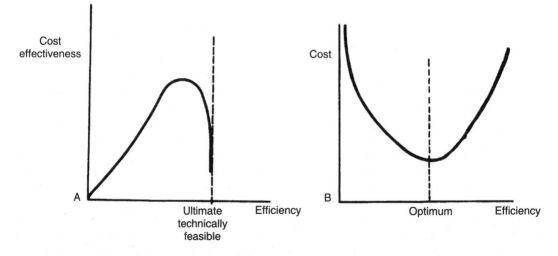

Fig. 7.2: The influence of efficiency on costs and cost effectiveness for a pumping system: A. How diminishing returns eventually defeat the benefits of seeking increased efficiency beyond certain levels. B. The variation of cost with efficiency.

of operation. Some components like pipes and transmission systems are most efficient (in terms of minimizing friction and hence losses) at very low rates of throughput, but they are then least productive and they will therefore have a point of 'optimum cost-effectiveness' where there is a good compromise between their productivity and their efficiency. Prime movers invariably have an optimum speed of operation; this is as true of humans and animals as it is of diesel engines or windmills.

Figure 7.3 shows three sets of curves; first, efficiency against speed for two prime movers (in this example electric motors might fit the speeds and efficiencies shown); second, a curve for a typical pump and lastly, for the combination of the prime movers with the pump. The efficiency of a combination of components is numerically the product (i.e. the multiplied result) of their individual efficiencies; e.g. a 30% efficient engine (0.3) with a 50% efficient pump (0.5) has a combined efficiency of:

$$0.3 \times 0.5 = 0.15 \equiv 15\%$$

The important point demonstrated in Fig. 7.3 is that the prime mover with the highest optimum efficiency is not in this case the best one to use with a particular pump. In the example, motor A has a best efficiency of 58% while motor B achieves 66%, yet, because the optimum efficiency of motor A occurs at a speed which coincides well with the optimum efficiency of the pump, the combined efficiency of that combination is better if the motor is direct-coupled to the pump; (motor B will drive the pump at a speed greater than its optimum, as at 1,500 rpm the pump has an efficiency of only 35%) so the best efficiencies of the two alternative combinations are:

1,000 rpm motor and pump:

$$0.58 \times 0.55 = 0.32 \equiv 32\%$$

1,500 rpm motor and pump:

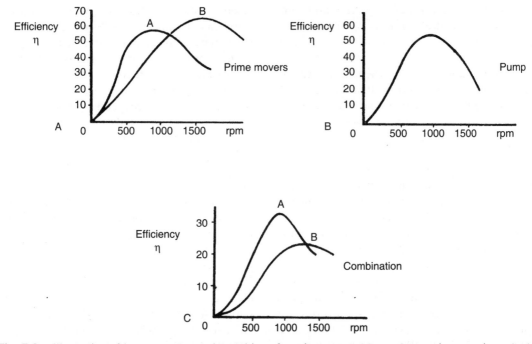

Fig. 7.3: Illustration of how correct speed matching of a prime mover to a pump can be more important that the basic efficiency of the prime mover. Here prime mover A is less efficient than B, but has a better speed match to the pump, and hence the less efficient prime mover provides a more efficient system.

$$0.66 \times 0.35 = 0.23 \equiv 23\%$$

This illustrates how it is generally more important to ensure that the design speeds of components match properly than to ensure that each component has the highest possible peak efficiency.

7.1.2 Transmission systems

Components often do not match effectively; i.e. their optimum speeds of operation are different. In such situations it generally pays, and it is sometimes essential, to introduce a speed changing transmission (for example, this is why cars have gearboxes). Also, in many situations the prime mover cannot readily be close to the pump, and some method is therefore necessary for transmitting its output either horizontally or vertically to the water lifting device.

Transmission principles
Power can be transmitted from a prime mover to a pump in a number of ways. The most common is a mechanical connection, which can either rotate (shafts, belts or gears) or reciprocate (pump rods or levers). Where power has to be transmitted some distance, then electricity, hydraulic pressure or compressed air can be used, since it is difficult to transmit mechanical power any distance, especially if changes of direction or bends are needed.

In all transmissions there is a trade-off between the force or torque being transmitted by the system (which demands robustness to resist it) and the speed of operation (which tends to cause wear and reduced life). Power, which is what is being transmitted, can be defined as the product of force and velocity. Mechanical systems that run at slow rotational or reciprocating speeds need larger forces to transmit a given amount of power, which in turn requires large gear teeth, large belts or large pump rods (for example) and these inevitably cost more than smaller equivalents. Where mechanical power is transmitted some distance, any reciprocating linkages need to be securely anchored; (even a 5 m diameter farm wind pump can pull with a

reciprocating force peaking at about 1 tonne). For this reason, most modern commercial systems involving lengthy mechanical links tend to use high speed drive shafts (for example surface mounted electric motors driving a rotodynamic pump located below the water or flood level as in Fig. 6.61 or Fig. 7.64B). A high speed drive shaft can be quite small in section because at high speed only a low torque is required to transmit the power. However a high speed drive needs to be built with some precision and to have good (and therefore expensive) bearings to carry it and to align it accurately so as to prevent vibrations, whirling of the shaft, premature wear and other such problems.

Electrical, hydraulic or pneumatic transmissions all have a common requirement demanding that their voltage, or pressure of operation ideally needs to be high to minimize the cross section of cable or of pipe needed to transmit a given power flow efficiently. High voltage cable (or high pressure pipes), need to be of a good quality and inevitably cost more per metre for a given cross section. Therefore, with all transmissions there is a trade-off between efficiency and cost; cheap transmissions can often reduce the capital costs but result in high recurrent costs due to their lower efficiency and greater maintenance and replacement needs, and vice-versa. It is therefore advantageous to match prime movers and pumps of similar speeds to avoid the cost and complication of speed-changing transmissions.

Mechanical transmissions
The most common need for a mechanical transmission is to link an engine or an electric motor with a pump. Generally such prime movers are used with centrifugal or other rotodynamic pumps which run at the same speed as the engine or motor; in such situations they can be direct-coupled with a simple flexible drive coupling as in Fig. 6.70 and Fig. 7.32. Many pumps are made integral with the motor driving them, with the impeller mounted on the motor shaft, so that no coupling is necessary.

It is important to appreciate why flexible couplings are used. As a general rule, there should never be more than two bearings on any shaft. If a shaft has two bearings along its length, this will locate it so that its centreline is fixed. A centrifugal pump will usually have two bearings on its shaft (as in Fig. 6.59), as will, say, an electric motor (as in Fig. 7.31). Now it is almost impossible to mount a pump and a motor on a frame so that centrelines of their shafts are exactly in line; with normal fabrication and machining tolerances they will always be out of line by a small amount, even if only a fraction of a millimetre. If an attempt is made to join the shafts together rigidly, each shaft will bend slightly. Because shafts are quite rigid, this bending will result in surprisingly large loads on the bearings, in addition to their normal working loads. If the pump is driven with this misalignment load locked in, the bearings in both the pump and the motor will quickly fail. A shaft coupling will have either a small amount of clearance in it, or a flexible element so that it can cope with a small amount of radial and angular misalignment without imposing excessive loads on the

bearings. Such a coupling should always be used when directly connecting the shafts of separate pump and prime mover units.

If the shafts do not need to be in line, then a belt drive can be used. Speed changes of up to about 4 : 1 can readily be achieved with wedge or 'V' belts as shown in Fig. 7.24 and Fig. 7.33. Figure 7.4 shows a two-stage V-belt drive where the total speed change can be as much as 4 : 1 on each stage. In this situation the total speed change is the product of the ratios for each stage. Where multiple V-belts are needed on one drive stage, as in Fig. 7.24 (showing four in use), it is best to use matched sets from a supplier, and always to renew all belts simultaneously so that they all share the load effectively; a more modern and convenient type of belt is the so-called poly-vee, which is similar to a whole lot of small V-belts fixed together edge-to-edge. Flat belts have less friction, and are more efficient than a set of V-belts. In the past, the belts used to be made of leather, but modern flat belts are made of synthetic materials. Toothed belts can also be used,

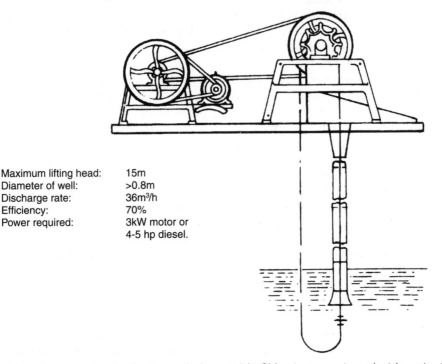

Maximum lifting head:	15m
Diameter of well:	>0.8m
Discharge rate:	36m³/h
Efficiency:	70%
Power required:	3kW motor or 4-5 hp diesel.

Fig. 7.4: A two-stage speed reduction transmission used in China to connect an electric motor to a chain and washer pump

having the advantages that tension adjustment is not critical, and there is no slip (so the pump is always driven at exactly the same speed as the motor).

A right angle drive may be created to drive a vertical shaft borehole pump (for example) either by using a 90° geared well head, or by using a twisted flat belt. To be successful twisted, belt drives need to have a generous distance between the pulleys in relation to their diameters or excessive wear will occur. V-belts have been successfully used with twist too, though manufacturers do not seem to recommend it.

If a speed change greater than about 4 or 5 to 1 is needed, then an alternative to multiple stages of belts (which introduce problems with belt adjustment) is to use gearboxes.

Other mechanical transmissions commonly used are reduction gearboxes with a pitman drive, similar in most respects to the wind pump transmission of Fig. 7.36. They consist of a rotary drive shaft which drives a single or pair of larger gear wheels via a small pinion; the large gear wheels drive a reciprocating cross-head or pitman slider via two connecting rods. The pump rod is connected to the cross-head or pitman. Mechanisms of this kind can be used to connect a diesel engine or an electric motor to a reciprocating piston pump. Other mechanical right-angle drives are illustrated by reference to Fig. 7.19, Fig. 7.20 and Fig. 7.21 (the large size necessary for making a strong enough drive from traditional materials is well-illustrated in Fig. 7.20).

When budgeting for a pumping system, it is important to know that the mechanical transmission can cost as much, and sometimes more, than the prime mover, especially if a geared or reciprocating well-head is used. The high cost is due to the stringent mechanical requirements for reliable operation and the volume of production usually being much lower than for engines or electric motors.

Electrical, hydraulic or pneumatic transmission
The use of a diesel-generating set (or wind-electric, solar-electric or hydro-electric unit) as a prime mover allows considerable flexibility in transmission (literally) since electric cable is all that is needed to link the prime mover to a motor-pump unit (which can even be submerged down a borehole as in Fig. 6.69 or Fig. 7.64A).

Other options, which are technically feasible, but more rarely used are hydraulic or pneumatic transmissions in which either a liquid (water or oil) or air are pumped through pipes to drive a pump. Examples of hydraulic transmissions are given with the jet pump in Fig. 6.74, or the positive displacement hydraulically activated pumps of Fig. 6.34. The air lift pump of Fig. 6.75 is an example of a pumping system which requires pneumatic transmission. Pneumatic diaphragm pumps are commercially available and tend to be most commonly used for construction projects, with an air supply from mobile engine driven air-compressors. They are not normally used for on-farm irrigation but there is no technical reason why they would be unsuitable. However, hydraulic and pneumatic transmissions tend to be inefficient and therefore such a system may have high running costs.

7.1.3 Fuels and energy storage

Power sources need energy, whether it is fuel for an engine, wind for a wind pump or sunshine for a solar pump. The main difference is that the provision of fuel can usually be arranged by the user, but nobody can make the wind blow or make the sun shine on demand. There is therefore an obvious qualitative difference between wind and solar powered devices that will only function under certain weather conditions and the rest that generally can be made to operate at any time they might be required.

Although the apparent randomness of wind or solar availability would appear to be a serious disadvantage, in reality the energy available over a period of a few days in a given location at a given time of the year does not vary much from year to year. The problem is more one of covering a mismatch that can occur between the rate at which energy is available and when the water is needed. This can be overcome either by choice of technique or by including a storage facility.

In most cases, where the output required is water, the most cost-effective solution is to introduce a storage tank. Drinking water supplies often include a storage tank anyway to give a feeder pressure to taps in the distribution pipework. Irrigation systems often do not have storage, and it is normally provided to overcome insufficient water from the pumping; in some cases the field itself can act as a storage tank. The other principal method for small-scale energy storage is to use lead-acid electrical batteries, but this becomes prohibitively expensive except when small amounts of energy of less than about 1–2 kWh need to be stored. The costs of tanks for storing water relate to their volume, while the costs of batteries relate to their energy capacity; therefore, at low heads when large volumes of water may need to be stored, but which involve little energy, electrical battery storage can be cheaper (and less demanding in terms of land utilization) than storage tanks. However, before considering the substitution of batteries for storage tanks, it must be remembered that batteries would need replacing a lot more often than the storage tank and generally also need much more maintenance. Ordinary car or truck batteries are not suitable for energy storage, because they can only withstand being discharged by about 30% repeatedly; they fail after a few cycles of full discharge and recharging. 'Deep-discharge' batteries are better, but are more expensive.

7.2 Human power

7.2.1 Human beings as power sources

Human power is an obvious first resort if any water lifting is required. In its simplest form, people will use buckets to carry water from one place to another. This is laborious, time consuming, and hard work, but nevertheless it is still the primary means for collecting drinking water and irrigating crops for millions of people. The mechanical output of a human body is small, so any human-powered water lifting is limited, but almost all pumping techniques are significantly more productive than carrying buckets. Where buckets are being used, introducing an appropriate water-lifting method can significantly increase the quantity of water delivered, as well as reducing the drudgery associated with pumping it. This section brings out the differences in the methods by comparing the efficiency and output of various devices.

Human power is very commonly used for pumping drinking water. It is quite suitable for such applications, as one person can readily lift sufficient water for a family in a few minutes. For irrigation, human-powered devices can be used, but they need to be worked for significantly longer periods to water a reasonable area of crop. Human power often offers the best means to initiate small-scale irrigation pumping because of its low first cost, and it can be quite appropriate for small vegetable plots. For other crops, and particularly for flooded rice paddy, human-powered irrigation is feasible for small areas, but demands many hours of hard pumping. In the longer term it is to be hoped that small farmers will be assisted to use more productive methods and other energy sources.

Efficiency as prime movers

In the whole small-scale pumping field it is difficult enough to make precise statements on pumping performance which are generally correct; nowhere is this more true than in the field of human powered water lifting devices and pumps. This is partly because human capabilities are very variable, but also because there is a multiplicity of pumps and water lifts of widely varying efficiency and ease of use.

People (and animals) derive their power from the calorific content of their food. Even when physically inactive the human body requires energy to run its basic metabolic functions, i.e. to power the heart and circulate blood, to work the lungs and digestive system, etc. Energy for muscle power is then an extra requirement on top of this. A typical food energy requirement is around 2,400 kcal, 10MJ or 2.8 kWh per 24 hours. Table 7.2 indicates the calorific values of various staple foods.

A person's muscular work capability per day is in the region of 200–300 Wh/d. Human beings therefore have an average overall efficiency

Table 7.2: The calorific values of various staple foods (Leech, 1975 [44])

Staple crop	Energy content (MJ/kg)	kg/day to provide 10 MJ
Dayak rice	10.4–11.4	0.92
Iban rice	13.3	0.75
Tanzanian rice	8.2	1.22
Maize (Africa)	4.2	2.38
Millet (Africa)	3.8	2.63
Sweet potato (Africa)	10.1	0.99
Cassava (Africa)	15.0	0.67
Yams (Africa)	9.5	1.05
Groundnuts/peanuts (Africa)	7.2	1.39

in the region of 7–11% for converting food energy to mechanical energy. This figure includes the basic metabolic energy requirement; the efficiency of the muscles for short but strenuous efforts can be as high as 20% or 30% [42], which compares well with internal combustion engines.

What fraction of the food produced from irrigation might be needed to 'power' the irrigator, if human energy is to be used? (Kraatz, 1981 [45]) (quoting Wood) gives a calculation of the food required by a man to generate the energy needed to irrigate a crop. For example, a rice crop needing 850 mm of water in 120 days, with a yield of 600 kg of rice from a 0.2 ha plot. With a 50% efficient water lifting device lifting the necessary water through 3 m head, the marginal cost of 'fuelling' the human prime mover for the irrigation pump was calculated to be 35 kg of rice or 6% of the expected total yield. An additional 35 kg would be needed to cover the basic metabolism of the person concerned, giving a total of 70 kg or 12% of the rice produced.

The Intermediate Technology Development Group's Water Panel (ITDG, 1983 [46]) gave a rule of thumb of a food requirement of 0.5 kg of rice per MJ of hydraulic work, plus 0.012 kg of rice per day per kg body weight. In the earlier example, the hydraulic requirement was 50MJ, which under the rule of thumb just quoted demands 25 kg of rice for pumping effort, and a 60 kg man would additionally need (0.012 × 60 ×

120 = 86 kg) of rice, giving a total requirement of 111 kg of rice, or 18% of the total crop produced.

Allowing for losses of rice, possible worse yields than that assumed, and the food requirements of the farmer's dependants, it is easy to see how hard it is to generate a surplus when cultivating staple crops on small land holdings. For example, if he has three dependants and loses just 20% of his crop through various forms of wastage, the farmer and his family will need to retain 60 to 90% of the harvest, depending on the method of estimating rice requirements used. Slightly worse wastage or a larger family would result in barely sufficient food for pure subsistence.

Productivity

Contrary to popular belief, human muscular energy is not cheap. The poor are forced to use human power, usually because they cannot afford anything better, since the cash investment required is minimized and therefore it is more 'affordable' than other options. As will be shown, almost any other source of power will pump water more cheaply unless only very small quantities are required.

The human work capability is around 250Wh/d, *so it takes four days of hard labour to deliver just one kWh;* this is an output which a small engine could deliver in less than one hour while burning less than one litre of petroleum fuel. So the farmer with a small mechanized pumping system has the equivalent of a gang of 20 to 40 men who will work for a 'wage' or running cost equivalent to say 1 litre of fuel per hour. Not surprisingly, any farmer who can afford it will sooner choose to employ an engine rather than 20 to 40 men. By using the idea of 'opportunity cost' this argument can be turned on its head to show the high price of human muscle power. The opportunity cost of human labour is the value it could have if the person were doing something else. If the farmer hired himself out for paid work, even if he were paid the low wage of US$1.00/day, this equates to an energy cost of about $4.00/kWh. Although this is a low wage for hard labour, even in some of the poorer countries, it represents an energy cost that is significantly more expensive than even new and exotic power sources such as solar photovoltaic panels.

Nevertheless, human labour is widely used for both household water and for irrigation pumping, and people devote a large amount of time and energy to it. It is reported that in Zimbabwe households may spend 300 hours per month with watering cans to irrigate crops. The willingness of people to spend so much time water lifting does not reflect the effectiveness of human power, but rather the poverty that deprives people of alternatives.

There is a further opportunity cost caused by diverting people from more important work to pumping water. The best asset people have is brains rather than muscle. If rural development is going to proceed, agricultural productivity is to improve, and economic standards are to be advanced, it is essential to introduce more productive power sources than human labour for all except the very smallest of land-holdings.

Power capability

Muscle power can handle quite large 'overloads' for short periods, but the power capability diminishes if more than a few minutes of activity are required. The power availability is also a function of the build, age, state of health and weight of an individual; finally the ability to produce power depends on the nature of the device being worked and the muscles that can readily be utilized. Table 7.3 indicates power outputs that may be expected for individuals of 20, 35 and 60 years age respectively over periods of operation ranging from 5 minutes to 3 hours, presumably with devices allowing much of the body to operate. Table 7.4 shows actual results from

handpump tests measured by the Blair Research Institute in Zimbabwe.

Therefore, although the actual output from any human powered pump is not precisely predictable, an approximate prediction can reasonably be made. Figure 7.5 gives a set of curves indicating the capability of from one to four people each providing 240 Wh per day of useful work through a pumping device with an efficiency of 60%. These curves probably represent what is generally achievable under favourable circumstances and indicate, for example, that the daily output per person if lifting water 5 m, is about 12

Table 7.4: Experimental measurements of hydraulic power output of people using a handpump to fill a 20 litre can (Morgan, 1983 [48])

Age (years)	Weight (kg)	Time (s)	Mean power (W)
Pump 1: pumping head 10.54 m			
9	34	173	12
14	54	74	28
14	54	77	27
16	50	69	30
18	55	59	35
20	68	70	29
29	82	100	21
33	65	55	32
47	75	48	43
Pump 2: pumping head 6.35 m			
9	33	51	29
11	31	48	28
11	31	68	18
10	55	60	20
10	32	66	19
14	37	55	22

Table 7.3: Power capability of human beings (Hofkes, 1981 [47])

Age (years)	Human power capacity by duration of effort (W)					
	5 min.	10 min.	15 min.	30 min.	60 min.	180 min.
20	220	210	200	180	160	90
35	210	200	180	160	135	75
60	180	160	150	130	110	60

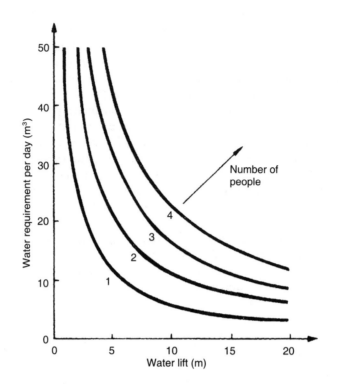

Fig. 7.5: The number of people required to pump a specified quantity of water at different lifts. The curves have been derived by assuming that a single person can provide 60 W of power for four hours per day, and that the pump efficiency is 60%.

m³. Note that these curves are for drawn pumping over an extended period, making them particularly relevant for irrigation. Handpumps for drinking water usage will be used for much shorter intervals, and the power levels will be somewhat higher; this is discussed below in Section 7.2.3.

The very fact that the output of people-powered pumping is so small can have some advantages. In some areas (such as in parts of Bangladesh) where diesel or electric-powered pumps are widely used to draw water from boreholes, the water table is dropping rapidly, with serious implications. Human-powered pumping simply cannot remove enough water to do this, and so helps to conserve water supplies.

Ergonomics
The actual useful output from a person depends a lot on the way the water lift or pump works; the most powerful muscles are the leg and back muscles while the arm muscles are relatively weak, so conventional hand pumps are less effective at 'extracting work' from a person than a device like a bicycle. Moreover, the 'ergonomics' of the design are important; the operator needs to be comfortable and not contorted into some difficult position, so the device should require a relaxed posture with the user well-balanced, and it should function best at a comfortable speed of operation. Utilization of the leg muscles will also often allow the operator to throw his or her weight behind the effort in order to gain further pedal pressure. (Wilson, 1983 [49]) reported that a rotary hand pump was improved in output by a factor of three (300%), by converting it from hand operation to foot operation (Wilson, 1983). The same article also promoted the bicycle as a supreme example of effective ergonomics; it uses the right muscles in the right motion at the right speed and applies human power through a light but strong

174

and efficient mechanism. Wilson makes the very valid point that what is needed is a pump which is as well designed, strong, efficient and easy to use as the bicycle. He quotes dynamometer tests as indicating that the average cyclist works at 75W when cycling at 18 km/h. Table 7.5 shows the flow rates that could be achieved at various lifts, assuming a water lifting device of only 50% efficiency, if this power rate could be sustained into a pedal-powered pump.

Table 7.5: Output from a pedal-powered pump with an input of 75 W and an efficiency of 50%

Head (m)	0.5	1.0	2.5	5.0	10.0
Flow (m³/h)	27.5	13.8	5.5	2.2	1.1

Good ergonomics is especially important for irrigation pumping, since the large quantities of water required mean that a human powered pump needs to be operated for several hours at a stretch; efficiency and ease of use are crucial. For this reason most irrigation pumps are in fact foot-operated. Hand operated devices are easier to install and can be lighter and smaller (since no one has to stand or sit on them and the forces that can be applied will not be so great anyway). Where pumps are used for water supply duties rather than irrigation, efficiency is less of a stringent requirement since any individual user will generally only operate the pump for a few minutes per day to fill a few small containers.

Therefore the criteria for defining a good human powered irrigation pump are significantly different from those for a water supply pump and it may be a mistake to use pumps for irrigation duties that have only been proved successful in water supply.

7.2.2 Traditional water lifting devices

Many traditional water lifting devices are particularly designed for low lift irrigation, and they are often foot-operated since it no doubt became apparent that this was the best method of harnessing human power.

The least-cost solution has always been a bucket or bag of water lifted when necessary on a rope; Fig. 7.6. The best that can be said for this technique is that with small plots the water can at least be applied with precision to individual plants, so at least efficient conveyance and distribution can partially compensate for the inefficiency of the actual water lifting. At low heads, the use of buckets and scoops (see also Section 6.3.1), led to the development of the swing-basket (Fig. 6.3), which can use two people and functions more rapidly, although only through very low pumping heads such as from canals into paddies. However, it is not an ergonomic device in that a lot of muscular effort goes into twisting the body, there is much spillage, and also water is lifted much higher than necessary. Nevertheless, two young boys using this technique, for example in Bangladesh, can complete 2,000 swings without a rest.

An improvement, obtained at the price of some slight complexity, is the use of suspended or pivoted devices such as the supported scoop (Fig. 6.4) and some which are also balanced such as the dhone (or dhoon) see-sawing gutters (Fig. 6.6), or the counterpoise lift (or shadoof) (Fig. 6.7). These are no longer portable since they need to be installed on a site, and they require a supporting structure which has to be attached securely to the ground, but they are far more efficient than such primitive devices such as buckets or swing baskets. Figure 7.7 shows how much superior a dhone is to a swing basket. A single dhone will lift 7.5 l/s at a lift of 0.75 m, which reduces to about 2 l/s at 1.5 m head. The dhone will move more than twice as much water as a swing basket at low lifts, and moreover using the power of only one person rather than two. Khan (1980 [50]) makes the point that many Bangladeshi farmers try and use a single stage dhone at too high a lift, and lose a lot of performance as a result; the optimum lift per stage is approximately 1 m.

Table 7.6 indicates how widely the dhone is used in Bangladesh, a country with very large areas offering the possibility of shallow lift irrigation, and it also shows clearly how much of

Fig. 7.6: Rope and bag water lift from a dug well (example from the Gambia) [40]

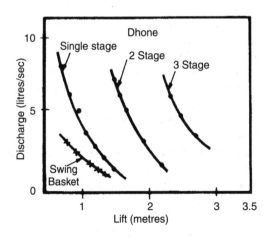

Fig. 7.7: Relative performances of the swing-basket and the dhone [50]

an improvement the dhone is over the swing-basket. The same table also indicates the characteristics relating to the counterpoise lift in a shallow hand-dug well (called a 'dugwell' in Bangladesh), and the 'MOSTI' (Manually Operated Shallow Tubewell for Irrigation), which is a No. 6 cast iron handpump mounted on a tubewell (see Fig. 6.19).

Despite being a considerable improvement on the swing-basket, the dhone is probably not as efficient as the various rotary devices described in Section 6.4, although it represents a good compromise between retaining simplicity and low-cost while achieving a useful output.

Rotary devices tend to be easier to work as they generate a smooth output and they therefore often can be driven with a comfortable pedalling motion of either the arm or, better, the

Table 7.6: Comparison of various irrigation water lifts in Bangladesh [50]

		Dhone	Swing bucket	Counterpoise bucket lift	MOSTI handpump
Area irrigated	(× 1000 ha)	392	65	4	20
	(% of total)	25	5	0.8	
Water source		surface	surface	hand-dug well	tubewell
Max. discharge	(m³/h)	7.5	2.3	0.6	0.8
Pumping head	(m)	0–1.5	0–1.8	0–4.5	1.5–6.0
Capital cost	(US$)	20	1.33	10	80
Working life	(years)	4	2	3	6
Command area (ha of dry season paddy)		1.6–2.0	0.4–0.6	0.3	0.2

legs. The various ladder pumps and flash-wheels are generally leg-powered (see Sections 6.4.6 and 6.6.1 plus Fig. 6.41 and Fig. 6.42), and they can often readily be powered in this way by several operators. While today Archimedean screws are usually hand operated (Fig. 6.15), in Roman times they were walked on rather like the treadwheel in Fig. 6.41, which no doubt was easier for the operator and far more productive.

7.2.3 Hand-operated pumps

Lever-operated handpumps, such as those described in Section 6.5.2, although less productive than footpumps, are the most common form of industrially manufactured manually operated water lift, and for that reason are very widely used. They are fairly cheap, and their installation is often paid for or subsidized by development organizations. The sort of duty the pumps can cope with depends on the design. Many lightweight pumps are intended for an individual family and for use for a few minutes a day. The more robust, VLOM handpumps (see Section 2.1.2) will withstand harder use, but are generally only worked for a few hours per day. Very few pumps are designed for the continuous use required for irrigation. Nevertheless, drinking water pumps are often used for watering crops, and this tends to make them break down frequently, and to shorten their lives considerably. Despite its name, the Manually Operated Shallow Tubewell for Irrigation (whose output is

given in Table 7.6) is a fairly light-duty pump that is somewhat overworked by irrigation use.

The forces involved in driving a piston pump with a lever have already been discussed in the sub-section 'Forces' of Section 6.5.1. So far as handpumps are concerned, Table 7.7 indicates the following maximum heads as being generally suitable for comfortable operation of various common sizes of handpump:

Table 7.7: Recommended maximum heads for various handpump cylinder bores [47]

Cylinder diameter		Maximum head	
(mm)	(in)	(m)	(ft)
51	2"	25	75'
63	2½"	20	60'
76	3"	15	45'
102	4"	10	30'

The load at any given head can be reduced by shortening the stroke of the pump, but the above recommendation applies with typical strokes in the region of 150 mm to 300 mm.

Figure 7.8 shows recommended performance criteria for handpumps, based on UNDP/World Bank work. People produce a higher work-rate when pumping against a higher head, and the graph is based on an output of 50 W at 7 m, rising to 75 W at 45 m head. These are conservative figures, allowing for children or weaker adults using the pumps; a fit adult will typically exceed 100 W, and may produce over 150 W against a high head.

The nomogram in Fig. 7.9 gives a means for determining handpump discharge. The method for using this is to rule a pencil line between the stroke length that applies (250 mm or 10" in the example) and the expected pumping frequency (40 strokes per minute in the example). Then if another pencil line is ruled from where the first line crosses the 'pivot line' through the appropriate cylinder diameter (76 mm or 3" in the example), the discharge is given on the left (46 l/min or 12 US gall/min in the example). No allowance is made for 'slippage' or leakage of water which will result in the discharge being less than the swept volume, so the result of using this nomograph is the maximum flow that might be expected; it may therefore be more realistic to reduce the result obtained by 10–20%.

Reciprocating lever-operated handpumps have other problems. Considerable wear and tear can result from operators ramming the levers into the stops at either end of the stroke, which gives rise to large forces in the mechanism. Operators also have to continually reverse the motion of a heavy lever (plus their arms), and this wastes energy. Rotary drive pumps, in which the piston is driven by a crank from a rotating drive wheel, overcome both these problems, and are

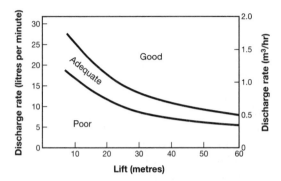

Fig. 7.8: Handpump discharge rate plotted against head. Pump efficiency is taken to vary from 45–70% as the head varies from 7–45 m [12]

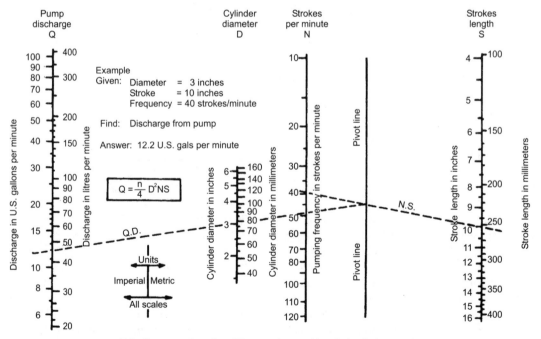

Note: Nomogram based on 100 per cent geometric cylinder displacement for single action, reciprocating handpumps (zero slip)

Fig. 7.9: Nomogram for calculating handpump discharge [47] (and McJunkin, 1977 [51])

Fig. 7.10: Rotary drive handpump (the Gambia)

often easier (and more efficient) to work (see Fig. 6.21 and Fig. 7.10). Here a flywheel smoothes the fluctuations and thereby makes the pump easier to operate, especially for long periods, because the cyclic loading involved in accelerating discrete cylinder-volumes of water up the rising main will be absorbed by the flywheel's momentum and therefore not be felt by the operator. Rotary pumps also tend to put less 'hammering' force into the mechanism because the rate at which the pump rod is accelerated and decelerated is more controlled; in lever pumps the operator can 'beat' the mechanism, and reverse the direction of motion too quickly, taking up the clearance or backlash in worn bearings and pivot, and giving rise to large impact forces.

The main disadvantage with rotary drive pumps is that they are relatively heavy and expensive due to their massive flywheel and crank mechanism, plus the supporting column that is needed. For pumping large quantities of water, as are required for irrigation, the improved ergonomics of the rotary drive is probably more advantageous than it is with water supply duties where no individual is likely to need to pump for more than a few minutes at any one time.

Bucket or piston pumps are not the only hand-operated pumps: joggle pumps (Section 6.7), progressive cavity pumps (Section 6.6.3), and rope-and-washer pumps (Section 6.6.2) all have hand-powered variants. Joggle pumps are, by their nature, reciprocating, but progressive-cavity and rope-and-washer pumps are naturally rotary devices. Figure 7.11 and Fig. 7.12 show hand-operated examples of these pumps.

The output of any human-powered pump can be increased if it utilizes more than just the arm muscles. The 'Rower Pump' is a simple piston pump that that uses the leg and body muscles as well as the arms in an action that resembles rowing a boat. The rower pump was developed

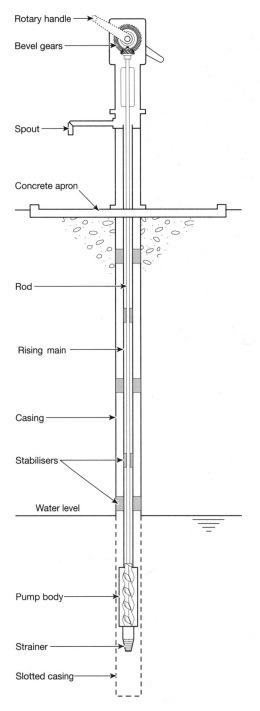

Rotary handle

Bevel gears

Spout

Concrete apron

Rod

Rising main

Casing

Stabilisers

Water level

Pump body

Strainer

Slotted casing

Fig. 7.11: A hand-operated progressive-cavity or Mono pump: a right-angle bevel-and-pinion gear in the head drives the vertical shaft down to the rotor at the base

in the late 1970s by the Mennonite Central Committee (MCC) working with farmers in Bangladesh, and is illustrated in Fig. 7.13. It consists of a PVC pipe rigidly fixed in an earth mound at an angle of 30° to the horizontal. It is a direct-action pump, with the piston directly connected to the handle. An innovative feature is the air chamber at the inlet to the pumping cylinder. This smoothes out the surges, leading to more steady flow both through the pump and up the well pipe (rising main), thereby making the pump easier to operate and giving increased pump efficiency.

The rower pump is claimed to pump 50% more water than the standard No. 6 lever handpump used in Bangladesh, with even better results at higher heads. Some test results are shown in Table 7.8, but it should be noted from these that the rower pump is only better if the air chamber is fitted to the rower pump and *not* to the No. 6, i.e. it is the air chamber that makes the difference, not the pump design. The claim is probably fair enough, in that No. 6 handpumps are not generally fitted with air chambers. It is significant that an air chamber makes such a difference to the No. 6 handpump, and shows that this fairly cheap addition to a pump is well worth it. (Air chambers are discussed in some detail in Section 6.7.2.) The rower pump is produced in 2" and 3" versions, though the larger size is only recommended up to 4 m head, beyond which it becomes somewhat heavy to use.

The rower pump was designed primarily for irrigation, and both the rowing action and the air chamber were included to make the pump easier to operate and to reduce fatigue when the pump is worked for extended periods. A measure of the success of the rower pump is that even when sold at a more-or-less commercial cost, and competing with the heavily subsidized UNICEF No. 6 pump, more than 50,000 units had been installed in Bangladesh by 1991. The development of the rower pump is a good example of the kind of useful innovative developments that can be successfully pursued by NGOs and educational institutions in this important field, as suggested earlier.

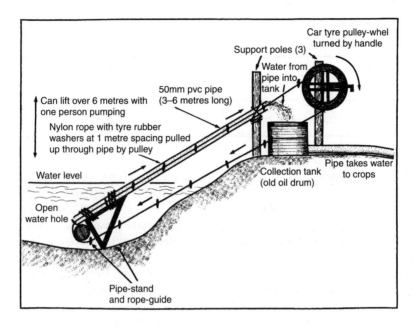

Fig. 7.12: A simple rope-and-washer pump used for irrigation [40]

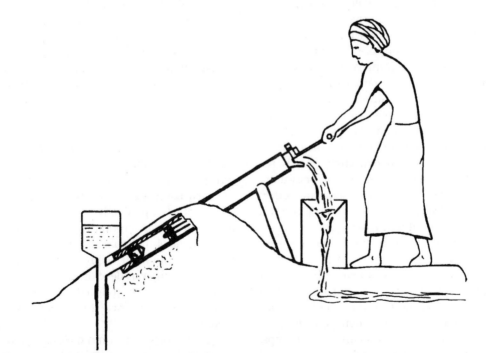

Fig. 7.13: A rower pump

Table 7.8: Comparison of the performance of a 2" MCC rower pump with the UNICEF No. 6 MOSTI handpump, pumping against head of 5–6.5 m (Klassen, 1981 [52])

Rower pump		No. 6 handpump		
without air chamber	with air chamber	without air chamber	with air chamber	
1.75	2.8	1.8	2.7	m³/h
7.7	12.3	8.0	11.7	US gall/min

7.2.4 Foot-operated pumps

As was stated above, many traditional pumps are foot-operated, utilizing the greater strength and endurance of the leg muscles. Humans can walk and carry heavy loads for many hours, and this action can be used to pump water for long periods without undue fatigue. There are a number of modern pumps that are also foot-operated.

The treadle pump (Fig. 7.14) is another small pump for irrigation that originated in Bangladesh (Barnes, 1985 [53]). It is a simple piston pump, but has two short cylinders operated by long beams or treadles. A rope and pulley arrangement between the treadles mean that one rises as the other goes down, so that when a person stands on the treadles they operate the pump with a walking action. One advantage of the treadle arrangement is that the operator can adjust his leverage by moving his position, for higher heads, the extra pumping force can be achieved by moving further away from the pivot. Operators do this automatically, and it means that a single size of pump can be used for a range of heads. For higher heads two people can work on one pump. For the original Bangladesh design one person could work satisfactorily up to 5 m head, and two people were needed for higher heads.

The construction of the treadle pump is very simple, so it can be made by almost any small workshop. The cylinders can either be made of standard plastic or metal tubes, but are often fabricated from steel sheet in order to utilize standard piston seals from other pumps, such as the No. 6 handpump. Unlike many other pumps, the treadle pump can be portable, and carried to

wherever it is needed. By nature the treadle pump is a suction pump, and is said to work with suction lifts of up to 7.5 m. Some versions of the pump have closed-top cylinders that allow the water to be pumped out under pressure, and can achieve a delivery head above the pump of 20 m or so, though this must be at rather low flows. The output is quoted at around 7 m³/h at heads of a metre or so, reducing to 3 m³/h at higher heads [35]. It is very much designed to be a low-head, high volume irrigation pump, rather than for lifting large distances. Since its development in the 1980s, around 500,000 units have been sold in Bangladesh alone, the design has been taken up in many other countries and remains in demand in regions such as West Africa (Snell, 2004 [54]).

A foot-operated diaphragm pump developed in the Philippines is shown in Fig. 6.37. This is another portable device for irrigation use. Its output is less than the treadle pump, but it is a simple and convenient pump for small applications.

Another, more unusual foot-operated pump is the Kangaroo Pump, shown in Fig. 7.15. This pump has a spring in the column, and is bounced, like a pogo stick. It uses the leg muscles in a slightly less productive way than the treadle pump, but by incorporating a spring it overcomes some of the problems of losing energy to reversing motion in reciprocating pumps. The kangaroo pump was developed in Holland, and though it has been introduced into Tanzania and other countries in Africa, it has not been widely used.

Just as a bicycle is a more efficient mode of transport than walking (provided a smooth track

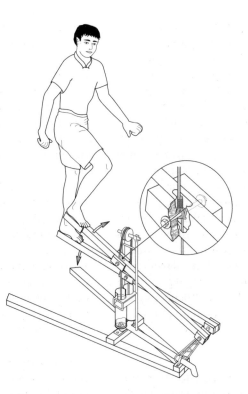

Fig. 7.14: The treadle pump

Fig. 7.15: The Kangaroo Pump

183

is available to ride on), pedalling can also be a more efficient way of powering equipment than a walking action. Table 7.5 shows the potential output from a pedal-powered pump using experimentally achieved power outputs and some assumed efficiencies. However, there are not many pedal-powered pump designs available, either commercially or as open designs. One problem with this is the difficulty of finding a suitable pump to match to pedal power. Pedal-power produces rotary motion, so it is most suitable for rotary pumps. Perhaps the most suitable pump is the rope-and-washer pump, and various bicycle-based designs have been made, in Nicaragua among other places. It is possible to connect a centrifugal pump to a bicycle, but there are two problems: first, very small centrifugal pumps are rather inefficient; second, it is difficult to get a high enough speed ratio for standard pumps.

7.3 Animal power

Animal power is primarily used for irrigation water lifting, not for community water supply. This is probably due to social factors associated with the water supply and ownership of animals. People traditionally look after their own household water needs, either fetching it from a source, lifting it from a well, or – in more recent times – pumping it from a handpump. Where water lifting is required, the needs of a family can easily be met by a few minutes' human-powered pumping. The output of an animal-powered pump would be more than was needed; it would not be worth the effort of coupling an animal to a pump just to obtain water for a single household. An animal-powered pump would be useful if the whole community's water was to be pumped, but working animals tend to be owned by families, not by communities. Rather than work through the issues of animal use, communities tend to jump from individually accessed water sources to mechanized, communally-owned, water supply systems. It is therefore most unusual for animals to be used for water supply, and this section on animal power deals primarily with irrigation water lifting.

The advantages of animal power over human power are twofold. First; draft animals are five to ten times more powerful than humans, so they can pump more water in a shorter time. Second; by freeing the operator from having to work the water-lifting device, he can often manage the water distribution system more effectively. In effect, the use of an animal provides the equivalent power of several people, at a fraction of the cost.

Some 200 million draught animals are deployed in developing countries, and these have an aggregate power capacity of about 75,000,000 kW. The majority of these animals are used in southern and south east Asia; 80 million draught animals are in use in India alone. Any mechanization programme to replace these animals would obviously have to be extremely large; but there is more immediate scope for improving the efficiency with which animals are used.

Animal powered irrigation is almost exclusively practised using traditional water lifting techniques pre-dating the industrial era. Although some attempts to produce improved mechanisms for the utilization of animal power have been made in certain areas during this century, there is little (if any) tendency to introduce animal powered water lifting anywhere where it has not been traditionally practised, although there seems good reason to believe it could usefully replace human labour for irrigation in many parts of the world where it is not already used (e.g. many parts of Africa). Instead, the trend has been either to make the quantum leap to full mechanization using engines or mains electricity or to make no attempt to improve on human power.

The main disadvantage of animal power is that animals need to be fed for 365 days of the year, yet the irrigation season usually only extends for 100 or at most 200 days of the year. In areas where water is close to the surface, and hence irrigation by animal power is feasible, there are usually high human population densities and a shortage of land. Since draught animals consume considerable volumes of fodder, a significant proportion of the available land can be absorbed simply to support the draught animals. Therefore it probably would be difficult to justify the use of animals for irrigation pumping alone, but generally there are other economic applications for them, such as transport, tillage, and post-harvest duties like threshing or milling which allows them to be employed more fully than if they were used exclusively for irrigation. In India and other countries where animal powered water lifting is widely practised, it is normal for the same animals to be used for transport and for tilling the land. They are often fed with agricultural residues, or are allowed to graze on fields left fallow for a season as part of a crop rotation.

Animals also serve other purposes; they are a non-monetary form of collateral that is important in the village economy in many regions, they produce by-products such as leather, meat and milk and of course in the Indian sub-continent in particular, their dung is widely used as a cooking fuel. So mechanization of irrigation pumps in lieu of draft animals is not necessarily a straightforward alternative.

7.3.1 Power capabilities of various species

Figure 7.16 gives the approximate water lifting capability of different numbers of oxen, assuming 60% efficiency from animal to water lifted, as might be achieved by one of the better types of water lifting device.

The typical power capabilities of various commonly used draught animals are given in Table 7.9. Some rules-of-thumb for healthy, well fed animals are that oxen, buffalo and light horses can produce draught forces of 10–12% of their body weight, camels 12–14%, and donkeys and heavy horses up to 16% (Pearson, 1991 [56]). Draught animals obviously require rest just as humans do, so it is common practice to work them on about three hour shifts, with a rest in between. Ten or 12 hours per day in total may be worked when necessary.

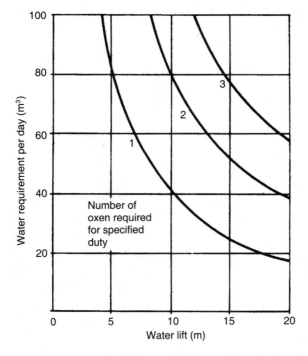

Fig. 7.16: The number of oxen required to lift a specified quantity of water at different lifts. The curves have been calculated by assuming that an ox can provide 350 W of power for five hours per day, and the efficiency of the water-lifting device is 60%.

185

Table 7.9: Power and drawbar pull of various animals [36] and (Birch, 1989 [55])

Animal	Weight (kg)	Draught force (kg)	Typical speed (m/s)	Power (W)
Heavy horse	700–1,200	50–100	0.7–1.2	500–1,000
Light horse	400–700	45–80	0.8–1.4	400–800
Mule	350–500	40–60	0.8–1.0	300–600
Donkey	150–300	20–40	0.6–0.8	75–200
Cow	400–600	50–60	0.6–0.8	200–400
Bullock/ox	500–900	60–80	0.5–0.7	300–500
Camel	500–1,000	80–100	0.8–1.2	400–700
Buffalo	400–900	60–100	0.5–1.0	600–1,000

In the days before mechanized power became widely available for agricultural use, considerable research was done into the effective use of animal power, particularly the horses that were common in Western countries. Hood, 1988 [57], discussing typical draught horses as used in the USA at the end of the twentieth century advocated the use of efficient mechanisms for coupling horses to water-lifts. He suggested that a team of two horses with an efficient water lifting device can typically lift 0.22 acre-feet per day through a head of 15 ft (270 m³/day through 4.6 m). He also cited various experiments completed at that time in Chennai, India (using bullocks), as an example for American farmers to emulate. In one of these, a device known as the Stoney Water Lift was tested and shown to have an animal-to-water mechanical efficiency of about 80%. This device was, in effect, an engineered version of the traditional circular mohte with two balanced buckets (see Fig. 7.17). Using a single Nellore bullock in a series of tests, it lifted between 2,000 and 2,500 Imperial gallons/hour through 22–23 ft (9–11.25 m³/h through 6.7–7.0 m). It was pointed out that although a high instantaneous efficiency was achieved by this two bucket lift, in the tests it was found that the animals were only actually performing useful

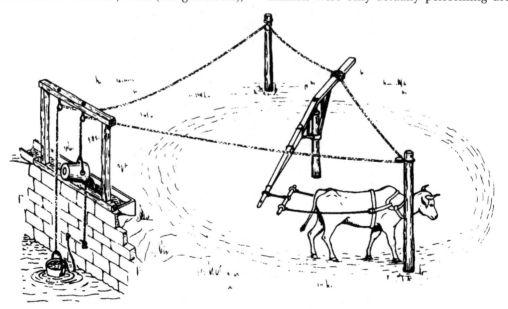

Fig. 7.17: Circular mohte using two buckets with flap valves in the bottoms

work for 60% of the duration of the tests, so the utilization was not as high as may theoretically be feasible; clearly the management of an animal powered water lift has a major influence on the daily productivity.

An important point is that all draught animals work best when subjected to a steady load that matches their pulling capability (although a horse, for example, can throw about one third of its weight into pulling for short periods – i.e. approaching three times the force it can sustain for a long time). Therefore, devices are needed which shield the animal from cyclic loading such as is experienced when a pump is driven by a crank (see explanation of cyclic torque requirements of piston pump in sub-section 'Forces' of Section 6.5.1).

7.3.2 Food requirements

Birch and Rydzewski [55] show that a cow in Bangladesh can be fed solely with forage and agricultural residues (although the latter had a value equivalent to US $0.30 per day in 1980, which was not a trivial sum) and that the same animal requires the residues from 0.77 ha of double-cropped agricultural land. Because of the general shortage of land and residual fodder in Bangladesh, it is unusual to use animals for water lifting in that country. The same authors carried out a similar calculation in relation to Egypt, where one hectare of land is needed to produce sufficient residue to support one animal, and the daily diet was valued at US $0.50.

7.3.3 Coupling animals to water lifting systems

The original method of using animals to lift water was some device such as the mohte (Fig. 6.10 and Fig. 7.18). Here animals walk in a straight line down a slope away from the well or water source while hauling water up in a bag or container. Traditional mohtes used a leather bag to collect the water, but in recent years more durable materials such as rubber truck innertubes (or, more rarely, steel oil barrels) have been used.

The mohte is simple to implement; the only mechanical component is a pulley and the only structure is the frame to hold the pulley. However, this key mechanical component is more complicated than might be expected due to the load on it, and demands considerable craftsmanship. The instantaneous efficiency of the mohte is high while the animal(s) are pulling; a disadvantage is the need to reverse the animals back up the ramp to lower the bucket. Sometimes two teams of animals are used, so that one is led back

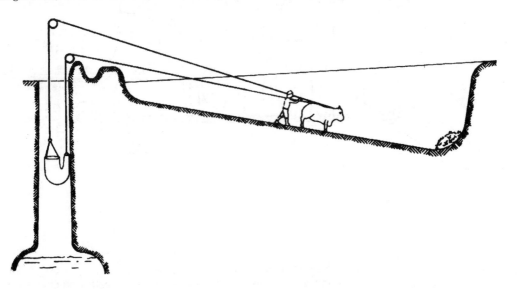

Fig. 7.18: A cross-sectional view of a mohte

to the top while one team descends; in order to do this, a man is needed at both ends of the ramp to harness and un-harness the animals at the end of each cycle. Using two sets of animals and usually two men and a boy, practically doubles the output, but even so inevitably, no action occurs during the harnessing and un-harnessing process.

The downhill slope helps use the weight of the animal partially to balance the weight of the full water container; it also applies a reasonably constant load to the animal for most of the journey down the ramp, from when the container leaves the surface of the water to when it starts to be tipped.

An improved version of the mohte, sometimes used in parts of India and (a few) in Sri Lanka, is the 'circular mohte'; Fig. 7.17. This involves attaching the animals to a sweep so that they can walk in a circle thereby allowing them to work continuously with less supervision. Because their weight can no longer partially balance the load, as they have to walk on level ground, two buckets are used so that the empty one descends while the full one comes up; this

at least balances the weights of the buckets and means that the water being lifted is the only large out-of-balance force to be handled. The main problem with this device is that the load on the sweep is cyclic, as the pull on the sweep by the chain will not be felt by the animals when the chain acts parallel to the sweep and it will reach a maximum when the chain is at right angles to the sweep; therefore the animals will have a tiring sinusoidal load to cope with. Also, the various pulleys and supporting posts need to be robust and well anchored, as the forces are quite large.

The Persian wheel (Fig. 6.11, Fig. 7.19 and Fig. 7.20) is a great improvement on the mohte, as its chain of buckets imposes an almost constant load on the drive shaft to the wheel. Persian wheels are usually driven by some form of right angle drive, such as in Fig. 7.19 and Fig. 7.20. The first is the most common, where the drive shaft from the secondary gear is buried and the animals walk over it; this has the advantage of keeping the Persian wheel as low as possible to minimize the head through which water is lifted. The second example is a traditional wooden Persian wheel mechanism where the

Fig. 7.19: A bullock-driven Persian wheel of a sort which is widely used in many parts of the world, particularly the Near East and southern Asia. The buckets are fixed together on chains which can loop down into water some distance below the wheel, in the manner of Fig. 6.11.

Fig. 7.20: A camel-driven Persian wheel showing an overhead drive mechanism

animal passes under the horizontal shaft. The sweep of a Persian wheel carries an almost constant load and therefore the animal can establish a steady comfortable pace and needs little supervision.

In Egypt, the sakia (see Section 6.4.3 and Fig. 6.14) is commonly used for low head applications instead of the Persian wheel, and it is driven in a similar manner via a sweep. It also has the advantage of applying a constant load to the animal, but is more efficient at very low heads.

The next development was for the sweep drive gear to be 'industrialized' and manufactured in large numbers from iron or steel to include an engineered set of gears. Figure 7.21 shows a mule harnessed to such a device in order to drive a chain and washer (or paternoster) pump which are widely used in China, where millions of Liberation Pumps, many of which were animal powered, were produced as an intermediate stage between human pumping and full mechanization. The Liberation Pump includes a mechanism driven by a sweep that is elegantly simple and made from steel castings (see Fig. 6.42 and Fig. 7.21). As detailed in Section 6.6.2, the Liberation Pump is capable of achieving a high efficiency of 70% in the animal-powered form illustrated, and it is compact enough to fit into quite a narrow well.

Another not unusual concession to modernization is the use of an old motor vehicle back-axle embedded in a concrete pillar as a means of obtaining a right angle drive from an animal sweep. An example of this is illustrated in Fig. 7.22, where a donkey is shown linked to an Archimedean screw (see also Section 6.4.4 and Fig. 6.15), although in the example illustrated the matching problem is not always solved satisfactorily. Again this is a compact and potentially efficient mechanism, as the Archimedean screw applies a completely steady load to the animal. It is clear that the same mechanism improvized

Fig. 7.21: An animal-powered Chinese Liberation Pump. A hand-operated version is shown in Fig. 6.42 and a motorized one in Fig. 7.4.

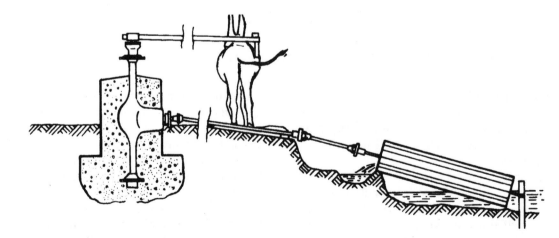

Fig. 7.22: The back axle from a car used as an animal-driven power transmission for an Archimedes' screw

from a car back axle could equally easily be coupled to a sakia, to a Persian wheel or to a chain and washer pump.

Another development in this field has been the appearance of a prototype animal-powered, but industrially manufactured double-acting diaphragm pump from Denmark. This has the advantage of having the sweep direct coupled to the pump, which acts as a suction pump. Therefore it is only necessary to bury the pipes carrying the water rather than a drive shaft and this device can be located up to 80 m away from the water source, which may in some cases be an advantage. This 'Bunger' sweep pump is claimed to lift 100 m³/day using two animals.

Although a sweep driven device avoids the problem of reversing animals as with a mohte, it suffers from the disadvantage that by forcing an animal to walk in a circle, even though the load may be steady, the tractive effort or pull is reduced to 80% of that which is feasible when the same animal walks in a straight line (Hood, 1988 [57]). A mechanism that can apply a steady load to the animal, but in a straight line, would be better. The simplest device of this kind is the tread-wheel; in some respects the principle is analogous to a mohte, with the animal 'walking on the spot' inside a large wheel, rather than up and down a ramp. This principle was taken further at the end of the nineteenth century in Europe and the USA through the use of 'Paddle wheel' animal engines, in which a horse would be harnessed on an inclined endless belt that it would drive with its feet. The disadvantage of these animal-carrying devices is that a mechanism is needed which not only has to transmit the maximum draw-bar pull of the animal, but additionally has to carry the full weight of the beast. Therefore a massive and robust construction is necessary which inevitably is expensive, and this probably is an example of where the search for maximum efficiency produces diminishing returns and is counter-productive.

7.4 Internal combustion engines

With the exception of a few rather rare rotary engines, all internal combustion engines are cyclic, reciprocating machines, with pistons that move within cylinders. The power is derived from burning a mixture of fuel and air within the cylinder, which pushes the piston down the cylinder as it expands. They are called 'Internal Combustion' engines because they burn their fuel within the working cylinder, as opposed to External Combustion engines (see Section 7.5) which burns their fuel in a separate firebox. Very small internal combustion engines will usually have just one cylinder, and large engines may have a considerable number. Small pumping engines will normally have between one and four cylinders.

The internal combustion engine is the common engine in vehicles around the world, and it is also by far the most common choice of prime mover for any stand-alone or mobile power source. Where no mains electricity is available, the internal combustion engine is also widely-used for water pumping. The main reasons for the widespread success of the internal combustion piston engine are its high power/weight ratio, compact size, ease of control (rapid response) and instant start-up capability. Mass production and decreasing fuel prices made small engines based on designs used for motor vehicles both cheap to buy and inexpensive to run. There has been a steady improvement in efficiency, reliability and ease of servicing, and a reduction in weight. Small, portable diesel and petrol engines are widely available in most countries, and many countries manufacture their own.

Fuels for internal combustion are not always available. Many developing countries are unable to import sufficient petroleum because they lack the foreign exchange to purchase it, and within many countries the supply may be patchy: fuel is available in towns and near roads, but difficult to find in remote areas. Poorly developed supply chains also mean that fuel is not consistently available, and may be unobtainable for months at a time. Almost everywhere, the most serious supply shortages are most prevalent in the rural areas, in other words, precisely where farmers are in need of power for irrigation pumping.

A major disadvantage of the internal combustion engine is its reliance on fossil fuels. Though internal combustion engines can be run off other fuels (this is discussed later), by far the majority run on oil derivatives. The huge world-wide supply network that has been built up to provide diesel and petrol for motor vehicles means that these fuels are generally easy to obtain, and this convenience often outweighs all other considerations. It is now accepted that burning fossil fuels releases the so-called 'greenhouse gases' which are responsible for global warming, and that this poses a serious threat to the planet, but as yet there has been little reduction in the use of oil-based fuels. The industrial economies of the world are underpinned by fossil fuel energy, and with that enormous petroleum infrastructure in place, change to other fuels is slow. It also means that when a villager in a developing country want a power source for water pumping, he often finds internal combustion engines – and the spares and servicing support for them – readily available, while more environmentally-friendly energy sources are unknown. Internal combustion engines also pollute the local environment. They tend to be noisy and smelly, particularly if they are badly manufactured or poorly maintained. Engines also need regular oil changes, and oil spillages or careless oil disposal can be a serious problem.

So internal combustion engines are a mixed blessing. They do offer unparalleled versatility: small, portable units can produce very respectable amounts of power; they can be bought off-the-shelf, taken home, and be running within a matter of minutes; though they are not cheap for a rural economy, mass-production makes them cheaper than many of the alternatives, and they are often cheap enough to pay for themselves in the benefits irrigation brings. While governments and NGOs are often keen to promote renewable energy, the effects of internal combustion engines on the global environment are often not of great concern for rural communities, and in any case their contribution to global warming is negligible compared with more industrialized economies. Local pollution may be an issue, but is secondary to the need for food and financial security. It is often only the problems of petroleum fuel supply that makes rural

communities consider alternatives to internal combustion engines.

The smallest internal combustion engines have an outputs of fractions of a kilowatt, and the largest have outputs of many hundreds of kilowatts. There are many different manufacturers of internal combustion engines, each of whom produce a range of different types, families and sizes of engines. The range of options can be quite bewildering, and the aim of the following sections is to describe the main categories of engine, and to present the relative merits of each. It is not a complete guide to the internal combustion engine, for which the reader is referred to standard textbooks. Another good source of information is engine manufacturers and dealers themselves, who often have a lot of good information in sales leaflets and brochures, and operating manuals.

7.4.1 Petrol or Diesel

The two main types of internal combustion engine are the petrol (gasoline or gas) engine, and the diesel engine. In technical parlance, the petrol engine is known as the Spark-Ignition engine (S.I.), and the diesel engine as the Compression-Ignition engine (C.I.). Both are common, and widely available, in a full range of sizes.

Petrol engines draw an air/fuel mixture into the cylinder, compress it, and then ignite it with a spark from a spark plug. They have a carburettor to mix the fuel in the correct ratio with the air, an ignition 'coil', to produce the high voltage spark, and a low tension circuit with a contact breaker ('points' or an electronic equivalent), which ensures the spark occurs at the right point in the cycle (which is a few degrees before Top Dead Centre, TDC, the point where the piston reaches the top of its travel). At best, a petrol engine will run at a fuel to shaft power efficiency of up to 30% (but see the comments in Section 7.4.9 below on typical working efficiencies). Petrol engines are quite fast-running, typically having top speeds of between 2,500 and 6,000 rpm.

As well as running on petrol (gasoline), S.I. engines can also be run on paraffin (kerosene), l.p.g. (liquefied petroleum gas) or other gases. To use gas, a modified carburettor has to be fitted. L.p.g. is supplied in cylinders, and is usually primarily propane or butane. Other gases that work are methane (such as biogas obtained from dung – see Section 7.10.8) and hydrogen. Transporting gas is more difficult than petrol, as it needs to be kept in a pressurized container. Refilling with fuel is also more difficult, involving swapping cylinders, and having the empty one recharged with a compressor.

A paraffin (kerosene) engine is very similar to a petrol engine; indeed most paraffin engines need to be started and warmed up on petrol, because paraffin will not vaporize adequately in a cold engine. Many paraffin engines have a separate compartment in their fuel tank for a small supply of petrol and a tap to switch the fuel supply from petrol to paraffin once the engine is warm; it is also important to switch back to petrol a few moments before stopping the engine so that the carburettor float chamber is refilled with petrol ready for the next time the engine has to be started. Some farmers start paraffin engines simply by pouring petrol into the air intake, but this practice is not to be recommended as it can cause a fire. The advantage of a paraffin engine is that paraffin is normally available for agricultural purposes in an untaxed, subsidized or lightly taxed form and it also contains approximately 10% more energy per litre than petrol. The latter also usually carries a motor fuel tax in most countries as it is mainly used for private cars; therefore fuel costs for paraffin are generally much lower than for gasoline. Paraffin is also much less dangerous to store in quantity as it is less inflammable and does not emit a potentially explosive vapour at normal temperatures. The paraffin supply is also used for lighting and cooking fuel in many rural households and is therefore a more generally useful fuel. Against this, paraffin engines need a lower compression ratio than petrol engines to avoid 'knocking', so they tend to be less fuel-efficient.

Diesel engines only draw air into the cylinder, and inject the fuel into the cylinders as a finely atomized spray when the piston is at the top of its stroke. Compressing the air causes it to heat up (to about 440°C), which is sufficient to ignite the diesel fuel spontaneously when it is injected. Diesel engines thus have a fuel injection pump on them instead of a carburettor, with fixed, metal, high-pressure pipes to carry the fuel from the pump to the injectors, and they do not need an electrical ignition system. Diesel engines work at higher pressures than petrol engines in order to generate the temperature required to ensure the sustained combustion of the fuel when it is injected. A diesel engine will typically have a compression ratio of around 14:1, where most petrol engines are between 8:1 and 10:1. To cope with these pressures, diesel engines have to be heavier and more robust than petrol engines, and this makes them more expensive. The fuel injection pump and injectors are also expensive, as they are precision components. To work efficiently the diesel fuel must be clean, and the fuel pump has to be carefully adjusted using special machinery. The results of poorly-adjusted diesel fuel systems are all too apparent on the roads of many countries, where trucks issue clouds of thick black smoke as they go along. The maximum efficiency that can be obtained from diesel engines is around 50% (for very large ships engines), though automotive engines achieve around 35%; this is better than petrol engines. Diesel is a heavier fuel than petrol, and is generally less heavily taxed than petrol. Diesel engines typically run slower than petrol engines, with conventional engines going 450–1,200 rpm, and sometimes much slower. More modern designs may go up to 2,500 rpm or even faster.

Although diesel engines are inherently more expensive to manufacture, they compensate for this by being more efficient in terms of energy delivered per litre of fuel used, more reliable, and more long-lasting (though more complicated to maintain in good running order). The main reasons for their better efficiency are first, the higher compression ratio, which results in a better thermodynamic cycle; second, fuel injection allows the diesel readily to run on a leaner fuel/air mixture than the equivalent petrol engine. A spark ignition engine cannot be designed to run at such a high compression ratio, or the fuel/air would ignite prematurely, causing 'knocking' or 'pinking' as the piston tries to compress the exploding mixture. Another less well known advantage of the diesel is that diesel fuel is 18% 'richer' in energy than gasoline per litre (mainly due to its higher density); Table 7.10 indicates the calorific value of the three main petroleum fuels. Since fuel is generally bought by the litre (or some equivalent volume measure such as gallons), rather than by its weight or by its energy value, you can buy 18% more energy per litre of diesel than with petrol. Therefore the diesel engine is a better power source, both because of its higher efficiency and because of its better durability when operated for long periods per day.

For pumping applications, however, the choice of petrol or diesel relates largely to the scale of pumping required. Where a small, lightweight, portable system is needed which will only be used for one or two hours per day, and where simplicity of maintenance is important,

and where 'affordability' matters – i.e. the farmer has only the minimum capital to invest, then a petrol or paraffin engine may be best, and for that reason is frequently used.

Table 7.11 compares the general attributes of the three main internal combustion engine options. It should be noted that diesels are subdivided into two main categories; 'low speed' and 'high speed'. The former run at speeds in the 450–1,200 rpm range and tend to be much heavier and more expensive in relation to their power rating than the latter which typically run at speeds in the 1,200–2,500 rpm range. The slow speed diesel tends to have a much longer operational life and to be better suited to continuous operation, or long duty cycles, but its initial purchase cost is much higher.

7.4.2 Four-stroke or two-stroke

Both petrol and diesel engines can be designed to run so that ignition takes place either every other revolution, (four-stroke or four-cycle) or every revolution (two-stroke or two-cycle).

Four-stroke petrol engines tend to be more efficient than two-stroke as the 'non-firing' revolution gives more time for inducing a fresh charge of fuel and also for effectively driving out the exhaust gases from the previous firing stroke (two-strokes tend to be less well 'scavenged' of residual exhaust gases). Two-stroke diesels do not suffer an efficiency penalty in the same way, but are not generally available in the small size range

Table 7.10: Comparison of the energy content of different petroleum-based fuels

Units	Petrol/ Gasoline	Paraffin/ Kerosene	Diesel/ Gasoil
MJ/l	32	36	38
MJ/kg	44	45	46
kWh/l	8.9	10.0	10.6
kWh/kg	12.2	12.5	12.8

Table 7.11: Comparison of small internal combustion engines

		Petrol/ Gasoline	Paraffin/ Kerosene	Diesel/Gasoil	
	Units			High speed	Low speed
Average fuel to shaft efficiency	(%)	10–25	10–25	20–35	20–35
Weight per kW of rated power	(kg)	3–10	4–12	10–40	20–80
Operating life	(h)	2,000–4,000	2,000–4000	4,000–8,000	4,000–8,000
Running speed	(rpm)	2,500–3,800	2,500–3,800	1,200–2,500	450–1,200
Typical daily duty cycle	(h)	0.5-4	3–6	2–10	6–24
Typical power ratings useful for small to medium pumping duties	(kW)	1–3	1–3	2–15	2–15

of relevance for small-scale irrigation. The two-stroke petrol engine tends to be high revving and lightweight; it usually has fewer components than a four-stroke, and therefore is cheaper to manufacture; typical applications are as moped engines. (An interesting feature of some two-stroke engines is that they can be run backward, which is impossible with a four-stroke set-up.) They are less suitable for irrigation pumping than four-strokes as they use more fuel and wear out more quickly. The mixing of lubricant with the fuel in two-strokes removes the need for oil changes, but is wasteful of lubricant, tends to cause a smoky exhaust, means the cylinder head needs to be 'de-coked' (cleaned of carbon deposits) more frequently, and introduces a risk of damage caused by an inexperienced operator failing to mix sufficient lubricating oil with the fuel or using the wrong type of oil. For these reasons, two-stroke petrol engines are tending to be phased out and replaced by four strokes.

7.4.3 Air or Water Cooling

About one-third of the heat produced when the fuel is burnt has to be dissipated through the walls of the cylinder and through the cylinder head; the two methods generally used for removing this heat and preventing the cylinder overheating are either by surrounding the cylinder with a water jacket which has water circulated through it and a separate radiator, or by having many cooling fins on the cylinder (to increase its effective surface area), and blowing air over the fins with a fan driven off the engine. A few small, low-powered, and old fashioned low-speed stationery engines have a water jacket with an open top and keep cool simply by boiling the water, which needs to be topped up from time to time, but most modern liquid cooled engines have their coolant circulated by a pump just like car engines.

Each method of cooling has its pros and cons. Water cooled engines tend to be quieter (because the water jacket dampens the vibrations) and the engine temperature is more easily regulated

through the use of a thermostat, than with air cooling. However, with water cooled engines, internal corrosion can occur, and water can leak out, evaporate or freeze. This last problem can be prevented by the use of anti-freeze (ethylene glycol) mixed with the cooling water in winter; most anti-freezes also contain corrosion inhibitor and are therefore useful to add to the cooling water even in climates where freezing is not likely to occur. Loss of coolant can cause severe engine damage if the engine is allowed to continue running when dry; various safety devices are available either to warn of overheating (caused by loss of coolant or for any other reason) and in some cases to automatically cut off the fuel supply and stop the engine. Air cooled engines obviously cannot lose their coolant, but it is important to ensure that their cooling fins do not get clogged with dust or dirt and that any cooling fan (when fitted) is clean and functioning correctly.

7.4.4 Cylinder arrangement

The smallest engines usually have a single cylinder, mounted vertically above the crankshaft. This is convenient for access to the main engine components and also allows an oil sump to be conveniently located where oil can drain down to it from the cylinder. A large flywheel is needed to provide the energy for the compression stroke, and to smooth the output, as excessive vibration can cause problems with parts resonating and fatiguing and nuts and bolts working loose. Single cylinder low speed diesels need particularly heavy flywheels because they have large heavy pistons and connecting rods which run at low speeds; traditional designs are 'open flywheel' (Fig. 7.23) while the more modern style of high-speed diesel engine usually has an internal enclosed flywheel (Fig. 7.24).

With larger sizes of engine it becomes feasible to have two or more cylinders. Twin cylinder engines have a smoother power output because the cylinders fire alternately and partially balance each other. Multi-cylinder engines

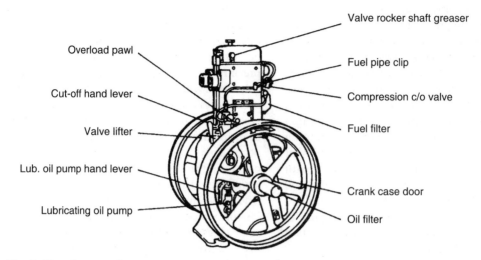

Fig. 7.23: An open-flywheel, low-speed, single-cylinder diesel engine

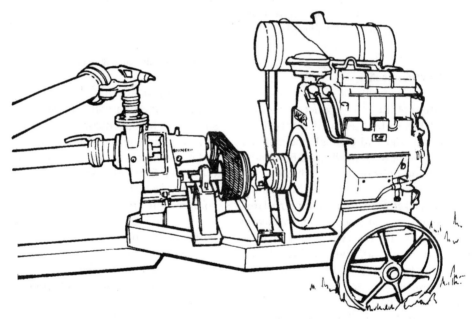

Fig. 7.24: A belt-driven three-cylinder Lister diesel engine coupled to a centrifugal pump via multiple V-belts

therefore run more smoothly and quietly than ones of the same power with fewer cylinders, but the more cylinders there are the more components are involved, so obviously a multi-cylinder engine will be more expensive and more complicated to overhaul and maintain for a given power level.

7.4.5 Relationship between size, speed and durability

A general characteristic of all internal combustion engines is that the smaller and lighter they are for a given power output, the lower will be their initial purchase price (which correlates to some extent with the weight) and the shorter will be their useful life. This is because a high power/weight ratio is normally achieved by running an engine at high speed; the faster an engine runs, the more air/fuel mixture it can consume and the greater will be the energy delivered. However, a faster machine will wear out more quickly simply because its moving and rubbing components travel further in a given number of hours of use, and they also tend to be more heavily loaded by the greater dynamic forces caused by high speed operation. There is therefore a trade-off between heavy, expensive and slow engines on the one hand, and cheap and fast ones of the same power rating. Therefore, small, lightweight engines are recommended for such duties where portability and low first cost are important. In most cases, especially if the engine is part of a fixed installation and to be used for lengthy duty cycles, it will generally be worth investing in a suitably heavy and slower machine in the interests of achieving better reliability and a longer operational life. In general, light petrol engines are restricted to duties requiring less than 500 hours running time per season.

7.4.6 De-rating

If an engine is run continuously at its Rated Power (which is the maximum power output the engine can achieve for short periods), premature wear will occur. All engines therefore require to be de-rated from the manufacturer's rated power. Small engines are usually de-rated to about 70–80% of their rated power; e.g. a 5 kW rated engine will be necessary to produce a continuous 3.5–4.0 kW.

The main reason for de-rating an engine is to prevent premature wear, but also the optimum efficiency for most engines is achieved at a speed corresponding to about 70–80% of its speed for maximum power. Therefore, de-rating an engine usually improves its specific fuel consumption (the fuel required per unit of output, which is equivalent to the efficiency of the engine).

Further de-rating is necessary at high altitudes or at high ambient temperatures;

recommendations to this effect are usually made by the manufacturer. Typically a further 10% de-rating is recommended for each 1,000 m above sea level, plus 1% for each 5°C temperature rise above 16°C at the engine air intake. Therefore at 2,000 m altitude and an ambient temperature of 26°C it would be necessary to de-rate an engine by say, 0.8 (generally) times 0.8 (for altitude) times 0.98 (for temperature) which totals 0.63 or 63% of rated power which would be the correct load to apply. Therefore a 2,000 W load would require an engine nominally rated at 2,000/0.63 or 3.2 kW (4.3 bhp) under those conditions.

Excessive de-rating is to be avoided, as (particularly with diesels) running at a fraction of the design power tends to cause coking of the cylinder. Also, the engine efficiency will of course be much poorer than normal under such conditions.

7.4.7 Special features and accessories

Many of the small engines (i.e. < 3 kW) used with small pumping systems have a hand crank starter or a pull-cord (recoil) starter (the former is more common with small diesels and the latter with small petrol engines). Diesels often include a decompression valve to aid starting, in which a cylinder valve can be partially opened to release the pressure when the piston comes up on the compression stroke, allowing the engine to be hand wound up to a certain speed, when the decompression valve is suddenly closed and the momentum of the flywheel carries the machine on sufficiently to fire the engine and start it off. Alternatively, engines can have an electric starter system, run off a battery.

Electric circuits on engines serve a number of functions. Spark-ignition engines have to have some circuitry to power the ignition system (though compression-ignition engines can be made without any electrics). Electricity can also be used to power a number of other devices, such as lights, or meters or safety cut-outs. If a battery is included in the system, then the electrics can be used for starting the engine through a starter motor. It used to be the case that larger engines had full-blown electric circuits with batteries and electric starters, and smaller engines had magnetos or dynamos that just generated electricity when the engine was running. It is now becoming much more common for even the smallest engines to have batteries and electric start.

If there is electricity on the machine, then it is well worthwhile having safety cut-outs. They can be used, for example, to shut down the engine if the oil or water levels drop, or if the cooling water overheats. They may seem like unnecessary complication, but they are not expensive, and can save the engine from catastrophic failure.

A vital, and often neglected accessory is the air filter, especially in dusty climates. Paper element filter (as used on most cars) need to have the paper element replaced regularly when it becomes clogged with dust or torn. Plastic foam filters can be washed to clean them, which is an advantage where spares are not easily obtainable. Another alternative is an oil bath filter. The latter is slightly more expensive, but can be effective and practical in an agricultural context, since at a pinch even old engine oil can be used to refill it. A worn or malfunctioning air filter can greatly reduce the useful life of an engine, a fact which is often not fully understood by farmers judging from the number of engines that can be found running without any air filter at all.

7.4.8 Installation

The smallest engines are supplied mounted on skids or in a small frame and therefore need no installation other than coupling their pump to the water conveyance system. However, larger machines, and many diesels, need to be properly installed, either on a concrete pad or on a suitable trolley or chassis. Most manufacturers will provide a detailed specification, when necessary, for the foundations of any engine-driven pumping system; this should be accurately adhered to. Note the comments in the sub-section 'Mechanical transmissions' of Section 7.1.2 about couplings when connecting the shafts of an engine with a pump; some sort of shaft coupling that can cope with mounting misalignment must be used.

The engine often needs to be installed in a small lockable building for security. It is essential however that any engine house is well ventilated and that the exhaust is properly discharged outside. This is not only to avoid the serious danger of poisoning the user with exhaust gases, but also to ensure the engine does not overheat. Similarly, engines with direct coupled centrifugal (suction) pumps sometimes need to be installed in a pit in order to lower them near enough to the water level to avoid an excessive suction lift. Considerable care is needed with such installations to ensure that neither exhaust nor oil fumes will fill the pit and poison anyone who enters it; carbon monoxide in internal combustion engine exhaust emissions can, and frequently does, cause fatal accidents. Care is also needed to ensure that the water level will never rise to a level where it could submerge the engine.

7.4.9 Efficiency of engine-powered pumping systems

This is a controversial subject where little reliable data on actual field performance exists in the literature. A few field tests have been carried out on 'typical' irrigation pumping systems, and in some cases surprisingly poor efficiencies were achieved. For example, in tests in Sri Lanka on three small (2–3 bhp), paraffin-fuelled pumping sets, total system efficiencies in the range 0.75–3.5% were recorded, although engine/pump efficiencies (without a pipeline) were between 2.6–8.8% (Jansen, 1979 [58]). Excessive pipeline friction losses obviously caused these very poor system performance results. Unfortunately, there is good reason to assume such losses are quite common.

Many of the reasons for poor performance can be corrected at little cost once it is recognized that a problem exists. But unfortunately, it is easy to run an inefficient pumping system without even realizing it, because the shortfall in output is simply made up by running the engine longer than would otherwise be necessary.

Figure 7.25 indicates the principal components of a small engine pumping system and the range of efficiencies that can typically occur for each. Some explanation of these may give an insight into how such poor total system efficiency can sometimes occur, and by implication, what can be done to improve it.

Firstly, fuel spillage and pilferage could perhaps result in anything from 0–10% of the fuel purchased being lost; i.e. 90–100% of fuel purchased may be usefully consumed as indicated in the figure. Spillage can occur not only when transferring fuel, but due to leaky storage, or very frequently due to either a leaky fuel line on the engine or leaky joints, especially on the

high pressure lines of a diesel engine. Well established fuel stains on the ground ought to give warning that something is wrong with fuel management. As the value of fuel increases, pilferage becomes increasingly a problem. One standard 200 litre drum of fuel is worth typically US$50–150; a small fortune in many developing countries.

Most basic thermodynamics textbooks state that petrol engines are 25–30% efficient, while diesels are 30–45% efficient. Similarly, manufacturers' dynamometer tests, with optimally tuned engines, running on a test-bed (often minus most

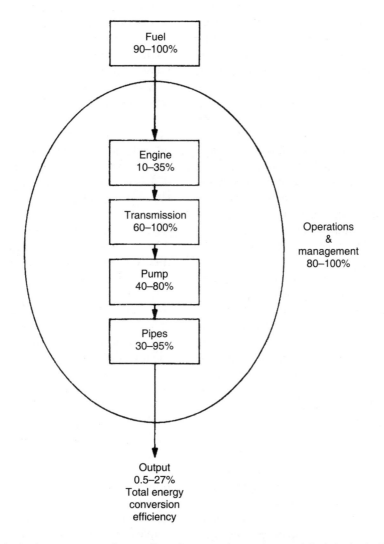

Fig. 7.25: The principal components of a small engine pumping system and their typical efficiencies

of their accessories), tend to confirm this. The difference between theory and reality is greatest with the smallest sizes of engines, which are inherently less efficient than larger ones, and the text-book figures quoted above really only apply to well-tuned engines of above about 10 kW power rating, and even then only when running the engine at one optimum speed. Such figures are in any case especially optimistic in relation to field operations. The smallest petrol engines also tend to vary in quality and 'state of tune', engine to engine, and can easily be as poor as only 10% efficient at around 1 kW power rating. Small diesels (the smallest are about 1.5 to 2 kW) will probably be better than 20% efficient as engines, but components like the injection pump, cooling fan and water circulating pump (all parasitic energy consumers) can reduce the fuel-to-useful-shaft-power efficiency to around 15% (or less) for the smallest engines. This large drop is because the parasitic accessories take proportionately more power from very small engines. Obviously engines are also only in new condition for a small part of their lives, and on average are worn and not well tuned, which also undermines their efficiency. Hence, depending on size, type and quality plus their age and how well they are maintained, engines may in reality be at best 35% efficient and at worst under 10% efficient.

Another source of loss is the mechanical transmission from the engine to the pump. In some cases the engine is direct coupled to the pump, in which case the transmission losses are negligible, but if there is any substantial change of speed, such as a speed-reducer and gearbox to drive a reciprocating borehole pump, then there will be noticeable transmission losses, particularly with small systems of less than 5 kW, where gearbox losses will be relatively large in relation to the power flow.

As discussed in the previous section, the most common type of pump used for irrigation with a small engine will be a centrifugal pump, either direct coupled or belt driven, usually working on suction (e.g. Fig. 6.70 and Fig. 7.24). If properly installed, so that the pump is operating close to its optimum head and speed, the pump

efficiency can easily exceed 60% and possibly be as high as 80% with bigger pumps. However there is a lot of scope for failing to achieve these figures: bad impeller designs, impellers damaged by cavitation, worn impellers with much back-leakage, and operating away from the design flow and head for a given speed will all have a detrimental effect and can easily singly, or in combination, pull the efficiency down to 25% or less. Given a reasonably well-matched and well-run system, pump efficiencies will therefore be in the 40–80% range, but they could easily be worse than this.

It is often not appreciated that the choice of delivery pipe can have a profound effect on system performance. Engines can deliver very high volumes at low heads, so pipe friction can grossly increase the total head across the pump, particularly with long delivery lines at low heads. When this happens, it is possible for the total head to be several times the static head, which multiplies the fuel requirement proportionately. Figure 5.5 allows this to be quantified; e.g. even a small portable petrol engine pump will typically deliver over 360 l/min or 6 l/s through 5 m head (600 W hydraulic output). The friction loss for each 100 m of delivery pipe with this flow and head will be approximately as shown in Table 7.12. (Inch sizes are used here simply because they are commonly used for pipes.)

These figures show that, for low heads at least, it is quite easy for the loss in the pipes to exceed the delivery head. It only takes 25 m of 2" pipe at 5 l/s for the pipe loss to be 5 m, which was the delivery head in our example. Figure 7.26 uses the losses from Table 7.12 to show the pipeline efficiencies for various length of pipes. For the smaller pipes the efficiency can be very low, down to 20% when 100 m of 2" pipe is used (i.e. in that case the pumped head is *five times* the static head so that five times as much fuel is needed compared with a 100% efficient pipeline). The situation gets proportionately less serious at higher static heads, because it is the ratio of pipe friction head to static head that matters; for example, at 20 m static head the above example would give the same friction head of 20 m which although unacceptably high would at least

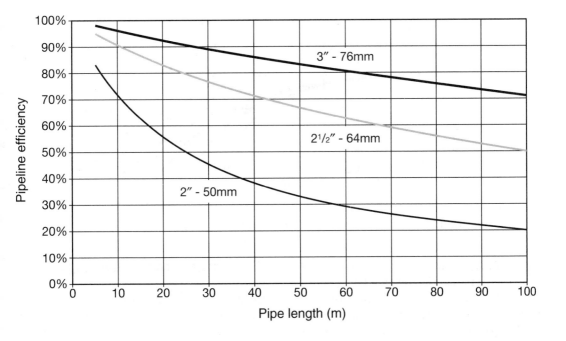

Fig. 7.26: Pipeline efficiencies for different pipe sizes for a flow of 5 l/s and a delivery head of 5 m

Table 7.12: Losses in pipes for a flow of 5 l/s

Pipe nominal internal diameter		Friction head per 100 m
2"	(50 mm)	20 m
2½"	(64 mm)	5 m
3"	(76 mm)	2 m

imply 50% rather than 20% pipeline efficiency. It is a common mistake to use pipework which is too small in diameter as a supposed 'economy', when larger pipe can often pay for itself in saved fuel within months rather than years. Also, some pumps which have a 2" discharge orifice may actually need a 3" pipeline if some distance is involved, yet uninformed users will usually use a pipe diameter to match the pump orifice size and thereby create a major source of inefficiency.

The performance curves in Fig. 7.27 indicates how centrifugal suction pumps can also suffer reduced performance as the suction head increases, mainly due to cavitation, particularly when the suction head is a large fraction of the total head. The figure shows how at 10 m total head, 6 m suction head causes a 20% drop in output compared with 3 m suction head. This is without any reduction in power demand, so the former system is 20% less efficient than the latter, simply due to suction losses. There is, therefore, a potentially large fuel cost penalty in applying excessive suction lifts (apart from the usual priming problems that can occur).

Pipe losses, whether due to friction or suction can therefore cause increased head and reduced flow and will typically have an efficiency in the 30–95% range, as indicated in Fig. 7.25.

The efficiency factors discussed so far apply to the hardware, while it is being run and water is being usefully applied to the field. Inevitably the system needs to run when water is not being usefully applied. For example, when starting up, any engine will often be run for a few minutes before the farmer can arrange the discharge to reach the correct part of the field, and water (and fuel) will be wasted. Similarly when rearranging the distribution system to deliver water to another part of the field, some wastage may occur. There is therefore a factor relating to the type of water distribution system and to the management skill

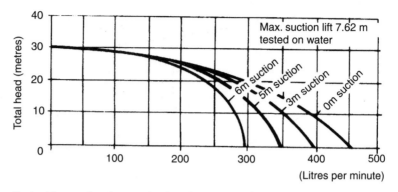

Fig. 7.27: The effect of increasing the suction head on output for a typical engine pumping set

of the farmer at applying the pumped water for as large a fraction of the time it is being pumped (or the engine is running) as possible. Even moderately good management could cause 20% loss compared with ideal usage, and really bad management can be much worse, so this efficiency is taken as ranging from 80–100% in Fig. 7.25.

When all the worst efficiencies suggested in Fig. 7.25 are compounded, they yield a theoretical worst total efficiency of 0.5% (which Jansen [58] and others have confirmed) while the best factors in Fig. 7.25 compounded together give 27%. The 'best' figure is only even theoretically feasible however for a larger diesel (over 5 kW), driving a pump at 10–20 m (or higher) head, which is rather higher than usual for most irrigation applications. Most smaller engine pumped irrigation systems therefore in practice probably achieve 5 to 15% total efficiency, with larger diesels operating at higher heads being towards the top end of this range and small paraffin or petrol engines at low heads being at (or below) the bottom.

The user should probably be satisfied if a small diesel system achieves 10–15% efficiency and a small petrol or paraffin fuelled system achieves 5–10%. *It is therefore important for any user to investigate the actual efficiency of any engine pumping system (by comparing fuel consumption against hydraulic energy output), so that if it is below par steps may be taken to find the causes and to correct them.*

7.5 External combustion engines

Until the late seventeenth century, human and animal muscle power, together with some limited applications of water and wind power, were the only sources of motive energy available to mankind. Then the steam engine was invented, harnessing the chemical energy of fossil fuels, usually coal, and releasing power that had hitherto only been dreamt of. Many of the early steam engines were initially designed for water pumping, for draining mine-shafts and land, as well as for water supply and irrigation. Steam engines were large, heavy, unwieldy bits of equipment, but the power they gave made them invaluable. They were a major factor in starting the Industrial Revolution, and began the widespread use of machinery that we see today.

The difference between internal and external combustion engines is, as their names suggest, that the former burn their fuel within the power cylinder, but the latter use their fuel to heat a gas or a vapour through the walls of an external chamber, and the heated gas or vapour is then transferred to the power cylinder. External combustion engines therefore require a heat exchanger, or boiler to take in heat, and as their fuels are burnt externally under steady conditions, they can in principle use any fuel that can burn, including agricultural residues or waste materials.

There are two main families of external combustion engines: steam engines, which rely on expanding steam (or occasionally some other vapour) to drive a mechanism, and Stirling engines, which use hot air (or some other hot gas). The use of both technologies reached their zeniths around 1900 and have declined almost to extinction since. However, a brief description is worthwhile, since:

- they were successfully and widely used in the past for pumping water;
- they both have the merit of being well suited to the use of low cost fuels such as coal, peat and biomass;
- attempts to update and revive them are taking place.

It is to be hoped that they may re-appear as viable options in the longer-term future.

The primary disadvantage of E.C. engines is that a large area of heat exchanger is necessary to transmit heat into the working cylinder(s) and also to reject heat at the end of the cycle. As a result, E.C. engines are bulky and therefore costly to construct compared with internal combustion engines. Also, since they are no longer manufactured, they do not enjoy the economies of mass-production available to internal combustion engines. They also will not start so quickly or conveniently as an internal combustion engine – because it takes time to light the fire and heat the machine to its working temperature, and once running they are much less responsive than internal combustion engines.

Due to their relatively poor power/weight ratio and also the worse energy/weight ratio of solid fuels, the kinds of applications where steam or Stirling engines are most likely to be acceptable are for static applications such as irrigation water pumping in areas where petroleum fuels are not readily available but low cost solid fuels are. On the positive side, E.C. engines have the advantage of having the potential to be much longer-lasting than internal combustion engines (100-year-old steam railway locomotives are relatively easy to keep in working order, but it is rare for internal combustion engines to be used more than 20 years or so). E.C. engines are also significantly quieter and free of vibrations than internal combustion engines. The level of skill needed for maintenance may also be lower,

although the amount of time spent will be higher, particularly due to the need for cleaning out the furnace.

Modern engineering techniques promise that any future steam or Stirling engines could benefit from features not available over 60 years ago when they were last in general use. Products incorporating these new developments are not yet on the market, but R and D is in hand in various countries on a limited scale; however, it will probably be some years before a new generation of multi-fuel Stirling or steam powered pumps become generally available.

7.5.1 Steam engines

Only a limited number of small steam engines are available commercially at present, and most are for general use, for steam enthusiasts, or for powering small pleasure boats. These engines tend to be manufactured by small companies in Europe and USA, though small steam engines are also made in Thailand and a number of other countries. A serious attempt to develop a 2 kW steam engine for use in remote areas was made by the engine designers, Ricardo, in the UK during the 1950s (see Fig. 7.81). That development was possibly premature and failed, but there is still interest in developing power sources that can run on biomass-based fuels (as discussed more fully in Section 7.10). However, small steam engines have always suffered from their need to meet quite stringent safety requirements to avoid accidents due to boiler explosions, and most countries have regulations requiring the certification of steam engine boilers, which is a serious, but necessary, inhibiting factor.

The principle of the steam engine is illustrated in Fig. 7.28. Fuel is burnt in a furnace, releasing hot gases that are used in a heat-exchanger to heat the water. In a 'water-tube' boiler the hot gases flow past a series of pipes carrying water, while in a 'fire-tube' boiler the gases are directed through tubes surrounded by water. In both designs, the heat is transferred to the water, causing it to boil and become steam. The water-tube boiler is the most common, being able to withstand high pressure in the water/steam circuit

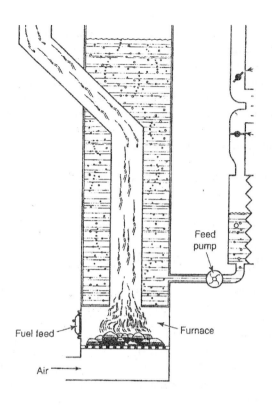

Fig. 7.28: Schematic arrangement of a condensing steam engine

more easily. Steam is generated under pressure, typically 5–10 atmospheres (5–10 bar). A safety valve is provided to release steam when the pressure becomes too high so as to avoid the risk of an explosion. A valve arrangement directs the high-pressure steam on to one side of the piston while venting the other side. The pressure differential forces the piston to move, and the high-pressure steam continues to fill the space behind it. The inlet valve closes at a certain point, but the steam usually continues expanding until it is close to atmospheric pressure before the exhaust valve opens to allow the piston to push the cooled and expanded steam out to make way for a new intake of high pressure steam. The valves are linked to the drive mechanism so as to open or close automatically at the correct moment. The period of opening of the inlet valve can be adjusted by the operator to vary the speed and power of the engine.

In the simplest types of engine the steam is exhausted to the atmosphere. This however is wasteful of energy, because by cooling and condensing the exhausted steam the pressure can be reduced to a semi-vacuum and this allows more energy to be extracted from a given throughput of steam and thereby significantly improves the efficiency. When a condenser is not used, such as with steam railway locomotives, the jet of exhaust steam is utilized to create a good draught for the furnace by drawing the hot gases up the necessarily short smoke stack. Condensing steam engines, on the other hand, either need a high stack to create a draught by natural convection, or they need fans or blowers.

Steam pumps can easily include a condenser, since the pumped water can serve to cool the condenser. The typical gain in overall efficiency from using a condenser can exceed 30% extra output per unit of fuel used. Condensed steam collects as water at the bottom of the condenser and is then pumped at sufficient pressure to inject it back into the boiler by a small water feed pump, which is normally driven off the engine.

A further most important advantage of a condensing steam engine is that re-circulating the same water reduces the problems of scaling and corrosion that commonly occur when a continuous throughput of fresh water is used. A clean and mineral-free water supply is normally necessary for non-condensing steam engines to prolong the life of the boiler. In many cases water treatment chemicals are needed to prevent premature boiler scaling.

The most basic steam engine is about 5% efficient (steam energy to mechanical shaft energy – the furnace and boiler efficiency of probably between 30 and 60% needs to be compounded with this to give an overall efficiency as a prime mover in the 1.5 to 3% range). More sophisticated engines are around 10% efficient, while the very best reach 15%. When the boiler and furnace efficiencies (30–60%) plus the pump (40–80%) and pipework (40–90%) are compounded, we obtain system efficiencies for steam piston engine powered pumps in the 0.5 to 4.5% range (which is actually not a lot worse than the efficiency of a pumping system powered by a small petrol engine).

Steam engines can be durable machines that can run off many different fuels. The main barrier to their use is that they are not widely available.

7.5.2 Stirling engines

The Stirling engine was originally developed by the Rev. Robert Stirling in 1816, whose main aim was to produce a safe engine that did not explode like the steam engines of the day. Tens of thousands of small Stirling engines were used in the late nineteenth and early twentieth century, mainly in the USA but also in Europe. At that time, they were known as 'Hot-Air Engines'. They were applied to all manner of small-scale power purposes, including water pumping. In North America they particularly saw service on the 'new frontier' (the 'Wild West'); which at that time suffered all the problems of a developing country in terms of lack of energy resources, etc.

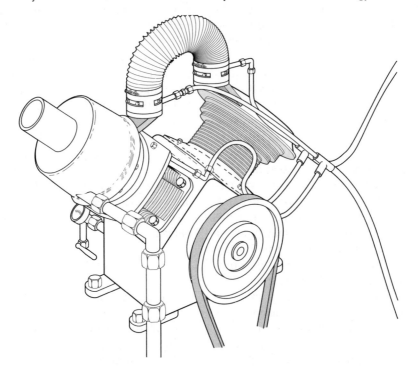

Fig. 7.29: A modern Stirling engine. This prototype was produced by IT Power as a power source for developing countries that could be run off biomass as well as fossil fuels

Rural electrification and the rise of the small petrol engine during and after the 1920s overtook the Hot-Air Engine, and their use declined. There was some interest in them as vehicle engines in the 1970s because of their quietness, low emissions and high efficiency, but technical difficulties were found in adapting them for such applications, and they were never put into production. Since then, a number of organizations have developed experimental Stirling engines for a variety of other applications, such as water pumping using biomass fuels, and small-scale electricity generation from solar energy. Few of these engines have become commercially available, though recently small multi-fuel Stirling engines have been marketed by the Stirling Technology Company in the USA. Nevertheless, Stirling engines are relatively simple and robust engines that can be run on almost any fuel. They are almost unique among heat engines in that they can be made to work quite well at fractional horsepower sizes, where both internal combustion engines and steam engines are relatively inefficient. All these attributes would seem to make them attractive for small-scale irrigation pumping in remote or rural areas, but unless they are produced commercially in reasonable volume, they will not compete with the convenience and cheapness of mass-produced internal combustion engines.

Stirling engines have a fixed mass of working gas trapped inside them, and use pressure changes caused by alternately heating and cooling this gas to produce power. Robert Stirling's original engine had one cylinder with two pistons inside it, but a number of different engine layouts have since been developed using the same basic cycle. The working gas may be air, or sometimes helium or hydrogen. The Stirling cycle has a high theoretical efficiency, and working engines have been made with efficiencies of 30–45% – better than small steam or internal-combustion engines. This good efficiency can be maintained even at fairly low temperatures and pressures. The forces appear and disappear relatively smoothly (there are none of the explosive expansions found in internal combus-

tion engines), and the combination of low stresses and low temperatures mean the materials used to make the engine are not too critical. The engines avoid the boiler explosion and scaling hazards of steam engines.

A critical component is the regenerator, which is a heat exchanger housed in the connecting tube between the cylinders. This absorbs heat from the hot gas leaving the displacement cylinder, and uses it to heat the cool gas as it comes back from the power cylinder. This avoids loosing heat in the cycle, and is important to give good efficiency. (Stirling called this element of the engine an 'economizer', for obvious reasons.)

Some insight into the mechanics of a small Stirling engine can be gained from Fig. 7.30, which shows a 1900 vintage Rider-Ericsson engine (a type which was manufactured in large numbers in the USA and in the UK from the 1870s until the early 1900s). The displacer cylinder projects at its lower end into a small furnace, and the displacement cylinder has a jacket of cooling water around it (this can be the pumped water if the engine is used for irrigation). The regenerator is a mass of metal gauze in the pipe connecting the cylinders.

An idea of the potential value of engines such as this can be gained from records of their performance; for example, the half horsepower Rider-Ericsson engine could raise 2.7 m³/h of water through 20 m; it ran at about 140 rpm (only) and consumed about 2 kg of coal per hour. All that was needed to keep it going was for the fire to be occasionally stoked, rather like a domestic stove, and for a drop of oil to be dispensed onto the plain bearings every hour or so. Many ran for several decades with minimal maintenance.

7.6   Electrical power

If a nearby connection is available to a *reliable* mains electricity supply, nothing else is either as convenient or more cost-effective for powering an irrigation pump. Unfortunately, the majority of farmers in developing countries do not have mains electricity close at hand, and even those

206

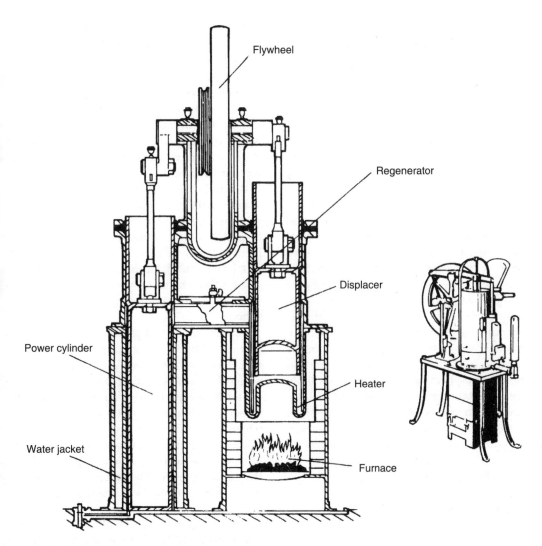

Fig. 7.30: The Rider-Ericsson hot air pumping engine

that do often find that the supply is unreliable. Electricity supply problems tend to be particularly prevalent during the irrigation season, because irrigation pumping tends to be practised simultaneously by all farmers in a particular district and can therefore easily overload an inadequate rural network and cause 'brownouts' (voltage reductions) or even 'blackouts' (complete power cuts). Therefore, there is a major inhibition for many electricity utilities in encouraging any further use of electricity for irrigation pump-

ing in developing countries where the electrical supply network is already under strain.

The real cost of extending the grid is very high, typically in the order of $5,000–15,000 per kilometre of spur, or around $750 per connection (Smith, 1996 [59]). Although connections in many countries have, in the past, been subsidized whatever the pricing policy of the utility, someone has to pay for it and the tendency today is to withdraw subsidies. Therefore, although an electric motor considered in isolation is an extremely inexpensive and convenient prime mover, it is only useful when connected to a lot of capital-intensive infrastructure, which needs to carry a substantial electrical load in order to be self-financing from revenue.

A further problem for developing countries in considering the mains electricity option is the high foreign exchange component in the investment; this is typically from 50–80%. Electricity generation in rural areas of developing countries tends to be by petroleum-fuelled plant (usually diesel generators) so this also is a burden on the economy. In fact a large fraction of many developing countries' oil imports goes to electrical power generation. The attractiveness of rural electrification as an investment for development is therefore being questioned much more now than it used to be. However it is not proposed here to deal with policy implications or macro-economic effects of the widespread use of electricity for irrigation pumping, other than to point out that it cannot be seen as a universally applicable solution to the world's irrigation pumping needs, because most countries will not be able to afford to extend a grid to all their rural areas in the foreseeable future. Even where such an option can be afforded, it is still necessary to question whether it is the most cost-effective solution for irrigation pumping bearing in mind the high infrastructure costs.

7.6.1 Sources and types of electricity

Batteries produce a steady flow of electricity known as 'direct current' or DC. Photovoltaic (solar) cells also produce DC. Electrical generators to produce DC are sometimes known as 'dynamos'; they require commutators consisting of rotating brass segments with fixed carbon brushes. Alternators are almost universally used today for the generation of electricity from shaft power. Alternators are simpler and less expensive than DC generators, but they produce a voltage that reverses completely several times per revolution. This type of electrical output, which is almost universally used for mains supplies, is known as 'alternating current' or AC.

AC mains voltage normally fluctuates from full positive to full negative and back 50 times per second (50Hz or 50 cycles/s) or in some cases at 60Hz. The current fluctuates similarly. Sometimes the current and voltage can be 'out of step', i.e. their peaks do not coincide. This discrepancy (or phase difference) is quantified by the 'power factor'; the output of an AC system is the product of the amps, volts and the power factor. When the amps and volts are in perfect phase with each other, the power factor is numerically 1. When the power factor is less than one (it frequently is 0.9 and sometimes less) then the useful power available is reduced proportionately for a given system rating. The rating of AC equipment is therefore generally given, not in watts or kilowatts (kW), but in volt-amps or kilovolt-amps (kVA). The useful power in kW will therefore be the kVA rating multiplied by the power factor.

Another important principle to be aware of is that it is considerably more economic to transmit electricity any distance at high voltages rather than low. A smaller cross-section of conductor is needed for a given transmission efficiency. This is analogous to water transmission, where higher pressures and smaller flow rates allow smaller pipes to be used for equal hydraulic power. However, electricity is potentially lethal, and the higher the voltage the more dangerous it becomes (AC voltages much above 240 V and DC voltages much above 100 V are considered dangerous – although it can of course kill at considerably lower voltages depending on the circumstances and state of health of the victim). Therefore, for safety reasons, 240 V AC or about 100 V DC are the maximum voltages used at the end-users' supplies and for electrical appliances.

The reason AC is generally used for mains applications rather than DC is that it has a number of important advantages:

- AC generators and motors are much simpler, less expensive and less troublesome, since they do not require commutators;
- AC voltages can be changed efficiently and with a high degree of reliability, using

transformers, but it is a technically much more difficult problem to change DC voltages; therefore AC can easily be transmitted efficiently at high voltages and then transformed to low, safer voltages close to the point of use;

- As a result of the advantages of AC, it has become the internationally used standard for mains supplies and virtually all mass-produced electrical appliances are designed for AC use.

It is sometimes necessary to convert AC to DC or vice-versa, for example to charge batteries (which are DC) from the AC mains or to run an AC appliance designed for the mains from a DC source such as a battery or a solar photovoltaic array. AC can quite readily be converted to DC by using a rectifier; these (like transformers) are solid-state devices that require no maintenance and are relatively efficient. A battery charger usually consists of a combination of a transformer (to step mains voltage down to battery voltage) and a rectifier to convert the low voltage AC to DC. Converting DC to AC is more difficult, and requires a solid-state electronic device called an inverter. In recent years inverters have become more readily available in the sizes required for small-scale pumping (up to a few kilowatts). The quality and price of inverters also varies a lot; if a good quality AC output is essential (and high efficiency of conversion) a more complicated and expensive device is needed. Cheap inverters often produce a crude AC output, are relatively inefficient, and maybe unreliable; they can also seriously interfere with radio and TV reception in the vicinity.

Different sources of electricity have very different costs, with mains electricity generally being the cheapest. Table 7.13 shows a few tariffs or costs per kWh of various electricity supplies. The cost of electricity in most developed countries is fairly consistent, but it varies considerably in developing countries. The cost of electricity from lead-acid batteries (car-type batteries) depends greatly on what is used to charge them, so no simple figures can be given. Dry cells (torch or flashlight batteries) do not provide enough power for pumping, but are, not surprisingly, prohibitively expensive anyway.

Table 7.13: Typical electricity costs from different sources (Inversin, 1995 [60]) and [59]

Source	Cost (US currency)
Mains electricity, developed countries average	10 cents/kWh
Mains electricity, developing countries	5–30 cents/kWh
Small diesel generator sets	40 cents/kWh
Lead acid batteries	$1/kWh
Dry cell batteries	$50–100/kWh

7.6.2 AC mains power

Mains electricity is generally supplied as alternating current (AC) either at 220 to 240 V and 50 Hz frequency or at 110 V and 60 Hz frequency for low power connections (including domestic ones) of up to about 10 kW. 220–240 V 50 Hz is standard in Europe and much of Africa and Asia, while the 110 V 60 Hz standard is used in the USA and many other areas.

When AC is supplied through two wires, it is known as single-phase. The two wires are not 'positive' and 'negative' but are 'live' and 'neutral'; there should always also be a third wire included for safety – the 'earth' or 'ground'. The latter is normally connected to the casing of any appliance or motor so that if any internal fault causes the casing to come into contact with the live supply, the leakage current will flow to earth (ground) and trip out the system or blow a fuse. Therefore if an electric pump keeps tripping or blowing fuses it is essential to have it checked to see if there is a short-circuit.

Mains power is normally generated as 'three-phase', in which the alternator transmits three 'single phase' AC outputs down three wires. Each phase is shifted by one third of a revolution of the alternator, so the voltage peaks in the three conductors do not coincide, but are evenly spaced out. The three phases, if equally balanced, will cancel each other out if fed through three equal loads, but in practice they are not usually perfectly balanced so there is normally a fourth return conductor called the neutral. A single phase

AC supply is simply a connection to one of the three 'lives' of a three-phase source with a return to its neutral. For this reason it is important in many cases not to confuse the live and neutral; also it is the live which should be protected by fuses or contact breakers.

At higher power levels, usually above 5 kW, and always above about 25 kW, it is normal to use three-phase AC. This is supplied mostly at 415 V line to line (Europe, Asia and Africa) or 190 or 440 V (USA, Canada and most of South and Central America).

7.6.3 Electric motors

An electric motor seems almost the ideal prime mover for a water pump. Power is supplied 'at the flick of a switch', and water is produced at a constant rate until the motor is turned off. Electric motors have relatively long service lives and usually need little or no servicing.

The cheapest and simplest type of electric motor is the squirrel cage induction motor which is almost universally used for mains electric power applications; see Fig. 7.31A and Fig. 7.32. Here there are no electrical connections to the rotating 'squirrel cage', so there are no brushes or slip rings to wear or need adjustment. Motors of this kind are available in either three-phase or single-phase versions. They run at a fixed speed depending on the frequency of the power supply and the number of poles in their stator windings. The most common type (which is usually the cheapest) runs at a nominal 1,500 rpm at 50 Hz (1,800 at 60 Hz), but other speeds are available. It is normal to direct-couple a motor to a centrifugal pump where possible (e.g. Fig. 7.32). Non-standard speed motors may be used where this does not suit the pump, or alternatively pulleys and belts may be used for speed reduction, such as in Fig. 7.33.

A problem with induction motors is that they normally need over three times as much current to start as they do for running at rated speed and power. This means that the peak current that can be supplied must be significantly higher than that needed for operation, which often causes not just technical but also financial problems, as some electricity tariffs are determined by the maximum current rating on a circuit. Recently

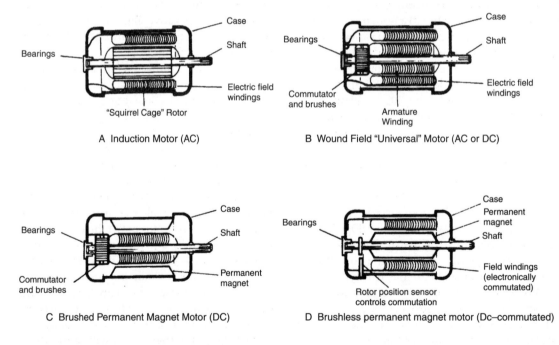

A Induction Motor (AC)

B Wound Field "Universal" Motor (AC or DC)

C Brushed Permanent Magnet Motor (DC)

D Brushless permanent magnet motor (Dc–commutated)

Fig. 7.31: The four main types of electric motor.

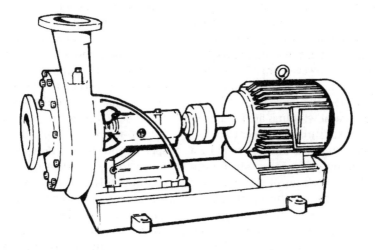

Fig. 7.32: A direct-coupled electric motor and centrifugal pump

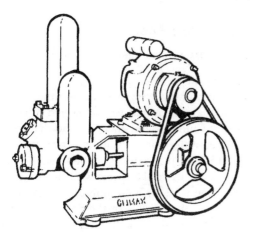

Fig. 7.33: An electric-motor powered, belt-driven piston pump (Climax) – note the air chambers provided to prevent water hammer

electronic starting devices have become available which limit the starting current while the motor runs up to speed and which in some cases also improve the overall efficiency of an electric motor.

Induction motors are typically 75% efficient for a 300 W size and may be around 85% efficient at 10 kW size (subject to having a unity power factor). They are not generally made in sizes significantly smaller than 100–200 W.

For very small-scale applications, the so-called 'universal motor' is most commonly used. The universal motor (Fig. 7.31B) is the 'classic' electric motor with a brushed commutator and wound armature. Fixed field coils produce the magnetic flux to run the motor. Motors of this kind can use either an AC or a DC supply and they are typically used for very small-scale power applications (in small power tools such as electric drills, and in some domestic appliances like washing machines, for example). They are more efficient than would be possible with a very small induction motor and their starting current is smaller in relation to their running current. They suffer, however, from needing periodic replacement of brushes when used intensively, as for pumping duties.

There are small-scale electrical power applications independent of a mains supply, which use a DC source such as a photovoltaic array, or batteries charged from a wind-generator. In these applications, a permanent magnet DC motor is the most efficient option (Fig. 7.31C). In these, permanent magnets replace the field coils; this offers higher efficiency, particularly at part-load, when field windings would absorb a significant proportion of the power being drawn.

Permanent magnet DC motors can be 75–85% efficient even at such low power ratings as 100–

200 W, needed for the smallest solar pumping systems. Most permanent magnet motors have brushed/commutated armatures exactly like a universal motor, which in the pumping context is a major drawback. However, brushless permanent magnet motors have recently become available (Fig. 7.31D). Here the magnets are fixed to the rotor and the stator windings are fed a commutated AC current at variable frequency to suit the speed of rotation; this is done by sending a signal from a rotor position-sensor, which measures the speed and position of the shaft and controls electronic circuitry, which performs the commutation function on a DC supply. Motors of this kind are mechanically on a par with an induction motor, and can be sealed for life in a submersible pump if required, but they are still produced in limited numbers and involve a sophisticated electronic commutator that makes them relatively expensive at the time of writing. With the increasing use of solar pumps they are likely to become more widely used and their price may fall.

Submersible pump motors, whether AC induction motors or DC brushless permanent magnet motors, are commonly filled with (clean and corrosion inhibited) water as this equalizes the pressure on the seals and makes it easier to prevent ingress of well water than if the motor contained only air at atmospheric pressure. Filling motors with water is obviously only possible with brushless motors, or short-circuits would occur. Another advantage of water-filled motors is that they are better protected from overheating.

There is a further discussion of the suitability of various type of electrical motor for pumping applications in sub-section 'Motor-pump sub-systems' of Section 7.8.3.

7.6.4 Electrical safety

Electricity is potentially lethal, especially if the contact is enhanced through the presence of water. Therefore, electricity and water need to be combined with caution, and anyone using electricity for irrigation pumping should ensure that all necessary protection equipment is provided; i.e. effective trips or fuses, plus suitable armoured cables, earthed (grounded) and splashproof enclosures, etc. Also all major components, the motor, pump and supporting structure should be properly earthed (or grounded) with all earth connections electrically bonded together.

It is vital that electrical installations should either be completed by trained electricians or if the farmer carries it out, he should have it inspected and checked by a properly qualified person before ever attempting to use it (in some countries this is in any case a legal requirement). It is also prudent to have some prior knowledge what action to take for treating electric shock; most electrical utilities can provide posters or notices giving details of precautions with recommendations on treatment should such an unfortunate event occur.

7.7 Wind Power

7.7.1 Background and state-of-the-art

Background

Wind power has been used for centuries. There is some evidence that wind-powered mills existed in China around 3000 BC, and that wind-powered water pumps were known in Babylon in 1600 BC. The origins of modern wind power seem to be in Persia, where wind is known to have been used for both mills and irrigation in Sistan (on the borders of the present-day Iran and Afghanistan) in the 10th century. These vertical-axis windmills and wind pumps spread through the Middle East, and as far East as China (Fraenkel et al., 1993 [61]).

The earliest European windmills appeared in France, Belgium and England in the 12th century, the idea having come from the Middle East during the Crusades, but European mills were horizontal-axis machines. Windmills were used widely, with around 10,000 in England, 18,000 in Germany, and 9,000 in Holland in the 19th century. As well as being used for milling, wind pumps were used for irrigation, and to reclaim land by pumping off seawater in low-lying areas of Holland and England. Smaller wind pumps, generally made from wood, were used to de-water polders (in Holland), and for pumping seawater in salt workings (France, Spain and Portugal). Though some windmills are still in use in places like Cape Verde (Fig. 7.34), the majority fell into disuse, as wind power was replaced by steam and then electricity.

The most widely used type of wind pump today is the so-called American farm wind pump (Fig. 7.35). This normally has a steel, multi-bladed, fan-like rotor, which drives a reciprocating pump linkage usually via reduction gearing (Fig. 7.36) that connects directly with a piston pump located in a borehole directly below. The American farm wind pump evolved during the period between 1880 and 1910 when many millions of cattle were being introduced on the North American Great Plains. Limited surface water created a vast demand for water lifting machinery, so wind pumps rapidly became the main general purpose power source

Fig. 7.34: An indigenous wooden wind pump for pumping seawater into saltpans on the island of Sal, Cape Verde

for this purpose. The US agricultural industry spawned a multitude of wind pump manufacturers and there were government-sponsored research and development programmes to evolve better wind pumps for irrigation as well as for water supply duties.

Other 'new frontiers' also took up the farm wind pump, and to this day more than a million steel farm wind pumps are in regular use, the largest numbers being in Australia and Argentina. It should be noted that the so-called American Farm Wind pump is rarely used today for irrigation; most are used for the purpose they were originally developed for, namely watering livestock and, to a lesser extent, for farm or community water supplies. They tend, therefore, to be applied at quite high heads by irrigation standards; typically in the 10 to 100 m range on boreholes. Large wind pumps are even in regular use on boreholes of over 200 m depth.

Wind pumps have also been used in S E Asia and China for longer than in Europe, mainly for irrigation or for pumping sea water into drying pans for sea salt production. The Chinese sail wind pump (Fig. 7.37) was first used over a thousand years ago, and tens of thousands, are still in use in Hubei, Henan and North Jiangsu provinces, though their use is declining. The traditional Chinese designs are constructed from wire-braced bamboo poles carrying fabric sails; usually either a paddle pump or a dragon-spine (ladder pump) is used, mostly at pumping heads of less than 1 m. Many Chinese windmills rely on the wind blowing in the same direction, because their rotors are of fixed orientation. Many hundreds of a similar design of wind pump to the Chinese ones are also used on salt-pans in Thailand (Fig. 7.38). However, the traditional wind pumps of China and S E Asia are being abandoned as the use of engines and mains power spreads.

Some 50,000 wind pumps were used around the Mediterranean Sea 40 years ago for irrigation purposes. These were improvized variations of the metal American farm wind pump, but often using triangular cloth sails rather than metal blades. These sail windmills have a type of rotor

Fig. 7.35: An all-steel 'American' farm wind pump

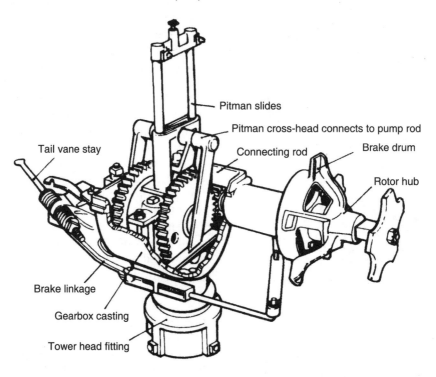

Pitman slides

Pitman cross-head connects to pump rod

Tail vane stay

Connecting rod

Brake drum

Rotor hub

Brake linkage

Gearbox casting

Tower head fitting

Fig. 7.36: The gearbox from a typical back-geared American farm wind pump

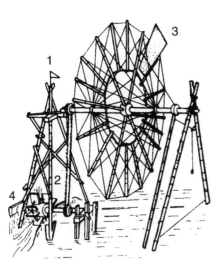

Fig. 7.37: A Chinese chain wind pump. 1. Flag (indicating wind direction). 2. Chain drive. 3. Sails (only one shown fitted for clarity). 4. Paddle pump.

which has been used for many centuries in the Mediterranean region, but today is often known as a 'Cretan Windmill' (see Fig. 7.39). During the last 30 years or so, increased prosperity combined with cheaper engines and fuels has generally led farmers in this region to abandon windmills and use small engines (or mains electricity where available). Around 6,000 wind pumps were in use quite recently in Crete itself, mostly with fabric sails, but the numbers have been declining rapidly.

The use of wind power for generating electricity was pioneered in Denmark at the end of the 19th century. Small aero-generators supplied electricity to many rural communities in America until grid electricity took their place in the 1930s. Thousands of small wind generators were bought for use in remote rural areas in many parts of the world. Similar machines, such as the 'windcharger' shown in (Fig. 7.40), are used today for charging batteries for lighting, radio communication, and as an alternative to a photovoltaic array for irrigation pumping in suitably windy areas.

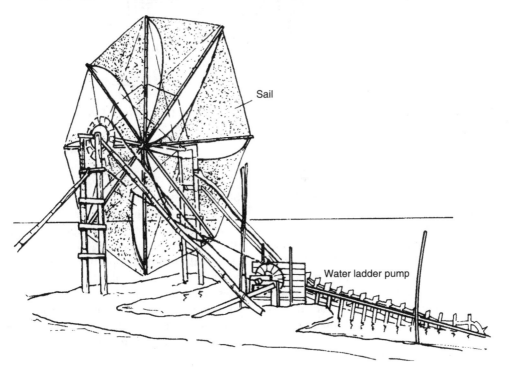

Sail

Water ladder pump

Fig. 7.38: A Thai wind pump

Fig. 7.39: A 'Cretan'-type of windpump used on an irrigation project in southern Ethiopia

Large wind turbines for electricity generation have been (and are being) constructed, to the extent that mushrooming wind farms were a new phenomenon of the 1990s. By the end of 2005 over 59000 MW of wind turbines had been installed worldwide and this is growing at more than 10% per annum. Figure 7.41 shows modern grid-connected wind turbines of the type used in wind farms; such units may have outputs of several megawatts, but smaller machines of about 50 kW may in future be of considerable relevance for larger scale irrigation pumping than is feasible with more traditional mechanical wind pumps.

State-of-the-art

There are two distinct end-uses for windpumps, namely irrigation or water supply. As a result, there are two distinct categories of windpump, because the technical, operational and economic requirements are generally different for these end uses. That is not to say that a water supply windpump cannot be used for irrigation (they quite often are) but irrigation designs are generally unsuitable for water supply duties.

Fig. 7.40: A Marlec Furlmatic 1803 340 W 12 V or 24 V wind electricity generator

Water supply windpumps need to be ultra-reliable, to run unattended for most of the time (so they also need automatic devices to prevent overspeeding in storms). They also should require minimum of maintenance and attention, and to be capable of pumping water generally from depths of 10 m to 100 m or more. A typical farm windpump should run for over 20 years with maintenance only once every year, and without any major replacements. This is a very demanding technical requirement, meaning typically that the windpump must average over 80,000 operating hours before anything significant wears out, which is four to ten times the operating life of most small diesel engines, or about 20 times the life of a small petrol engine. Windpumps to this standard therefore are usually industrially manufactured from steel components, and drive piston pumps via reciprocating pump rods. Inevitably they are quite expensive in relation to their power output, because of their robust construction. But American, Australian and Argentine ranchers have found the price worth paying for windpumps that run and run without demanding much attention to the extent they can almost be forgotten about for weeks at a time. This inherent reliability for long periods is their main advantage over practically any other form of pumping system.

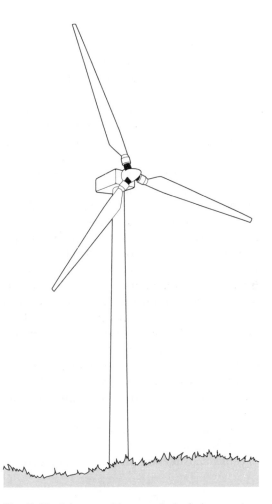

Fig. 7.41: A large, grid-connected wind generator

Irrigation duties on the other hand are seasonal (so the windmill may only be useful for a limited fraction of the year), they involve pumping much larger volumes of water through a low head, and the intrinsic value of the water is low compared with drinking water. Therefore, any windpump developed for irrigation has to be as cheap as possible and this requirement tends to override most other considerations. Since irrigation generally involves the farmer and/or other workers being present, it is not so critical to have a machine capable of running unattended. Therefore, windmills used for irrigation in the past tend to be indigenous designs that are often improvized or built by the farmer as a method of low-cost mechanization (e.g. Fig. 7.37, Fig. 7.38, and Fig. 7.39).

If standard farm water-supply windpumps (Fig. 7.35) are used for irrigation, usually at much lower heads than are normal for water supply duties, there are difficulties in providing a piston pump of sufficient diameter to give an adequate swept volume to absorb the power from the windmill. Also most farm windpumps have to be located directly over the pump, on reinforced concrete foundations, which usually limits these machines to pumping from wells or boreholes rather than from open water. A suction pump can be used on farm windmills with suction heads of up to about 5–6 m from surface water (see Fig. 7.42 for typical farm windpump installation configurations). Most indigenous irrigation windpumps, on the other hand, such as those in China, use rotary pumps of one kind or another which are more suitable for low heads; they also do not experience such high mechanical forces as an industrial windpump (many of which lift their pump rods with a pull of over 1 tonne, quite enough to 'uproot' any carelessly installed pump).

Most farm-windpumps, even though still in commercial production, date back to the 1920s or earlier and are therefore heavy and expensive to manufacture, and difficult to install properly in remote areas. Recently, various efforts have been made to revise the traditional farm windpump concept into a lighter and simpler modern form. Figure 7.43 shows the 'IT Windpump', which is half the weight of most traditional farm windpump designs of a similar size, and is manufactured in Kenya as the 'Kijito' in Pakistan as the 'Tawana' and in Zimbabwe as the 'IT Windpump'. Modern designs like this are fabricated from standard steel stock by small engineering companies and cost only about half as much as traditional American or Australian machines of similar capability. It is possible therefore that through developments of this kind, costs might be kept low enough to allow the marketing of all-steel windpumps that are both durable like the traditional designs, yet cheap enough to be economic for irrigation.

7.7.2 The wind resource

Power in the wind
Wind is moving air, and its power comes from the energy of motion, or kinetic energy, of the air mass. A windmill removes power from the wind by slowing it down. Any windmill rotor will have a certain area facing the wind, and the

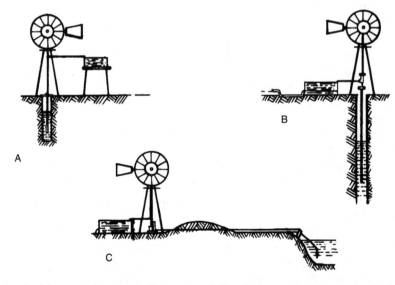

Fig. 7.42: Typical farm windpump configurations: A. Borehole to raised storage tank; B. Well to surface storage tank; C. Surface suction pump

Fig. 7.43: The IT Windpump, made in Kenya as the 'Kijito' and in Pakistan as the 'Tawana'

maximum possible wind energy available to it is given by the kinetic energy that passes through that area. The total power available is the energy that passes through per second. This is expressed mathematically as:

$$P = \frac{1}{2}\rho \cdot A \cdot V^3$$

P   –   power available in the wind (W)
ρ   –   density of air (kg/m³)
A   –   cross-section, or swept area of a windmill rotor (m²)
V   –   instantaneous free-stream wind velocity (m/s)

Note that the power is proportional to the wind speed cubed. A rotor cannot remove all this power from the wind, because it cannot stop the air completely. (If it did, the air behind the rotor would be stationary, and no more could pass through!) It can be shown that the maximum amount of power that can be withdrawn is about 60% of the total wind energy, which happens when the wind is slowed to one third of its upstream speed.

The density of air is approximately 1.2 kg/m³ at sea level, so putting this figure into the equation above the power in the wind at sea level is:

$$P = 0.6 \cdot A \cdot V^3$$

P   –   power in the wind at sea level (W)
Because of this cubic relationship, the power availability is extremely sensitive to wind speed; doubling the wind speed increases the power availability by a factor of eight, as shown in Table 7.14.

This indicates the very high variability of wind power, from around 10 W/m² in a light breeze up to 41,000 W/m² in a hurricane blowing at 144 km/h. This extreme variability greatly influences virtually all aspects of system design. It makes it impossible to consider trying to use winds of less than about 2 m/s, since the power available is too diffuse, while it becomes essential to shed power and even shut a windmill down if the wind speed exceeds about 10–15 m/s (25–30 mph or 40–50 km/h) as excessive power then becomes available which would damage the average windmill if it operated under such conditions.

The power in the wind is a function of the air-density, so it declines with altitude as the air thins, as indicated in Table 7.15.

Table 7.14: Power in the wind as a function of wind speed in units of power per unit area of wind stream

Wind speed	(m/s)	2.5	5	7.5	10	15	20	30	40
	(km/h)	9	18	27	36	54	72	108	144
	(mph)	6	11	17	22	34	45	67	90
Power density	(kW/m²)	0.01	0.08	0.27	0.64	2.2	5.1	17	41

Table 7.15: Variation of air density with altitude

Altitude above sea level	(ft)	0	2,500	5,000	7,500	10,000
	(m)	0	760	1,520	2,290	3,050
Density correction factor	n	1.00	0.91	0.83	0.76	0.69

Because the power in the wind is so much more sensitive to velocity rather than to air density, the effect of altitude is relatively small. For example the power density of a 5 m/s wind at sea level is about 75 watts/m^2; however, due to the cube law, it only needs a wind speed of 5.64 m/s at 3,000 m a.s.l. to obtain exactly the same power of 75 W/m^2. Therefore, the drop in density can be compensated for by quite a marginal increase in wind velocity at high altitudes.

Areas suitable for windpumps

Windpumps need a minimum amount of wind before they will start to work. There is obviously a certain amount of friction and inertia to overcome before any windpump can turn, but the minimum working windspeed is mainly set by the relationship between the sizes of the pump and the rotor. A big rotor powering a small pump would start turning in very light winds, but would go too fast as soon as the wind picked up, and it would need to be furled or stopped in any reasonable wind to stop it breaking. In order to utilize the stronger winds, there is a trade-off which means that the windpump does not work in light winds. This is discussed in more detail in the subsection 'Matching rotors to pumps'. Most windpumps will not start at wind speeds much below 3 m/s, and they will furl between 12 and 15 m/s.

The wind can be extremely variable; some days will have storms, some days will be completely calm. However, though the wind is unpredictable on a minute-by-minute or an hour-by-hour basis, the average windspeed at a given location over any given month of the year will not differ much from one year to the next. So, if mean monthly windspeed figures are available, taken over a number of years, a reasonable prediction of the performance of a windpump should be possible.

If an economic analysis is done, it can be shown that windpumps typically require an average 'least windy month' windspeed of about 2 to 2.5 m/s to begin to be competitive. Because of the cube relationship between windspeed and energy availability, the economics of windpumps are very sensitive to windspeed. Table 7.16 gives general guidelines as to when windpumps are the best options from another reference.

If the mean wind speeds at a site exceed about 4 m/s, then windpumps are one of the most cost-effective pumping options (compared with engines or any other prime movers), but they are not at all cost-competitive where mean windspeeds are below 2 m/s.

A first step, then, in deciding whether windpumps are likely to be useful is to look at the mean wind speed for the location. Figure 7.44 gives an approximate indication of the world's windspeed distribution pattern. Any attempt to present information for the whole world obviously neglects local terrain differences, but it can be seen that much of the world, with the exception of the centres of the major land-masses, and the equatorial forested regions, is suitable for deploying windpumps. As a rule of thumb, areas that are free of trees (e.g. coastal areas, savannah grasslands, semi-deserts and deserts) tend to be

Table 7.16: Economic viability of windpumps compared with other water lifting techniques for various average wind speeds during the critical months when water is required [19]

Average monthly windspeed (m/s)	Economic viability of windpumps
<2	Generally not viable
2–3.5	Possible, depending on local costs
>3.5	Generally good
>5	Usually the best option

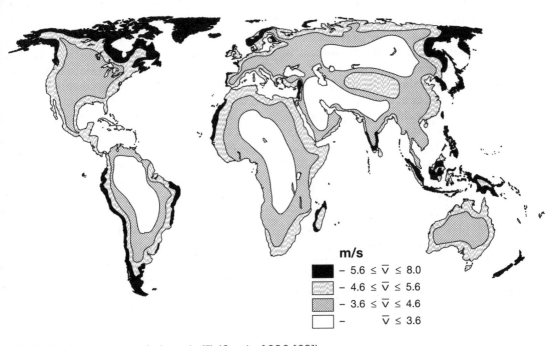

Fig. 7.44: Annual mean windspeeds ($\bar{v}$) (Gasch, 1996 [62])

windy and suitable for windpumps, while forested and wooded areas not only have less wind but trees make siting of windmills difficult unless very high towers can be used.

Various studies on the potential market for windmills in different parts of the world, plus numerous country-specific studies of meteorological data, suggest that quite a number of developing countries have areas with adequate wind speeds for the use of windpumps. Some of these are listed in Table 7.17.

There are also many small islands which are not listed but which invariably have adequate wind regimes due to the proximity of the open ocean. Indeed most coastal locations have adequate sea breezes for windpump operation.

Wind measurements and wind records
If windpumps are already in use in a particular area, then the sizing of another one is best done by looking at the experience of existing users. If a nearby site looks better or worse in terms of exposure to the wind, then some suitable allowances can be estimated to compensate, without too much risk of serious misjudgement. Usually, in such situations where windpumps are

Table 7.17: Developing countries with area with potential for windpumps. The first column shows countries that have moderately widespread use of windpumps already [61]

Argentina	Algeria	Lebanon	Peru
Cape Verde Islands	Brazil	Libya	Somalia
China	Chad	Madagascar	Sri Lanka
Cyprus	Chile	Mali	Sudan
Kenya	Columbia	Malta	Syria
Morocco	Djibouti	Mauritania	Tanzania
Namibia	Ecuador	Mauritius	Tunisia
Senegal	Egypt	Mexico	Turkey
South Africa	Ethiopia	Mongolia	Uruguay
Thailand	Haiti	Mozambique	Yemen
Tunisia	India	Niger	Zambia
Zimbabwe	Jordan	Oman	
	Korea, N and S	Pakistan	

reasonably common, the suppliers will be able to recommend a suitable size to suit the duty requirement on the basis of past experience.

It is less easy to pioneer the use of windpumps in any particular area; in such situations, it is necessary to obtain some estimate of the local wind regime. A check should be made to find the nearest meteorological station, which may be a weather station, an airport, a seaport, a university, or a research station. Unfortunately, most small rural meteorological stations were not set up primarily to log wind data, and more often than not they have incorrectly sited anemometers. Often the anemometers are on 2 m tall masts and are surrounded by trees or buildings. Any readings from such a site are almost useless for wind energy prediction purposes yet, unfortunately, they are often logged, and incorporated in the national data-base, where they distort the apparent wind regime so far as its value for wind power is concerned.

Therefore, when using data from a local rural meteorological station, it is strongly recommended that a visit should be made to the station to check whether the data were measured in an acceptable manner to make them of value. Data from international airports (or from major meteorological stations) are usually reliable, as the anemometers are normally located at the World Meteorological Organisation (WMO) recommended height of 10 m, and they will be unobstructed. This is especially true at airports where wind behaviour is of considerable interest from the point of view of aircraft safety. Most such stations log wind speed and direction data continuously on either paper charts or on magnetic tape. If reliable data is available, some allowance will need to be made for the exposure of the proposed windpump site relative to the meteorological station.

If there is no local data, there may be some for the wider area. With the upsurge of interest in the use of wind for generating electricity, some organizations do produce detailed maps specifically showing average wind power figures. One such map is shown in Fig. 7.45, showing annual mean power 50 m above the ground (somewhat higher than most windpumps). Note that local variations in terrain may give rise to actual power figures 50–100% different from those shown on this large-scale map. Similar maps may be available for areas within countries, with other maps showing monthly averages. Where such data are available, it provides an easy means of estimating the wind water-pumping potential; unfortunately, such mapping tends only to cover more developed countries. These maps are derived from windspeed data, processed to predict the power density.

The most basic format for national wind statistics is as in Table 7.18 which shows average wind speeds collected over a number of years, for each month, for a selection of meteorological stations in India. The Indian irrigation season typically occurs in the dry period from January to May, so by inspection it is possible to identify places with seemingly adequate wind regimes during this period; i.e. with monthly means preferably exceeding 2.5–3 m/s.

If wind records are not available from a sufficiently close or representative existing meteorological station, then it is necessary to set up an anemometer and log wind records for at least one year and preferably two to three years. Obviously, this is not a recommendation so much for the small farmer wanting one small windpump, but rather for institutional users contemplating a large investment in wind power, which needs to be soundly based on objective wind records. Ideally, about three years of records are required to obtain reasonably representative averages, as mean monthly wind speeds can vary by 10–20% or so from one year to the next. The need for this is of course greater in areas which are thought to be 'marginal' for the use of windpumps. Therefore, in places which are decidedly windy; i.e. with mean wind speeds almost certainly in excess of 4 m/s, there is no great risk in guessing the mean wind speed when ordering a windpump, and it probably is not worth the trouble and cost of carrying out long-term wind measurements in advance. It is possible to 'fine tune' the original guess, if it turns out not to be sufficiently accurate, simply by changing the stroke or the pump size. Subsequent windmills can be ordered on the basis of

222

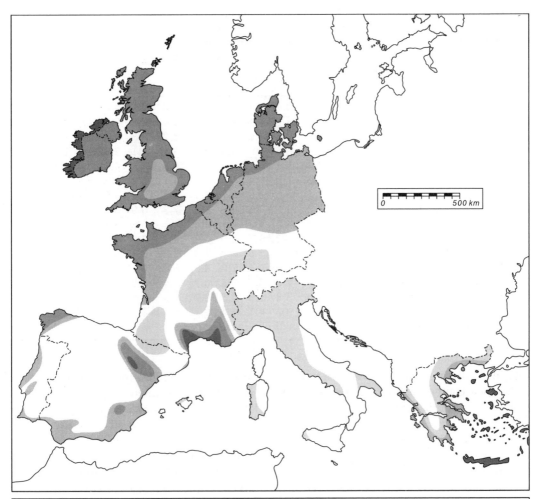

Wind resources[1] at 50 metres above ground level for five different topographic conditions

	Sheltered terrain[2] ms⁻¹	Wm⁻²	Open plain[3] ms⁻¹	Wm⁻²	At a sea coast[4] ms⁻¹	Wm⁻²	Open sea[5] ms⁻¹	Wm⁻²	Open sea[5] ms⁻¹	Wm⁻²
	> 6.0	> 250	> 7.5	> 500	> 8.5	> 700	> 9.0	> 800	> 11.5	> 1800
	5.0-6.0	150-250	6.5-7.5	300-500	7.0-8.5	400-700	8.0-9.0	600-800	10.0-11.5	1200-1800
	4.5-5.0	100-150	5.5-6.5	200-300	6.0-7.0	250-400	7.0-8.0	400-600	8.5-10.0	700-1200
	3.5-4.5	50-100	4.5-5.5	1000-200	5.0-6.0	150-250	5.5-7.0	200-400	7.0-8.5	400-700
	< 3.5	< 50	< 4.5	< 100	< 4.5	< 150	< 5.5	< 200	< 7.0	< 400

1. The resources refer to the power present in the wind. A wind turbine can utilize between 20 and 30% of the available resource. The resources are calculated for an air density of 1.23 kg m⁻³, corresponding to standard sea level pressure and a temperature of 15°C. Air density decreases with height but up to 1000 m a.s.l. the resulting reduction of the power densities is less than 10%.
2. Urban districts, forest and farm land with many windbreaks (roughness class 3).
3. Open landscapes with few windbreaks (roughness class 1). In general, the most favourable inland sites on level land are found here.
4. The classes pertain to a straight coastline, a uniform wind rose and a land surface with few windbreaks (roughness class 1). Resources will be higher, and closer to open sea values, if winds from the sea occur more frequently, i.e. the wind rose is not uniform and/or the land protrudes into the sea. Conversely, resources will generally be smaller, and closer to land values, if winds from land occur more frequently.
5. More than 10 km offshore (roughness class 0).
6. The classes correspond to 50% overspeeding and were calculated for a site on the summit of a single axisymmetric hill with a height of 400 metres and a base diameter of 4 km. The overspeeding depends on the height, length and specific setting of the hill.

Fig. 7.45: Average wind power map for Europe (Troen and Lundtang Peterson, 1989 [63])

Table 7.18: Average windspeed tables for various locations in India, showing a typical presentation of long-term (30 year) wind data as monthly and yearly averages (NAL, 1978 [64])

Location			Average wind speed (m/s)												
			Jan	Feb	Mar	Apr	May	Jun	Jul	Aug	Sep	Oct	Nov	Dec	Year
28°37'N	77°13'E	New Delhi	2.2	2.8	3.1	3.1	3.6	4.2	2.8	2.5	2.8	1.7	1.9	2.2	2.7
29°27'N	79°41'E	Mukteshwar	3.1	3.4	3.6	4.1	4.6	4.3	3.4	2.8	2.8	2.8	2.9	2.9	3.4
22°30'N	88°20'E	Kolkata	1.1	1.4	2.3	3.6	4.5	3.4	3.2	2.8	2.3	1.4	1.1	1.0	2.4
24°48'N	85°00'E	Gaya	1.7	1.9	2.5	2.8	3.3	3.3	3.1	3.1	2.5	1.7	1.4	1.4	2.4
19°49'N	85°54'E	Puri	3.3	4.4	5.7	6.7	7.3	6.5	6.5	5.5	4.4	3.4	2.8	2.9	4.9
19°20'N	85°00'E	Gopalpur	2.8	3.6	5.0	6.4	6.9	4.7	4.7	4.2	3.3	3.1	3.1	2.8	4.2
27°06'N	72°22'E	Phaloch	2.8	2.4	3.6	3.9	5.7	7.1	6.6	5.4	4.6	3.2	3.3	2.3	4.2
22°42'N	75°54'E	Indore	2.8	3.0	3.6	4.3	6.8	7.5	7.3	6.0	5.1	2.7	2.1	2.0	4.4
17°45'N	73°07'E	Harnai	3.9	3.9	4.2	4.7	4.7	4.4	6.1	5.8	3.6	2.8	3.1	3.1	4.2
16°24'N	73°25'E	Devgarh	3.6	3.9	4.2	4.7	5.0	5.8	8.1	7.2	4.2	3.1	3.1	3.1	4.7
22°18'N	70°53'E	Rajkot	3.6	3.9	5.3	5.6	7.2	7.8	7.8	6.4	4.7	3.3	3.1	3.1	5.1
22°48'N	74°18'E	Dohad	3.5	2.8	3.6	4.7	7.2	8.3	8.1	6.1	3.1	2.5	1.9	1.9	4.4
17°22'N	78°26'E	Hyderabad	3.2	2.5	2.8	3.1	3.3	6.7	6.1	5.0	3.6	2.5	2.2	1.9	3.5
15°54'N	74°36'E	Belgaum	3.1	3.3	3.3	3.9	5.3	6.7	7.2	6.4	5.7	2.8	3.1	3.3	4.4
11°00'N	76°54'E	Coimbatore	2.9	3.0	3.3	4.1	6.4	9.1	8.6	8.6	5.6	4.5	2.6	2.8	5.1
10°50'N	78°43'E	Tiruchirapalli	2.8	2.2	2.5	2.8	4.7	8.1	9.7	7.2	5.3	3.1	2.5	3.1	4.5

experience with the first one. However, if it turns out that there is just not enough wind, no amount of tampering with the stroke or pump sizes will adequately correct that misjudgement.

The most simple method of measuring mean wind speeds is to install a cup-counter anemometer which simply sums the kilometres (or miles) of wind run just as a car odometer sums kilometres of road run. By noting the time when each reading is taken, and dividing the difference between two readings by the time interval, it is possible to determine the mean wind speeds over the time period. A mechanical cup-counter anemometer of meteorological office quality costs around US $300 (without a mast – the mast can be improvized with 2" water pipe and guy wires). Ideally, such instruments should be read three times per 24 hours, in the early morning, at mid-day and in the evening to allow the diurnal pattern of wind to be recorded. This allows the mean wind speeds for the mornings, afternoons and night periods to be separated. Failing this, an early morning and an evening reading should be taken each day to allow day and night averages to be calculated. Once-a-day or once-a-week readings, providing they are consistently and accurately logged, are however a lot better than nothing, although they will not show diurnal patterns at all.

The effort involved in analyzing raw, continuously recorded data is formidable, so with the recent upsurge of interest in windpower, numerous electronic data loggers have come onto the market which can record wind data in a form that is convenient for 'wind energy prospectors'. A commonly used approach is to log the frequency with which the wind speed is measured to be blowing within a series of pre-defined speed 'bins', such as 0–5 km/h, 5–10 km/h, 10–15 km/h, and so on. If more accurate results are wanted, then narrower bins may be defined to improve the resolution, but this of course requires a more sophisticated logger or more analytical work afterwards. Some dedicated loggers will give average power readings too.

The most useful starting point for any sophisticated attempt to predict the performance of a windpump in a given wind regime is to create or obtain a velocity-frequency histogram which shows the percentage of the time that the wind blows at different speeds (as in Fig. 7.46). This has been constructed from hourly wind data by adding up how many hours in the month, on average, the wind was recorded as having been blowing at a velocity within each pre-defined 'bin'; for example, in Fig. 7.46, the bins are at 1 m/s intervals, and there were about 6 hourly records of 1 m/s wind, 35 hourly records of 2 m/s, and so on. Clearly an electronic data-logger that automatically measures and records the frequency of wind speeds in predetermined bins makes this task much easier.

It is also quite common to present wind data as a velocity-frequency curve. These are in effect fine resolution velocity-frequency histograms. The wind regime of a given site is characterized by the velocity-frequency curve which will have a similar shape every year and will not vary very much from one year to the next. Velocity frequency curves can be synthesized by a sophisticated mathematical process using what is known as a Weibull Probability Distribution Function, which, providing certain parameters are correctly selected, will produce a passable correlation with natural empirically-measured wind regime curves; the analysis required is beyond the scope

of this book and is dealt with in the European Wind Atlas [63], and other references.

The best information that is ever usually available is an hour-by-hour wind frequency distribution curve for the site. Ideally, this will have been analyzed to give monthly average wind power, or at least monthly mean wind speeds and the percentage of calm per month. For irrigation pumping, it is of critical importance to consider the wind regime during the month of maximum water demand; annual averages are not good enough for this.

The relationship between average wind speed and wind energy
Windpumps are for pumping water, and so the output we are interested in is the quantity of water pumped in a given period. This is directly related to the energy put into the windpump, which in turn is related to the energy in the wind during that period. If the total amount of wind energy that passes through the rotor area in the period is known, then it should be possible to predict the water output. An average wind power map such as Fig. 7.45 would give an indication of this. In most cases, wind power is not

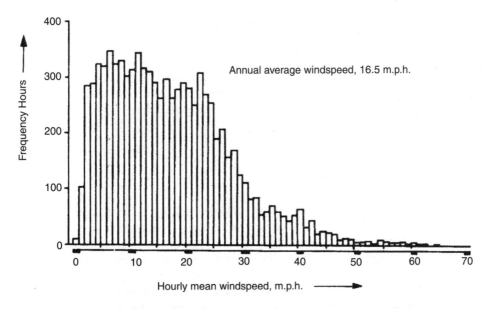

Fig. 7.46: A wind velocity-frequency histogram [60]

225

measured, and the only figures to hand are average wind speeds. Average wind speeds are obviously related to the total wind energy, and it looks as if it should be possible to predict wind energy from average speed. Unfortunately, the subject is more complicated than it might at first appear.

Imagine two identical windmills situated at two different sites operating for one month. It is quite possible for the average windspeed to be the same at both sites, and yet for the energy output of the two windmills to be quite different. The reason for this is that the power depends on the cube of the windspeed. One site might have had nearly constant wind all month. The other might have achieved the same average speed by having half the month calm and half the month blowing a gale. The power output during the half month of strong winds will be much more than the output of a full month of moderate winds. It is important to appreciate that the actual energy available in the wind over a month is always considerably *more* than the power you would calculate by assuming the wind blew at the average speed for the whole month.

In order to find the energy available at a potential windpump site, you need to know more than just the average windspeed. This is one reason why wind measurements are done at short intervals. Even then, converting wind speed measurements to available power is a complex subject, because it depends on the variability and the frequency of the sampling (this is dealt with more fully in Lysen, 1983 [65]). Fortunately, some generalizations can be made. Suppose the monthly energy is estimated by multiplying the power of the average monthly wind speed by one month. Typically, the actual power available will be double this estimate. The actual factor by which the average power exceeds the instantaneous power corresponding to the mean windspeed can vary from around 1.5 to 3 and depends on the local wind regime's actual variability pattern. The greater the variability the greater this factor.

In summary, then, for any specific wind regime, the energy available will be in some proportion to the mean wind speed cubed, even if the actual proportion differs depending on the location. We shall discuss later in this section how to determine the useful energy that can be obtained from a wind regime with respect to a particular windmill.

Variation of wind speed with height
The speed of the wind increases with height. The rate of increase is dependent partly on the height and partly on the nature of the ground surface. This is because rough ground, with many uneven trees, bushes or buildings, causes turbulence, while a flat and obstructed surface like a lake, the sea or a flat grassy plain allows the air to flow smoothly which results in higher windspeeds nearer to the surface. The relationship between windspeed and height can be estimated as follows:

$$\frac{V}{V_r} = \left(\frac{H}{H_r}\right)^a$$

where V is the wind velocity at height H and V_r is a reference wind velocity measured at height H_r. The exponent 'a' is a function of the surface roughness, as given in Table 7.19 (Lipman et al., 1982 [66]).

For example, if there is high grass and small bushes, and a mean reference windspeed of 5 m/s recorded at the standard meteorological office recommended height of 10 m, this can be adjusted to obtain the mean windspeed at $H = 20$ m windmill hub height as follows:

$$\frac{V}{5} = \left(\frac{H}{10}\right)^{0.19}$$

from which $V = 5.7$ m/s. A gain of 0.7 m/s from mounting a windmill at 20 m rather than at 10 m may sound small in relation to the cost of the extra high tower required, but it should be noted again that the energy available at those two heights will be related to the *cube* of the velocities (assuming optimally matched pumps in each case) and will therefore be:

Table 7.19: Values of height factor 'a' for different terrain

Type of terrain	a
smooth water or flat sand	0.10
low grass steppe	0.13
high grass and small bushes	0.19
woodlands and urban areas	0.32

$$\left(\frac{5.7}{5.0}\right)^3 = 1.48$$

This shows that a 48% increase in energy availability can be gained in terrain of that type from using a 20 m tower instead of a 10 m tower (or a windmill with a smaller rotor could be used to gain the same energy – in this case the rotor area could be reduced so that a windmill with 20% smaller rotor diameter on a 20 m tower would be used compared with one on a 10 m tower). The effect is illustrated in Fig. 7.47.

The effect of obstructions

Any obstruction to the wind has a wake downwind of it, which may extend for up to 20 or 30 times its height. The wake is depleted of wind energy compared with the surrounding wind, and is turbulent. For example a large mango tree (or a similar rounded, well-leafed tall tree) can have a wake which even 200–300 m downwind has 10% less wind energy than either side of it. Sharp edged and irregular obstructions such as rock outcrops, cliffs and escarpments, or large buildings can cause more violent turbulence that, apart from depleting the energy available, can cause damage to a windmill located nearby. Obstacles also cause turbulence up-wind of themselves, for a distance of between two and five times their height. This means a windpump must not be place too close to trees or buildings that are down-wind of it.

It is normal to recommend that windmills are mounted so that the rotor is at least 200–300 m from any significant obstruction to the wind. Ideally, if obstructions like trees or buildings are nearby, the rotor should be mounted on a high enough tower so its bottom edge is a clear 5 m or more above the highest point of the obstruction. In reality, it is often impossible to avoid obstructions, so the least that can be done is to try and locate the windmill so that it is unobstructed from the direction of the prevailing wind.

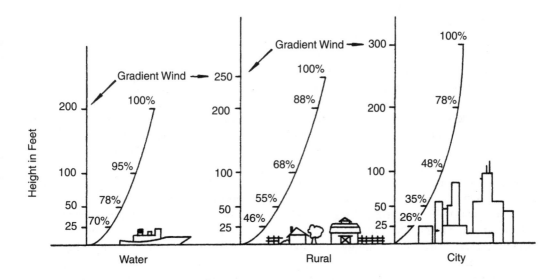

Fig. 7.47: The variation of windspeed with height over various terrains [61]

227

Because the wind lifts to go over an obstruction, siting windmills with large obstructions nearer than 100–200 m downwind should also be avoided.

One special form of obstruction is a hill. It is well known that the wind is stronger at the top of a hill than on a plain, and in fact the wind speed on an isolated hill can be considerably more than on surrounding flat land. There will also be a dead area for wind in front of the hill, and a turbulent area behind it. Since water is rarely found on hill tops it is hard to make use of the increased windspeed there, but windpumps should not be sited directly at the foot of a hill, either upwind or downwind.

7.7.3 Principles of wind energy conversion

Converting wind power to shaft power
There are two main mechanisms for converting the kinetic energy of the wind into mechanical work; both depend on slowing the wind and thereby extracting kinetic energy. The crudest, and least efficient, technique is to use drag. Drag is developed simply by obstructing the wind and creating turbulence, and the drag force acts in the same direction as the wind. Some of the earliest and crudest types of wind machine, known generically as 'panamones', depend on exposing a flat area on one side of a rotor to the wind while shielding (or turning the sails) on the other side; the resulting differential drag force turns the rotor.

The other method, used for all the more efficient types of windmill, is to produce lift. Lift is produced when a sail or a flat surface is mounted at a small angle to the wind; this slightly deflects the wind and produces a large force perpendicular to the direction of the wind with a much smaller drag force. It is this principle by which a sailing ship can tack into the wind, or sail at speeds greater than the wind. Lift mainly deflects the wind, extracting the energy without causing much turbulence, making it a more efficient method of extracting energy from the wind than drag.

It has been noted above that the theoretical maximum fraction of the kinetic energy in the wind that could be utilized by a 'perfect' wind turbine is approximately 60%. This occurs when the wind is slowed to one-third of its initial speed by the rotor. Any attempt to slow the air more means it cannot leave the rotor quick enough, and the incoming air is increasingly deflected away round the sides instead of passing through the blades. In reality, the efficiency achieved by the best wind rotors is only around 50%.

Horizontal and vertical-axis rotors
Windmills rotate about either a vertical or a horizontal axis. All the windmills illustrated so far, and most in practical use today, are horizontal axis, but some vertical axis machines exist. These have the advantage that they do not need to be orientated to face the wind, since they present the same cross-section to the wind from any direction; however, this is also a disadvantage as under storm conditions you cannot turn a vertical axis rotor away from the wind to reduce the wind loadings on it.

There are three main types of vertical axis windmill. Panamone differential drag devices (mentioned earlier), the Savonius rotor or 'S' rotor (Fig. 7.48) and the Darrieus wind turbine (Fig. 7.49). The Savonius rotor consists of two or sometimes three curved interlocking plates grouped around a central shaft between two end caps; it works by a mixture of differential drag and lift. The Savonius rotor has been promoted as a device that can be readily improvised on a self-build basis, but its apparent simplicity is more perceived than real as there are serious problems in mounting the inevitably heavy rotor securely in bearings, and in coupling its vertical drive shaft to a positive displacement pump (it turns too slowly to be useful for a centrifugal pump). However, the main disadvantages of the Savonius rotor are two-fold:

- It is inefficient, and involves a lot of construction material relative to its size, so it is less cost-effective as a rotor than most other types;
- It is difficult to protect it from over-speeding in a storm and consequently flying to pieces.

The Darrieus wind turbine has airfoil cross-section blades (streamlined lifting surfaces like the wings of an aircraft). These could be straight,

Plan of three and two bladed
Savonius rotors

Fig. 7.48: A Savonius rotor vertical-axis windpump in Ethiopia. It was found to be less cost-effective than the Cretan windpump of Fig. 7.39 [39]

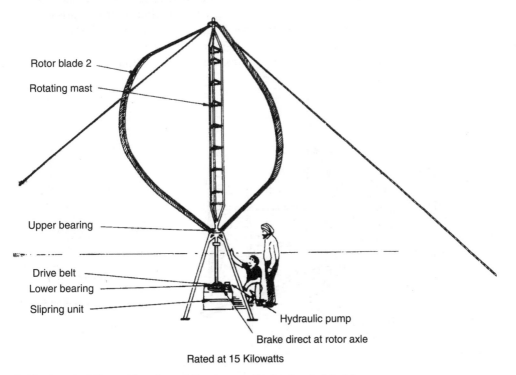

Rotor blade 2

Rotating mast

Upper bearing

Drive belt

Lower bearing

Slipring unit

Hydraulic pump

Brake direct at rotor axle

Rated at 15 Kilowatts

Fig. 7.49: A typical Troposkien-shaped Darrieus vertical-axis wind turbine

giving the machine an 'H'-shaped profile but, in practice, most machines have the curved 'egg-beater' or Troposkien profile as illustrated. The main reason for this shape is because the centrifugal force caused by rotation would tend to bend straight blades, but the skipping rope or Troposkien shape taken up by the curved blades can resist the bending forces effectively. Darrieus-type vertical axis turbines are quite efficient, since they depend purely on lift forces produced as the blades cross the wind (they travel at 3 to 5 times the speed of the wind, so that the wind meets the blade at a shallow enough angle to produce lift rather than drag). The Darrieus turbine was predated by a much cruder vertical axis windmill with Bermuda (triangular) rig sails from the Turks and Caicos Islands of the West Indies (Fig. 7.50). This helps to show the principle by which the Darrieus works, because it is easy to imagine the sails of a Bermuda rig producing a propelling force as they cut across the wind in the same way as a sailing yacht when tacking; the Darrieus works on exactly the same principle.

Vertical axis windmills are rarely applied for practical purposes, although they are a popular subject for research. The main justification given for developing them is that they have some prospect of being simpler than horizontal axis windmills and therefore they may become more cost-effective. This still remains to be proved.

Most horizontal axis rotors work by lift forces generated when 'propeller' or airscrew like blades are set at such an angle that at their optimum speed of rotation they make a small angle with the wind and generate lift forces in a tangential direction. Because the rotor tips travel faster than the roots, they 'feel' the wind at a shallower angle and therefore an efficient horizontal axis rotor requires the blades to be twisted so that the angle with which they meet the wind is constant from root to tip. The blades or sails of slow speed machines can be quite crude (as in Fig. 7.34) but for higher speed machines they must be accurately shaped airfoils (Fig. 7.40 and Fig. 7.41); but in all three examples illustrated, the principle of operation is identical.

Efficiency, power and torque characteristics
Any wind turbine or windmill rotor can be characterized by plotting experimentally derived curves of power against rotational speed at various windspeeds; Fig. 7.51A. Similarly, the torque produced by a wind rotor is characterized by a set of curves such as in Fig. 7.51B.

The maximum efficiency coincides with the maximum power output in a given windspeed.

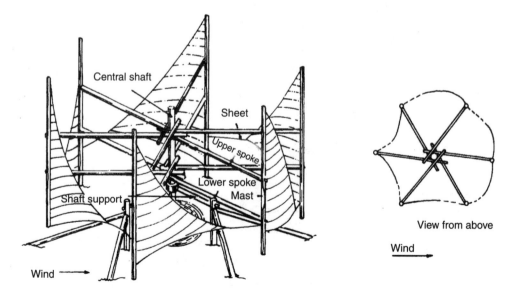

Fig. 7.50: A vertical-axis sail rotor in the Turks and Caicos Islands (UN-ESCAP, 1981 [67])

Efficiency is usually presented as a non-dimensional ratio of shaft-power divided by wind-power passing through a disc or shape having the same area as the vertical profile of the windmill rotor. When expressed as a fraction, rather than a percentage, this ratio is known as the 'Power Coefficient', C_p, and is numerically expressed as:

$$C_p = \frac{P}{\frac{1}{2}\rho \cdot A \cdot V^3}$$

P – rotor power output (W)
ρ – air density (kg/m³)
A – rotor area (m³)
V – wind speed (m/s)

The speed is also conventionally expressed non-dimensionally as the 'tip-speed ratio' (λ). This is the ratio of the speed of the windmill rotor tip to the speed of the wind, and is numerically:

$$\lambda = \frac{\omega \cdot R}{V} = \frac{2\pi N}{60} \cdot \frac{R}{V}$$

R – rotor blade tip radius (m)
ω – rotor rotational speed (rad/s)
N – rotor rotational speed (rpm)

When the windmill rotor is stationary, its tip-speed ratio is also zero, and the rotor is stalled. This occurs when the torque produced by the wind is below the level needed to overcome the resistance of the load. A tip-speed ratio of 1 means the blade tips are moving at the same speed as the wind (so the wind angle 'seen' by the blades will be 45°) and when it is 2, the tips are moving at twice the speed of the wind, and so on.

The torque coefficient, C_t, is a non-dimensional measure of the torque produced by a given size of rotor in a given wind speed (torque is the twisting force produced by the rotor on the drive shaft), and is defined as:

$$C_t = \frac{T}{\frac{1}{2}r \cdot A \cdot V^2}$$

where T is the actual torque at windspeed V for a rotor of that configuration and radius R.

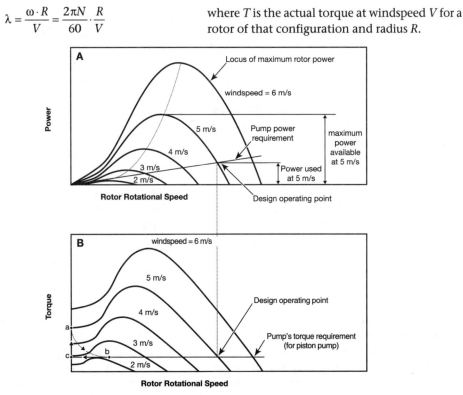

Fig. 7.51: Power and torque curves for different wind speeds as a function of rotational speed

231

The C_p versus λ curves for different types of rotor are shown in Fig. 7.52. The second set of curves show the torque coefficients, C_t.

Rotor solidity
'Solidity' (s) is a term for the proportion of a windmill rotor's swept area that is filled with solid blades. It is generally defined as the ratio of the sum of the width, or 'chords' of all the blades to the circumference of the rotor; i.e. 24 blades with a chord length (leading edge to trailing edge) of 0.3 m on a 6 m diameter rotor would have a tip solidity of

$$\sigma = \frac{no.\ of\ blades \times chord\ length}{rotor\ circumference} = \frac{24 \times 0.3}{\pi \cdot 6}$$

Multi-bladed rotors, as used on windpumps, (e.g. rotor **B** in Fig. 7.52) are said to have high 'solidity', because a large proportion of the rotor swept area is 'solid' with blades. Such machines have to run at relatively low speeds and will therefore have their blades set at quite a coarse angle to the plane of rotation, like a screw with a coarse thread. This gives it a low tip-speed ratio at its maximum efficiency, of around 1.25, and a slightly lower maximum coefficient of performance than the faster types of rotor such as **D**, **E** and **F** in the figure. However, the multi-bladed rotor has a very much higher torque coefficient at zero tip-speed ratio (between 0.5 and 0.6) than any of the other types. Its high starting torque (which is higher than its running torque) combined with its slow speed of rotation in a given wind make it best suited to driving reciprocating borehole pumps.

In contrast, the two or three-bladed, low-solidity, rotors **E** and **F** in Fig. 7.52, are the most efficient, (with the highest values for C_p), but their tips must travel at six to ten times the speed of the wind to achieve their best efficiency. To do so they will be set at a slight angle to the plane of rotation, like a screw with a fine thread and will therefore spin much faster for a given windspeed and rotor diameter than a high solidity rotor. They also have very little starting torque, almost none at all, which means they can only start against loads which require little torque to start them, like electricity generators (or centrifugal pumps) rather than positive displacement pumps.

All this may sound academic, but it is fundamental to the design of wind rotors; it means that multi-bladed 'high-solidity' rotors run at slow speeds and are somewhat less efficient than few-bladed 'low solidity' rotors, but they have typically five to twenty times the starting torque which is an essential requirement to start a piston pump.

Matching rotors to pumps
High solidity rotors are typically used in conjunction with positive displacement (piston) pumps, because, as explained in the 'Forces' subsection of Section 6.5.1, single-acting piston pumps need about three times as much torque to start them as to keep them going. Low solidity rotors, on the other hand, are best for use with electricity generators or centrifugal pumps, or even ladder pumps and chain and washer pumps, where the torque needed by the pump for starting is less than that needed for running at design speed. Table 7.20 indicates the relative characteristics and C_p values for various typical wind rotor types so far described.

Figure 7.51 shows the load lines for a positive displacement direct-driven pump superimposed on wind rotor output curves. A positive displacement pump requires a more-or-less constant torque when running, and so appears as a horizontal line on the torque graph **B**. On the power graph **A** the power required to drive the pump appears as a straight rising line.

The most common sort of pump used in a windpump is a reciprocating piston pump, which, as stated above, has a higher starting torque than running torque. On graph **B**, the pump will only start when the torque reaches the value 'a', and as it subsequently speeds up it will follow the dashed line a-b till it reaches the constant torque line. Note that a-b represents a transient condition that only occurs momentarily when the windpump starts to rotate. Point 'a' corresponds to a windspeed of about 5 m/s, which is the speed required before it starts. Once it is running, the windpump will continue to turn

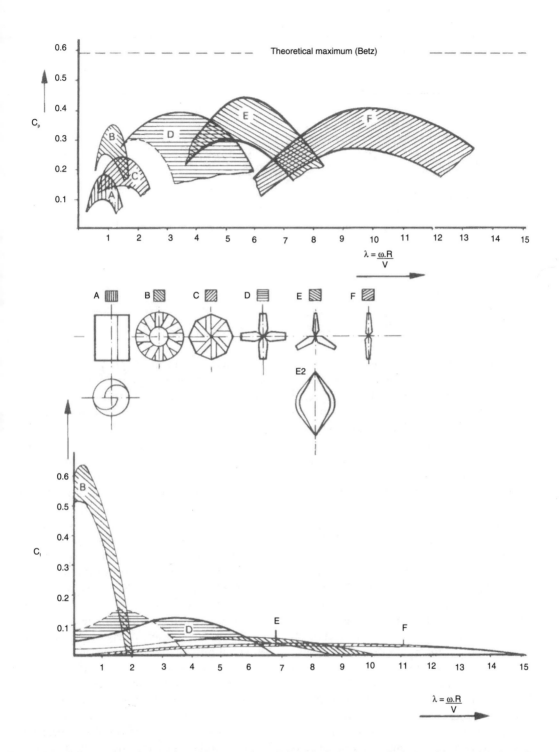

Fig. 7.52: The power and torque coefficients, C_p and C_t of various types of wind turbine rotors plotted against tip speed ratio, λ [65]

Table 7.20: Comparison between different rotor types

Type	Performance characteristics		Manufacturing requirements	Power coeff.	Solidity	Optimum tip-speed ratio
	Starting torque	Speed		C_p	s	λ
Horizontal-axis						
Cretan sail or flat paddles	medium	low	simple	0.05–0.15	50%	1.5–2.0
Cambered plate fan (American farm windpump)	high	low	moderate	0.15–0.30	50–80%	1.0–1.5
Moderate speed aero-generator	low	moderate	moderate, some precision	0.20–0.35	5–10%	3–5
High speed aero-generator	almost zero	high	precise	0.30–0.45	<5%	5–10
Vertical-axis						
Panemone	medium	low	simple	<0.10	50%	0.4–0.8
Savonius	medium	moderate	moderate	0.15	100%	0.8–1.0
Darrieus	small or zero	moderate	precise	0.25–0.35	10–20%	3–5

even if the windspeed drops to just below 3 m/s, represented by point 'c'. (Because the rotor torque is proportional to the square of the windspeed, if the pump starting torque is three times the running torque, the starting windspeed will be $\sqrt{3}$ = 1.73 times the minimum windspeed.) As a rule-of-thumb, windpumps are generally designed to start at around three-quarters of the mean windspeed. For very windy sites, the three-quarters rule may give too high a starting speed, say 6 or 7 m/s, which could lead to the pump being mechanically overloaded, though such sites are rare.

This windpump is nominally designed for a windspeed of 5 m/s, marked as the 'design operating point' on both graphs. It is immediately obvious on graph A that this operating point is well below the maximum power that can be obtained from the rotor in a 5 m/s wind. Consequently, the windpump is only using a fraction of the windpower available in the 5 m/s wind. At first sight this seems like a very bad match of pump and rotor, but it is in fact unavoidable, and a direct consequence of the compromise between starting and running. The only way of using more power at 5 m/s is to use a pump which requires more torque. This increases the

slope of the pump line graph A, but it also moves the horizontal line in graph B upwards. The bigger pump needs a higher windspeed to start, and so will run for less of the time. Pump torque can be increased either by using a larger diameter pump, or by increasing the stroke of the pump (by increasing the radius of the crank driving it). For a given rotor, the choice is between having a windpump that runs even in light winds, but has a modest output, or one that only starts in strong winds but then gives a high output.

The difference between the power available and the power used arises from a mismatch between the prime mover (the windmill rotor) and the load (the pump). The proportion of the power available from the rotor in a given windspeed which is usefully applied is known as the 'matching efficiency'. Figure 7.51 illustrates how this mismatch becomes progressively worse as the wind speed increases. This mismatch is actually less serious than it may seem, since the time when the best efficiency is needed is at low windspeeds when, fortunately, the best efficiency is achieved. When a windmill is running fast enough to be badly matched with its pump, it means that the wind is blowing more strongly than usual and the chances are that the efficiency, although theoretically reduced by bad matching, will be more than adequate, as the extra pumping speed will compensate for the reduction in efficiency.

It might be thought that centrifugal pumps would match better with a windmill than positive displacement pumps, but in practice their efficiency falls rapidly to zero below a certain threshold running speed at a fixed static head. In other words, centrifugal pumps do not readily run with adequate efficiency over as wide a speed range as is necessary to match most windmill rotors and they are therefore not generally used with windmills (except through intermediate electrical transmission which can modify the relationship between the pump and windmill speeds). Some attempts have been made to use progressive cavity or Mono pumps with windmills, but these pumps also have a high starting torque, due to friction.

When generators are used as a load, instead of pumps, a much better match can be obtained. Wind generators therefore tend to have a better matching efficiency over their whole range of operating speeds than windpumps; the interested reader is referred to a text on this subject, such as (Lysen, 1983 [65]).

The operating characteristic of a typical windpump, given in Fig. 7.53, shows how if the start-up windspeed is V_s, a windpump can run down to a slightly lower windspeed V_{min} (as explained earlier, assuming the use of a piston pump). It reaches its best match with the rotor at windspeeds close to V_{min} (in theory at $0.8V_s$ [65])) which is the design windspeed, and then increases its output almost linearly with windspeed to V_r (its rated windspeed). At still higher windspeeds means must be introduced to prevent it running even faster, or the machine may over-speed and be damaged or destroyed; various methods for doing this are discussed in the next section. At very high windspeeds, the only safe course of action is to make the windmill 'reef', 'furl' or 'shut-down'; the figure shows how this process commences at a windspeed V_f (furling speed) and is completed at windspeed V_{sd} (shut-down).

It is the high starting torque of piston pumps that makes high-solidity rotors most suitable for them. High solidity rotors are slow speed, high torque, and can get a reasonable size piston pump started. American farm pumps typically had a solidity of about 80%. A number of recent attempts to make improved windpumps have gone for low solidity rotors because they are lighter, cheaper, and more efficient. Many of these designs have run into problems. They are difficult to match with reasonable pumps because of their lower torque, and they tend to damage themselves by going too fast. It is really the pump that is the starting point of windpump design and the rotor and other components have to be matched to it.

Small rotors go faster than large ones of the same type, but reciprocating pumps can only be worked at quite low speeds. Typically, pumps are worked at 30–50 pumping strokes per minute, and if they exceed about 60 strokes per minute they can end up bending the piston rod (this was discussed in the sub-section 'Mechanically driven borehole pumps'). Even for high-solidity rotors this means that windpumps cannot have the crank mechanism directly on the rotor shaft if the rotor has a diameter of less than about 4.5 m. A means of overcoming this is to use a gearbox, and these were common on farm windpumps (see Fig. 7.36). Gearboxes would normally be enclosed, with an oil bath to lubricate the gears, though open graphite impregnated gears were used on at least one design. When an oil sump is used, the oil needs checking and topping up every few months. The IT Power Small Windpump shown in Fig. 7.54 uses an unusual design of gearbox with a high enough reduction to allow a quite small rotor to be used. This concept dates back to a Canadian double-acting windpump that outperformed all others in tests conducted at trials in 1903, and uses modern materials and components to achieve high performance with little need for maintenance.

Gearboxes can adjust the speed between the rotor and the pump, but they do not help with the mismatch between the starting and running

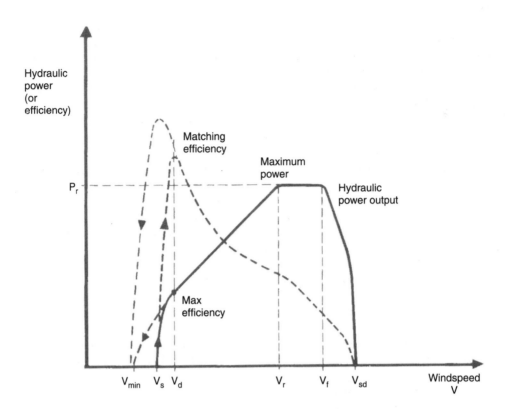

Fig. 7.53: The operating characteristics of a windpump showing how the power output and matching efficiency vary with windspeed. V_{min}: *stopped*; V_s: starting; V_d: *maximum afficiency*; V_r: rated; V_f: *furling*, V_{sd}: shut-down.

requirements. Many attempts have been made to design mechanisms that overcome mismatch, as it is one of the most obvious defects of windpumps. Some of these give some benefits, but every design produced so far has disadvantages as well. One approach is to attempt to fit heavy weights, often made of concrete, on the crank opposite to the pump rod. These counterweights effectively help to start the pump, which can reduce the starting torque to around 1.6 times the average torque, so that the windpump starts at a lower windspeed. Their disadvantage is that they require larger, stronger (and more expensive) rotor shafts and bearings, because they double the inertial load at high speeds. Some direct-drive windpumps achieve the same effect by putting weights in the rotor blades on one side, deliberately making the rotor out-of-balance (which is acceptable if the speed is not allowed to go too high). Other designs replace such counterweights with an arrangement of springs. An alternative approach is to introduce a controlled leak across the piston of the pump by putting a small hole in it that allows the piston to move slowly at a much reduced force, and lets the pump get started. When working, the leakage through the hole is small in comparison with the pumped flow. An improvement on this idea is the 'floating piston', which has a buoyant, floating element in the piston assembly; when the piston movement is slow, this floats up and uncovers a hole in the piston, allowing the piston to rise freely, but as the speed picks up the float is forced down onto the hole, sealing it again. It should be said that none of these modifications to improve starting torque are regularly

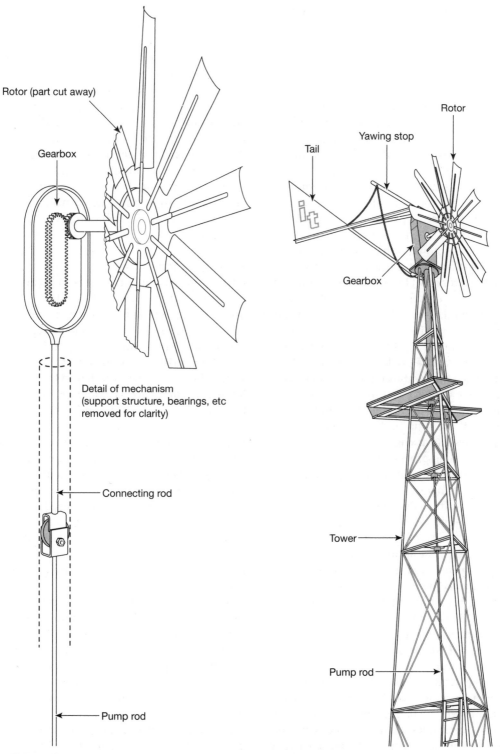

Rotor (part cut away)

Gearbox

Detail of mechanism
(support structure, bearings, etc
removed for clarity)

Connecting rod

Pump rod

Tail

Yawing stop

Rotor

Gearbox

Tower

Pump rod

Fig. 7.54: The IT Power Small Windpump, showing the novel gearbox arrangement

used in practice, as they often cause problems of reliability.

Methods of storm protection and furling

Windmills must have a means to limit the power they can deliver, or else they would have to be built excessively strongly (and expensively) merely to withstand only occasional high power outputs in storms. Sailing ships 'take in canvas' by wholly or partially furling the sails (manually) when the wind is too strong, and Cretan sail windmills and other such simple traditional designs generally use exactly the same technique; fewer sails are used in high winds or else the sails are partially rolled around their spars. Metal farm windmills, however, have fixed steel blades, so the solution most generally adopted is to mount the rotor offset from the tower centre (Fig. 7.55) so that the wind constantly seeks to turn the rotor behind the tower. Under normal conditions the rotor is held into the wind by a long tail with a vane on it. This vane is hinged, and fixed in place with a pre-loaded spring (as illustrated). When the wind-load on the rotor reaches a level where the force is sufficient to overcome the pre-tension in the spring, the tail will start to fold until the wind pushes the rotor around so that it presents its edge to the wind, as in Fig. 7.55. This furling process starts when the rated output is reached and if the windspeed continues to rise, it increases progressively until the machine is fully furled (i.e. rotor completely turned edge-on to the wind). Most windpumps furl in windspeeds from about 8–12 m/s. When the wind drops, the spring causes the tail vane to unfold again and turn the rotor once again to face 'square' to the wind. On commercial farm windmills, this action is normally completely automatic. Other designs have a manual furling mechanism that swings the rotor round in the same way, but which is operated by a chain or cable from the ground.

Wind-generators and other wind turbines with high speed, low-solidity rotors often use a mechanism which changes the blade pitch. An alternative technique used on some wind turbines is for air-brake flaps to be automatically deployed to prevent overspeed.

Larger wind turbines do not use tail vanes to keep them facing the wind, as they cannot stand being yawed as fast as might occur if there is a sudden change in wind direction. Instead they usually have a worm-reduction gear mechanism similar to that in a crane, which inches them round to face the wind; this can be electrically powered on signals from a small wind direction vane, or it can use the mechanism used traditionally on large windmills for several centuries, where a sideways mounted wind rotor only catches the wind and thereby drives the orientating mechanism every time the main rotor is at an angle other than at right angles to the wind direction.

Windpump construction

A windpump that is left in operation year-round will be subject to a very high number of pumping strokes. A typical windpump, turned by the wind on average 15 hours per day, will run for about 55,000 hours in 10 years, and will total about 66 million pumping strokes. Farm windpumps might be expected to have lives 2–3 times this or longer. Windpumps are also subject to violent weather conditions, and frequently to extended periods of neglect. For any piece of machinery to withstand this sort of life it has to be very robust. Bearings, gears, and other wearing parts must be sized to keep the bearing pressures small, and the whole structure needs to be heavily built to resist fatigue failure. A failing of many modern windpump designs is that they are too light, and do not have sufficient safety margins to survive for extended periods; the same problem applies to many homemade windmills.

Windpumps always mount the rotor on the top of a tower. This is most commonly made of steel components bolted together. Wood can be used for smaller pumps, and was used for American farm pumps, though the wood has to be of good quality and well treated for larger windpumps. The strength of a tower is primarily determined by the need to stay standing in a storm, rather than for supporting the rotor when it is working. This is because the wind force is proportional to the square of the windspeed, so

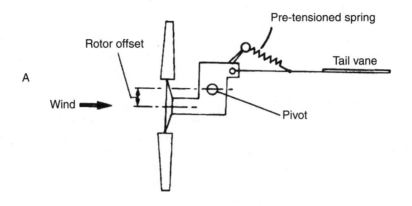

A

Rotor offset

Pre-tensioned spring

Tail vane

Wind ➡

Pivot

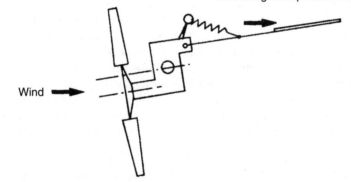

B

Increasing wind pressure on tail

Wind ➡

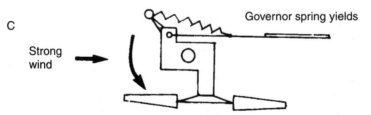

C

Governor spring yields

Strong wind ➡

Rotor swings edge-on to wind until windspeed falls

Fig. 7.55: A typical windpump storm protection method in which the rotor is yawed edge-on to the wind (plan view)

in the very high winds experienced during a storm the force on the tower is very high, even though the rotor mechanism is furled. The weight and design of the rotor actually make little difference to the strength required for the tower.

7.7.4   Windpump performance estimation

General principles
To size a windpump correctly will usually require an estimate to be made of the week-by-week or month-by-month average output requirement. One method for making such an estimate is to combine the performance characteristics of the windpump with hourly average wind-speed data. An example is given in Table 7.21. The inputs are the number of hours that the wind blows within each average speed range (or 'bin', to use the common jargon) from meteorological data, and the manufacturer's figures for windpump output at these windspeeds. The total output for each speed bin is obtained by multiplying the output per hour at that speed and the number of hours at which that speed is likely to occur. By adding together the output for each speed bin we arrive at the total annual output. This example is

for a whole year, but it is also valuable to repeat the calculation for each month. The importance of doing this is that the least windy month can have a mean windspeed of as little as half the annual mean wind speed, so the available wind energy in the least windy month can be less than 20% of what can be expected for a mean windspeed equal to the annual average wind speed. Therefore, if annual averages are used, a considerable margin of safety is necessary to allow for 'least windy month' conditions.

A graphic way of achieving the same result as used in Table 7.21 is illustrated in Fig. 7.56. Here the wind velocity frequency histogram (preferably for a month at a time), A, is multiplied by the windpump performance characteristic, shown in idealized form in B; in this example a windpump is assumed which starts at a nominal 2 m/s, produces 3 kW of output at its rated speed of 5 m/s and is fully furled at 9 m/s. A windpump performance histogram using similar speed 'bins' to diagram A is constructed over the windpump performance characteristic. Finally the wind velocity distribution histogram is multiplied by the windpump's histogram to arrive at a performance prediction histogram, C. To illustrate the mechanics of multiplying two histograms together, the

Table 7.21: An example of calculation of annual windpump output in a table, for a particular windpump and site. This combines the wind regime for the site, recorded as the number of hours of each particular band or 'bin' of windspeeds in the year, and the windpump manufacturer's output figures for each band

Wind speed (m/s)		Annual duration (h)	Output rate (m³/h)	Total output (m³)
over	to			
0	3.15	600	0.3	180
3.15	3.60	500	1.4	700
3.60	4.05	500	2.3	1,150
4.05	4.50	400	3.0	1,200
4.50	4.95	500	3.7	1,850
4.95	5.40	450	4.2	1,890
5.40	5.85	450	4.7	2,115
5.85	6.30	450	5.2	1,560
6.30	6.75	300	5.7	1,710
6.75	–	300	6.0	10,200
Annual Totals:		1,700		22,555

first speed bin in **A** is 200 h, the first in **B** is zero kW, so their product in **C** is zero kWh; the second is 600 × 0 = 0, the third is 750 hours × 0.5 kW = 375 kWh, the fourth 800 h × 1.5 kW = 1200 kWh, and so on.

Simple 'rule-of-thumb' approach

The problem with the above methods is that the result is only as good as the wind and performance data used, which all too often are unreliable. Therefore, if only approximate data are available, it becomes pointless subjecting such vague data to a precise and time-consuming analysis. Hence a simpler rule of thumb may be more appropriately used, (and is often useful anyway as a cross check on other methods). This method was originally proposed by (Lysen, 1983 [65]), and provides a reasonable method of estimation.

The rule of thumb assumes that a windpump system will, on average, be 17% efficient in converting wind energy into hydraulic output, which in many cases is probably not a bad estimate (the losses in a windpump system and the total efficiency that can be expected are discussed in more detail in the sub-section 'Overall system efficiency' below). The average hydraulic output power for a windpump of about 17% average efficiency will be:

$$P = \eta \cdot \frac{1}{2} \rho \cdot A \cdot V^3 = 0.17 \times \frac{1}{2} \rho \cdot V^3$$

where P is in W/m² of rotor area. Because the density of air at sea level is approximately 1.2 kg/m³, it follows that:

$$P = 0.17 \times \frac{1}{2} \times 1.2 \times V^3$$
$$= 0.1V^3$$

This can be expressed in terms of rotor diameter as:

$$P = 0.1 \times \frac{\pi D^2}{4} \cdot V^3$$

P –   hydraulic output power (W)
D –   rotor diameter (m)
V –   average wind speed (m/s)

The hydraulic energy output is the power multiplied by the time. This means that the daily hydraulic energy output (for a period of 24 hours), if expressed in watt-hours, will be 0.1V³ multiplied by 24:

$$E = 24 \times 0.1V^3$$

E –   hydraulic energy output per day (Wh/m² of rotor area)

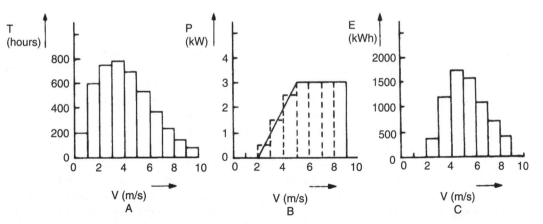

Fig. 7.56: An example of the calculation of the energy output of a windpump using the velocity frequency distribution of the wind, A, and multiplying it by the windpump performance characteristic, B, to obtain the total, C

241

If this is multiplied by the rotor area in square metres, it gives the daily hydraulic energy output. Dividing the number of watt-hours per day by 2.725 converts this to a daily 'cubic metres-metre' product, or $m^3 \cdot m$ (i.e. output in cubic metres times head in metres).

The reason for using the rather strange units of $m^3 \cdot m$ as a measure of energy is so that the energy output can be converted easily to a volume of water pumped at a particular pumping head, as discussed in Section 5.6. The conversion factor is:

$$1000[W \cdot h] = 1[kW \cdot h] = 367[m^3 \cdot m]$$

So for every 1 kWh of hydraulic energy output per day, there would be 36.7 m³ of water lifted through 10 m in the day, or 3.67 m³ through 100 m, etc.

Overall system efficiency

Table 7.22 indicates the efficiency factors relating to windpumps, and shows that between 7 and 27% of the value obtained for the energy in the wind (using the mean wind speed) can be converted to hydraulic energy. The first row makes allowance for the energy in the wind being greater than is predicted from mean windspeed measurement; this was explained earlier in the sub-section 'The relationship between average wind speed and wind energy'. The total energy in the wind typically exceeds the energy calculated from the mean windspeed by a factor of about 2 (or 200%), and is almost always in the range 180–250%.

A windpump rotor does not succeed in catching all the energy there is in the wind. In light winds the rotor will not turn, and in heavy winds it will be furled or partially furled. Furthermore, the match of the rotor with the pump is only good at certain windspeeds, so considerable energy is lost in stronger winds (see the sub-section 'Matching rotors to pumps'). When it is working, the rotor only delivers a proportion of the kinetic energy in the wind to the shaft, typically 25–30% for better designs of windpumps (see the 'Forces' sub-section of Section 6.5.1, and the C_p values in Table 7.20). Then the drive

Table 7.22 Factors affecting windpump system efficiency

Factor	Typical efficiency (%)
Ratio of actual energy in the wind to energy calculated from mean wind speed	180–250%
Amount of available energy that can be utilized by the rotor	30–50%
Rotor to shaft efficiency	25–30%
Shaft to pump efficiency	92–97%
Pump	60–75%
Total efficiency of energy conversion based on mean wind speed	7–27%

system has losses of a few per cent, and the pump itself is only 60–75% efficient. The combined effect of all these factors it that a windpump can utilize between 7% and 27% of the calculated total wind energy.

This result indicates that the figure of 17% overall efficiency used to produce the $0.1V^3$ rule of thumb described in the sub-section 'Simple "rule-of-thumb" approach' above may vary with different windpumps and wind regimes by about plus or minus 10% of the total energy available. Therefore, the rule of thumb coefficient used of 0.1, and hence the predicted output using this method, may generally be expected to be within the range of 0.6 to 1.6 times the result obtained by using 0.1 and the mean wind speed.

Wind requirements for economic operation

A convenient method for costing and comparing windmills is to estimate the total installed cost of a system as a function of rotor area (e.g. in dollars, or other currency, per square metre of rotor). Since the energy output is a function of the wind regime combined with the system efficiency and its rotor area, the unit cost of the rotor area will give an indication of the cost of energy in a given wind regime if a uniform system efficiency is assumed (or upper and lower limits such as indicated in the previous section may be used).

Wind pump prices correlate quite closely with the area of rotor being purchased. Experience with the IT Power Small Windpump has shown that, with local manufacture in developing countries, installed pumps can cost $250–350/m² of rotor area, though in some countries, notably China, the cost can be considerably less. Prices for industrially manufactured windpumps are generally higher, but not greatly so. The main reasons for encouraging local manufacture are usually to save foreign exchange, to avoid customs duties, and to promote local capability and employment. 'Do-it-yourself' windpumps, built in the village, such as are used in Thailand are very much cheaper, but the cost depends very much on what assumptions are made on the value of the construction labour. Small wind generators tend to be two to three times as expensive as windpumps per unit of rotor area.

Combining these costs with the previously given performance assumptions will show that at current prices, most windpumps need mean winds speeds in the region of 2.5 to 3 m/s to begin to be economically attractive, and wind generators need 3.5 to 5 m/s. Moreover the cube law ensures that the economics of windmills improves dramatically at higher windspeeds, making them a most economically attractive technology in most wind regimes having mean windspeeds exceeding say 5 m/s.

Windpump manufacturers' performance claims
The easiest method of estimating the performance to be expected from a windpump is to use manufacturers' data as printed in their brochures. For example, Fig. 7.57 shows a table and performance curves for the 'Kijito' range of windpumps, based on the 'IT Windpump' and made in Kenya by Bob Harries Engineering of Thika (see Fig. 7.43). The table indicates the average daily output to be expected at different pumping heads for the four sizes of Kijitos in three different average speeds, defined as 'light' 2–3 m/s, ' medium' 3–4 m/s and 'strong' 4–5 m/s while the curves reproduce these results just for the 'medium' wind speeds. It is interesting to note how sensitive windpumps are to windspeed; the smallest machine with a 12 ft (3.7 m) rotor will perform in a 5 m/s wind almost as well as the largest machine (24 ft or 7.3 m) does in a 3 m/s

wind; this is because there is 4.6 times as much energy per unit cross-section of a 5 m/s wind as in a 3 m/s wind as a result of the cube law.

A problem with manufacturers' performance claims is that some brochures include inaccurate, unreliable or even incomplete data. For example, it sometimes is not clear what wind speed applies for the manufacturers' claimed outputs. There is a tendency for manufacturers to quote performance figures for unusually high average wind speeds, no doubt because this makes the performance look more impressive, and they then give rules of thumb which in some cases do not seem accurate for reducing the outputs to more realistic levels for more common wind speeds.

The difficulty inherent in monitoring the performance of a windpump often prevents users from actually checking whether they are getting what they were promised. If a cup-counter anemometer and a water meter is available, it is possible to measure the wind run and the water output over fixed periods of time (either 10 minute intervals or daily intervals – short-term and long-term – is recommended). The mean wind speed and mean water output over these periods can be logged and then plotted as a scattergram. When enough points are obtained on the scattergram, a 'best-fit' curve can be drawn to obtain the performance characteristic. It is recommended that institutional users and others who need to procure numerous windpumps should seek performance guarantees from their supplier and should make some attempt to verify whether the performance is being achieved, for example, in the manner just suggested. In some cases sub-optimal performance can occur simply because the wrong pump size or wrong stroke has been used, and considerable improvements in performance may result from exchanging the pump for the correct size or from altering the stroke.

7.8 Solar power

Virtually all the energy we use derives from the sun originally, whether it comes to us via plants, animals, water or wind power, or from fossil

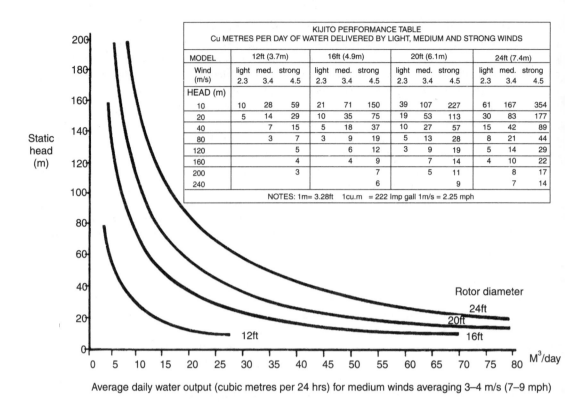

KIJITO PERFORMANCE TABLE Cu METRES PER DAY OF WATER DELIVERED BY LIGHT, MEDIUM AND STRONG WINDS												
MODEL	12ft (3.7m)			16ft (4.9m)			20ft (6.1m)			24ft (7.4m)		
Wind (m/s)	light 2.3	med. 3.4	strong 4.5	light 2.3	med. 3.4	strong 4.5	light 2.3	med. 3.4	strong 4.5	light 2.3	med. 3.4	strong 4.5
HEAD (m)												
10	10	28	59	21	71	150	39	107	227	61	167	354
20	5	14	29	10	35	75	19	53	113	30	83	177
40		7	15	5	18	37	10	27	57	15	42	89
80		3	7	3	9	19	5	13	28	8	21	44
120			5		6	12	3	9	19	5	14	29
160			4		4	9		7	14	4	10	22
200			3			7		5	11		8	17
240						6			9		7	14
NOTES: 1m= 3.28ft 1cu.m = 222 Imp gall 1m/s = 2.25 mph												

Average daily water output (cubic metres per 24 hrs) for medium winds averaging 3–4 m/s (7–9 mph)

Fig. 7.57: Manufacturer's performance data for the Kenyan-made 'Kijito' windpump range based on the IT windpump (see also Fig. 7.43)

fuels. The earth as a whole receives a huge amount of energy from the sun, and it is an obvious step to try and harness the sun's energy directly.

7.8.1 Background and state-of-the-art

There are two main methods for converting solar energy into power for driving a pump. In practice, the only commercially available method is photovoltaic, or PV, technology, where solar cells are used to convert sunlight into electricity. The other method is to use solar energy to power various types of heat engines. The most feasible routes for applying solar power to pumping water and various means of harnessing solar energy are shown in Fig. 7.58.

Although the photovoltaic effect was discovered in 1839 (by Edmond Becquerel in France), the first reasonably efficient solar cells were only made in 1954. Since then, PV technology has

become widespread. Most people are familiar with the tiny solar cells used to power hand-held calculators and other small electronic goods, and have seen solar panels used for powering telecommunications equipment away from grid electricity. On the other hand, solar-powered engines are rarely seen, even though they date back more than 100 years.

The first successful solar thermodynamic systems were developed in France during the mid-nineteenth century. By 1900 most of the development effort had shifted to the USA, where several people were seeking to develop commercially viable solar pumping systems. However, although several solar steam engines were successfully demonstrated, their cost was several times as much as a conventional steam engine of the same power, which limited their commercial success (even though their fuel was, of course, free). This work culminated in the construction in 1914, by an American called Frank Shuman, of

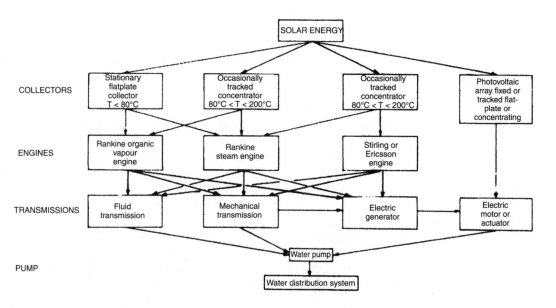

Fig. 7.58: Feasible options for solar-powered water pumping systems

what even today remains one of the largest and, for that matter, most technically successful solar thermodynamic pumping systems ever built. Developed in the USA, but installed at Meadi in Egypt to pump irrigation water, this unit incorporated hot water storage and could therefore drive an irrigation pump for 24 hours per day. After a few teething troubles, the Meadi solar pump was shown to develop 40 kW, and it could pump up to 1,300 m³/h (360 l/s). Under Egyptian conditions at that time the plant could pay back in competition with a steam engine in 2 years, and could completely pay for itself in 4 years. Enormous interest ensued, and ambitious plans to install similar solar pumps in other parts of the world were initiated, but the First World War broke out and Shuman, the driving force behind solar pumps at that time, died before it ended. The cheap oil era and the widespread development of rural electrification in the USA that followed led to a lack of interest in solar power for pumping until the oil price increases of the 1970s.

Numerous researchers initiated laboratory research work on solar thermodynamic systems during the 1970s, and SOFRETES, a French company, began manufacturing a low temperature solar pumping system, nominally capable of

about 500–1,000 W of pumped output, which was distributed with French government support to a number of developing countries in the late 1970s on a pilot demonstration basis. Also, a number of quite large solar thermal installations, some for pumping water and some for electricity generation, were completed in the USA and in Africa. Unfortunately, the majority of these latter-day solar thermodynamic systems performed poorly, and many also proved troublesome to operate reliably under field conditions. Today the French company that produced the solar thermodynamic systems is no longer in business and no other manufacturer has a proven solar thermodynamic pumping system commercially available, although experimental work on large-scale solar thermodynamic electricity generation continues in the USA and Europe.

As long ago as 1979, a global project was initiated by the World Bank and funded by the UNDP (United Nations Development Programme) specifically to evaluate small-scale solar pumps for irrigation. Field trials were conducted in Mali, Sudan and the Philippines, and it was decided to select solar pumps which were at least nominally commercially available and which showed reasonable prospects of being able

245

to function adequately in the field. When bids were invited from suppliers all over the world, it transpired that only one solar thermodynamic solar pump was available for procurement by the project in 1980, and this only barely fulfilled the minimum requirements to justify field testing it. Despite a century of development, with early signs of promise, small-scale solar thermodynamic systems had not really succeeded. In contrast, no less than eleven solar photovoltaic pumps were short-listed from a still broader choice. As the UNDP projects proceeded the emphasis moved from the use of solar pumps for irrigation to their use for water supply duties, where they are more immediately economically viable. The information from this work, and subsequent development is gathered together in (Barlow et al., 1993 [68]), which is intended to help those seeking more detailed information on selecting and sizing solar pumps.

Photovoltaic systems use cells which can convert sunlight directly to electricity. This technology had its origins at the Bell Laboratories in the USA in the early 1950s. Solar photovoltaic cells were originally developed to power space satellites, which in common with many rural parts of the earth's surface, need a small, independent power supply. This technology therefore started at the frontiers of science on an 'expense-no-object' basis. This meant that the earliest terrestrial solar power cells, which became available in the 1960s, were prohibitively expensive for such mundane applications as water pumping.

The basic material of PV units is silicon, which is cheap (sand is mainly silica, which is silicon dioxide), but the production process is complicated, and requires sophisticated, and expensive, manufacturing facilities. Over the years, there has been a lot of optimism in PV circles, with predictions of new technologies leading to cheap, mass-produced units that are competitive with other energy sources but, as yet, no such development has emerged. There has been a steady improvement in the efficiency of PV units, which, combined with improvements in manufacturing methods and economies of scale as production volumes have increased, have led to a slow but steady fall in the price. Figure 7.59 shows a record of decline in the price of solar modules per watt of output up to 1996 (W_p is the power output under standard conditions, defined in the sub-section 'Photovoltaic properties' below), and the improvement of efficiency. The 1996 price was about $4.3/$W_p$, and by 2005 this had dropped to $3/$W_p$. These reductions in price will mean that solar power becomes progressively more attractive for water pumping.

Small-scale water pumping is one of the more attractive applications for solar power. PV units that are portable, or at least easily transported, are of a size that can readily power small pumps. For drinking water systems, the pumped water can be stored in tanks, so provided the average amount of sunshine is sufficient, it does not matter if it shines at a particular time. For irrigation, solar radiation tends to be at its most intense when the need for pumped water is greatest. For both applications, the energy supply is available at the point of use, making the users independent of fuel supplies or electrical transmission lines. Good PV technology can be highly reliable, working for many years without attention. Solar pumping is already used on a limited scale for drinking water systems, and under the right conditions it is an economically viable option. It is less common for irrigation pumping, and tends only to be used in special cases. If the price of PV does fall as predicted, it will become economically comparable with other options, and much more common.

7.8.2 The solar energy resource

The average value of solar irradiance just outside the earth's atmosphere is 1,353 W/m^2. As solar radiation passes through the atmosphere it is attenuated so that the maximum level normally recorded at sea level is about 1,000 W/m^2. This is made up of two components: the direct beam radiation from the sun, and the diffuse radiation consisting of light scattered by the atmosphere to give a bright sky and clouds.

The combination of direct beam and diffuse radiation is called the global radiation. The level of global radiation varies through the day

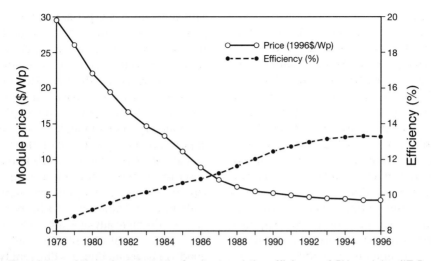

Fig. 7.59: The history of the price per watt of output and the efficiency of PV modules (IT Power, 1997 [69])

because the path length the light has to take through the atmosphere is greatest when the sun appears low in the sky in the early morning and late afternoon and least at solar noon. For the same reason there are variations with both season and latitude. The total solar radiation received in a day can vary from about 0.5 kWh/m² on a sunny northern winter day to over 6.0 kWh/m² on a sunny day in the tropics or in arid or mountainous regions. Obviously on a cloudy day the direct solar energy reaching ground can be close to zero. On a really clear day, diffuse solar energy reaching the ground may only be 15 to 20% of the global irradiance, but on an overcast day it is nearly 100%.

Because of this variability of solar irradiation at different locations and times, the performance of solar pumping systems will be strongly influenced by where they are located, the time of the year and weather conditions. However, just like with wind, solar energy tends to be consistently available at any particular location from one year to the next; in other words, analysis of past solar energy records allows quite accurate prediction of available solar energy and hence of system sizing. To some extent it is easier to achieve accuracy with solar energy prediction than with wind energy prediction since it is less affected by local site conditions (providing the site is not actually shaded by trees), and any errors in solar energy measurement have much less influence on overall system performance than comparable percentage errors in wind speed recording.

7.8.3 Photovoltaic systems

Photovoltaic systems depend on a property of certain semi-conductors to generate electricity when exposed to light. Photons of light above a certain energy (below a certain wavelength) can knock electrons from their normal positions in the atomic structure into a 'excited' state. These can be collected by conductors set into the material, and harnessed to produce a current in an external circuit. The physical principles are explained in more detail in textbooks and other references on photovoltaic power.

Practical photovoltaic systems consist of 'modules' which contain the semiconductor generating units or 'cells' in an enclosed, weatherproof frame, with a transparent front surface to let the light in. Collections of modules are put together in an 'array', oriented to maximize the capture of the available sunlight; small arrays are illustrated in Fig. 7.64.

247

Types of module

At first sight, most PV modules all look rather similar, with a the semiconductor sealed behind glass in a rectangular unit. When looking to purchase modules, it will be found that some are significantly more expensive than others. There are three main types: mono-crystalline silicon, multi-crystalline silicon, and amorphous silicon. New, non-silicon types such as cadmium telluride and CIS, have recently become available too. As these technologies have different efficiencies, they are normally sold according to their output. A system using modules with a lower efficiency, such as amorphous silicon, will require a larger number of modules than one using higher-efficiency, crystalline-silicon modules.

Most commercially-available PV cells are made from silicon, and the different types arise from different manufacturing methods. There are two main groups: first, those that are made by slicing layers from crystals of silicon, and, second, those that are made by depositing a thin layer or film of silicon onto another material. Currently, crystalline-silicon cells form the basis of the majority of the modules sold, they are the most efficient, and they have a proven track record. Thin film technologies have the potential of giving mass-produced, low-cost modules.

Mono-crystalline silicon cells are made by growing a crystal of purified silicon (usually 100–150 mm in diameter) and sawing this into wafer-thin slices (see Fig. 7.60). The slices are round, but they are often trimmed to make them nest together better in the module. These slices are then 'doped' by having impurities added to the back surface, to create a 'junction' between the layers with different electrical properties. A metal film is added to the back, and a pattern of conductors to the front, to collect the current. An anti-reflection surface is put on the front. Light falling on the cells produces a potential difference (or voltage) across the junction. Each cell (Fig. 7.61) can only develop about 0.4 volts when under load, (0.6 V on open circuit), so strings of cells are normally connected together in series to produce a more useful voltage, typically 14–16 V. Individual cells are delicate, and expensive, and need to be protected, so they are housed in a sealed module.

This generally has a special toughened, low-iron glass cover (sometimes given a matt finish to minimize reflection), and a metal or glass rear surface. The cells may be simply sandwiched between the glass and the rear plate, or encapsulated in plastic. The whole assembly is sealed to prevent the ingress of water (or anything else).

Mono-crystalline modules have a distinctive appearance, being made up of bluish-grey individual cells. As can be appreciated from the brief description above, the production process is lengthy, involving many delicate stages, and the costs are high. These cells have the best efficiency of any commercially-available cell. This means the power output of a small module can be as good as a larger module of a different type. Good quality mono-crystalline panels are very reliable, with lives of over 20 years, and are even sold with 20 year guarantees. As might be expected, this type of panel is also the most expensive.

Multi-crystalline silicon cells are produced in a similar way to mono-crystalline cells, but a cast block of silicon is used instead of a single crystal. The cells look different, having a patchy appearance arising from the different crystal areas within them. Multi-crystalline cells are a little cheaper than mono-crystalline, but have efficiencies a few per cent lower. The characteristics and reliability are similar. Overall, they have similar cost-effectiveness to mono-crystalline cells.

Amorphous silicon modules are made up of thin layers (1–10 mm) of silicon deposited onto a glass or clear plastic sheet and divided into bands 10–12 mm wide, with a backing plate. They look quite different from crystalline modules, with the semiconductor appearing as very dark-brown or black strips that run the length of the module. Amorphous silicon has a lower efficiency than crystalline silicon, and has the major technical disadvantage that the performance degrades over the first few months of operation (see Fig. 7.62). The voltage produced by the modules after 3 months can be 30–50% less than the initial production voltage, under the same conditions. As with crystalline-silicon modules, it is important that the modules are sealed; if even a small amount of moisture seeps in, the efficiency of the units drops off dramatically. Though most

Stage 1
Grow silicon crystal
Pull or cast into blocks
Saw into wafers

Stage 2
Polish wafer
"Dope" to enhance
  PV properties
Treat to reduce light
  reflection
Add electrical contacts

Stage 3
Connect cells together
Encapsulate
Add glass front, weather proof backing and seal edges
  to protect from elements
Add frame (usually) to provide strength and a means of
  support
Add junction box to allow easy connection

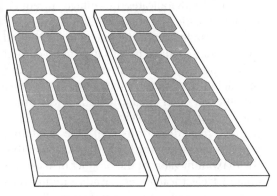

Stage 4
Interconnect modules to give required power
Attach to controller

Now ready to supply electricity

Fig. 7.60: Production process for a crystalline-
silicon photovoltaic module

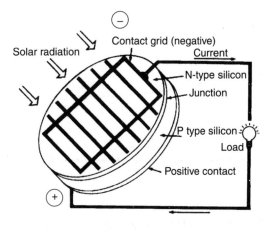

Fig. 7.61: The construction of a crystalline-
silicon photovoltaic cell

modules are rigid, glass-and-metal units, there has been some work on all-plastic modules, particularly for putting solar panels on building roofs. Modules are produced in the form of light plastic roof tiles, and flexible sheets like roofing felt.

Standard amorphous silicon modules are slightly cheaper, for a given output, than crystalline ones, but the stabilized efficiency is only about one-half to a third of a crystalline module, so a larger area of panel is required to generate the same power. A greater area requires more space, and a larger structure to mount it on, which adds to the cost of the system. Amorphous silicon modules are usually sold 'light-soaked', so that the power is close to the stabilized level, or at least they should be rated for the stabilized value; it is worth ensuring that this is the case when buying them.

Multi-junction cells use a number of thin films of amorphous silicon laid on top of each other and designed so that each catches a different frequency in the sunlight, so increasing the overall energy caught; they have stabilized efficiencies of around 10%. Various other types of cell have been developed that use non-silicon semiconductors. Two that have recently become commercially available are cadmium telluride (CdTe) and CIS (Copper Indium Disellenide).

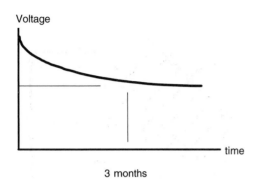

3 months

Fig. 7.62: The fall-off of voltage of over time for amorphous silicon PV cells

It should be noted that PV technology is developing fast, and it is not clear which type of solar module will, in the long term prove the best. Some experts consider that thin-film technology will eventually become the standard, because it holds out the prospect of cheap mass production.

Solar PV modules are actually very valuable pieces of equipment. At a price of \$4.30/Wp, a standard 50 Wp module, which is a small and very portable item, will cost \$215 – a considerable sum in many countries. A serious worry, as their high intrinsic value becomes more widely known and a 'second-hand market' develops, is the possibility of theft; this is already a problem in some areas.

Photovoltaic properties
The output of a PV module varies with the amount of light available, the colour of the light, the temperature, and with the atmospheric conditions. In order to obtain a meaningful comparison between different modules they are tested under standard conditions, which include a light strength of 1,000 W/m² and a cell temperature of 25°C. This light strength is about the maximum value of sunlight found anywhere on the earth's surface, and so the voltage and power measured under these conditions are called 'peak volts' or 'peak watts', Vp and Wp respectively. It requires specialist equipment to produce the standard conditions, which makes it very hard to check

whether solar modules are producing the power they are supposed to.

The performance characteristics of individual mono-crystalline-silicon solar cells are shown in Fig. 7.63. It can be seen that the efficiency of energy conversion is just over 15% in this example. This means that a sunlight power of 1,000 W/m² on modules with a surface area of 1 m² at 25°C will yield about 150 W of electrical output. Compared with other prime movers, this is a low conversion rate, turning what sounds to be a reasonable power density, 1 kW/m², into a rather modest amount of useful energy. Unfortunately, the efficiency of solar cells gets even less as they get hotter, as shown in Fig. 7.63A. Most solar cells attain temperatures in the range 50–70°C in full sunlight conditions, but their power rating is generally quoted by manufacturers at the standard temperature of 25°C. They therefore will never achieve their rated output in practice under normal sunshine, but sizing methodologies, such as are described later, take account of this discrepancy. (The rule-of-thumb method used in the sub-section 'Rule of thumb method for sizing a solar pumping system' below assumes it takes 1,200 W/m² of radiation to produce the rated power Wp at normal working temperatures, instead of the 1,000 W/m² at 25°C.)

Figure 7.63B indicates the voltage-current (V-I) characteristic of a solar cell, under 1,000 W/m² solar irradiance. At the one extreme the cell can be short-circuited to get a maximum current I_{SC} (the short-circuit current) of about 36 mA/cm² of cell, but the voltage will be zero. At the other extreme, on open circuit, there is zero current, but an open-circuit voltage, V_{oc} of about 0.60 V per cell, (regardless of its size). The maximum power occurs when the load applied is such that the maximum value of the product of V and I is obtained (electrical power in watts is numerically volts times amps). This occurs near the 'knee' of the V-I curve at around 0.48 V per cell, as indicated by the dotted curve showing power. As the efficiency is exactly proportional to the power output, the efficiency curve is identical in shape to the power curve.

The sun usually shines with a strength of less than 1,000 W/m², and Fig. 7.63C indicates how,

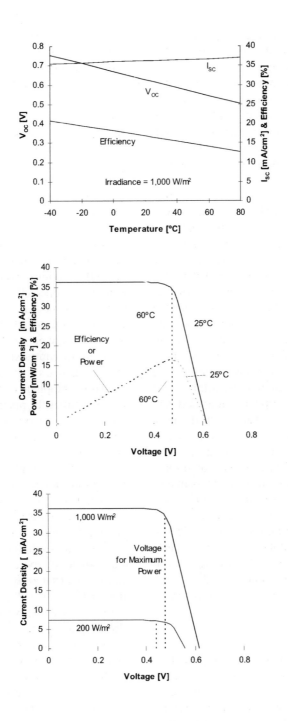

Fig. 7.63: The performance characteristics of silicon photovoltaic cells A. The dependence of efficiency, short-circuit current, I_{sc}, and open circuit voltage, V_{oc}, on cell temperature (at 1,000 W/m²). B. The effect of cell temperature on the *V-I* and *V-P* characteristic (at 1,000 W/m²). C. The effect of the change in irradiation on the *V-I* characteristic.

251

if the irradiance is reduced by say 80% to 200 W/m^2, the current density declines proportionately, but the voltage characteristic stays more-or-less the same. The power from a cell is therefore almost linearly proportional to the intensity of illumination from the sun. Because a voltage is produced even in low levels of irradiance, solar photovoltaic systems can function in low levels of sunlight, depending on the nature of the electrical load and what the threshold power for starting happens to be.

The different PV technologies all have characteristics of the form of Fig. 7.63, but the values are different. The best efficiency obtained from a mono-crystalline cell in a laboratory is around 20%. Top commercial mono-crystalline cells currently achieve 15–16%, and it is predicted that this will increase to around 18% by the year 2010. Module efficiencies are somewhat lower, because of the gaps between the cells, reflection from the glass, and wiring losses; current commercial modules achieve around 14%. Poly-crystalline cells are typically a couple of per cent less efficient than mono-crystalline.

As noted before, the output of amorphous silicon modules degrades over time, with the peak output power decreasing by 30–50% over the first few months of operation (see Fig. 7.62). Voltage, power and efficiency figures should be quoted for the stabilized figures, but sometimes manufacturers' figures are overestimated. A typical stabilized module efficiency is 4–6%, which is considerably less than crystalline-silicon modules. Cadmium-telluride modules have stabilized efficiencies of around 6%. It is claimed that multi-junction thin-film silicon modules will soon be in production with stabilized efficiencies of about 8%.

Solar arrays
Modules are mounted on a supporting structure in a frame and this assembly is known as a photovoltaic array which can simply be connected by electric cable to the motor/pump sub-system. Examples of four typical types of solar photovoltaic pumping systems are shown in Fig. 7.64.

In a few cases arrays have been developed which track to follow the sun; this of course increases the amount of sunlight intercepted as the array will always face the direct beam radiation. However, the complication and expense of providing mechanical tracking has not generally been found worthwhile so it is not common practice. A few portable, or semi-portable small-scale solar pumping systems exist in which the arrays can be manually orientated by moving them bodily; here some significant advantage at little effort or cost is gained by facing the array(s) south east in the morning and south west in the afternoon when in the northern hemisphere (or NE and NW respectively in the southern hemisphere).

Most arrays are generally designed to carry the modules at a fixed tilt angle which maximizes the amount of sunlight received over the year. It so happens that the theoretical angle for this to be achieved coincides with the angle of latitude of the location. This angle which will place the array perpendicular to the sun at solar noon on the equinoxes, and will therefore make the divergence of the sun's rays from perpendicular to the plane of the array a minimum at all other times. In practice, the actual angle for the array is sometimes varied so as to bias the optimization to suit a season having more cloud cover; for example, in areas with a marked rainy season it may be advantageous to incline the array more normal to the sun in that season, and sacrifice a little solar energy in the dry season when perhaps more energy than necessary can be intercepted. Also, although mounting the array at zero angle (i.e. horizontal) is the optimum angle for the equator, it is normally recommended that arrays be mounted at angles of at least 10° so that there will be good rainwater run-off, which helps to keep them clean. It is often advantageous to have an array with a capability of having its angle adjusted manually every few months, as this can improve the output by 10% or more over the year.

A few manufacturers have produced solar photovoltaic systems with concentrating collectors, using mirrors or lenses to intensify the strength of sunlight on the cells. This allows a smaller area of cells to be used, but the added expense of mirrors or lenses can negate any saving on cells.

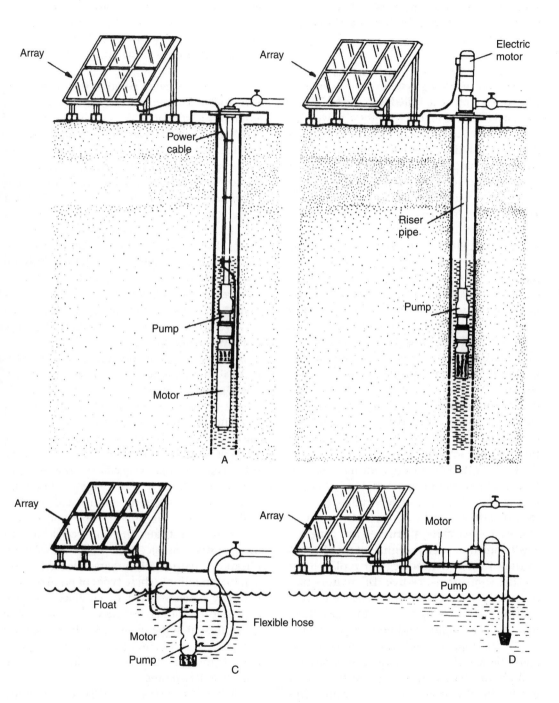

Fig. 7.64: Examples of solar pump configurations: A. Submerged motor/pump set. B. Submerged pump with surface motor. C. Floating motor/pump set. D. Surface motor with surface-mounted pump.

Concentrating collectors also have other disadvantages, in that the units need to track the sun to work efficiently, and the optical surfaces need to be kept clean.

Motor-pump sub-systems

Photovoltaic pumping systems require, in addition to the array, a so-called 'sub-system' which consists of at least an electric motor powering a pump. Figure 7.64 illustrates various commonly used configurations that can comprise a photovoltaic pumping system. Figure 7.65 shows schematically the necessary (and optional) components of a solar photovoltaic pumping system and how they interact.

Because the output from an array is DC (direct current), either a DC electric motor needs to be used, or alternatively an inverter can be used to convert the DC to AC so as to allow a standard, mass-produced, low-cost, AC electric motor to be used. It used to be the case that inverters were expensive and inefficient, but inverter efficiency has now been improved, and the costs reduced. Dedicated solar-pumping units usually have special variable-frequency inverters which are electronically controlled to optimize the matching between the motor-pump unit and a solar panel. The extra power these units can extract from the panels can more than pay for them in many situations.

Where DC motors are used, the most efficient types are permanent magnet motors, where the flux is provided by magnets rather than an electro-magnetic field coil. A problem with DC motors is that carbon brushes are generally needed and these are a potential source of trouble as they wear and need regular replacement. Brushless, maintenance-free, DC motors have recently been developed however, which have electronic circuitry to perform the same function as a commutator and brushes (see Section 7.6.3). This type of motor is becoming increasingly common for solar pumping applications.

A photovoltaic array will give its best output if it is run, at a given level of irradiance, with voltage and current as close as possible to the 'knee' of the module characteristic (see Fig. 7.63B). Pump-motor units will also have an optimum speed and load for a given current and voltage level. The aim of a solar system design is to match the motor-pump characteristic as closely as possible to the module characteristic, so that both are operating under optimal conditions.

The most common solution to matching arrays and motor-pump units (and to allow for variations in their load lines when operating off the design head, for example), is to use electronic Maximum Power Point Tracking (MPPT). This can adjust the voltage and current that the array sees so that the array is working at its maximum power point. It then takes the electrical power it received and converts it to the optimum voltage, current and frequency for the pump motor. This is all done electronically, with a microprocessor controlling the matching. This approach results in extra cost, plus a small parasitic power loss inherent in any extra component (1–2%), but in many cases, particularly with positive displacement pump systems, it greatly improves performance.

Some years ago, it was common to use centrifugal pumps with solar pumping systems. These could be matched well with PV module output without the need for electronic controllers. They had the extra advantage of low starting torques, so that they began pumping at low levels of sunlight. The disadvantage is that centrifugal pumps are not very efficient as small units. Centrifugal pumps are still used for solar pumping, often with electronic control and MPPT as well, but as electronic units have become cheaper and more sophisticated there has been a move to using positive displacement pumps for solar applications, particularly progressive cavity and diaphragm pumps. These types of pump do not naturally match well with PV modules, and have high starting torque, but they are considerably more efficient in the small sizes suitable for solar pumping. Using electronic controllers overcomes the matching problem, as well as improving the starting at low power.

Much of the discussion in Section 7.6 in the context of mains (or generating set) electricity applies to the motors and pumps of photovoltaic electric systems. For example, combined

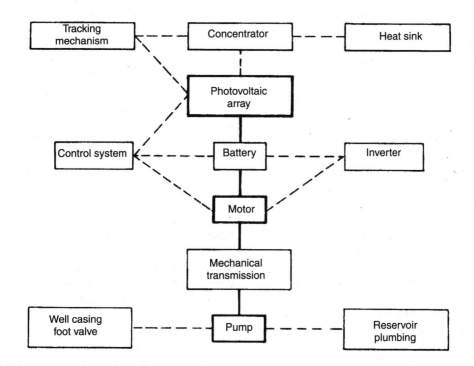

Fig. 7.65: A schematic representation of the components of a photovoltaic solar pumping system; the essential components are shown with heavy lines, and the options with broken lines

submersible motor-pump units may be used (either the borehole type or surface water type) which need either AC or brushless DC motors, since they are sealed and the brushes cannot easily be changed. The electronic control for submersible pumps will often be above ground. For irrigation duties, generally at low heads, the most common and useful system is a submersible motor pump unit, usually suspended from a float for pumping surface water. Any pump used for solar pumping should be self priming, otherwise the user would have to re-prime it every time a cloud passed by.

Because solar panels are relatively expensive, the energy they produce is very valuable, and so any losses in the pumping system should be kept to a minimum. For this reason, it is best to have direct-coupled motors and pumps, rather than inefficient mechanical drives. It is obviously possible to use surface-mounted motors driving submerged pumps via a long shaft, but the friction losses consume quite a proportion of the available power.

A controversial technical question is whether batteries should be used with solar pumps. They are not often used because their life under tropical conditions tends to be limited, and they need regular topping up with distilled water unless even more expensive sealed batteries are used. It is much cheaper and easier to store water rather than electricity.

Each component of a PV pumping system causes a loss and an inefficiency; the power flow through a typical photovoltaic pumping system is illustrated in Fig. 7.66. This diagram shows the best system efficiency currently available, and it can be seen that just over 9% of the incident radiation energy is converted to useful hydraulic output. Efficiencies of this order are currently only obtainable by positive displacement pumps driven by electronically-controlled, permanent-magnet, brushless, low-voltage DC motors, operating at higher heads (50–70 m). The electric-to-hydraulic, or wire-to-water, efficiency of the controller/pump/motor units is around 70% (and it is predicted that this could rise to 75% in a few years). Systems based on diaphragm pumps achieve wire-to-water efficiencies of around 45%. Older-style centrifugal pumps with inverters and AC motors operating at lower heads (10–25 m) give efficiencies of 20–40%. The differences in efficiency between different systems are clearly significant. The poorer systems will need more than two-and-a-half times the area of solar panels than the better systems. If thin-film panels were used with a centrifugal pump system, the solar panel area would need to be seven times more than the same output high-efficiency system!

Solar pumping systems are usually bought off-the-shelf, complete with modules. This means that it is not too difficult to achieve the higher efficiencies, provided reasonable attention is paid

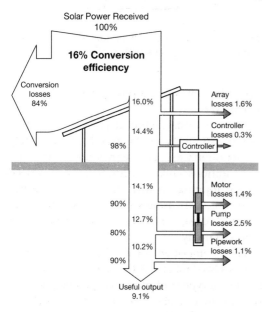

Fig. 7.66: Losses in a solar-photovoltaic pumping system. This shows the best efficiencies for commercially-available components in 1997. The 16% solar conversion efficiency refers to the cell efficiency, module efficiency (here shown as array efficiency) being 14.4% (IT Power, 1997 [70]).

to the installation, and the pipework losses are not too high. Installations are found in the field working at good efficiency. It is also true that many units are not nearly as good as they should be, and research has found that system efficiencies of 2–3%, or worse, are not uncommon.

It is notable that efficiencies have improved enormously in the last 10 years or so, and look set to continue to do so. This improvement has been accompanied by a halving of prices in real terms that has made solar pumping much more economic than it used to be. Efficiency is an important factor in selecting a solar pump, because with the high price of photovoltaic arrays, low efficiency implies a need for a proportionately larger and more expensive array.

To illustrate the financial difference an improvement in efficiency can mean, consider the example of a 350 Wp photovoltaic array powering an 80% efficient motor. If a 70% efficient motor were used instead, then 400 Wp would be required, necessitating buying an extra 50 Wp module costing around $215 more. Since the difference in cost between an efficient motor and an inefficient one is usually much less than this, it is obviously worth buying the best motor available. This decision is of course usually made by the system manufacturer and not the user, but the well-informed user can at least question the choices made by manufacturers by studying their specifications before buying.

Solar pump performance estimation
Accurate sizing of a solar pump array is necessary to minimize the array size for a given duty and thereby to achieve the most cost-effective system possible. If there is doubt about the sizing, a technically acceptable approach is to use a larger-than-necessary system in order to guarantee an adequate output, but the cost will increase approximately in proportion to the power rating of the system. Unnecessary over-sizing results in significant extra cost, but accidental under-sizing leads to an inadequate system to meet the pumped water demand.

Solar pumps used for irrigation generally need to be sized for the critical month when the system is most heavily loaded in relation to energy available. This is usually the month of maximum irrigation water demand, which fortunately is generally one of the sunniest months, since crop irrigation water demand and solar energy are well correlated. A solar water pump for drinking water supply duties, on the other hand, is likely to need to deliver a more or less constant daily output, which in such a case would make the least sunny month the critical month for sizing purposes.

Figure 7.67 gives an example of mean monthly solar energy availability plotted on the same histogram as mean monthly gross irrigation water requirement for the Lake Chad region of Africa. It can be seen from this that the month of June is not the sunniest month, but it is the critical month in terms of solar irrigation pump sizing as that is when the water demand is largest in relation to the energy availability. The sunniest month, April, is not a critical month as it is too early in the growth cycle for the crop in question (cotton), while the fields are fallow in the second sunniest month of March.

A solar pump located in Chad for water supply, rather than irrigation, duties is more likely to need to deliver a constant daily water output, which would make the least sunny months of August, December or January critical. It is interesting to note that August is probably low in solar energy because of cloud cover due to the beginning of the rainy season (which also reduces irrigation water demand), but December and January are low in solar energy because of the seasonal effect of winter, Chad being north of the equator.

Determination of the critical month, and the mean daily water demand and mean daily solar irradiation for that month are the starting points to size a solar pump, (and hence to estimate its likely cost). Irradiation figures can be obtained from most national meteorological departments, and they are also published covering the whole world, for each month in references such as Barlow et al., (1993 [68]), in some of the brochures of several of the larger manufacturers of solar photovoltaic power systems, and from sources such as the World Meteorological

Organisation. Unlike wind data, solar irradiation is not much affected by local topography, so even maps that cover large areas or whole regions can be used to make a reasonably accurate judgement of the irradiation for a particular location.

References such as these [68] give a detailed explanation of rigorous methods for solar photovoltaic system sizing, but for most purposes a reasonable estimate can be made using a rule-of-thumb approach. In any case, all photovoltaic system manufacturers maintain computer models which they use for sizing systems; these generally include a world-wide data-base, so when requested to provide a quotation they can minimize the system size so as to price competitively. Therefore the potential purchaser is well advised to request quotations from several sources and to compare the size estimates and prices which are quoted.

Care should be taken, however, to avoid simply choosing the least expensive system and thereby possibly obtaining one which is possibly undersized for the required duty. Solar pump economics are discussed in more detail in Chapter 8.

Rule of thumb method for sizing a solar pumping system
A rule-of-thumb method may be used to obtain an approximate idea of the size and cost of a photovoltaic array, as follows:
- Estimate the peak daily hydraulic output (in kWh) required, using either Fig. 5.12 or the following formula:

$$E_{hyd} = \frac{Q \cdot H}{367}$$

E_{hyd} – peak daily hydraulic energy output (kWh/d)
Q – output required (m³/d)
H – total pumped head (m)
E.g., for a drinking water system requiring 5.8 m³ of water pumped through a total head of 60 m, the energy requirement per day is (5.8 × 60)/ 367 = 0.95 kWh (hydraulic) per day. (See Section 5.6.)

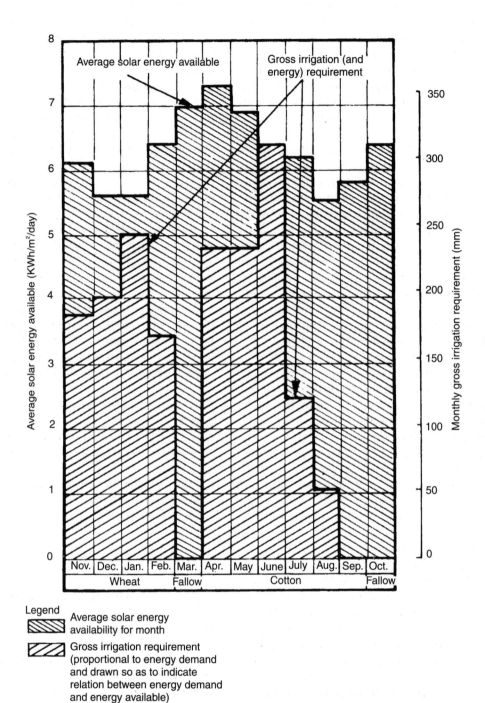

Fig. 7.67: Solar energy available compared with crop irrigation demand for the Lake Chad region

- Assume a figure for the sub-system efficiency, i.e., the efficiency of conversion of electricity to hydraulic output (wire to water). This is sometimes given in manufacturer's brochures or in technical studies (IT Power,1997 [70]). As a rough guide, efficiency is related to the head, with higher head units (30–60 m) achieving 50–70%, medium head units (15–30 m) giving 30–50%, and lower head units (2–15 m) giving 20–30%.
- Divide the daily hydraulic output by the sub-system efficiency to arrive at the daily electrical energy demand for the system, e.g., in the example above, using a sub-system efficiency of 60%, 0.95 kWh/0.60 = 1.58 kWh (electrical) per day.
- Look up the mean extra-terrestrial radiation for the latitude being considered in Table 7.23. If we take Dakar, Senegal, in West Africa as an example, this is at approximately 15°N, which gives a figure of 9.73 kWh/m² per day. Refer to the map in Fig. 7.68 and note the approximate Clearness Index for the location in question, e.g., Dakar is in the zone between 60 and 70%, at say 63%. The radiation needs to be multiplied by the relevant Clearness Index of 63%, which yields 9.73 × 0.63 = 6.1 kWh/m² per day on average. To allow for below average months and the inaccuracies possible with this estimating technique, it is prudent to reduce this value by 20% for solar pump sizing purposes to give, say 0.8 × 6.1 = 4.9 kWh/m² per day (0.8 being 100% less 20% expressed as a decimal factor).

To summarize this; take the extraterrestrial irradiation for the latitude, multiply by the Clearness Index given on the map, and finally reduce by a 20% margin of safety.

- Take the daily electrical energy requirement, divide it by the daily irradiation per square metre, and multiply the result by 1,200 W/m² to get the approximate peak watt rating required for the array, e.g., in the above example it is (1.58/4.9) × 1,200 = 387 Wp.
- Different manufacturers make different module sizes, but suppose 40 Wp units are available. It is then necessary to divide the answer by 40, and round up the answer to an integer

Table 7.23: Daily mean irradiation outside the atmosphere at various latitudes on the earth

Latitude	Daily mean extra-terrestrial irradiation (kWh/m²)
0°	10.04
5°	10.00
10°	9.90
15°	9.73
20°	9.49
25°	9.19
30°	8.82
40°	7.93
50°	6.87
60°	5.71

(whole) number of modules, e.g., in our example with 40 W modules we get 387/40 = 9.7, therefore 10 × 40 Wp modules would be needed, giving a true array rating of 400 Wp.

Typical *complete* solar pumping system costs can be estimated on the basis of US$8–18 per Wp for drinking water systems over 400 Wp. These figures are of course approximate, as is the sizing methodology outlined, but with the above example we can see that a 400 Wp system is likely to cost in the region of US $3,200–7,200.

These costs are likely to come down further during the next decade by perhaps 25 to 50%, as the volume of photovoltaic manufacturing increases. This will significantly affect the economics of solar water pumping, and readers are advised to find up-to-date costs for comparing solar power with other options.

7.8.4 Thermodynamic systems

As discussed above, solar-thermodynamic pumping systems, although experimented with for over a century, remain generally immature and 'non-commercial'. For this reason they are dealt with rather briefly here. There is always the chance of some future breakthrough that might make them worthy of reconsideration.

Thermodynamic systems can be sub-divided into three main categories according to their operating temperatures: low and medium

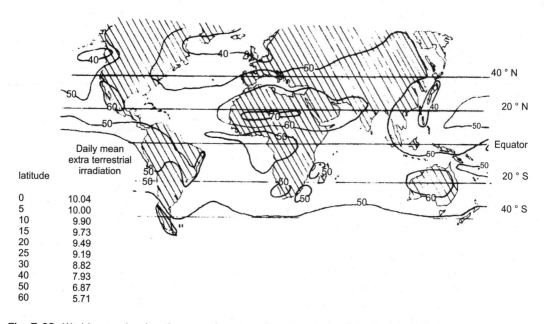

latitude	Daily mean extra terrestrial irradiation
0	10.04
5	10.00
10	9.90
15	9.73
20	9.49
25	9.19
30	8.82
40	7.93
50	6.87
60	5.71

Fig. 7.68: World map showing the annual average Clearness Index for solar irradiation

temperatures using a 'Rankine' or steam engine, and higher temperatures using a Stirling engine.

As indicated in Fig. 7.58, thermodynamic pumping systems always include a solar collector, which collects solar heat and transfers it to a working fluid, an engine, which takes heat from the working fluid and converts this to shaft power, and a transmission system, to connect the engine to a pump.

Low temperature thermodynamic systems use what are called 'flat plate collectors', which usually consist of a flat absorber panel containing passages through which the working fluid circulates. These are generally painted matt black and mounted in a shallow insulated housing behind a glass window of similar area to the panel. The absorber panel is mounted at an angle to the ground of approximately the latitude of the location, and facing towards the equator. This has the effect of maximizing the amount of solar energy received by the absorber.

The glass window readily admits light, but inhibits the outflow of the heat that is produced; this is commonly known as 'the greenhouse effect'. This effect can be enhanced with double-glazing, but this also increases the costs, since the glass is one of the more expensive components. Similarly, the absorber panel can be coated with a special 'selective surface' that also enhances the efficiency of absorption of solar radiation, but at increased cost compared with regular black paint. Flat plate collectors of this kind can only achieve working temperatures of up to about 80°C, but more usually will operate at about 60°C. Flat plate collectors are therefore used with low-boiling point working fluids such as ammonia, the freons (fluorohydrocarbon fluids which are used in air conditioning and refrigeration circuits, but which in recent years are being phased out due to the fact that escaped freons attack ozone in the upper atmosphere and cause serious environmental problems) or even butane (the latter poses a fire hazard if it leaks). However, even with low boiling point fluids, the efficiency of a Rankine engine will be very low, because the thermodynamic efficiency is, for fundamental physical reasons, a function of the temperature difference between the hot vapour admitted to the engine and the cool vapour that is exhausted. The exhausted vapour can only be cooled to the condenser temperature, which will generally be the temperature of the pumped water which is usually used to cool the condenser. Therefore it is only possible to achieve a temperature difference (sometimes known as 'delta T' or 'ΔT') of about 30°C with flat plate collectors.

If higher temperatures are required it becomes necessary to focus, or concentrate, the sunlight on a smaller area than it would naturally fall on. This is normally achieved by using a parabolic mirror. The simplest arrangement is a line focusing parabolic trough collector, which focuses the light falling on it into a line, as in Fig. 7.69; greater temperatures and concentration factors can be achieved with a 'point focus' parabolic dish concentrator. These offer improved thermodynamic efficiency in terms of a greater ΔT (line focusing achieves 100–200°C while point focusing achieves 200–500°C). Unfortunately focusing or concentrating solar collectors have two major disadvantages (which apply equally to the use of focusing with photovoltaics as well as with thermodynamic systems):

- they need to be aimed at the sun so that the sun's rays are focused accurately on the heat absorber; the greater the concentration, the greater the accuracy with which the device must be aligned with the sun. To do this requires a mechanical means to make the collector track the sun;
- they can only focus direct rays (beam radiation) and therefore cannot make use of scattered light (diffuse radiation) which is available to flat plate collectors. In areas with haze, atmospheric dust, high humidity or scattered clouds there is much diffuse radiation, often amounting to as much as 30% or more of the total solar irradiation, which is not accessible to a concentrating collector but can be used by a flat plate collector.

Therefore, although a concentrator improves the thermodynamic efficiency of a solar pumping system, and thereby reduces the area of solar collector needed to achieve a given power output, the added complication increases the cost per square meter of solar collector and also reduces the available solar energy by limiting usage to direct beam radiation. One analysis (Halcrow/IT Power, 1981 [71]) indicated that a compromise of using low concentrating factor line focusing collectors appears to be the most cost-effective approach with current solar collector costs, but that future technical developments could make point-focus systems competitive if a clever, low cost and reliable parabolic dish and sun tracking mechanism is developed. But this would only apply in locations (such as deserts) with a higher than average proportion of direct beam radiation.

Figure 7.69 is a schematic diagram of a solar thermal pumping system, showing the energy flow and the principal losses. A good solar collector will typically collect 60% of the solar energy falling on it. Of this 60%, about 7% will be converted to shaft power and the rest is lost as rejected condenser heat, feed pump and expander losses, and finally perhaps 50% of what is left, i.e. 3.5% of the original input, will be converted into useful hydraulic pumped power. This is an example of the better types of small solar thermal systems; many that have been developed are not nearly as good as this in practice and unfortunately quite a few seem to achieve only 0% efficiency most of the time!

7.9   Water power

7.9.1   The use of water power for pumping

Hydropower is a potentially attractive source of energy for water pumping. Unlike fossil fuels or grid electricity, it is free, and there are no problems with fuel supply chains. Unlike solar and wind power, it can be available all the time, day and night, all year round. Hydropower is a clean, reliable form of renewable energy, and small water-powered schemes generally have negligible impact on the environment.

The main shortcoming of water power for pumping is that it requires a suitable site, and places with suitable sites do not often need pumped water. Regions which are suitable for hydropower are generally those which have plentiful rainfall anyway, which puts the water directly where it is needed. Also, to obtain power from a stream, the water either has to drop a cer-

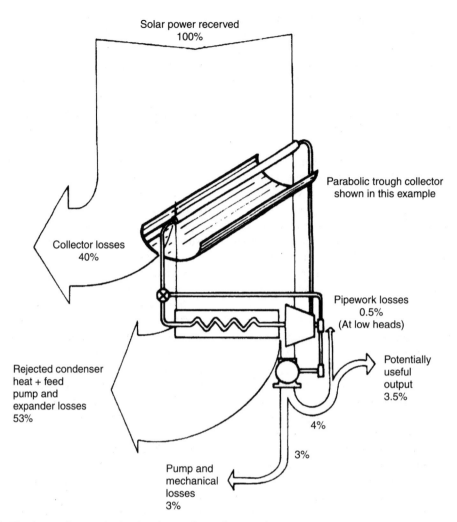

Fig. 7.69: The losses in a typical solar thermodynamic pumping system

tain distance, or there must be a reasonably strong current. In mountainous or hilly areas, where streams do fall steeply, it is often possible to let water flow by gravity to where it is needed: springs or small streams can be piped directly down to the villages or community water supplies, and fields can be irrigated by diverting water from streams or rivers into canals that follow contours around the hillsides.

Water-powered pumping is primarily used for irrigation rather than drinking water supply. The reason for this is that streams or rivers that are large enough to power turbines are not generally clean enough to drink. Water sources that are potable tend to be small, with insufficient power to do much pumping. The exception to this is the ram pump, which is a low-power device that is often used for community water supply, as well as smaller irrigation schemes.

The main applications for water-powered pumping will be in lowland areas, using the currents of large rivers, or low-head drops on streams and irrigation canals, as a power source to irrigate land which would not be accessible to gravity water flow. An obvious important application, common in China, is to extend the command area available to a gravity irrigation scheme, taking in higher land above a dam. In some arid regions, or regions with dry seasons, there are large perennial rivers where the river current can be utilized to lift water which would otherwise flow past parched fields. Even in some wetter and more mountainous areas there are situations where water power could allow irrigation of terraces or plateaux that are inaccessible to gravity flow; this can be of importance where flat land with soil suitable for cultivation is scarce.

When there is a suitable site for water power close to where water is needed, hydro-powered pumping can be an excellent option. It has already been stated that water is a free energy source. It is easy to predict the power available, and though flow may vary through a year, it does not vary much on a day-to-day basis. The energy density in streams and rivers is quite high, so whereas windpumps need large rotors and tall towers to capture the relatively diffuse energy in moving air, and solar power requires large arrays of photovoltaic modules to give enough power to pump from sunlight, water power can produce several kilowatts quite readily from small units. Because of the favourable power-to-size ratio of a hydro system, they are generally cost-effective. Turbines tend to be mechanically simple and robust, having long working lives and only requiring limited and simple maintenance. As a result hydro-power can be one of the most reliable and economic sources of power for those fortunate enough to have a suitable resource available.

7.9.2 General principles

Power

All water power applications involve removing energy from falling or flowing water. The power available in flow falling through a certain head is:

$$P = 9.8 \times Q \cdot H$$

P – power available in the flow (W)
Q – flow (l/s)
H – head (m)

This equation used litres per second and gives power in Watts. If Q is put in m³/s, then it gives power in kilowatts: in other words there are theoretically 9.8 kW available for a flow of 1 m³/s per metre drop. The actual output will be reduced by multiplying by the system efficiency; e.g. a device with an efficiency of 50% will produce half the available power.

Water current turbines do not rely on head, but are like windpumps in that they extract kinetic energy. The equation for the energy available in a flowing stream is exactly the same as for wind:

$$P = \frac{1}{2} \rho \cdot A \cdot V^3$$

P – power available in the current (W)
ρ – density of water (1000 kg/m³ for fresh water)
A – swept area of a current turbine rotor (m²)
V – instantaneous current velocity (m/s)

From this the power densities can be calculated, as shown in Table 7.24. It is interesting to compare this with Table 7.14, which gives the equivalent result for wind. The density of fresh water is about 800 times greater than that of air, which means that a 1 m/s river current has the same power as a 9.4 m/s wind.

Efficiency

The efficiency of hydro-powered systems is high. A good small turbine will typically be 70% efficient and even water wheels and other more primitive devices tend to be 30 to 60% efficient, as indicated in Table 7.25. Note that in all cases shown in Table 7.25, except turbine-pumps and hydraulic ram pumps, we are considering the conversion simply of water power to shaft power; pumping water then requires the addition of a pump or water lifting device which in turn will have further inherent losses.

7.9.3 The water power resource

From the water power equation above it can be seen that the two key parameters required to estimate the power potential of a water resource are head and flow. Techniques for measuring head and flow are discussed in some detail in most references on micro-hydro power, such as Inversin (1986 [72]) and Harvey et al., (1993 [34]).

Head

The static head is the most straightforward to measure; it needs some equipment, such as:

- A length of hosepipe with a pressure gauge (1 m of water $\equiv$ 0.1 kg/cm^2 $\equiv$ 0.098 bar $\equiv$ 1.42 p.s.i. $\equiv$ 9.81 kPa); the hosepipe is completely filled with water with its open end submerged in the upper water source and the other end fitted with the pressure gauge is held at the lower level to measure the actual static head.
- A water-filled hosepipe and calibrated rods, to measure down the hill in a series of steps (see Fig. 7.70A); a spirit level, dumpy level, or Abney level, may be used in a similar way.
- Surveyor's levelling equipment (theodolite or Abney level) and a tape measure, used to measure the head as a series of angles and distances (see Fig. 7.70B).
- Altimeters/barometers (for higher head applications): pressure-sensing altimeters need to be compensated for changes in atmospheric pressure between height reading, and for this reason may not be very accurate. GPS-based altitude measurement can also be used.
- Any available large-scale contoured maps or site plans.

Table 7.24: Power density in water currents as a function of water velocity

Velocity	(m/s)	0.5	1.0	1.5	2.0
	(knots)	1.0	2.0	3.0	4.0
Power density	(kW/m^2)	0.06	0.5	1.7	4.0

Table 7.25: Typical efficiencies of various small hydropower prime movers. Efficiencies are shown for water power to shaft power, except for the two marked *, where the efficiency is to pumped hydraulic output

Type of device	Typical efficiency range
Undershot water wheel	20–40%
Vertical shaft water mill	20–35%
Poncelet undershot or breast wheel	50–65%
Overshot water wheel	50–70%
Impulse turbine (e.g. Pelton, crossflow)	70–85%
Reaction turbine (e.g. Francis, propeller)	60–80%
Turbine-pump*	35–50%
Hydraulic ram pumps*	30–60%
River current converter	15–30%

Flow

Determining the flow of a stream is a little more complex. Stream flow varies through the year depending on the catchment area feeding it. Flows will be higher during a monsoon or wet season than in a dry season. Melting snow or glaciers in mountains may increase the flow even when it is not raining. Different streams also have different flow characteristics, depending on how quickly rainwater runs-off into them. Some streams get nearly all their flow directly from rain; this happens when the catchment area is made of steep, rocky or impermeable ground. Streams of this sort tend to flood violently, and may dry up completely when it is not raining. Other streams are fed mainly by springs coming from underground where the water may have been held for months as it percolates through the layers. This type of stream will have a consistent flow, varying little even when it rains, and possibly not even being reduced much by an extended dry period.

Techniques for predicting river flow rely on knowing the area of the stream catchment being considered (which can be found from maps), the rainfall in the catchment area, and the run-off characteristics for the terrain. The first two figures can be used to calculate the total amount of water falling within the catchment area of the stream, and a run-off coefficient will tell the proportion of that water that will flow out of the area in the stream (the remainder of the water

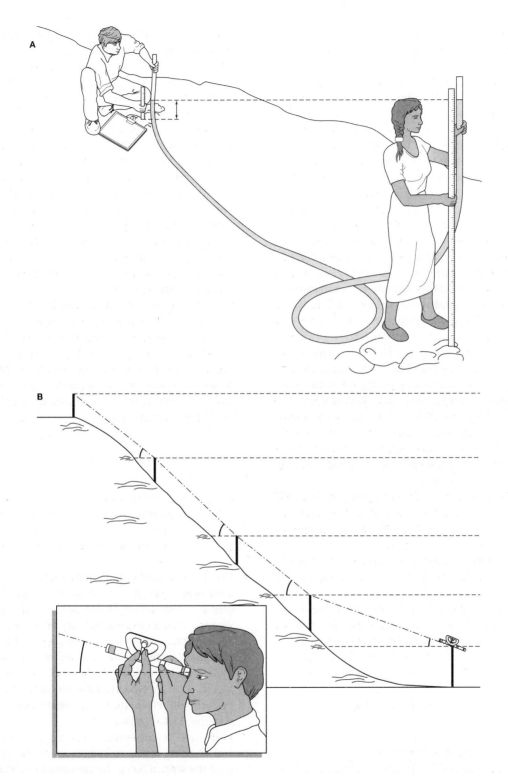

Fig. 7.70: Various methods of measuring head. A. Using a level or hosepipe. B. Measuring angles.

will evaporate, or be taken up into plants, etc.). As with wind data, some countries and regions have good information on rainfall, but many have sketchy and rather inaccurate figures. If there is a hydro-electric scheme in the neighbourhood, this will often have good hydrological data. Local or national meteorological stations may also be able to help. National authorities often have flow data extending over many years for large rivers, but are less likely to record flows in smaller streams. Run-off coefficients may be known for the area, or for similar sites in the same region, but are all too often unobtainable or plain inaccurate. If good rainfall and run-off data are available, then the reader is referred to additional reading [72] for further details on prediction methods. It should be noted that local variations can make big differences to the actual flow found in a stream. A number of organizations publish rainfall and run-off characteristics for various regions, but the results obtained from such data can be misleading. It always pays to check predicted flow with measurements of stream flow over as long a period of time as possible. Historic data for a wider region can be useful to give an idea of the order of variation that can be expected. It is helpful to know how often floods are experienced, and how large they are, for example.

In most cases small water-pumping sites will be on smaller streams, and it will be necessary to measure the flow. The following list gives some of the methods of doing this.

- Dam the stream and measure the overflow by measuring the time to fill a container (Fig. 7.71A).
- Measure the height of water going over a rectangular weir made from metal sheet, wood or concrete (triangular or trapezium-notch weirs may also be used). See Fig. 7.71B. For a rectangular weir the flow can be found from:

$$Q = 1.8 \cdot (L - 0.2 \cdot h) \cdot h^{3/2}$$

Q — flow (m³/s)
h — head over weir (m)

- Estimation of the stream velocity with a float. This method is used in streams where it is not

practicable to build a weir. Measure the depth of the stream at equal intervals across its width (at a point where the stream is straight and uniform), as in Fig. 7.71C. Then time a float drifting down the centre of the measured section. This gives the speed of the current at the centre of the stream; the mean velocity will be 0.6–0.85 of this figure. A rough, rocky stream bed requires a factor of 0.6, while smooth muddy surfaces require a factor of 0.85. The flow is calculated from the product of the mean velocity and area of stream cross-section using appropriate units: e.g. velocity in m/s × cross-section in m² gives the flow rate in m³/s. A current meter, or ship's log, if available, can be a more convenient way of measuring the velocity.

- Use a triangular-section velocity-head rod to measure the flow and depth at regular intervals across a stream, and calculating the flow from these measurements (Fig. 7.71D). The average velocity of the stream over the depth being measured can be calculated from the height by which the flow 'backs-up' on the bluff side of the rod [72].

$$h_{velocity} = \frac{v^2}{2 \cdot g}$$

$h_{velocity}$ — velocity head (m)
v — average velocity over depth of stream (m/s)
g — acceleration due to gravity, (9.8 m/s²)

- Use the 'salt gulp' conductivity method. Pour a measured quantity of salt solution into the centre of the stream at one point, and measure the change in conductivity of the water some distance downstream with an electrical conductivity meter. The data can then be used to determine the flow rate. Specialist salt-gulp meters have become available recently which perform the calculations automatically and give the flow as the output.

Flow can be measured over an extended period by using a stream gauge. To do this the flow of the stream has to be measured or calculated for various water levels, using one of the

266

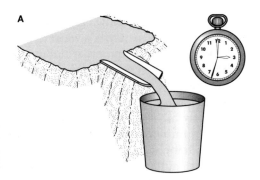

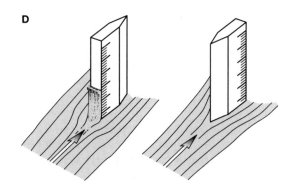

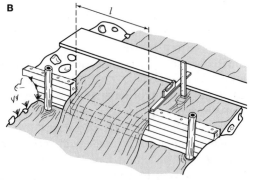

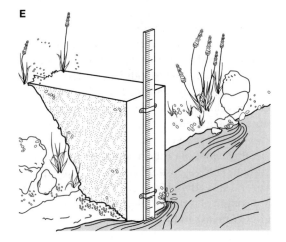

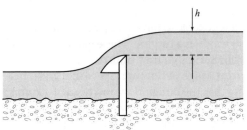

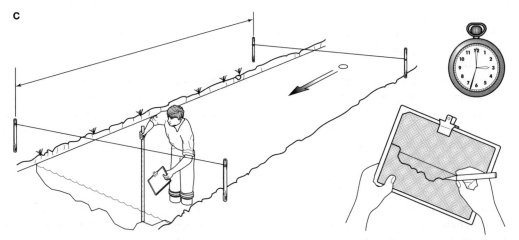

Fig. 7.71: Various methods of measuring stream flow: A. Filling a container. B. Using a weir. C. The float method. D. A velocity-head stick. E. Stream gauge.

267

methods above. In its simplest form, a stream gauge is simply a post with marking on it to show the water level. To measure the flow, the height of the water level is read off the gauge, and then the flow is determined by referring to the previous calibration measurements. The measurements can be automated by using an electronic or mechanical (clockwork) meter to record the water level. In this way the flow in a stream can be measured over a year, or ideally over several years, to find the average variation during different seasons or from month to month.

As well as determining the useful flow during the periods when pumping is required, it is important to assess how prone a stream is to flood damage. Many mountain streams have short duration flood flows that are 50 or more times the normal, and such floods can do severe damage to a pumping station. Local knowledge is often invaluable in this respect, as villagers will generally know how often a stream floods, and what the worst level was.

A final word of caution is that it is difficult to estimate flow or current velocity accurately by eye, and it is advisable to measure it, preferable by a couple of different methods, before relying on a stream to produce enough power for pumping.

7.9.4 General types of turbine for water lifting

As with pumps, there are families of different types of turbine to deal with different types of situation. Note that while turbines can be used for low-powered pumping applications of a few kilowatts, some of them can have variants for large hydroelectric stations that produce hundreds of megawatts. The comments here concern small units only, and so, for example, high head means 100–200 m or so, not 1,500–2,000 m that might be found in a big hydro scheme.

Propeller turbines are used at low heads (typically up to 5 or 10 m). A typical small fixed blade propeller turbine is shown in Fig. 7.72A. These are only adequately efficient over a narrow range of flows. Where variable flow and power is needed, adjustable gates are provided and the turbine runner may have fixed or adjustable

blade pitch. The latter is known as a Kaplan turbine and is more efficient over a wider range of flows than a fixed pitch propeller turbine. But adjustable pitch runner blades are expensive, and therefore are only normally applied for larger-scale installations.

For slightly higher heads (10–50 m), a number of other turbines can be used. One is the crossflow turbine (alias the Banki, Michell, or Banki-Michell turbine after the men who invented and developed it, or the Ossberger turbine after the main company that produced it). Here a jet of water impinges on a set of curved blades mounted between two discs, travels through the centre of the rotor and emerges from the far side again; Fig. 7.72C. Turbines of this kind do not run full of water and are known as impulse turbines in that they derive their rotation from deflecting a jet of water. Simple crossflow turbines can be made with very basic workshop facilities, and have been used for microhydro power in a number of developing countries.

It is possible to run a standard centrifugal pump backwards as a turbine. These make rather cheap turbines, though they only run efficiently over a narrow range of flow and speed at a given head. Note that the design flow and head of a Pump as Turbine is different from the pump design flow and head (for more details, see Williams, 1995 [73]). A dedicated turbine that looks rather like a pump is the Francis turbine, shown in Fig. 7.72B. The flow travels radially inward from the spiral casing, and exits from the middle of the rotor or 'runner'. A series of guide vanes direct the water from the casing into the runner; in more simple units these vanes are fixed, but more complex units have movable vanes which can maintain the efficiency of the turbine over a range of operating conditions. Francis turbines can have very high efficiencies, but have rather complex shapes, and tend to be expensive.

Pelton and Turgo turbines both work by squirting jets of water from nozzles onto the runner. Fig. 7.72D shows a Pelton turbine, which has a set of buckets mounted around the runner wheel. Each bucket has a central splitter which splits the jet in two and directs it almost back in the

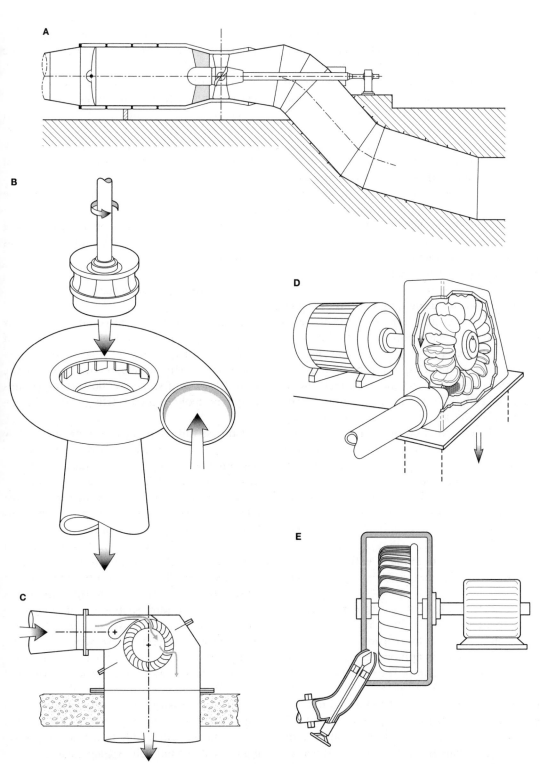

Fig. 7.72: Examples of the main types of hydropower turbine: A. Propeller. B. Francis. C. Crossflow. D. Pelton. E. Turgo.

direction it came from and outwards from the rim of the wheel. The jets in a turgo turbine hit the runner at an angle, and the water exits on the other side (Fig. 7.72E). Turgo turbines would typically be used from 30–100 m, with Pelton turbines able to go 30–200 m or more.

In books on turbines, a distinction is often made between 'impulse' and 'reaction' turbines. Impulse turbines are those that work at atmospheric pressure, with air inside the casing, converting the momentum of a jet of water to useful power; Pelton, turgo and crossflow turbines are impulse turbines. Reaction turbines run full of water, and dissipate pressure across the runner as well as removing momentum; Francis, Kaplan and propeller turbines are reaction turbines.

The reasons for using different turbine types at different heads and flows relate to the efficiency and speed of rotation that is required. Low head turbines, such as propeller turbines, tend to have a high rotational speed in relation to the velocity of the water travelling through them, and to take high flows. High head turbines generally go slower and take lower flows. For any specific site combination of head and flow, the choice of turbine depends on the speed required to drive the pump (or generator, or whatever), the efficiency that the turbine can achieve, the cost, and the availability. The operating ranges of the different turbine types overlap, and several different types can be suitable for a particular location. A full discussion of turbine selection will be found in standard textbooks on hydro-turbines, and in outline in Harvey et al. (1993 [34]).

The shaft of a turbine can be connected directly to a generator, which then can be used to power electric pumps for irrigation, or it can be directly coupled to an appropriate centrifugal or other rotodynamic pump. The route via electricity is of interest in that irrigation water pumping is highly seasonal, and a system which produces electricity can in many cases perform useful duties other than irrigation, such as providing light at night, post-harvest processing, etc. However electricity generation inevitably involves a higher level of engineering sophistication and investment than is inherent in powering a simple pump. Also, any hydro-electric plant needs to be well protected from flooding, while a simple turbine powering a pump is much less liable to damage and can therefore be more simply installed. There are also losses of efficiency inherent in converting shaft power to electricity, transmitting the electricity and then converting it back to shaft power; this could absorb 25 to 40% of the energy converted.

The chosen approach must depend on the size of the hydraulic resource, and the potential for satisfying other economic applications, plus of course the financial and organizational resources of the user community.

7.9.5 Chinese turbine-pumps

The Chinese have taken the combination of turbines and pumps to the logical conclusion of producing a large range of integrated turbine-pump units. This development started in the early 1960s, and some 60,000 turbine pumps were reportedly in use irrigating 400,000 ha by 1979.

Chinese turbine-pumps are generally for low head applications, where the hydro-power source will often be a canal fall in an irrigation scheme or a weir on a canalized river giving a head in the region of 1–5 m. Therefore the turbine most commonly used is a fixed pitch propeller turbine, which is appropriate for low heads. This is generally mounted with a vertical shaft, with fixed vanes directing the flow into it; it tends to be at its most efficient over a narrow range of flow rates. A centrifugal pump impeller is mounted on the same shaft as the turbine, back-to-back as in Fig. 7.73A. Where a high head water supply is needed, multi-stage centrifugal pumps may be connected to the turbine as in Fig. 7.73B. In some cases an extension drive shaft can be fitted, as in Fig. 7.74; this allows the turbine to be used as a general power source at times when there is no demand for irrigation water. For example it can readily be applied to powering a small rice mill, oil expeller, generator, etc. This can greatly enhance the economic value to be gained from the installation.

A large variety of different sizes and models of turbine pumps are made by numerous small manufacturers in China, and attractively low prices have been quoted for the export market. Table 7.26 indicates the range of sizes of single stage turbine pumps manufactured by a typical production unit, the Youxi Turbine-Pump Plant, Fujian.

Table 7.27 indicates the performance of a selection of small low-, medium- and high-head turbine-pumps, including estimates of shaft power and efficiency. The overall efficiency is in the range 32–50% for the models considered; this implies that the turbines and pumps have individual efficiencies in the 56 to 71% range, assuming roughly equal efficiency for each. Other models exist with claimed overall efficiencies as high as 58%.

Because fixed pitch propeller turbines only have a narrow operating range where high efficiency can be achieved, it is important that they are accurately sized to suit the flow and head. Where varying flow conditions occur, it is usual to install several small units rather than one large one. This means each unit can always be run near to its optimum flow condition by shutting them down one by one to cater for reduced flows. A good design strategy is to install two units, one with twice the flow capacity of the other; then both are used under the maximum flow condition. With this arrangement, the larger turbine can take 2/3 of the maximum flow on its own, and the smaller can take 1/3. This therefore allows efficient operation at 1/3, 2/3 and full-flow. Higher heads or higher flows are commonly catered for by connecting turbine pumps in series or parallel.

Turbine pumps are typically installed on a concrete platform built into a weir, as in Fig. 7.75. Therefore, although the turbine-pump unit is inexpensive, depending on the site, civil workings are likely to represent the largest cost-element. Pipes also will be expensive, but then for a given flow they will be equally expensive regardless of the choice of pumping system.

Cost comparisons within China show that irrigation using turbine pumps is significantly cheaper than driving pumps with electric motors or small IC engines. System costs in other countries would depend on the cost of the

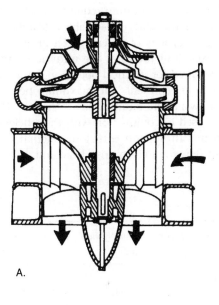

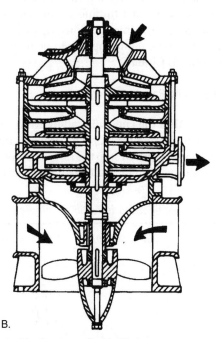

A.

B.

Fig. 7.73: Cross-sections through two turbine pumps: A. Single-stage. B. Multi-stage.

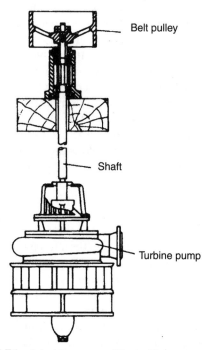

Fig. 7.74: A turbine pump fitted with an extension driveshaft (shown part sectioned)

turbine-pump units locally, but the Chinese experience does show that turbine pumps can be very attractive for suitable locations. It is worth noting that turbine pumps appear to be manufactured only in China.

7.9.6 Hydraulic Ram Pump (or Hydram)

A ram pump uses the energy in falling water to develop high pressure for pumping. It works by slamming a valve shut to stop the flow in a pipe, which creates very high 'water hammer' pres-

sures. These high pressures are then used to push a small fraction of the amount of water that flows through the pump to a much higher level. The operation of a ram pump is discussed in some detail in Section 6.10.

Ram pumps are low power devices. A small ram pump will usually have an input power of less than 50 W, and very large ram pumps rarely go over 500 W. Their useful output comes from their persistence; they work day and night without stopping. Even then, the output is limited, and so ram pumps are more often used for drinking water systems than for irrigation. They can be useful for irrigating crops with a limited water requirement, such as vegetables.

When installing ram pumps, it is important to appreciate several points. Firstly, they require falling water to operate them, and so are suitable for springs or streams in hilly areas; they cannot be powered from lakes or slow rivers without a head drop. Secondly, the available flow needs to be much greater than the flow to be pumped. Thirdly, the water pumped is the same as the water that powers the ram pump, so if a dirty stream is used, the pumped water will also be dirty.

The size of ram pump required can be estimated from the tables below. Table 7.28 indicates the input capacity of different sizes of hydram; the lower limit indicates the minimum input flow required for practical operation, while the upper limit represents the maximum possible drive flow a hydram can efficiently handle. This can be used in conjunction with the efficiency equations in Section 6.10.1 to calculate the output flow for a given drive head and delivery head.

Table 7.26: Specifications for various Chinese turbine-pump models

Model	Drive head (m)	Drive flow (l/s)	Delivery head (m)	Delivery flow (l/s)	Net weight (kg)
20–6	1–4	88–180	6–24	6–12	59
30–6	1–4	210–420	6–24	21–42	155
40–6	1–4	370–740	6–24	37–72	290
60–6	1–4	684–1,354	6–24	70–142	985
60–16	1–6	650–1,620	16–96	25–57	1,374

Table 7.27: Performance data for small turbine pumps

Turbine pump model		Drive head (m)	Drive flow (l/s)	Delivery head (m)	Delivery flow (l/s)	Shaft power (kW)	Overall efficiency (%)
High yield	10-0	0.5	15	3	0.8	0.047	32.8
High yield	20-4	0.5	60	2	7.8	0.203	
	20-6	1.0	84	6	6.0	0.57	42.8
High yield	30-6	1.0	190	6	16.0	1.34	50.6
Low head ZD680	10-6	1.0	20	6	1.2	0.13	
	10-4	4.0	40	24	2.4	1.0	36.0
Low head ZD 680	20-6	1.0	81	6	6.4	0.56	
	20-6	6.0	198	36	15.5	8.18	47.0
Low head ZD 680	30-10	6.0	446	60	19.2	19.25	
	30-16	6.0	446	96	11.2	19.25	43.0
Medium head Z 540	Z20-6	5	139	30	10.0	4.62	
	Z20-6	14	232	84	16.0	21.6	42.0
High head ZD 440	G20-6	12	172	72	11.0	14.4	
	G20-6	20	222	120	14.0	30.9	38.0
High lift	40-6	0.5	238	3	20.9		
	40-6	5.0	750	30	66.1		
High lift	40-17	1.0	333	17	3.3		
	40-17	6.0	815	102	8.5		

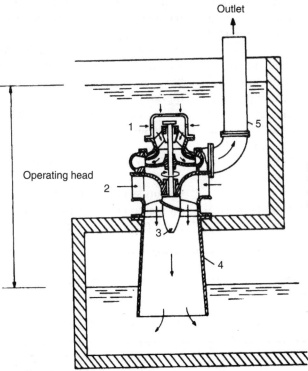

1 – pump intake
2 – turbine intake
3 – turbine runner
4 – draft tube
5 – pump discharge pipe

Fig. 7.75: A typical turbine-pump installation

In a typical hydram installation, a supply head is created by digging a small contoured diversion canal off a more steeply-falling stream. For very small heads it is normal simply to create a weir and to install the hydram directly below it. The drive pipe itself needs to be a certain length in order to generate a sufficiently long pressure spike when the valve closes. Publications give wildly differing recommendations for the optimum length and angle of the drive pipe, which probably indicates that they are not too critical. The drive pipe length should be at least 100 times its own diameter, and probably not more than 1,000 times its diameter (at which length the friction losses would be significant); some give the optimum as 500 times the diameter [35]. The slope of the drive pipe also has to be kept within certain limits. Jeffery et al., 1992 [43] recommends that the length of a drive pipe should be between 2 and 4 times the drive head (corresponding to a slope of between 15° and 30°), but some commercial manufacturers recommend ratios of 5 : 1 and even 8 : 1.

Except for the low heads, the drive pipe should be made of good quality steel, to resist the fatigue stress during operation. A suggested pressure rating for a drive pipe is twice the delivery pressure. The pipe should be straight, as any bends would have strong sideways forces induced in them by the water hammer pressure, which could cause the pipe to move around and break. In any case, the ram pump body needs to be firmly fixed down, as the beats of its action apply a significant shock load. In most installations the ram pump is bolted down to a concrete foundation.

The delivery head is normally kept between 5 and 25 times the drive head. For a given drive flow and head, the higher the delivery head, the lower the output, and if the delivery head is more than 25 times the drive head the output will fall to a trickle. The maximum height that can be lifted also depends on the construction of the pump. Most steel or cast iron pumps can deliver up to 100 m, though a few manufacturers produce pumps for up to 200 m. Plastic pumps would typically be limited to 40 m. The delivery pipe can be made from any material capable of carrying the delivery pressure. The delivery pipe should be sized to keep the friction losses reasonable; if it is too small the output flow will be restricted, but if it is too large it will be very expensive. Losses of 5–10% are reasonable. It is recommended that a hand-valve or check-valve (non-return valve) should be fitted in the delivery line near the outlet from the ram pump so that the delivery line does not have to be drained if the hydram is stopped for adjustment or any other reason. This will also minimize any backflow past the delivery valve in the air-chamber and improve the efficiency.

If the output of one ram pump is insufficient, the flow can be increased by having a combination of pumps – either multiples of the same size, or a large and a small pump. Multiple pumps are a good idea anyway, as they allow the output to be varied without the need for re-tuning (by closing down one or more pumps) and give increased reliability of supply if one pump breaks down or needs servicing.

7.9.7 Water wheels and norias

The undershot water wheel is probably the oldest method of extracting energy from rivers. In many cases the device simply dips into the river

Table 7.28: Ranges of typical ram pump drive (input) flows for various drive pipe bores (Tacke, 1986 [74])

Nominal dia. of drive pipe	(in)	bore:	1¼	1½	2	2½	3	4	5	6	7	8
	(mm)	bore:	32	40	50	65	80	100	125	150	175	200
Flow	(l/min)	from:	7	12	27	45	68	136	180	364	545	770
	(l/min)	to:	16	25	55	96	137	270	410	750	1,136	1,545

and is turned by the movement of the current; see Fig. 7.76. In the example illustrated, from Vietnam, the entire structure is made of bamboo. Bamboo tubes with one end closed are mounted around the rim of the wheel. The bamboo tubes dip into the river and re-emerge filled with water, which they carry round to near the top, where the water pours out into a trough. Devices of this kind are quite widely used in S. E. Asia, including China, Japan and Thailand as well as Vietnam, and are known as 'Noria'. Figure 7.77 shows a Chinese version and illustrates the principle and method of construction. The Noria is similar in many ways to the Persian Wheel discussed earlier in Section 6.4.1.

The biggest shortcoming of the Noria is that they need to be of a diameter somewhat greater than the head; this makes them fine for low head applications, but they become large and cumbersome for higher lifts. The example illustrated in Fig. 7.76 is 10 m in diameter and is claimed to be able to irrigate about 8 ha. There is a small weir just visible in the illustration which creates a head of about 100 mm at the base of the wheel which significantly improves the performance. The 10 m diameter Vietnamese Noria turns at the rate of about 1 revolution in 40 seconds and delivers water, typically, at the rate of 7 l/s. Although the Noria is attractive in being relatively inexpensive and also being capable of manufacture in the village, the sites where they may be used are limited and they are particularly prone to damage by floods. Therefore annual repair costs quoted for Vietnamese Norias can be as much as 30–50% of the capital cost of the installation. However, under Vietnamese conditions the same source indicated that some sample installations which were surveyed produced a return for the users in terms of value of grain production in the range 24–60% over the estimated costs.

A modern version of the Asian Noria is the floating coil pump, versions of which have been tested in Kenya, Sudan and Mali by various organizations (see Fig. 7.78 and Fig. 6.17). The principle of the coil pump is explained in Section 6.4.5. These experimental river current powered irrigation pumping systems consist of floating undershot water wheels (mounted on floating pontoons made from empty oil barrels), and by using a coil pump it is possible to use a small diameter water wheel to lift water to a considerable height (around 10–15 m is possible from a 2–3 m diameter rotor).

The claimed performance of a prototype floating coil pump tested on the River Nile near Juba was 0.7 l/s against 5 m head with a river current velocity of 1.2 m/s. Quite high current velocities in the range from 1–2 m/s (2–4 knots) seem necessary for devices of this kind. The Sudan prototype device was made from steel and wood, with flexible plastic pipe for the coil pump and cost $350 when built in the early 1980s. In both cases the considerable length of flexible pipe required accounted for about one-third of the total cost.

The Royal Irrigation Department of Thailand also developed a floating, undershot waterwheel device similar to those just described, but in this case the wheel is mechanically linked to a conventional piston pump by means of sprockets and chains. It requires a minimum current velocity of 1 m/s with a river flow of at least 0.6 m³/s, and is claimed to be capable of pumping between 0.3 l/s to a 60 m head and 1.5 l/s to a head of 15 m.

A general problem with water wheels is that if the drive is taken from the main shaft, the costs become high in relation to the power available, because large slow-moving (and therefore expensive) mechanical drive components are needed to transmit the high torque involved. Also, with shafts only turning at 1–5 rpm (which is typical of waterwheels) either very large pump swept volumes are required or a lot of gearing up is necessary to drive a smaller pump at an adequate speed; either way the engineering is expensive in relation to the power. Therefore water wheels, although apparently offering simple solutions, are not always easy to adapt for powering mechanical devices such as pumps.

7.9.8 River current turbines

Undershot water wheels are an inefficient means to exploit river currents since the bulk of the

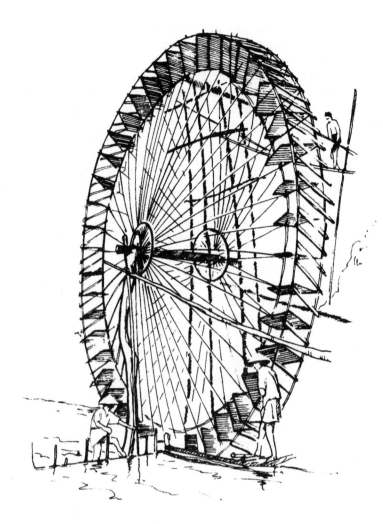

Fig. 7.76: A bamboo water wheel, Vietnam

machine is external to the water at any one time, and therefore provides no power. There have been a number of attempts to develop improved water-current devices, but despite the number of designs that have been tried, there are very few commercially-available current turbines. Most of the turbines tried have been for generating electricity.

A river-current turbine that was being used to supply drinking water in Juba, southern Sudan, is shown in Fig. 7.79. It uses an inclined-axis rotor, completely submerged in a river below a floating pontoon that is moored to the bank with cables. Being situated in the main stream of the river, away from the banks, the water it pumped was reasonably clean. The minimum current speed for which this design of turbine is viable is 0.6 m/s, when it will deliver 2 l/s of water through a head of 4 m, equivalent to a hydraulic output of around 80 W. At higher current speeds (above 2 m/s), the turbine can produce up to 2 kW. The maximum head a single unit can pump is 25 m, though a number of pumps can be placed in series to obtain higher heads. The capital cost

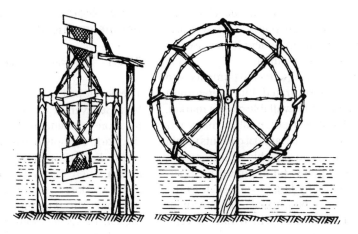

Fig. 7.77: A small-scale Chinese Noria

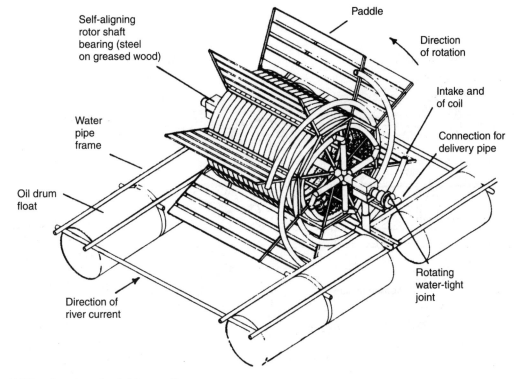

Self-aligning
rotor shaft
bearing (steel
on greased wood)

Paddle

Direction
of rotation

Water
pipe
frame

Intake and
of coil

Connection for
delivery pipe

Oil drum
float

Direction of
river current

Rotating
water-tight
joint

Fig. 7.78: A water wheel driven coil pump

of the turbine was $4,500, excluding pipe, pontoon and mooring. This turbine replaced diesel-powered pumps, which suffered from fuel supply problems before being completely destroyed in unrest in 1992. Further details of this type of turbine are given in Garman, 1986 [75].

An early experimental prototype of this turbine (using a Darrieus-type vertical axis rotor – see the sub-section 'Horizontal and vertical-axis rotors' in Section 7.7.3), was developed by IT Power as an irrigation pump. This was also tested in southern Sudan, where it was used to irrigate a 6 ha vegetable garden.

The potential for using a river to pump its own water has been demonstrated, but river-current turbines are not readily available on the market. The considerable power potential in many rivers, canals and for that matter tidal currents would suggest that there is considerable scope for using water currents to power pumping devices, particularly because many large rivers (such as the Nile, Euphrates, Zambesi, Indus), flow through regions which are arid or which have several months of dry season.

7.10 Biomass and coal (non-petroleum fuels)

7.10.1 The availability and distribution of fuels

The developed world runs mainly on petroleum because, even at today's prices, oil is cheap and far more convenient than any alternative. But, the world's supply of easily recovered petroleum is fast diminishing and we are moving towards an era when supply will no longer exceed the demand. Already, many developing countries can no longer afford to import sufficient oil for their present needs, let alone to satisfy expanded future energy demand.

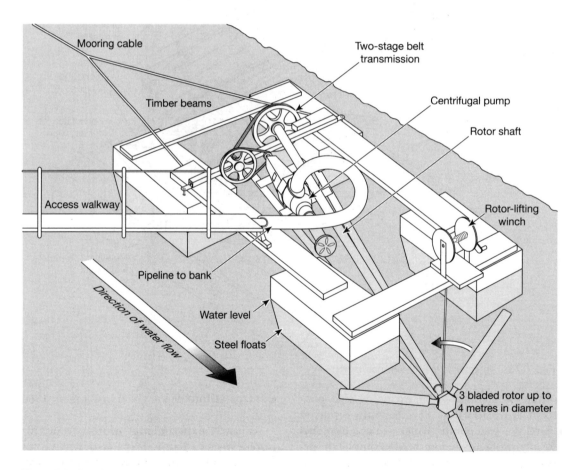

Fig. 7.79: The Garman river-current turbine pump

The main fuel alternatives to petroleum are fossil fuels, such as gas, coal, lignite and peat, plus the 'biomass fuels', which are derived from recently-living (rather than fossilized) organic material, such as wood, plant crops and animal dung. Estimates on world coal reserves vary, but there is general agreement that the amount of coal energy available is of the order of ten times the total for oil, so although oil shortages due to physical depletion can be expected within decades, coal should remain available for centuries. In fact it is increasingly being realized that the need to control greenhouse gases and atmospheric pollution will constrain the use of coal long before the reserves are exhausted.

Considered as a global resource there is no shortage of biomass, since:

- the total energy usage by man is only about 7% of the world's natural rate of photosynthetic energy storage (i.e. the solar energy stored in plant matter);
- the stored biomass on the earth's surface at present is approximately equivalent to the entire proven fossil fuel reserves (oil, coal and natural gas).

Biomass, in the form of firewood, charcoal, agricultural residues, or dried animal dung is already the main energy resource for over 2,000 million people, comprising the majority of the poorer half of humanity. It is estimated that biomass accounts for about 14% of the world's primary energy demand, the total amount of fossil-fuel energy and energy from renewable sources used by man (Hall et al., 1993 [76]). In developing countries biomass represents 35% of the primary energy supply. Certain poorer countries depend on biomass fuels at present for over 90% of their energy needs (i.e. mainly for cooking fuel). It has been estimated that 58% of energy use in Africa, 17% in Asia and 8% in Latin America is currently met from biomass energy (Kristoferson et al., 1991 [77]). Therefore biomass is already a huge and vital economic resource, although it is usually used in traditional ways and on a small scale. Biomass is still rarely used for the production of shaft power via heat engines, and even less so for water pumping.

The main reason that biomass is so widely used in rural areas is that it is free, and locally available. Firewood can often be extracted from forests or scrubland near villages, and crop residues and animal dung are a by-product of agriculture. Collecting and storing fuels such as firewood can be a time-consuming activity, especially as deforestation makes usable wood more scarce, but the fact that no money has to be paid for it makes it the primary fuel for many poorer people. Biomass may be less well suited for larger scale exploitation, as it is bulky and of low commercial value, so transporting it to where it is needed may not be economic.

Biomass fuels are becoming increasingly scarce. Rapid population growth is leading to a depletion of biomass resources. Increasing demand for land for agriculture is primarily responsible for this, but the additional demand for fuel also puts pressure on natural vegetation. Climatic change has also aggravated the situation in some regions, such as the African Sahel and Haiti. Lack of firewood leads to increasing use of lower quality fuels such as dung. Dung is a major household fuel in many areas of South Asia, and in India 21% of households already rely on dung for their cooking energy needs (Ravindranath and Hall, 1995 [78]). Where dung was previously used as a fertilizer, its use for fuel means that soil quality declines, making both crop and biomass production more difficult in an ever-deepening cycle.

Biomass is a versatile source of energy that can be converted to 'modern' forms such as liquid and gaseous fuels, electricity, and process heat. Biomass energy is not restricted to small-scale usage, but can be used for large power plants. Modern biomass systems can be set up in virtually any location where plants can be grown or domestic animals reared. Much of the R and D on large-scale biomass utilization has focused on its use as a petroleum substitute (e.g. alcohol for powering cars in Brazil), to address the 'oil crisis' of the rich, rather than the 'wood crisis' of the poor. Some of these latter developments, involving the large-scale production of biomass fuels, give rise for concern as to the impact they might have on the capability of countries to feed their populations. For example, Table 7.29 indicates the land requirements in Brazil to fuel a car compared with those to feed a person. This shows that even a medium sized car doing 12,000 km per year needs a land area to produce its alcohol fuel sufficient to feed 14 people on a subsistence diet. Brazil is actually a net exporter of food, and so can afford to use land for fuel, but the situation may be different for countries that need to import food.

This issue of food crops versus energy crops is an important one, but it is not always a problem. Where crop residues are used as fuel, the production of food and energy can be complementary; many crops produce residues with an energy value, e.g., sugarcane bagasse, rice hulls, maize cobs, coconut husks, oil palm husk and fibre, groundnut shells, coffee and cotton husks. Table 7.30 provides crop residue figures for a selection of different crops, as does Table 7.32.

Many biomass fuels can be grown on arid or marginal land that is unsuitable for food crops. Where the fuel crop is used for irrigation pumping to produce food crops, especially in a small-scale 'on-farm' process, then the overall food output of the land can increase, even allowing for the area used to grow dedicated biomass fuel (a numerical example is given in Section 7.10.3).

Some research and development has been done on the application of small modern biomass technologies in rural decentralized areas of developing countries. Nepal, India and China, for example, are well known for their rural biogas programmes. More recently, gasifiers using energy crops and crop residues are being installed in parts of India for drinking and small-scale irrigation.

7.10.2 The nature and calorific value of fuels

All fuels involve the combustion of carbon and, usually, hydrogen with atmospheric oxygen to produce mainly carbon dioxide and water, plus heat. As far as heat production is concerned, the relative merits of various fuels are best summarized in terms of the calorific value of total heat released when they are burnt; see Table 7.31. This

Table 7.29: Land requirements in Brazil to produce grain for food or for fuel alcohol (Brown, 1980 [79])

Grain crop used	Quantity required (kg/year)	Cultivated land area (ha)
Subsistence diet	180	0.1
Affluent diet	700	0.4
Medium sized car	2,800	1.4
Large (US) car	6,600	3.2

Table 7.30: Crop residue production

Crop	Fuel residue
	(as % of total crop weight)
Rice	20%
Maize	30%
Groundnut	33%
Cotton	235%
Sugarcane	33%
	(yield)
Coconut	shell −135 g; fibre −164 g; pith − 264 g
Mulberry	10 t/ha/yr

can be expressed in energy per unit weight or per unit volume, but in the end, what matters most is the energy per unit cost. Also of importance with biomass fuels grown as a fuel crop is their productivity, which obviously affects their cost-effectiveness. This must clearly depend on many factors such as location, soil fertility, nutrient supplements, precipitation and/or water supplements, species or species mix, and seed or planting stock quality. There are numerous studies that show that a mixed wood plantation is likely to provide better biomass productivities than monocultures. Table 7.32 shows the range of estimated productivities of woody biomass under different management situations. The most productive areas for photosynthetically produced material are the forested regions; agricultural land is typically only half as productive per hectare in terms of biomass generation. It must be noted that forests are only productive if biomass is harvested at a sustainable rate, leaving the ecosystem intact. Cutting down a forest produces a huge initial harvest, and the land will be highly fertile for a year or two following, but production rates will decline steeply thereafter. Table 7.33 shows some typical stable photosynthetic production rates for different types of land usage, while Table 7.34 gives calorific values for a variety of fuels, both fossil and biomass. Fossil fuels tend to be more consistent in their properties than biomass. The calorific value of biomass fuels is particularly influenced by the moisture content of the fuel. For example, air-dried wood, which normally has a moisture content of 25% will produce 50%–100% more heat than 'green' freshly cut wood with a moisture content of 50%.

Oven-drying of wood increases the heat yield further (but requires expenditure of heat); fuel, once oven-dried, has to be kept in warm dry conditions before being burnt or it will reabsorb atmospheric moisture. Therefore there is a good case to be made for utilization of waste heat from any biomass engine system to help dry its own fuel supply. Both the production rates and the calorific values of different cultivated biomass crops are highly variable; Table 7.35 indicates examples of measured yields of potential fuel crops.

7.10.3 The potential for using biomass to fuel irrigation pumps

Biomass ought to be an ideal energy resource for irrigation, since the whole point of irrigation is to produce more biomass, usually for food rather than for fuel. A simple calculation confirms that it is possible, at least in theory, to grow more than enough biomass to fuel an engine and produce an additional food crop, even without considering using food-crop residues. For

Table 7.31: Typical energy content of various cereal crop residues [44]

Crop	Typical crop yield (tonne/ha)	Residue yield (tonne/ha)	Calorific value of residue (GJ/ha)	(kWh/ha)
Rice	2.5	5.0	90	25,000
Wheat	1.5	2.7	49	14,000
Maize	1.7	4.3	76	21,000
Sorghum	1.0	2.5	45	12,000
Barley	2.0	3.6	65	18,000
Millet	0.6	2.0	36	10,000

Table 7.32: Estimates of woody biomass productivity under different management situations (oven dry weight)

Management situation	High (tonnes/ha/year)
No improvement in genetic stock + no fertilizer application + no extra water	2–5
Genetic improvement of planting stock + no fertilizer application + no extra water	4–10
Genetic improvement of planting stock + no fertilizer application + extra water	20–30

Table 7.33: Photosynthetic carbon production rates (Earl, 1975 [80])

Type of land	Net biomass production (tonne/ha)	Total world annual natural production (giga-tonne)
FOREST		
Temperate deciduous	10	8
Conifer and mixed	6	9
Temperate rain forest	12	1
Tropical rain forest	15	15
Dry woodlands	2	3
Sub-total		36
NON-FOREST		
Agricultural	4	6
Grasslands	3	8
Tundra	1	1
Deserts	1	3
Sub-total		18
TOTAL		54

Table 7.34: Approximate heat values of various fuels

Fuel	Calorific value per unit weight (MJ/kg)	Calorific value per unit volume (MJ/m³)
Fossil fuels		
Petrol/gasoline	44	32,000
Fuel oil	44	39,000
Paraffin/kerosene	45	36,000
Diesel/gas oil	46	38,000
Coal tar/asphalt	40	40,800
Anthracite coal	35	56,000
Bitumous coal	33	42,900
Lignite (brown) coal	30	37,500
Peat	20	18,200
Coke	28	22,400
Natural gas (methane)	56	40*
Coal gas	9	20*
Propane (cylinder gas)	48	90*
Butane (cylinder gas)	47	120*
Biomass fuels		
Oak wood	18	14,400
Pine wood	20	10,000
Acacia wood	16	11,000
Charcoal	28	11,000
Sunflower stalks	20	10,000
Wheat straw	18	–
Beef cattle manure	14	–
Methanol (methyl alcohol)	20	19,000
Ethanol (ethyl alcohol)	28	28,000
Biogas (65% methane)	20	23*
Wood gas (typical producer gas)	–	5*
Vegetable oil	39	32,000

* The calorific value per unit volume of these fuels appears very low because they are normally gaseous.

example, considering the irrigation system sized in Fig. 5.12, where 3 ha is irrigated with 8 mm of water on average per day over a pumping head of 10 m. Assuming that irrigation is necessary on 200 days per year, Fig. 5.12 indicates an average shaft-power requirement of 13 kWh/d, or in this case 2,600 kWh per year. If the power system can produce shaft power from fuel at 10% efficiency (which is possible at this power size) then the gross fuel requirement is for 26,000 kWh or 94 GJ. It can be seen from Table 7.31 that this requirement could often be met simply from cereal crop residues for 3 ha, but if a fuel crop was grown (because, for example the residues were needed for other purposes, such as cooking fuel) then just 0.1 to 0.2 ha of eucalyptus (for example) would produce this fuel requirement. Therefore, the entire irrigation energy demand could be met from a fuel crop occupying in this example less than one tenth of the area to be cultivated. And 10 m lift with 200 days per year irrigation is a more demanding irrigation energy need than would apply in many cases.

There are examples of villages where biomass is used to fuel irrigation pumping, such as in Tumkur District in Southern India, but these are comparatively rare. The main reason for this is that the technology for cost-effective pumping is not readily available, and few farmers will even be aware that the option exists. The rest of this chapter sets out to review biomass-fuelled pumping options and their advantages and disadvantages.

7.10.4 Technical options for using biomass fuels for irrigation pumping

All biomass fuels are ultimately burnt so as to power an appropriate internal or external combustion engine. There is, however, a plethora of options available for preparing, processing or modifying raw biomass for more effective use as a fuel, as shown in Fig. 7.80. Generally these involve a trade-off between enhancing the properties of the biomass as a fuel on the one hand, and extra cost combined with losses of some of the original material. No particular route can be said to offer advantages over any other, rather there are 'horses for courses'; some are better than others in specific applications and situations.

It can be seen from Fig. 7.80 that there are three primary categories of biomass raw materials:

Table 7.35: Potential yield and energy content of selected crops

Crop	Location	Annual dry matter yield (tonne/ha)	Calorific value of residue (GJ/ha/yr)	Equivalent tonnes of oil (t/ha/yr)
Sunflower	Russia	30	530	12
Forage sorghum	Puerto Rico	69	1,210	28
Hybrid corn	Mississippi, USA	13	250	6
Water hyacinth	Florida, USA	36	630	14
Sugarcane (average)	Florida, USA	39	680	16
Sugarcane (experimental)	California, USA	72	1,250	29
Sudangrass	California, USA	36	630	15
Bamboo	SE Asia	11	210	5
Eucalyptus	California, USA	45	790	19
Eucalyptus	India	39	678	16
Eucalyptus	Ethiopia	48	834	19
American sycamore	Georgia, USA	8	160	4
Algae (pond)	California, USA	88	1,520	36
Tropical rainforest	typical	41	710	17
Subtropical deciduous forest	typical	24	420	10

- solid woody, ligno-cellulose material and dry residues;
- wet vegetation, residues and wastes;
- oil-bearing seeds and resins.

In most cases these need some kind of processing before use; at the very least they need to be dried.

7.10.5 Direct combustion of solid biomass fuels

As indicated in Fig. 7.80, solid fuels may be treated in a number of ways. The most straightforward is to burn them as solids, as, for example, using wood in the firebox of a steam engine boiler. Historically, a huge range of solid fuel furnaces and boilers existed, but today only a few manufacturers make them for small power systems. Medium-sized furnaces and steam plants are readily available for use in tropical agro-industrial process plants such as sugar refineries, though these are, unfortunately, much larger than is appropriate for powering small-scale irrigation pumps.

For small systems, the fuel can simply be fed into a furnace by hand. An example of an engine using this type of furnace is the 2 kW experimental steam engine developed in the early 1950s by Ricardo, shown in Fig. 7.81. Furnaces of this kind will typically burn 2–3 kg/h of wood per kilowatt of shaft output, assuming the power is produced via a small steam engine. The small Stirling hot-air engine shown in Fig. 7.30, dating from USA around 1900, has a similar heating arrangement.

There are some difficulties in designing a furnace that will handle any fuel; quite different grate arrangements are needed to cope with particulate fuels such as sawdust or rice hulls, as compared with large lumps such as logs or coal. Therefore it is important to use equipment able to accept the proposed fuel. For example, there are furnaces designed especially to handle fuels like sawdust or rice hulls, which would clog up a conventional grate arrangement; in one such type known as a 'Kraft Furnace', the furnace and storage hopper are combined so that the outer surface of the mass of sawdust burns and the partially burned gases are drawn through a multitude of small passages into a secondary combustion chamber, where combustion is

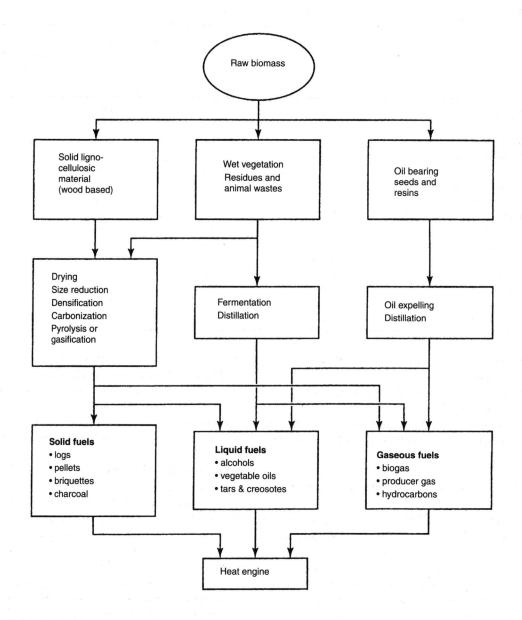

Fig. 7.80: Routes for processing biomass fuels

completed. The International Rice Research Institute (IRRI) in the Philippines has developed a small-scale 'fluidized bed' burner for rice hulls which pumps air through the hulls to separate them and supply sufficient oxygen for them to burn.

7.10.6 Gasification of solid biomass fuels

Instead of burning solid fuels directly, woody biomass may be pyrolized to yield either combustible gas (which may be used for an internal combustion engine), or volatiles that may be

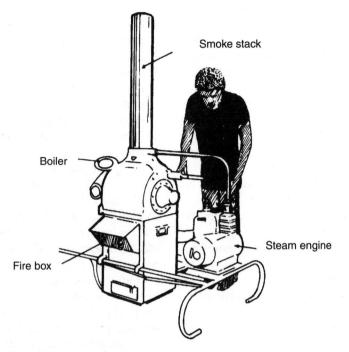

Fig. 7.81: A 2 kW Ricardo steam engine

condensed to yield a limited quantity of liquid fuels. The purpose of gasification is to convert some of the energy of an inconvenient solid fuel into a more convenient gaseous fuel. The main advantage of gaseous fuels is that they can generally be used with internal combustion engines and not just with rare steam or Stirling engines.

The first commercially successful internal combustion engine powered by a gasifier was built by Lenoir in France in 1860 and ran on coal, and the technique was widely used at the beginning of the last century. It was again widely used during the 1939–45 World War, when some 700,000 gasifiers were in use for powering motor vehicles due to shortages of petroleum. The subsequent cheap-oil era curtailed their use almost completely, but a number of manufacturers in various countries still make gasifier or producer gas units. For example, India has around 500 small (5 and 10 hp) 'wood-gas' water-pumping systems.

The process involves the heating of a solid, carbonaceous fuel to drive off inflammable volatiles and to produce carbon monoxide (CO) from a reaction between the carbon and the carbon dioxide generated by primary combustion. Moisture in the fuel, plus carbohydrates in the biomass also react with carbon to yield further carbon monoxide plus free hydrogen, and some of the free hydrogen reacts with carbon to produce methane. Any source of heat may be used to gasify biomass fuels, but usually the heating process is by partial combustion; i.e. the fuel is burnt to heat itself. The chemical make up of producer gas is typically:

17% CO; 18% H_2; 14% CO_2; 2% CH_4; 49% N_2

and its calorific value will be approximately 5 MJ/m³. Because of the high proportion of inert nitrogen and carbon dioxide, this is only one-eighth of the energy per unit volume of natural gas, such as methane. The calorific value can be enhanced by injecting steam into the gasifier, or by using moist fuel; this yields more hydrogen, but with small systems it is difficult to do this in an optimal manner without actually extinguishing the primary combustion. A similar effect can be achieved by controlling the moisture in the fuel, with a moisture content of around 12% being optimal; the performance of gasifiers is quite sensitive to the moisture content of the fuel.

Although the calorific value of producer gas is low, the quantity of air required for combustion is also low, so that the thermal value of a stoichiometric mixture, as is required to be induced into an engine for optimum combustion, of producer gas and air is better than might be expected, as indicated in Table 7.36.

A wide variety of materials can be used in gasifiers. The main groups are:
- Agricultural crop residues: straw, stubble, hulls, cobs, stalks, coconut shells, sugarcane bagasse, cotton stover, etc.
- Wood: fuelwood, bark, woodchips, charcoal
- Fossil fuels: peat, coke, coal
- Dry animal waste: poultry litter
- Organic household refuse.

Some combustible materials do not work well in gasifiers because they clog together to form dense layers. This cools the combustion, and leads to the formation of tar. Some sorts of straw do not work well, sawdust is a poor feedstock, and woodchips need to be more than a few millimetres in size to work.

Types of gasifier

A producer gas generator is usually a vertically mounted cylinder which is loaded with fuel from the top (see Fig. 7.82). The fuel falls under gravity to replace burnt and gasified material in the lower fire zone. The figure shows three main types of gasifier that are used for small plants:
- **Up-draught**, in which air is introduced at the bottom and the feedstock has the products of gasification passing through it.
- **Down-draught**, in which the volatiles are drawn downwards through the hottest part of the combustion zone; this has the effect of cracking any tars and complex chemicals and thereby gasifying them more effectively than with an up-draught unit.
- **Cross-draught**; these have a small, intensely hot zone fed from an air nozzle or tuyere.

The first of the above options, the up-draught gasifier, is simplest, but it produces gas with a lot of carry-over of tar and volatiles that can rapidly damage an internal combustion engine. This is a particular problem if it is burning raw biomass fuels containing a lot of volatiles. Tar-problems can be reduced in up-draught units by using pre-pyrolized fuels like charcoal or coke, but this adds to the cost of the process. Up-draft units are good at handling moisture in the fuel, because the hot gases pass through the new fuel feedstock and dry it.

Down-draught gasifiers produce a cleaner output, and are more commonly used to power small internal combustion engines. They are not as good at drying out the fuel, because the combustion gases do not pass through it, and neither can they handle small or particulate fuels so well, since these easily fall through the grate and clog it.

Cross-draught units produce very intense heat in a small area, which results in effective gasification of volatiles and tars, but there are often problems with the nozzle burning. A solution for this is to water-cool the nozzles, but this makes the device rather more complicated.

Fixed-bed, internally-heated gasifiers of the type described above can only be made up to around 200 kW. There are many other types of gasifier, such as the fluidized-bed gasifiers where air is blown through the fuel, and retort-type gasifiers which are heated externally, but these designs are for much larger plants than are needed for small-scale pumping.

Table 7.36: Comparison of the thermal values of gas and gas-air mixtures for producer gas and methane

Fuel gas	Thermal value (MJ/m^3)	Thermal value of air-fuel mix (MJ/m^3)
Natural gas (CH_4)	40	3.5
Producer gas	5	2.5

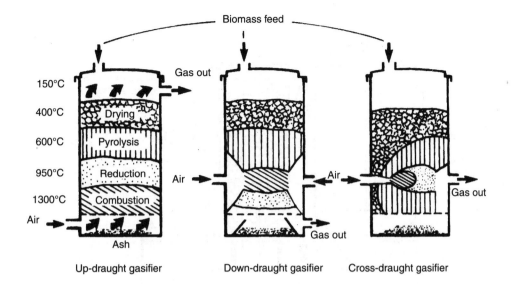

150°C	Drying
400°C	
600°C	Pyrolysis
950°C	Reduction
1300°C	Combustion

Biomass feed

Gas out

Air

Air

Ash

Up-draught gasifier   **Down-draught gasifier**   **Cross-draught gasifier**

Gas out

Air

Gas out

Fig. 7.82: The three main types of gasifier

Producer gas cleaning

Before producer gas can be used in an internal combustion engine, it needs to be effectively cooled and cleaned of impurities including ash, unburnt fuel dust, tar and acidic condensates, as otherwise any significant carry-over of these materials will quite rapidly destroy the engine. Obviously the more ash and tar in the original fuel, the more of a problem there is in cleaning the output gas. Therefore fuels having an ash content greater than 5–6% are not recommended for use in producer gas units for internal combustion engines. Also, the high performance gasifiers necessary to run small internal combustion engines tend to be sensitive to inconsistencies in the fuel, so that regularly sized, low ash fuels are best. Charcoal provides one of the best fuels for gasifiers, being almost pure carbon in itself, but materials such as coconut shells and maize cobs are both relatively effective gasifier fuels.

The methods used for gas cleaning vary; water or air coolers are generally used to reduce the gas temperature to near ambient conditions, and cyclones, spray scrubbers, filters packed with a wet matrix of wood-wool, steel swarf, coir fibre and other materials have been tried. Ineffective gas cleaning remains the 'Achilles heel' of small gasifier systems, being a major cause of premature engine failure.

A typical small producer gas irrigation pumping system is illustrated schematically in Fig. 7.83. Here a down-draught gasifier is used, with wet coke as a primary filter and cotton waste as a secondary filter for the gas.

Engines for use with gasifiers

After cleaning, the producer gas is mixed with air metered in the appropriate quantity. The resulting mixture can then be induced into the inlet manifold of most standard internal combustion engines. Spark ignition engines are capable of running exclusively on producer gas, but diesel engines will not fire when run purely on producer gas, and need to be run with at least a small amount of diesel fuel so that the timed injection fires the mixture at the appropriate moment. Therefore they can be run as pilot fuel engines in which diesel is used to start up and continues to be used in quantities normally necessary just for idling, with producer gas making up the main part of the fuel supply. The amount of diesel required depends on the size of the engine. For engines of a few kilowatts,

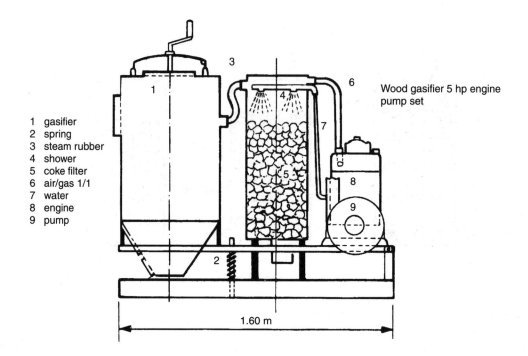

1 gasifier
2 spring
3 steam rubber
4 shower
5 coke filter
6 air/gas 1/1
7 water
8 engine
9 pump

Wood gasifier 5 hp engine pump set

Fig. 7.83: An experimental 3 kW producer-gas irrigation pumping system (Damour, 1984 [81])

around 20–30% of diesel fuel (by weight) will be required in order to sustain ignition. Much larger engines require less diesel.

The low calorific value of producer gas compared with petroleum fuels generally leads to a marked reduction in power output, often by as much as 30 to 50% below the rated power using petroleum. An approximate idea of the fuel requirements using producer gas compared with conventional diesel operation, is given in Table 7.37.

Operation and maintenance of gasifiers
A draught is needed to get a gasifier going. This is usually provided by a hand (or electric) driven fan. The early gas is too dirty to be used in an engine, and should be burnt off in a flare. This flame can be inspected to make sure that there are no particles burning in it, which are seen as red flecks in an otherwise blue flame. When the flecks stop, the gas is ready for use in the engine. Before starting the gasifier it is necessary to ensure that there is no residual gas from the last

time the system was run which could explode. The producer gas unit needs to be refuelled before the fuel in the hopper reaches a level of less than about 300 mm above the fire zone, or gas production may not be reliable.

Care is needed with gasifiers. Producer gas is extremely toxic due to the carbon monoxide present; a unit must never be used in enclosed conditions where producer gas could build up. There is also significant risk of explosion and/or fire when opening the unit to refuel it. Opening the gasifier often causes a small blow-back ex-

Table 7.37: Comparison of fuel consumption of various gasifier fuels with diesel

Quantity of fuel required to produce 1 kWh of shaft power		
Gasifier fuel		*Diesel fuel*
Charcoal	*Hardwood chips*	
1–1.3 kg	2–3 kg	0.3–0.5 kg

plosion, so while an experienced operator can open the hopper and refuel safely, inexperienced operators can often be recognized by their singed eyebrows!

The gasifier, and gas cleaning system, must be regularly cleaned out and any leaks must be repaired immediately. Experience with motor vehicle gasifiers during the Second World War suggested that as much as one hour per day is needed to clean and prepare a gasifier for operation. This is probably the main reason for their general replacement as soon as petroleum fuels became more readily available.

7.10.7 Liquid biomass fuels

There are two main categories of liquid fuels derived from biomass that are relevant to powering small engines for water pumping: alcohols and oils.

Alcohols

There are two varieties of alcohol that can be used to run internal combustion engines: methanol (methyl alcohol) and ethanol (ethyl alcohol). For a petrol/alcohol-mixture fuel, standard engines can be used. Alcohols are relatively harmless inside the engine, and burn cleanly. Methanol used to be known as 'wood alcohol' because it was produced by the destructive distillation of wood, but is now always made from carbon monoxide and hydrogen from natural gas in an industrial process at high pressure. The traditional fermentation was inefficient and unproductive, and is not economically viable. Ethanol, which is the type of alcohol found in wines and other drinks, can be produced by yeast fermentation of natural sugars or other carbohydrates such as starches, either from purposely-grown fuel crops or from wastes and residues.

Current activities to produce fuel alcohol focus on large-scale processing of a number of different crops (see Table 7.38). Sugarcane, maize, and cassava have all been used, and a wide range of other plants are being considered, such as alfalfa, clover, hemp and a variety of grasses. Sugars can be fermented directly, but cellulose first requires hydrolyzation, usually with acids, to

change it into sugar. There is as yet no technically and economically viable small-scale process for fuel-alcohol production, so the use of alcohol by farmers must generally depend on a national programme in their countries. They may also be in a position to grow the fuel crops for the programme, so such programmes could be more important for farmers than simply providing an alternative fuel.

There are a number of problems inherent in the large-scale production of fuel alcohol. Obviously the food versus fuel argument, as outlined in Section 7.10.1, is important. Secondly, there can be problem disposing of the large volumes of 'distillery slops' produced by large-scale ethyl alcohol production, though these can be used as fertilizers on fields or used to produce fuel gases in large-scale anaerobic digesters (biogas digesters are discussed in Section 7.10.8). Finally, the product is only marginally economic compared with gasoline. The cost of alcohol derived from sugarcane in Brazil in 1991 was about $0.23/litre, compared with $0.20/litre for petrol, although it is predicted that the price may continue to fall by anything up to 23% (Johansson et al., 1993 [83]). In the USA, the price of cellulose-derived alcohol was around $0.40–0.50/litre, though this has been falling. At current costs, the main justifications for using alcohol are to use locally-produced fuel instead of imported oil, and to replace fossil fuels with a renewable energy source. Nevertheless, a number of alcohol fuel programmes have been initiated. By far the largest is in Brazil, where over 14,000 million litres of ethanol are produced per year as an

Table 7.38: Alcohol (ethanol) yield from various crops (Bassam, 1998 [82])

Crop	Alchohol yield (litres per tonne of biomass)
Molasses	270
Sugarcane	70
Sweet sorghum	80
Sweet potato	125
Cassava	180
Corn	470

289

automotive fuel. In Zimbabwe, all 'petrol' is blended with alcohol to produce 'Gasohol'. The USA also has a substantial production of alcohol (from maize) and a major research programme.

Oils

There are two types of vegetable oils that show promise as fuel for internal combustion engines: these are expressed oils from seeds, and the saps or latex from certain succulent plants and trees.

Some successes have been reported with running diesel engines on vegetable oils. Tests have been run on seed oils from peanut, rape, soybean, sunflower, coconut, safflower, jojoba, hemp, crambe and linseed. Sunflower oil, in particular, shows promise as a fuel for diesel engines. The main problems relate to the much higher viscosity of vegetable oils compared with diesel gasoil; this makes it difficult to start a diesel on vegetable oil, but once warm it will run well on it. Tests have shown that the performance is little affected, but fuel consumption on vegetable oil is slightly higher, due to its lower calorific value. Slow-running, heavily built diesel engines with a prechamber (indirect injection) are best suited to running on vegetable oil. There is a tendency for engines run on unmodified vegetable oils to coke up, leading to reduced power and eventual engine failure if no corrective action is taken. Tests on an Indian engine running on physic nut oil showed that the fuel injectors need to be cleaned at the same interval as the oil changes (Metzler, 1995 [84]). Tests have also shown that rape seed oil can be used both for fuelling and lubricating a small diesel engine, which can be another significant cost saving for the operator.

Chemical treatment of vegetable oils to turn them into an ethyl or methyl ester has been found to overcome most of these problems and to actually give a better engine performance than with diesel oil, combined with less coking than with diesel [84]. Also, blends of sunflower oil with diesel fuel appear to reduce or eliminate some of the problems experienced with pure sunflower oil.

Large-scale processing of vegetable oil can crack the oil in much the same way as is done with crude oil, to produce veg-gasoline as well as veg-diesel. During the Second World War, China developed an industrial batch cracking process for producing motor fuels from vegetable oils, mostly tung oil. The China Vegetable Oil Corporation of Shanghai was able to produce 0.6 tonne of veg-diesel, 250 litres of veg-gasoline and 180 litres of veg-kerosene per tonne of crude vegetable oil.

It is possible to extract vegetable oil 'on-farm' on a small scale and to consider using this to reduce diesel fuel requirements, although obviously any vegetable oil needs to be extremely well filtered before it can be used in an engine. Another approach would be production on a small-industry basis, in which the extraction unit procured seed from a district for oil production on a more economic scale. Typical yields for sunflower seeds are 700–1,800 kg/ha. It is possible to express between 0.30–0.43 litres of oil per kg of seed, depending on the technique. Small-scale presses will produce the lower level of yield while large screw presses and solvent extraction are needed to achieve the upper level. This implies that from 210–770 l/ha can be produced. The development of more efficient on-farm oil seed expellers could make this a potentially viable process in many areas. In fact a combination of efficient cultivation and efficient oil extraction could yield in excess of 1 tonne/ha of vegetable oil.

Therefore, the use of oil-seed as a feed-stock to produce diesel fuel certainly looks technically feasible. However the economics remain more doubtful, since the value of refined vegetable oils on the international market is generally higher than that of diesel fuel. However, the price differential is strongly dependent on the taxation applied to the different fuels, and in some countries biodiesel is similarly priced to diesel, and may even be cheaper.

7.10.8 Gaseous biomass fuels

'Biogas' is the term used to describe the naturally occurring gas that results from the fermentation of organic materials in the absence of air. It lends itself to small-scale on-farm use, and there is considerable experience with this technique in a number of countries, making it the most immediately practicable means for powering a conventional internal combustion engine from biomass.

Biogas is produced naturally by a process known as anaerobic digestion, which is the action of bacteria on water-logged organic materials in the absence of air. Biogas occurs naturally as 'marsh gas', an inflammable gas that bubbles out of stagnant marshes or bogs. Gas is produced in a similar way in the digestive system of cattle and other animals. The process can be harnessed by feeding animal waste into a sealed container or 'digester'. One such digester is shown in Fig. 7.84. The animal waste is mixed with water, and sometimes with a small amount of vegetable residue, to form a slurry that is put into the digester through the inlet pipe (the various components of the feedstock are described in the sub-section 'The biogas production process' below). The digestion process occurs naturally, due to bacteria that occur naturally in the animal waste. At the end of the digestion a sludge is left at the bottom of the digester, which can be removed through the outlet pipe. This process is continuous: there is no need to stop the digestion process in order to fill or empty the digester. It is possible to make 'batch' digesters, which are filled, generate gas, and then emptied; because gas production from such units 'peaks' noticeably and then tails off gradually, and because of the 'down-time' involved in emptying and refilling a batch digester, a reasonable number of units are required to ensure that gas is always available. Batch biogas digesters are obviously much less convenient than the continuous type, and are consequently quite rare.

Biogas consists of about 60% methane, a non-toxic and effective fuel gas similar to many forms of natural gas; the remaining 40% is mainly inert carbon dioxide with traces of hydrogen, hydrogen sulphide, etc. Raw biogas has a calorific value of about 23 MJ/m^3, which is considerably better than producer gas (see Table 7.34), and can be used to run engines without further treatment. It is sometimes necessary to remove water vapour from the gas to get satisfactory engine performance, and to prevent rust in the system; this can be done by having a cooled U-tube in the gas outlet pipe with a drain so that it can be emptied periodically. It is possible to remove the

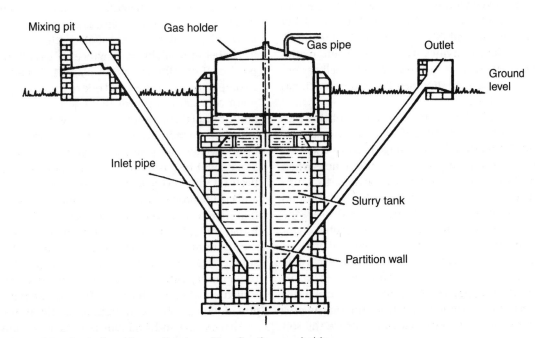

Fig. 7.84: An Indian biogas digester with a floating gas holder

291

carbon dioxide (by bubbling raw biogas through a solution of slaked lime, calcium hydroxide) to produce a gas with a calorific value of around 40 MJ/m^3, which is comparable with methane. There is little reason for doing this to run an engine directly, but is required if the gas is to be compressed for storage.

Biogas is an attractive fuel for use in internal combustion engines since it has no difficult pollutants that can damage them (unlike producer gas). Biogas from pig dung or sewage can have a hydrogen sulphide content of up to 4%, which gives sulphuric acid when it burns that cause faster-than-average corrosion in the exhaust system; it is generally cheaper to replace the exhaust as necessary than to try and remove the hydrogen sulphide. Biogas does have good anti-knock properties and can safely be used with high compression ratio spark ignition engines as the sole fuel. To make the best use of biogas requires a spark ignition engine with a compression ratio approaching that of a diesel. Some special biogas engines have been built, which run on 100% biogas more efficiently than with an unconverted gasoline engine. Biogas can be used in diesel engines, but some diesel fuel needs to be mixed with it to obtain ignition – gas self-ignites only at several thousand °C. For 3 kW engines, around 20% of diesel will be required; much larger engines require less. Some manufacturers, such as Kirloskar in India, sell gas engines, which are modified diesel units with gas carburettors.

An important further advantage of this process, especially in the context of irrigation pumping, is that the digested sludge makes a good fertilizer, so that unlike the situation where when biomass is totally burnt, it is possible to return much of the original material to the land and thereby improve the soil quality and displace the use of chemical fertilizers. The anaerobic digestion process makes the nitrogen and various other chemicals in the feedstock more accessible for plant growth than the normal aerobic (in air) composting process. Also, unlike artificial fertilizers, the sludge left over from the biogas process contains humus that can improve the soil structure. This process also is useful as a method for treating sewage or disposing of other unpleasant or potentially dangerous organic wastes as well as for producing fertilizer and fuel gas. Anaerobic digestion is a standard sewage treatment process which kills most water-borne pathogens harmful to people and converts the effluent to a relatively innocuous and odourless liquid which can easily be sprayed or poured onto the fields.

Anaerobic digestion is quite widely used for large-scale city sewage plants, but it is also increasingly being applied on farms. The first reasonably widespread farm use was in France during the Second World War, when farmers built concrete digesters to produce methane to replace petroleum fuels which were unobtainable for them at that time. More recently, efforts have been made to popularize the use of biogas in Asia, mainly in China, but also in India, Nepal and some of the S.E. Asian countries. Commercial farm biogas units have also gone into production in various countries, including the USA, Denmark, UK, Australia and Tanzania as well as the main users of the technology, China and India.

Although the widespread use of biogas only started in China in the early 1970s, within ten years some seven million biogas units had been installed (van Buren, 1979 [85]), with the majority being in Sichuan Province. A large proportion of the Chinese biogas plants failed after a comparatively short period due to the development of small leaks from the digester, particularly around the manhole cover 'plug' at the top, and there were indications that only 1 million, or about 15%, were still in operation by 1980. Since 1980 biogas or rural energy offices have been set up at every level of government to try and ensure proper installation. Around 2.57 million digesters are said to have been installed in India, though again only around half of these are thought to be working. Nepal has had a smaller-scale but somewhat more successful programme, with around 50,000 digesters installed, most of which are the fixed-dome type, and of which 90% are thought to be still in use.

Figures 7.84 and 7.85 illustrate the two main types of small-scale biogas digester, developed originally in China and in India respectively. The Chinese type of digester consists of a concrete-lined pit with a concrete dome, entirely below ground. It is completely filled with slurry, and once gas begins to form, it collects under the dome and forces the level of the slurry down by up to about 1 m. The gas pressure is consequently variable depending on the volume of gas stored, but by using a simple manometer on the gas line it is possible to measure the gas pressure and thereby gain an accurate indication of the amount of gas available. The Indian digester is more expensive to construct because it has a steel gas holder, on the other hand it is less likely to leak than the Chinese design which requires high quality internal plastering to avoid porosity and hence gas leaks. With the Indian design, gas collects under the steel gas holder, which rises as it fills with gas. The height that the gas holder rises out of the pit indicates how much gas is available; in this case the pressure is constant. Corrosion of the steel gas holder is a problem with this design; the inside of the holder does not rust because it contains oxygen-free methane, but the outside at the point where it is continually being submerged in slurry and then exposed to the air can rust through in a couple of years without adequate protection.

Most other biogas programmes around the world involving small-scale digesters have been based on one or other of these two designs, though various improvements and innovations have been made. Nepal has a very successful biogas programme based on a modified version of the Chinese fixed-dome type digesters, which is described in detail in Fulford (1988 [86]).

The biogas production process
The biogas process requires an input material provided as a liquid slurry. The amount of solids is usually kept between 8–12% to allow the slurry to flow into and out of the digester; digesters can use slurry with solid contents of up to 30%. It is important to use materials that break down readily; highly fibrous materials like wood and straw are not easily digested by the bacteria, but softer feedstocks like dung and leaves react well to the process. Also some feedstocks are more productive than others as indicated by Table 7.39, and some producers of feedstock are more productive than others as indicated by Table 7.40.

For optimum performance the internal temperature of the digester needs to be in the mid-30s centigrade and certainly over 25°C, moreover temperature conditions need to be as steady as possible. The digestion process generates a

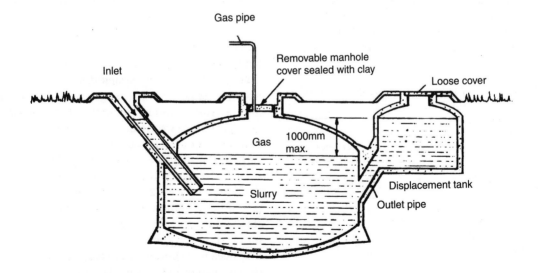

Fig. 7.85: A Chinese fixed-dome biogas digester

293

small amount of heat, but in cooler climates or seasons the unit needs to be well insulated and may need heating when cold spells occur. The average retention time for solids for the complete process is normally 20 to 40 days. With continuously operating (as opposed to batch) digesters, the actual digester size has to be equal to the design retention time in days multiplied by the daily input rate; i.e. with a 30-day retention time and 1 m³/day of input, the digester volume needs to be 30 m³. The longer the retention time and the warmer the digester, the more complete the process and the more energy per kg of volatile solids is obtained, however the larger and more expensive the digester needs to be. Hence the sizing and retention time are usually a compromise between keeping costs reasonable and obtaining complete digestion. The loading rate and the moisture content are related; too thin a slurry takes up more volume and needs a bigger digester than necessary, while too thick a slurry needs to be mechanically loaded and removed, limits mixing, and tends to solidify and clog up the unit. Another important criterion is the carbon/nitrogen ratio; for efficient digestion the process requires between 20 and 30 parts of carbon to be present per part of nitrogen. Certain carbon-rich materials like leaves or grass benefit, therefore, from being mixed with nitrogen-rich substances such as urine or poultry droppings. Alternatively ammonia or other nitrogen-rich artificial chemicals may be added to a digester running on mainly vegetation to obtain a better ratio and help the process. Finally, the output to be expected will be in the range 0.1–0.7 m³ per kg of volatile solids input per day. Table 7.41 gives the principal operating parameters of typical continuous biogas digesters.

Because biogas digesters have the capability of storing at least a 12 hour supply of gas, an engine can be used that draws gas at quite a high rate. In fact the size of engine is not critical since it is only the number of hours it will run that are governed by the digester gas capacity. Transporting biogas is technically difficult. In China it is quite often piped several hundred metres through plastic tubes. Unlike propane or butane, it is not possible to compress biogas into a liquid at normal temperatures and the only ways to transport it as a gas are either in high pressure cylinders, which of course require a high pressure compressor to charge them, or in a plastic bag. Figure 7.86 shows how small two-wheel tractors in China are powered from a bag of biogas carried on an overhead rack. The unit in the figure is towing a trailer tank full of biogas digester sludge and it also carries a pump driven off the engine for pumping the sludge onto the field as fertilizer via a spraying nozzle. An interesting option for irrigation by biogas power is to combine the digester sludge and the irrigation water in order to perform three functions simultaneously; i.e. irrigation, the application of fertilizer and waste disposal.

Sizing example

Biogas typically has a calorific value of about 6.4 kWh/m³, so it is quite straightforward to estimate the daily volume of biogas needed to perform a given pumping requirement. A worked example of how to do this is given below, which indicates how a 3 ha small-holding could be irrigated using biogas generated from the wastes from 20–30 pigs, 5–10 cattle, 500–700 poultry or a community of 80–200 people. The production rate of biogas can be enhanced by mixing vegetation with the animal wastes, although extra nitrogen, which could be in the form of urine, may need to be introduced to balance the excess carbon present in the vegetable wastes.

Table 7.39: The biogas yield from various fresh feedstocks

Feedstock	Gas yield (m³/kg)	Energy yield (MJ/kg)
Sewage sludge	0.3–0.7	6–17
Pig dung	0.4–0.5	8–11
Cattle dung	0.1–0.3	2–6
Poultry droppings	0.3–0.5	6–11
Poultry droppings and paper pulp	0.4–0.5	8–11
Grass	0.4–0.6	8–14

Table 7.40: Quantities of excreta from various species

Source of waste	Volatile solids yield (kg/animal/day)	Biogas yield (m³ / animal/day)	Energy yield (MJ / animal/day)
Humans (including cooking waste)	0.1	0.03–0.07	0.6–1.7
Pigs	0.6	0.24–0.30	4.8–6.6
Cattle	4.0	0.40–1.20	8–24
Poultry (× 100 birds)	2.2	0.70–1.10	13–24

Table 7.41: The principal operating parameters for farm biogas digesters (Meynell, 1982 [87])

Operating temperature	30–35°C
Retention time	20–40 days
Loading rate (volatile solids)	2–3 kg/m³/d
Operating moisture content	85–95%
Specific gas production	0.1–0.7 m³/kg/d
Feedstock carbon/nitrogen ratio	20–30

Requirement: 8 mm of water per day pumped through a head of 6 m onto 3 ha.

Engine and pump: A petrol engine coupled to a pump assumed to be 10% efficient (fuel to hydraulic power).

Biogas: Calorific value assumed to be 6.4 kWh/m³.

The volume of water required is:

$$Q = 3 \times 10^4 \times 0.008 = 240 \text{m}^3 / \text{day}$$

The energy requirement to lift this water through 6 m is:

$$E_{hyd} = \frac{Q \cdot H}{367} = \frac{240 \times 6}{367} = 3.92 \text{ kWh / day}$$

(see Section 5.6)
Assuming a system efficiency of 10%, the fuel energy requirement is:

$$E_{fuel} = \frac{3.92}{0.1} = 3.92 \text{ kWh / day}$$

Hence the daily biogas requirement will be:

$$Q_{biogas} = \frac{39.2}{6.4} = 6.13 \text{ m}^3 / \text{day}$$

This requires a biogas digester of at least 20 m³ capacity. From Table 7.40 it can be calculated that this can in turn be obtained from:

- 20–30 pigs, or
- 5–15 cattle, or
- 600–900 poultry, or
- 100–200 people.

The same table shows that the digester will generally need to be fed 10–20 kg of input material (volatile solids) per day, or rather more if some types of cattle dung are used. The addition of some vegetables to the waste, providing it did not unduly upset the carbon/nitrogen ratio, could allow the same volume of gas to be produced from possibly two-thirds to three-quarters the number of livestock or people.

The example therefore shows that this process needs significant inputs of waste material to yield even quite modest amounts of pumped water. Therefore, looked at just in energy terms, the economics tend to be at best marginal in comparison with petroleum fuels, but when the fertilizer value plus the waste disposal benefits are factored in, the process frequently comes out as being economically worthwhile.

It is difficult to generalize on the economics of biogas since many factors that are locality-specific are involved. However there is no doubt that the process offers significant economies of scale. For example a survey of biogas units in India found a payback period, using a 10% discount rate, of 23 years for a 1.7 m³ (60 cu.ft.) plant

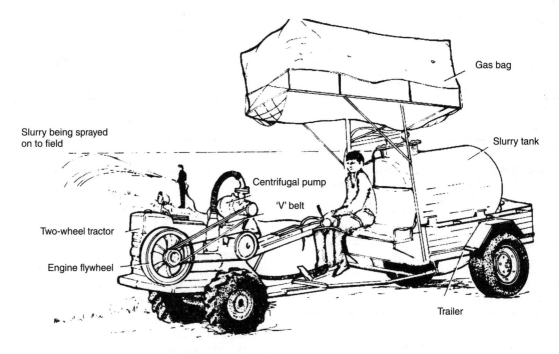

Fig. 7.86: A Chinese two-wheel tractor running on biogas and being used to pump digester slurry onto a field

which improved to 7, 4 and 3 years respectively with 2.8, 5.7 and 8.6 m³ units (100, 200 and 300 cu.ft). The sizes of plants needed to run small engines are much bigger than this and are therefore likely to be more cost-effective. Various studies have indicated that, in China, the value of the fertilizer output usually surpasses the value of the energy produced by the process. The waste disposal and sanitation aspects of the process are also important justifications for its use.

8

THE CHOICE OF PUMPING SYSTEMS

Suppose you have decided that you need a water pumping system. You have investigated the various pump options available, and the alternative power sources. There are probably quite a large number of options that are possible. How do you decide between them?

Any choice of this sort will have a financial and a non-financial side to it. It is, therefore, essential to make sure that the project is financially viable, because if you cannot afford it, or if it does not pay back, you cannot do it. Finance is not, however, the only consideration, and is frequently not the most important element in the decision. There are other factors, such as reliability, availability of spare parts or maintenance skills, ease of use, and vulnerability to theft, which can have a major impact on whether the use of a particular system is sustainable or not. These factors are difficult to quantify, but must be considered.

This chapter has two main parts. Section 8.1 deals with the financial and economic aspects of choosing a pumping system, while Section 8.2 covers the other considerations. The financial section is longer, not because it is more important, but rather because it is covering analysis methods which need some explanation. If you follow through the methods and analyze various pumping options it will lead to a numeric comparison between them. It might show that one option can pay for itself in, say, three years, while an alternative could take 10 years. This is useful information, and will be helpful in deciding which system to choose, but it must be treated with caution. The calculations may look like they are accurate to the nearest cent or rupee, but the results are only as accurate as the assumptions made at the beginning. Furthermore, a system that looks to be incredibly profitable on paper will be worse than worthless if it breaks down after a month and there are no spare parts available to repair it. The choice of pumping system should be made with the best information and after the best analysis possible, but in the end it will be a matter of judgement.

8.1 Financial and economic considerations

The objective of most methods of financial or economic analysis is to arrive at a figure for the true cost-effectiveness. The costs will be a mixture of capital costs associated with purchasing and installing the system, and running costs such as purchasing fuel, paying for operators, and maintaining the equipment. The 'life-cycle costs', which are the total of all the costs incurred during the life of the system, can then be compared for different systems, and the costs can be compared with the 'life-cycle benefits' to see whether it is worth doing the project at all.

As stated before, there are two main types of costs relating to any system; its first cost (or capital cost), and its recurrent costs or 'Operation and Maintenance' (O and M) costs. So far as the first cost is concerned, the over-riding consideration in most rural communities is whether it is affordable as a cash payment and if not, whether they can obtain finance on acceptable terms. The institutional user will no doubt have access to finance and will be more concerned to ensure that there is an adequate return on the investment. The O and M costs can vary considerably both within and between technologies and will no doubt increase with time due to inflation. Generally speaking, all options for pumping water represent a trade-off between capital costs and recurrent costs; low first cost systems usually have high recurrent costs and vice-versa.

8.1.1 Calculation of costs and benefits: present values and discounted cash flow

Clearly, extra expenditure at the procurement stage may save recurrent costs throughout the life of the system. But how do you compare a petrol engine that is cheap to buy but has high running costs over a short life, with an expensive solar-powered pump which costs almost nothing to run over many years? One method would be to add up the total purchase cost of each system and to divide it by the expected life of the system. This would give a cost per year, which could be compared. For example, suppose the petrol-engine system costs $900, needs $500/year to operate it, and only lasts for three years before it wears out. An equivalent PV solar-pumping system might last 10 years and only cost $500 every 5 years for maintenance, but costs $5,000. The cost of the petrol-engine system over its three-year life is $900 + 3 × $500 = $2,400, which is equivalent to $2,400/3 = $800 per year. The solar pumping system costs $5,000 + 2 × $500 = $6,000 over 10 years, or $600 per year, which is cheaper. This example makes the solar pumping system seem more attractive.

The problem with the simple analysis above is that it neglects the changing value of money. The effect of inflation and bank lending interest rates can make the petrol-engine option seem more attractive, even if it really is not. What is needed is a method of calculating the effect of inflation and interest rates.

We are all familiar with inflation, which means that prices generally rise. For example, a litre of diesel fuel may be anticipated to cost, say, 10% more next year than it does today. If we are planning to spend $100 this year on fuel, we will need to spend $110 next year. Another way of putting this is that the future value of $100 will only be worth 100/110 of its present value, or $90.09. The decrease in value of a sum over one year for the general case can be expressed as:

$$FV = \frac{PV}{(1+i)}$$

FV – Future Value of a sum after one year at inflation rate 'i'
PV – Present Value of a sum
i – inflation rate

After two years:

$$FV = \frac{\left[\dfrac{PV}{(1+i)}\right]}{(1+i)} = \frac{PV}{(1+i)^2}$$

And after 'n' years:

$$FV = \frac{PV}{(1+i)^n}$$

Whereas inflation decreases the value of money, the interest on a bank deposit account increases it. Each year the value goes up as interest is paid. The general equation for this is:

$$FV = PV \cdot (1+r)^n$$

r – interest rate

Both the inflation and interest rate equations tell us what the present value of a sum of money now will be after 'n' years. We can rearrange them to tell us what the present value of a future sum will be. So, for inflation:

$$PV = FV \cdot (1+i)^n$$

What this says is that we need more money now to have a given sum in the future after inflation has decreased its value.

For interest rates:

$$PV = FV \cdot \frac{1}{(1+r)^n}$$

This indicates that a small sum now will become a larger sum in future if interest is paid.

Inflation is going to affect any pumping project; fuel costs, spare parts, labour… all these things will cost more in the future. Interest rates will obviously affect the project if a loan is needed to purchase the equipment. It is less obvious, however, that the interest rate affects the value of the money even if no loan is needed. This is because of the 'opportunity cost' of the money. If you did not use a certain amount of cash that you had 'in your pocket' to buy the pumping system, you could put it into a deposit account at a bank, and earn interest. By investing this money in capital equipment, you are effectively loosing this interest that you could earn, and this is a cost of the project. The general points are that money available in the future is worth less than if it were available now, and that money invested in a pumping project is no longer available to earn interest from a bank.

If both inflation and interest rates apply to a project (as they usually do) then the present value equations can be combined to give:

$$PV = FV \cdot \left(\frac{1+i}{1+r} \right)^n$$

It is more convenient to combine the interest and inflation rates into a 'discount rate', such that:

$$1 \left(\frac{1}{1+d} \right) = \left(\frac{1+i}{1+r} \right) \Rightarrow d = \left(\frac{r-i}{1+r} \right)$$

d – discount rate
r – interest rate
i – inflation rate

This shows that the effective rate of interest for a project is roughly the difference between the interest rate and the inflation rate. This is reasonable, since the value of savings in a bank only increases in real terms if the interest rate is more than inflation. The present value equation then becomes, simply

$$PV = \frac{FV}{(1+d)^n}$$

$$FV \times \frac{1}{(1+d)^n} = FV \times discount\ factor$$

The results of this equation can be presented in a table of discount factors such as Table 8.1.

For example, to find the present value of $1,000 to be paid in 10 years time at a discount rate of 10%, the relevant PV factor is looked up in the Table 8.1 (it is 0.386) and multiplied by the sum of money in question to give, in this example 0.386 × $1,000 = $386.

A series of payments can be treated in the same way. If it can be anticipated that $1,000 needs to be paid, say, now and then every five 5 years (to pay for a replacement diesel engine, for example) for the running costs of a system (for example), then the PV factors for years 0, 5, 10, 15, 20 and 25 at the relevant discount rate can be looked up in Table 8.1, added together and multiplied by the sum in question. In this case, the factors are 1 for year 0, 0.621 for year 5, 0.386 for year 10, and so on, and the calculation for a 10% discount rate would be:

$$(1 + 0.621 + 0.386 + 0.239 + 0.149 + 0.092) \times \$1,000 = \$2,487$$

This procedure works, but is a little tedious, particularly if a long series of payments has to be dealt with. Since it is common in a project for there to be regular annual payments and income over a number of years, it is common to use a shortcut called the 'annuity equation' which gives the mathematical sum of a series of PV calculations. The 'annuity equation' calculates the present value of a regular series of payments over a given number of years:

$$PV = A \cdot \left[\frac{(1+d)^n - 1}{d \cdot (1+d)^n} \right] = \frac{annuity}{annuity\ factor}$$

PV – present value of a series of annual payments
A – annual payment amount
d – discount rate

The results of this equation can also be presented in the form of a table, as shown in Table 8.2. (The annuity factor here is defined slightly differently to the discount factor in the PV equation above in keeping with conventional accounting use, so that standard tables of annuity factors such Table 8.2 can be used.)

299

Table 8.1: Discount factors for single sums

Year	1%	2%	3%	4%	5%	6%	7%	8%	9%	10%	12%	15%	20%	25%
						Yearly discount rate, d								
1	0.990	0.980	0.971	0.962	0.952	0.943	0.935	0.926	0.917	0.909	0.893	0.870	0.833	0.800
2	0.980	0.961	0.943	0.925	0.907	0.890	0.873	0.857	0.842	0.826	0.797	0.756	0.694	0.640
3	0.971	0.942	0.915	0.889	0.864	0.840	0.816	0.794	0.772	0.751	0.712	0.658	0.579	0.512
4	0.961	0.924	0.888	0.855	0.823	0.792	0.763	0.735	0.708	0.683	0.636	0.572	0.482	0.410
5	0.951	0.906	0.863	0.822	0.784	0.747	0.713	0.681	0.650	0.621	0.567	0.497	0.402	0.328
6	0.942	0.888	0.837	0.790	0.746	0.705	0.666	0.630	0.596	0.564	0.507	0.432	0.335	0.262
7	0.933	0.871	0.813	0.760	0.711	0.665	0.623	0.583	0.547	0.513	0.452	0.376	0.279	0.210
8	0.923	0.853	0.789	0.731	0.677	0.627	0.582	0.540	0.502	0.467	0.404	0.327	0.233	0.168
9	0.914	0.837	0.766	0.703	0.645	0.592	0.544	0.500	0.460	0.424	0.361	0.284	0.194	0.134
10	0.905	0.820	0.744	0.676	0.614	0.558	0.508	0.463	0.422	0.386	0.322	0.247	0.162	0.107
11	0.896	0.804	0.722	0.650	0.585	0.527	0.475	0.429	0.388	0.350	0.287	0.215	0.135	0.086
12	0.887	0.788	0.701	0.625	0.557	0.497	0.444	0.397	0.356	0.319	0.257	0.187	0.112	0.069
13	0.879	0.773	0.681	0.601	0.530	0.469	0.415	0.368	0.326	0.290	0.229	0.163	0.093	0.055
14	0.870	0.758	0.661	0.577	0.505	0.442	0.388	0.340	0.299	0.263	0.205	0.141	0.078	0.044
15	0.861	0.743	0.642	0.555	0.481	0.417	0.362	0.315	0.275	0.239	0.183	0.123	0.065	0.035
16	0.853	0.728	0.623	0.534	0.458	0.394	0.339	0.292	0.252	0.218	0.163	0.107	0.054	0.028
17	0.844	0.714	0.605	0.513	0.436	0.371	0.317	0.270	0.231	0.198	0.146	0.093	0.045	0.023
18	0.836	0.700	0.587	0.494	0.416	0.350	0.296	0.250	0.212	0.180	0.130	0.081	0.038	0.018
19	0.828	0.686	0.570	0.475	0.396	0.331	0.277	0.232	0.194	0.164	0.116	0.070	0.031	0.014
20	0.820	0.673	0.554	0.456	0.377	0.312	0.258	0.215	0.178	0.149	0.104	0.061	0.026	0.012
21	0.811	0.660	0.538	0.439	0.359	0.294	0.242	0.199	0.164	0.135	0.093	0.053	0.022	0.009
22	0.803	0.647	0.522	0.422	0.342	0.278	0.226	0.184	0.150	0.123	0.083	0.046	0.018	0.007
23	0.795	0.634	0.507	0.406	0.326	0.262	0.211	0.170	0.138	0.112	0.074	0.040	0.015	0.006
24	0.788	0.622	0.492	0.390	0.310	0.247	0.197	0.158	0.126	0.102	0.066	0.035	0.013	0.005
25	0.780	0.610	0.478	0.375	0.295	0.233	0.184	0.146	0.116	0.092	0.059	0.030	0.010	0.004

For example, suppose you want to calculate the present value of a series of regular payments of $180 per year over a 15 year period at a 4% discount rate. The annuity factor from Table 8.2 is 0.090, so the present value of the payments is $180/0.090 = $2,000.

Note that this annuity equation is the form for annual payments at the end of the year, after interest is due. For a series of payments where the first payment is at the beginning of the first year, the equation becomes:

$$PV = A \cdot (1+d) \cdot \frac{\left[(1+d)^n - 1\right]}{d \cdot (1+d)^n}$$

$$= \frac{annuity}{(annuity\ factor) / (1+d)}$$

This is $(1 + d)$ times the other equation. Table 8.2 can still be used provided the annuity factor is divided by $(1 + d)$.

Present value can be calculated with built-in functions in spreadsheets. In Excel, present values can be calculated using the PV function, with the inputs $PV(d,n,-A,0)$ for payments at the end of the years, $PV(d,n,-A,1)$ for payments at the beginnings of the years.

We now have the basic tools for comparing the value of transactions whenever they occur in the life of the project. All the sums of money

Table 8.2: Annuity factors for annuities, a regular series of annual payments

							Yearly discount rate, d							
Year	*1%*	*2%*	*3%*	*4%*	*5%*	*6%*	*7%*	*8%*	*9%*	*10%*	*12%*	*15%*	*20%*	*25%*
1	1.010	1.020	1.030	1.040	1.050	1.060	1.070	1.080	1.090	1.100	1.120	1.150	1.200	1.250
2	0.508	0.515	0.523	0.530	0.538	0.545	0.553	0.561	0.568	0.576	0.592	0.615	0.655	0.694
3	0.340	0.347	0.354	0.360	0.367	0.374	0.381	0.388	0.395	0.402	0.416	0.438	0.475	0.512
4	0.256	0.263	0.269	0.275	0.282	0.289	0.295	0.302	0.309	0.315	0.329	0.350	0.386	0.423
5	0.206	0.212	0.218	0.225	0.231	0.237	0.244	0.250	0.257	0.264	0.277	0.298	0.334	0.372
6	0.173	0.179	0.185	0.191	0.197	0.203	0.210	0.216	0.223	0.230	0.243	0.264	0.301	0.339
7	0.149	0.155	0.161	0.167	0.173	0.179	0.186	0.192	0.199	0.205	0.219	0.240	0.277	0.316
8	0.131	0.137	0.142	0.149	0.155	0.161	0.167	0.174	0.181	0.187	0.201	0.223	0.261	0.300
9	0.117	0.123	0.128	0.134	0.141	0.147	0.153	0.160	0.167	0.174	0.188	0.210	0.248	0.289
10	0.106	0.111	0.117	0.123	0.130	0.136	0.142	0.149	0.156	0.163	0.177	0.199	0.239	0.280
11	0.096	0.102	0.108	0.114	0.120	0.127	0.133	0.140	0.147	0.154	0.168	0.191	0.231	0.273
12	0.089	0.095	0.100	0.107	0.113	0.119	0.126	0.133	0.140	0.147	0.161	0.184	0.225	0.268
13	0.082	0.088	0.094	0.100	0.106	0.113	0.120	0.127	0.134	0.141	0.156	0.179	0.221	0.265
14	0.077	0.083	0.089	0.095	0.101	0.108	0.114	0.121	0.128	0.136	0.151	0.175	0.217	0.262
15	0.072	0.078	0.084	0.090	0.096	0.103	0.110	0.117	0.124	0.131	0.147	0.171	0.214	0.259
16	0.068	0.074	0.080	0.086	0.092	0.099	0.106	0.113	0.120	0.128	0.143	0.168	0.211	0.257
17	0.064	0.070	0.076	0.082	0.089	0.095	0.102	0.110	0.117	0.125	0.140	0.165	0.209	0.256
18	0.061	0.067	0.073	0.079	0.086	0.092	0.099	0.107	0.114	0.122	0.138	0.163	0.208	0.255
19	0.058	0.064	0.070	0.076	0.083	0.090	0.097	0.104	0.112	0.120	0.136	0.161	0.206	0.254
20	0.055	0.061	0.067	0.074	0.080	0.087	0.094	0.102	0.110	0.117	0.134	0.160	0.205	0.253
21	0.053	0.059	0.065	0.071	0.078	0.085	0.092	0.100	0.108	0.116	0.132	0.158	0.204	0.252
22	0.051	0.057	0.063	0.069	0.076	0.083	0.090	0.098	0.106	0.114	0.131	0.157	0.204	0.252
23	0.049	0.055	0.061	0.067	0.074	0.081	0.089	0.096	0.104	0.113	0.130	0.156	0.203	0.251
24	0.047	0.053	0.059	0.066	0.072	0.080	0.087	0.095	0.103	0.111	0.128	0.155	0.203	0.251
25	0.045	0.051	0.057	0.064	0.071	0.078	0.086	0.094	0.102	0.110	0.127	0.155	0.202	0.251

paid out or received in the life of a project can be multiplied by a factor to bring them to today's prices. Regular series of payments or receipts can be multiplied by annuity factors from Table 8.2, and individual sums can be multiplied by discount factors from Table 8.1. This then allows us to compare different schemes. Various methods of making comparisons are dealt with in the following sections.

This sort of analysis is known as Discounted Cash Flow, or DCF, because the cash flows over the life of the projects are 'discounted' back to their present values for comparison. It is a useful tool, and the only real drawback is the choice of an appropriate discount rate, '*d*'. This involves prediction of the interest and inflation rates into the future – obviously not an exact science.

A further point to note about annuity tables is that they can also be used to calculate the repayments on a loan over a given period at a given interest rate. So if a loan of $2,000 is taken out for a 15 year period at an interest rate of 4%, the annual repayments would be $2,000 × 0.090 = $180. This will be seen to be a variant of the result of the previous example. What it says is that taking out a loan of $2,000 now at 4% costs the same in today's money as paying out $180 per year for 15 years to meet expenses as they arise.

8.1.2 Defining the variables: discount rate, period, costs and benefits

The discount methods outlined above give a technique for including the value of money in financial calculations about a project. It takes a little while to become familiar with the principles behind them, but the methods themselves are fairly straightforward. However, as soon as you come to apply DCF methods to a real situation, you will discover problems in assigning values to the variables in the equations. What is a realistic discount rate? Will this rate be the same over the life of the project? Over what period should the calculations be done?

The choice of discount rate used for analysis effectively reflects the analyst's view of the future value of money. A high discount rate implies that money available now is much more useful than money available in the future, while a low discount rate is more appropriate when longer term considerations lie behind an investment decision. The implications of this are that low discount rates favour the use of high-first-cost low-operating-cost systems, which cost a lot now in order to save money in the future, while high discount rates make low-first-cost high-operating-cost systems look good by making the high future costs seem less important.

The length of period (n) selected for analysis can affect the answer, so it is normal to use a long period in order to minimize this effect; this will normally need to be 15 to 20 years or more because at normal discount rates, costs more than about 20 years into the future become discounted to such small levels that they cease to affect the results very much. Obviously, short-life equipment will need replacement during the period under analysis, and this is taken account of by adding the discounted value of the capital costs of future replacements to the operating costs as part of the life cycle costs.

While it is obvious that the discount rate and calculation period have to be chosen, at first sight it might be thought that the costs and benefits of a project are well-defined. However, it will soon be found that it is not always possible to work out a numeric value for all the costs and income. Suppose you are comparing a treadle pump with a small petrol-engine-driven pump. The costs of the engine are easily accessible, because they have to be paid for with money; the engine has to be purchased, and then will need fuel, oil, filters, spare parts, and so on. The treadle pump has to be purchased, but how do you charge for the operator if it is worked by the farmer or his family? No money is involved in the transaction. One way of doing it would be to use the labour rate that the people could earn if they hired themselves out for work. Another way is to put a value on the other agricultural or domestic work they would be doing for the family. There is no hard-and-fast rule as to how this should be done, and using different rates will produce different results. In the end, it is a matter of judgement as to how valuable the farmer thinks his labour is. The same problem applies when using animals part time when they would be on the farm anyway, even if they were not used for water pumping.

The income or benefits from a pumping system may be similarly hard to define. A community water supply system installed by a village for its own benefit may have no monetary income at all. Sometimes a nominal user fee is collected to cover maintenance, but this is not a realistic assessment of the value of the water. Perhaps a value could be put on the time saved by the women and children who do not now have to carry water from a source some distance away. In a case such as this, where it is hard to put a figure on the benefits, it may be best only to consider the costs, as in the Life Cycle Cost analysis of the sub-section *'Life-cycle costs and unit-output costs'* in Section 8.1.3 below. The choice then would be the 'least cost' solution. For irrigation systems, the benefits are often in terms of the crops rather than the value of the water. The income then would be the extra value of the crops grown compared with if there were no irrigation.

Where actual monetary expenditure and income is involved, this should be used. Where the costs and benefits are less tangible, either use an estimated value, or use a comparison method that ignores the undefined items.

8.1.3 Financial comparison methods

Having explained the methods of equating future costs and payments to the present, it remains to use these techniques to arrive at a means for comparing the relative economic merits of different systems. There are in fact four commonly used techniques for making economic appraisals:

Life cycle costs and unit-output costs
At the start of Section 8.1.1, an example was given of dividing the total cost of a system by its lifetime to find a cost per year. The result was of limited use because it did not take into account the value of the money tied up in the project. Now we have the tools to convert costs to their present day value, this analysis can be done with more accuracy.

To work out a life cycle cost, all the costs associated with a scheme should be converted to present values and added together. This gives the total present value cost of the system. If this life cycle cost is then divided by the expected life of the system, we get an annual cost. By generating this figure for the different pumping options, a comparison can be made between them.

Further breakdown of the figures may be needed if the outputs or the heads of the different options are significantly different. If the heads are the same, the annual life cycle costs should simply be divided by the volume of water pumped in a year. Where the head and the flow are different, the annual life cycle cost should be divided by the head-flow product (i.e. $m^3.m$) to give the cost of unit quantity of water lifted through unit head. Care must be taken that you are comparing like with like.

It is important to note that life cycle costs are purely a criterion for comparison. They do not indicate whether a specific water pumping system is actually economically viable (for example whether the value of additional crops gained from pumping irrigation water may actually exceed the cost of pumping the water).

Net present value (npv) or net present worth
The Net Present Value (NPV) of a project is simply the sum of the present values of all the income *minus* the present values of all the costs. It should always be made clear what discount rate has been used to arrive at the NPV, because this assumption obviously affects the result. The more positive the value of the NPV, the better the financial return of the project. Calculating the NPVs of various options allows them to be compared financially. Note that the dependence of the NPV on the discount rate means that this is not simply a comparison of the different technologies, but depends upon the assumption of the prevailing economic conditions. Different interest or inflation rates could make different technologies more attractive. Net Present Value is sometimes referred to as Net Present Worth.

The NPV of a project differs from the life cycle costs in that it includes the income or benefits of the system, not just the expenditure. A negative NPV would indicate that the project consumes money rather than generates it, while an NPV of zero show a project where the costs equal the benefits.

Benefit/cost ratio
A variation on the concept of Net Present Value is to calculate the total life cycle benefits and the total life cycle costs and then to divide the former by the latter to obtain the Benefit/Cost Ratio. If this ratio is greater than one, then the benefits exceed the costs and the option is worthwhile. The same criticisms apply to this as to the Net Present Value approach, since the result is strongly influenced by non-technology-specific factors such as the choice of discount rate.

Internal rate of return
Internal Rate of Return is difficult to calculate, but provides a criterion for comparison independent of any assumptions on discount rates or inflation. It is therefore a purer method for comparing technologies. The Internal Rate of Return can be defined as the discount rate which will give a Net Present Value of zero (or a Benefit/

Cost ratio of 1); i.e., it is the discount rate which exactly makes the benefits equal the costs. To calculate Internal Rate of Return requires finding the discount rate to achieve a Net Present Value of zero; this is usually determined by trial and error, by recalculating the Net Present Value for different discount rates until the correct result is achieved. It is tedious to do this manually, but various standard computer spread sheets are widely available which make it a relatively easy task. The advantage of the Internal Rate of Return as a selection criterion is that it is, in effect, the discount rate at which an option just breaks-even. If the Internal Rate of Return is higher than the actual discount rate, then the option can be said to be economically worthwhile. Obviously, the higher the Internal Rate of Return of an option, the more attractive it is as an investment, since it basically says whether you do better to leave your money in the bank or invest it in an irrigation pumping system, or whatever.

8.1.4 Economic analysis

It is important to distinguish between 'financial' and 'economic' assessments of technologies. The discussions in this chapter are primarily concerned with a financial assessment that will be useful to those implementing water-pumping schemes. It deals with the actual costs an individual or a community is likely to experience in installing and operating a water system. An economic assessment, on the other hand, seeks to look at 'absolute' costs and benefits and therefore considers costs and benefits as they would be, if unaffected by taxes, subsidies or other local influences; the object is to arrive at a valuation of the technology in pure terms, excluding any local financial conditions. The value of an economic assessment is more for policy makers and those who need to compare technologies. In contrast, a village community, or a farmer, should do a financial assessment which takes account of conditions within his local economy, such as subsidies and taxes and the local market price of the final product harvested as a result of irrigation. The economist and the local people

may therefore come to quite different conclusions as to what is 'cost-effective'.

A term which may be found in literature on the economics of water-pumping is 'shadow pricing'. Economists recognize that there are so-called 'opportunity costs' associated with cash transactions; for example, although for most analytical purposes the exchange rate of a local currency will be taken at the official rate, in practice this does not always reflect its real value in terms of purchasing power. The opportunity cost of using foreign currency is therefore often higher than the exchange rate would suggest. It is therefore legitimate in a comparative analysis to penalize options involving a lot of foreign exchange to a greater extent than would apply simply by using the prevailing exchange rate. The normal method of doing this is to multiply the actual financial cost by a so-called 'shadow price factor'; where there is a shortage of a commodity (e.g. frequently, diesel fuel) it will have a shadow price factor greater than unity, conversely where there is a surplus (such as being able to use unskilled labour), then a shadow price factor of less than one may be applied to unskilled labour wages. For example the shadow price of diesel fuel may in some rural areas of developing countries be as much as four times the real price, while the ready availability of unskilled labour may allow it in reality to be costed at as little as 70% of its real wage level for economic comparisons. Tables of shadow prices specific to different countries, and even to regions of countries have been developed, but the concept of shadow pricing is complex and is probably best left to economists. However the principles of shadow pricing should at least be borne in mind, since items with a high opportunity cost may go into regular short-supply and cause operational problems.

8.1.5 A procedure for a cost appraisal of an irrigation pumping system

Figure 8.1 outlines a method that can be used to compare the costs of alternative water lifting techniques. This step-by-step approach is based on life-cycle-costing of the whole system. It takes

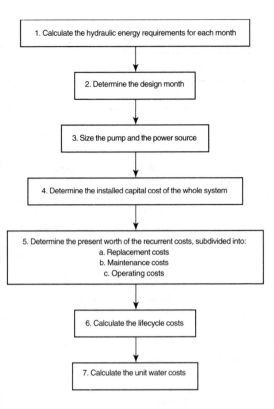

```
┌─────────────────────────────────────────────────────────────────┐
│  1. Calculate the hydraulic energy requirements for each month    │
└─────────────────────────────────────────────────────────────────┘
                              ↓
        ┌─────────────────────────────────────────┐
        │  2. Determine the design month           │
        └─────────────────────────────────────────┘
                              ↓
        ┌─────────────────────────────────────────┐
        │  3. Size the pump and the power source   │
        └─────────────────────────────────────────┘
                              ↓
    ┌───────────────────────────────────────────────────┐
    │  4. Determine the installed capital cost of the     │
    │     whole system                                    │
    └───────────────────────────────────────────────────┘
                              ↓
┌─────────────────────────────────────────────────────────────────┐
│  5. Determine the present worth of the recurrent costs,           │
│     subdivided into:                                              │
│           a. Replacement costs                                    │
│           b. Maintenance costs                                    │
│           c. Operating costs                                      │
└─────────────────────────────────────────────────────────────────┘
                              ↓
        ┌─────────────────────────────────────────┐
        │  6. Calculate the lifecycle costs        │
        └─────────────────────────────────────────┘
                              ↓
        ┌─────────────────────────────────────────┐
        │  7. Calculate the unit water costs       │
        └─────────────────────────────────────────┘
```

Fig. 8.1: A step-by-step procedure for a cost appraisal of a water-pumping system

into account all the identifiable costs, but ignores benefits gained by the users of water.

An integrated approach which considers the system as a whole, from the water source, to the point of application on the field is recommended, i.e. including the water source costs (such as well digging) and water distribution costs (such as digging ditches or purchasing pipes or sprinklers).

8.1.6 Example: comparison of petrol, diesel, wind and solar-powered pumps

A simple worked example is included as Table 8.3. The first step is to determine the hydraulic energy requirements. Suppose we wish to irrigate 0.5 ha to a depth of 10 mm each day, while pumping through a static head of 4 m in the month of maximum water demand. Reference to Fig. 5.12 indicates that this requires a net daily

hydraulic energy output of 0.545 kWh (factoring down by ten from the scale used in the figure). Alternatively, the following relationship, also explained in Chapter 5, may be used:

$$E_{hyd} = \frac{Q \cdot H}{367}$$

E_{hyd} – Hydraulic energy (kWh/d)

Allowance must now be made for distribution losses; for convenience it is assumed that all systems being compared involve the same distribution efficiency of 60%. Then the gross hydraulic energy requirement is (0.545/0.6) = 0.91 kWh/d. It should be noted that in reality, different distribution efficiencies might occur with different types of system, which would result in different energy demands.

The next step is to determine the design month; this is generally the month of maximum average water demand if the power supply is unaffected by climatic conditions (e.g. for engines), but where the energy resource is the wind or the sun, it becomes necessary to compare the energy demand with the energy availability and the design month will be the month when the ratio of energy demand to energy availability is highest. Supposing in this case that the design month does coincide with the month of maximum water demand in all examples, then using the assumptions in Table 8.3, we arrive at the sizing for the systems. The petrol engine needs to be sized to meet the demand without having to run for too long in a day: a 2 kW engine can meet the peak demand in just under six hours, which is reasonable. The diesel engine in this case will be of the smallest practical size, 2 kW. The petrol, wind and solar pumps need to be suitably sized to match the demand with the resource.

The next step is to estimate the installed capital cost of the system, generally by obtaining quotations for appropriately sized equipment. Some 'typical' values, valid at the time of writing, have been used. The product of size and cost factor gives the installed capital cost, which for simplicity is assumed to include the water source

Table 8.3: Analysis of unit water costs for four types of irrigation pumping system

Parameter	Assumptions and results			
	Petrol	Diesel	Wind	Solar
Price of fuel delivered on field	$0.60/l	$0.50/l		
Critical month mean irradiation				5.8 kWh/m²
Critical month mean windspeed			3.5 m/s	
Sizing assumption	1 kW 8% efficient, fuel to water	Minimum size available = 2 kW 12% efficient, fuel to water	0.1 V³ W/m² see sub-section 'Simple "rule-of-thumb" approach' in Section 7.7.4	See sub-section 'Rule of thumb method for sizing a solar pumping system' in Section 7.8.3 35% mean motor-pump efficiency
Requirement to produce peak daily water output	1.2 l/d petrol	0.7 l/d diesel fuel	8.8 m² rotor area	380 Wp array
Requirement to produce annual irrigation output	129 litres petrol per year	70 litres diesel per year	As above	As above
Capital cost assumption (total power system and pump including source and distribution)	$650 (engine + pump)	$1,800 (engine + pump)	$300/m² of rotor area	$10/Wp of array
Life of system	3 years	7 years	15 years	15 years
Storage tank capacity	2 × 200 l fuel in secured shed	2 × 200 l fuel in secured shed	40 m³ water tank	30 m³ water tank
Cost of storage	$280	$250	$600	$450
Life of storage	15 years	15 years	15 years	15 years
Life-cycle system costs	$2,414	$3,441	$3,282	$4,239
Life-cycle storage costs	$347	$310	$744	$558
Total life-cycle capital costs	$2,761	$3,751	$4,026	$4,796
Annualized system costs	$266	$379	$361	$476
Annualized storage costs	$38	$34	$82	$61
Annual O and M costs	$220	$200	$50	$50
Annual fuel costs	$78	$36	–	–
Total annual cost	$602	$650	$493	$578
Unit cost of water	$0.118/m³	$0.127/m³	$0.097/m³	$0.114/m³

Operational requirement:
10mm of water lifted 4 m to cover 0.5 ha (peak irrigation demand), giving a peak daily hydraulic energy requirement of 0.91 kWh/d. Annual requirement is mean of 67% of peak for five months, which is 5,094 m³/year.
Petrol and diesel calorific values from Table 7.10.
For simplicity, assumed water source costs are identical in all four cases; although in reality this may not necessarily be correct.
Financial parameters (for all cases) $d = 10\%$, $n = 25$ years, $i = 0$.

and distribution system in all cases. Some storage facility is likely to be needed in all cases; a secure lock-up holding two 200 litre oil drums is assumed for the diesel while a low cost compacted soil bund with a lining is assumed for water storage for the wind and the solar systems, holding 40 and 30 m³ respectively. In the case of petrol and diesel systems, the cost of storage includes the notional investment in stored fuel (assuming on average that the storage is at 50% capacity and amortizing a continuous investment in 200 litres of fuel).

The actual useful life of the systems and storage is assumed, as indicated in the table, as are financial parameters for the discount rate and the period for analysis. All systems are analyzed over a 'life cycle' of 25 years. The life cycle costs may be determined by working out the present values of the first system and all subsequent replacement ones (using factors from Table 8.1) and adding them all together. Table 8.3 shows the system and storage life cycle costs separately, but they could also be combined. The life-time costs are then converted back to an equivalent annual payment using the factors of Table 8.2; in this case a 25-year period and 10% discount rate gives a factor of 0.11; the each life-cycle cost is multiplied by this figure.

The combined system and storage annualized costs represent the annual investment or 'finance' costs. Different systems also have recurrent costs consisting of O and M (Operation and Maintenance) costs, and sometimes fuel costs. When the finance, O and M and fuel costs are added, we obtain the gross annual cost of owning and operating each system.

Where an identical useful output is to be produced, then the gross annual cost is sufficient for ranking purposes. In reality, however, different cropping strategies may apply for different irrigation systems, resulting in different crop irrigation water demands and different benefits (in terms of the market values of the crops). Therefore it is useful to divide the gross annual cost by the gross annual irrigation water demand to arrive at an average unit cost for water from each option.

In this example, the wind pump comes out marginally better than the others, but all the costs are quite close. The differences are small enough for another technology to be preferable if other, non-economic factors are taken into account. It must be stressed that this is but one simple example which should not be blindly used to draw any conclusions on the relative merits of engines, wind and solar pumps generally. The costs used in the table may not even approximate to locally-prevailing costs in a given area. Even varying totally non-technology-dependent parameters such as the discount rate, the period of analysis, the water demand or the head could significantly change the results and rankings obtained. Changing the technical performance parameters also has a profound effect.

8.1.7 Relative economics of different options

A procedure similar to that just described has been followed to analyze a representative selection of the types of water lifting systems described earlier in this paper.

Most studies attempting this kind of analysis use a single assumption for each and every parameter and compound these to arrive at a single answer, as in the example just given. This is often presented as a single curve on a graph for each option. The trouble with this approach is that errors are compounded and may not cancel out, so the result could be very misleading. In an attempt to minimize this problem, the approach in this case has been to choose a low and a high parameter at each and every decision point; i.e. a plausible pessimistic and a plausible optimistic one. Two sets of calculations are then completed for each technology, to produce a pessimistic and an optimistic result, which when graphed gives two curves. It is then reasonable to assume that the real result is likely to lie between the two curves and the results are therefore presented as a broad band rather than a thin line. Therefore, where the broad band for one technology lies wholly above or below another it is reasonable to assume the one with the lower band is almost certainly the cheaper option. In most cases the options overlap considerably and in such situations other considerations than water cost should dictate the decision.

Table 8.4 lists all the systems considered and gives the principle assumptions used for calculating the cash flows. The capital cost assumptions are intended to include the entire system as defined in the previous section; i.e. not just a prime-mover and pump, but all the accessories that are necessary and appropriate for each type of technology and scale of operation.

To eliminate one parameter, the output was calculated for each option, not in terms of volume of water pumped, but in terms of hydraulic energy output; this effectively combines the volume of water pumped and the head, since units of $m^3.m$, or cubic metre-metres were used. However it should be realized that this is only valid for comparing similar systems; it is not realistic to compare systems operating at radically different heads, such as a 100 m borehole pump with a 10 m head surface-suction pump, purely on the basis of $m^3.m$. To convert a figure in $m^3.m$ to flow at a specific head it is only necessary to divide by the head in question; e.g. 10 $m^3.m$ could be 2 m^3 pumped through 5 m head.

To convert a unit cost of, say, 5 cents/$m^3.m$ to obtain a cost per unit of water, it is necessary to multiply by the head in question; e.g. that energy cost at 2 m head represents a water cost of 10 c/m^3.

The final results are presented in terms of output cost versus the hydraulic energy demand. This is because the unit costs of different options, and hence the economic rankings, are sensitive to the size of system used. Therefore the choice of technology will differ depending on the scale of operation; systems that are economic for larger scale operations are often uneconomic on a small scale, and vice-versa.

Figures 8.2 to Fig. 8.7 show the results for the different options analyzed. In some cases, such as solar and wind powered pumping systems, the variability of the energy resource was allowed for by recalculating the band of results three times, i.e. for a mean of 10, 15 and 20 MJ/m^2 per day (2.8, 4.2 and 5.6 kWh/m^2 per day) of solar irradiation and, similarly for three mean

wind-speeds of 2.5, 3.0 and 4.0 m/s. The lower levels chosen are deliberately selected because they are sub-marginal conditions, while the middle level was judged to be marginal rather than attractive for the technologies concerned; so the results of all except the 20 MJ/m^2 per day (for solar) and the 4.0 m/s (for wind) examples would not be expected to show these technologies particularly favourably.

A problem with the figures is that they had to be plotted on a log-log scale, because of the large ranges of power and cost considered. Otherwise, either a very large sheet of paper would be needed to show the results, or the results at the lower end, which are of great interest to many people, would have been compressed to insignificance. The trouble with log-log scales is that the eye interprets distances linearly, so they can be misleading if viewed without much thought. This makes it difficult to compare the various options shown in Fig. 8.2 to Fig. 8.7. Therefore, Fig. 8.8 has been provided as a simplified composite of these results, using mean values (between the highs and lows) of the other graphs (to avoid too much of a confusion of curves) and moreover it was plotted against linear axes over a necessarily smaller size range, up to only 1,000 $m^3.m/day$. This range is of most interest as the relative rankings do not change much once an energy demand of about 1,000 $m^3.m/day$ is exceeded.

Another, perhaps more easily interpreted presentation of these results is given in Fig. 8.9, where histograms of the cost spread for each system at daily energy demands equivalent to 100, 1,000 and 10,000 $m^3.m$ are given, and compared linearly rather than logarithmically for ease of comparison. (To put this in perspective, this is equivalent to 20, 200 and 2,000 m^3 per day at 5 m head, or half those amounts at 10 m head, etc.) This set of histograms also reintroduces the 'optimistic' to 'pessimistic' spread for each technology, which was omitted in the previous comparison of Fig. 8.8. It is important not to lose sight of the possible range of costs applicable to any given technology, especially as in some cases the band of possible costs is very wide even on the basis of quite plausible assumptions in all cases.

Table 8.4: Cost and performance assumptions used for comparison of alternative pumping methods

Type of system Capital cost	Life (years)	Maintenance (per annum)	Operating cost
SOLAR PV Sized for irradiation levels of 20 MJ/m²/d in design month. Peak water requirement in design month twice average. *Wp* is array rating in peak watts. Pumping 365 days/year			
High		$50 + $0.05 × *Wp*	Nil
Motor/pump sub-system efficiency of 30%			
Module: $3 × *Wp*	10		
Motor and pump: $400 + $1 × *Wp*	5		
Rest of the system: $1,000 + $2 × *Wp*	20		
Low		$100 + $0.05 × *Wp*	Nil
Motor/pump sub-system efficiency of 70%			
Module: $6 × *Wp*	15		
Motor and pump: $500 + $1.5 × *Wp*	7.5		
Rest of the system: $1,500 + $2 × *Wp*	15		
WIND A_{rotor} is the swept area of the rotor in m². Sized for a mean windspeed '*V*' of 3 m/s in the design month. Peak water requirement in design month twice average. Mean hydraulic power = $0.1.V^3$ W/m² Pumping 365 days/year			
High		$50 + $2.5 × A	Nil
System cost: $400 × A	20		
Low		$100 + $3 × A	Nil
System cost: $200 × A	10		
DIESEL P_{shaft} is the engine power (kW), either 2.5 kW or 10 kW. Efficiency rises linearly from zero to stable value in first ½ hour. Engine efficiency 40% of total efficiency. Calorific value of diesel fuel is 38 MJ/l. Pumping 250 days/year.			
High		$400	$0.80/l of fuel
Fuel to hydraulic efficiency = 3% + 0.7% × P_{shaft}			
System cost: $1,900 + $8.6 × P_{shaft}	5		
Low		$200	$0.40/l of fuel
Fuel to hydraulic efficiency = 13% + 0.7% × P_{shaft}			
System cost: $950 + $4.3 × P_{shaft}	7.5		
PARAFFIN/KEROSENE Engine size 1 kW. No. of engines to suit demand. Same efficiency assumptions as for diesel. Calorific value of paraffin is 36 MJ/l. Pumping 250 days/year.			
High		$200	$0.80/l of fuel
Fuel to hydraulic efficiency = 2%			
Single engine system cost: $600	2		
Low		$100	$0.40/l of fuel
Fuel to hydraulic efficiency = 6%			
Single engine system cost: $200	5		

BIOGAS

G is energy content of gas produced (MJ/d). Biogas unit
sized to suit S.I. engine as above. Pumping 250 days/year.

High		$20	$0.03/MJ of gas
Gas holder: $137 + $1 \times G$	5		
Pump: $600	5		
Rest of the system: $91 + $1.89 \times G$	10		
Low		$20	$0.03/MJ of gas
Gas holder: $137 + $1 \times G$	5		
Pump: $200	5		
Rest of the system: $91 + $1.89 \times G$	10		

OXEN

Hydraulic output = 200 W/animal. Work for 8 h/d $\equiv$
588 m³.m/day/animal maximum. Pumping 200 days/year

High		$20	$1.25/animal/day
Animal: $125	10		
Pump: $100	5		
Low		$20	$0.75/animal/day
Animal: $250	10		
Pump: $100	5		

HUMAN

Hydraulic output = 37 W/person. Work for 4 hours
per day $\equiv$ 54 m³.m/day/person maximum.
Pumping 200 days/year

High		$20	$1/man/day
Pump: $200	6		
Low		$20	$0.30/man/day
Pump: $200	4		

TURBINE

Hydraulic output = 350 W
Operates 24 hours/day, 365 days/year

High		$20	Nil
Civil works: $2,000	30		
Turbine-pump unit: $200	10		
Low		$20	Nil
Civil works: $200	20		
Turbine-pump unit: $200	5		

RAM PUMP/HYDRAM

Hydraulic output = 100 W
Operates 24 hours/day, 365 days/year

High		$5	Nil
System cost: $3,000	30		
Low		$5	Nil
System cost: $1,000	10		

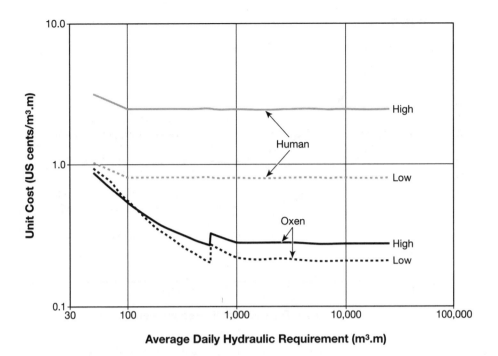

Fig. 8.2: Comparison of the costs of water-pumping using human and animal power

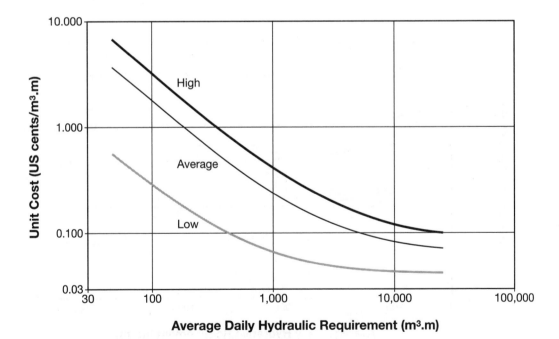

Fig. 8.3: Cost of water pumping using pumps powered by mains electricity at various costs

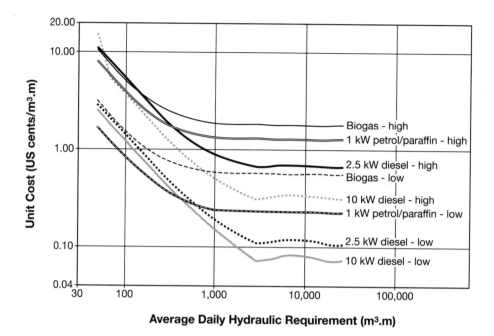

Fig. 8.4: Comparison of the costs of water pumping using biogas, petrol/paraffin (gasoline/kerosene) and diesel pumping sets

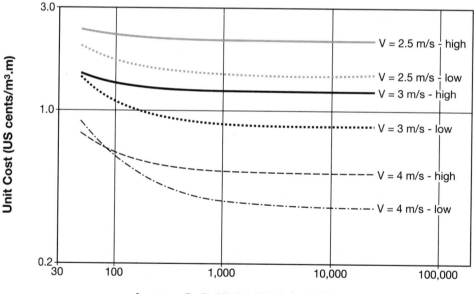

Fig. 8.5: Comparison of the costs of pumping using windpumps at various mean windspeeds

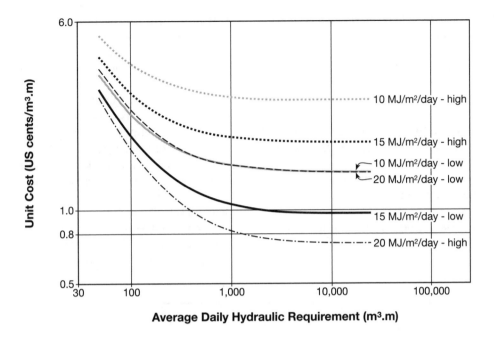

Fig. 8.6: Comparison of the costs of pumping using solar PV at various mean insolation levels

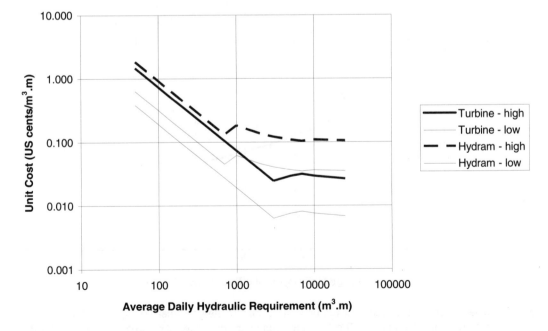

Fig. 8.7: Comparison of the costs of water pumping using turbine pumps and hydrams

8.1.8 Conclusions to be drawn from economic analysis

The economics for most options are size-sensitive, so that what is correct at 100 m³.m/day is not generally true for a hydraulic requirement of 10,000 m³.m/day.

Low unit-output cost options which apply almost right across the entire size range of interest include:

- mains electricity; providing it is already close to the field so only minor connection costs are incurred;
- hydro-powered devices (rampumps or turbine pumps); but these require suitable site conditions;

- windpumps; for locations with high mean wind speeds of 4 m/s or greater;
- animal power; which is a cost-competitive option, but does not generally seem a realistic new option where animal traction has not traditionally been used;
- human power is cost-competitive in very small-scale applications (under 100 m³.m/day); but only if a very low 'opportunity cost' is assigned to human labour, and this conflicts with many development goals.

Where land-holdings are so small that the demand is less than 100 m³.m/day, then human power is relatively inexpensive and animal power appears to be competitive. Solar and windpumps are both potentially competitive and

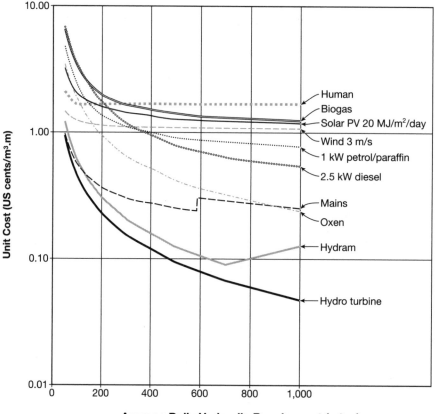

Fig. 8.8: Mean values of the results of the previous graphs plotted for linear scales for daily requirements of up to 1,000 m³.m only. Jumps in the curves show where it is necessary to introduce an extra pumping unit in order to meet the demand

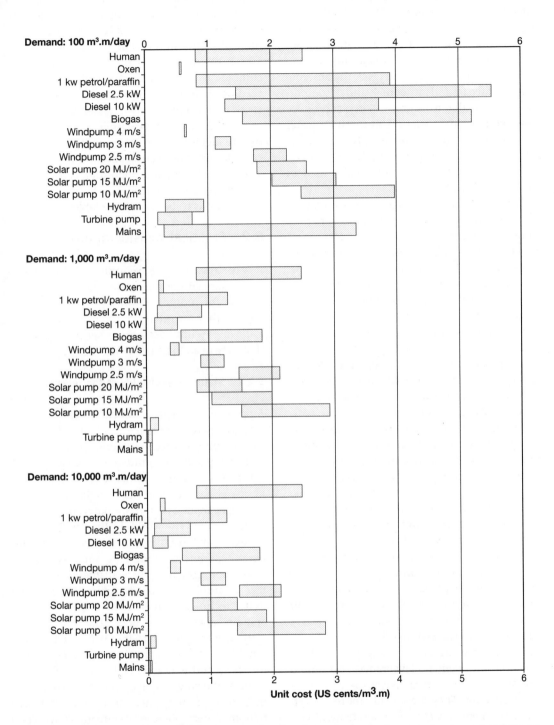

Fig. 8.9: Histogram showing the typical range of unit water-pumping costs against volume requirement for various pumping options

315

so are petrol/kerosene spark ignition engines, providing they are reasonably efficiently sized and operated. Diesel power is not generally cost-effective for such small energy demands. Although the renewables in some cases appear competitive at this small demand level, the absolute costs of water are still rather high and it is important to ensure that irrigation will in fact produce a profitable yield in relation to the high water costs involved. It may be better to try to consolidate a single larger water system shared between several such small land holdings, where such an option is feasible.

At the medium size range analyzed, namely 1,000 m^3.m/day, all the options are generally more cost-effective than they are at 100 m^3.m/day energy demand, and there is an overlap between most options. Animal power, windpower (properly sited with V greater than 4 m/s), water power, and mains electricity appear marginally the best options, closely followed by diesel and internal combustion engines (only if efficiently operated).

At the large size range of 10,000 m^3.m/day, diesel power comes into its own, and unless mains electricity or water power is available, diesel will probably be the best option.

It should be noted that the low cost option for a given type of prime mover is not necessarily the one with the cheapest capital cost. Replacement, operating and maintenance costs can all make what seems initially to be a cheaper option more expensive in the long term. This is the case, for example, for the PV pumping and oxen examples considered here.

Therefore, in summary, mains electricity (but only if no significant connection costs are involved) or water power are most economical. Wind power is next most attractive if wind speeds are high (but it is decidedly unattractive with low or uncertain winds). Solar power is generally expensive but fills a useful gap in the 100–1000 m^3.m/day demand level range, and should become increasingly attractive as the cost of solar systems fall. They are already more cost effective than engines at very small demand volumes. Engines have a very wide band of uncertainty relating to their unit costs at small energy demand levels, ranging from competitive to unacceptable. Spark ignition engines are more attractive in the small to medium range of 100–1,000 m^3.m/day while diesel engines become more competitive at energy demands exceeding around 1,000 m^3.m/day. Biomass-fuelled spark ignition engines will generally cost more to run than kerosene or gasoline fuelled engines (where fuel is at world prices), but will be worth considering where petroleum fuels are either not available or have a high opportunity cost. Clearly, in such cases a suitable low-cost biomass fuel resource needs to be readily available.

8.2 Practical considerations

It was stressed at the beginning of this chapter that financial considerations are not the only criteria for judging a water-pumping project; indeed, they are often not the major factor. The following sections deal with other considerations that may need to be taken into account.

8.2.1 Status or availability of the technology

A primary consideration in choosing a pumping technology is whether it is available. Of the various options discussed in this book, some are widespread, but some are limited to small geographical areas. The relatively 'high-tech' options, such as small internal-combustion engines or solar PV, tend to be made by international companies with outlets around the world. In theory, these technologies can be obtained anywhere. At the other extreme, some technologies, such as Chinese turbine pumps, are only available in one country. The turbine pump is an interesting example, as it is technically an excellent option for a suitable site, appears to be most attractive economically, and has proved itself in wide use in southern China, but is currently only manufactured in China and is not generally exported. Again, some of the very simple human-powered or animal-powered pumps may only be found in certain small areas where local craftsmen have learnt the skill of making them. Mains-powered electric pumps will be sold in the towns of almost every country, but this is of no use if there is no grid in the rural area where water is needed.

Some of the pumping options discussed in this book are not just geographically limited, but are historically limited; they used to be available, but are no longer. Small steam engines and Stirling engines fall in this category. Both appear to have great potential for small-scale water projects, but are not commercially available anywhere. In the case of the Stirling engines, they were widely used in the past, and there seems no intrinsic reason why they should not be economic and effective pumping machines today if they were manufactured in quantity, but it is believed that no company currently offers a viable Stirling engine for sale. Stirling engines would only be an option if some organization or company decided to invest in their production.

Even when a technology is commercially available, there are still problems in implementing it. Perhaps the greatest difficulty is finding information on new or unfamiliar products. Any individual, community or organization who wishes to install a pumping system will need information in order to procure the correct size and specification of system, to install it correctly, and to operate and maintain it effectively.

It is probably best if all but the more adventurous (and wealthy) of small farmers play safe and stick to familiar and 'available' technologies where help, advice and spares are readily available and risks are minimized. However, if everyone took this advice, new and potentially better technologies would never become available. It is worth suggesting that governments, international aid agencies, and any other institutions with a commitment to the development of water supply and small-scale agriculture, take risks in this area on behalf of their rural populations to test and demonstrate any technologies that appear promising.

Problems must be expected with pilot projects. It is therefore vital to measure, monitor and record the behaviour of any innovative systems that are tried. Even if no serious problems occur, unless such pilot projects are properly monitored it will not be possible to come to any conclusion as to whether the new technology being tried is competitive with what it is supposed to replace.

Actual performance monitoring is important, but so are qualitative comments on operational aspects, such as maintenance or installation difficulties, or shortcomings as perceived by the user. Feedback on these aspects needs to be absorbed by the manufacturers and developers of this kind of equipment so that the necessary improvements can be set in hand, otherwise development will be delayed.

8.2.2 Capital cost versus recurrent costs

As explained previously, low recurrent costs tend to have to be traded for high capital costs. High capital costs represent a real barrier for small farmers to take up new technology, even if the unit output costs are competitive. Worse, low capital costs are often an incentive to install inefficient systems (e.g. small kerosene pumps sets with inadequately sized distribution pipe). Where there is a good case for farmers to be encouraged to use a high capital cost technology (even to move from spark-ignition to diesel engines), then it will generally be necessary for appropriate credit facilities to be made available as an incentive.

Renewable energy systems, with their high capital costs and low recurrent costs may be of particular interest to institutions having access to grant or aid finance for capital items, because they do offer a means for investing in low recurrent costs. Many rural institutions face major problems with meeting the recurrent costs of running conventional pumping systems, so in some situations it may make sense to introduce high capital cost equipment simply to reduce the maintenance and fuel budgets and thereby to produce a more sustainable project.

8.2.3 Operational convenience

This factor varies considerably with different types of pumping system. For example, a wind pump will be highly dependent on adequate wind to operate, so if high-risk crops are grown, where the provision of water on demand is vital to the survival of the crop, then a large (and consequently expensive) storage tank will be necessary to ensure water is always available. Alternatively, less risky (and probably less valuable) crops could be grown with only a small storage tank, or even with no storage at all. Therefore the flexibility of the device, or its controllability, must be taken account of as it affects such fundamental decisions as the choice of crop to grow under irrigation.

Other factors relate to aspects such as size and portability. Small engines and small solar pumps may be quite portable, which means they can be moved around to irrigate with only short, but effective distribution pipes, while a wind pump, a larger engine, or a hydram will inevitably have to be fixed. However small portable items are also vulnerable to theft in some regions, which makes the relatively large and fixed installation less at risk in that context.

Few options can rival the operational flexibility of an internal combustion engine system in terms of rapid start up, portability, provision of power on demand, etc., but of course one of the reasons for looking at the other options is that the internal combustion engine generally suffers the major drawback of needing petroleum fuels. So the operational shortcomings of many of the alternatives need to be weighed against the fuel needs and the likely future availability and cost of fuel.

8.2.4 Skill requirements for installation, operation and maintenance

If a water-pumping system is to work correctly, it must be installed correctly. Likewise, the long-term sustainability of a system depends on having an operator with sufficient skill to work it, and a capable mechanic to mend it if it breaks down or needs adjustment.

Two key factors apply here: the absolute skills required, and the level of familiarity with the equipment. Machinery that is familiar will seem simple, even though it is actually quite complicated. In absolute technical terms, there are no water-lifting technologies more technically

demanding than the diesel engine, yet mechanics in most towns in the world will completely overhaul a diesel engine without a second thought. If the same mechanic is presented with a solar PV pump to mend – actually a much simpler job – he is likely to be nervous and unsure of what to do. The difference is not in the complexity of the task, but in his familiarity with it. It should be recognized that lack of familiarity with a technology strongly influences people to avoid it. There is a need to learn about an unfamiliar technology before dismissing it as too complicated. It is often not appreciated that renewable energy technologies are basically fairly simple.

When an unfamiliar technology is introduced, some training will be needed for all concerned. It should be borne in mind that operators and mechanics do not always need to understand the basic principles of a device in order to work on it; few diesel mechanics understand the first principles of a diesel engine, but this does not stop them working on one! The level of support available from manufacturers or suppliers is most important in this respect. Most successful technologies have become widely used because they were promoted and supported by the commercial interests that market them. Even the simplest technologies stand little chance of being taken up unless they are effectively promoted. This means making sure that early users are properly supported and helped through any problems.

Often there are trade-offs between the amount of skill needed and the amount of maintenance/ operational intervention required. Solar pumps need very little maintenance, so even if an overhaul is a specialized and slightly tricky task, a skilled mechanic will only need to be called out every few years. Internal combustion-engine pumps need quite frequent and sometimes technically sophisticated maintenance functions, but because the technology is so widespread there are many people capable of performing these. The cruder types of village-built wind pumps need a great deal of adjustment and running repairs, but to the people who are familiar with them, these present little inconvenience or difficulty.

8.2.5 Durability, reliability and useful life

Durability, reliability and a long operational life usually cost money 'up front', but they also are frequently a good investment in terms of minimizing costs. Perceptions on the value of capital or the choice of discount rate will usually control decisions on these aspects, but it is best to use a financial analysis to quantify the cost-effectiveness of buying high-quality equipment. Many who have analyzed the cost of operating machinery in remote areas, particularly engines, have concluded that their performance, not only in terms of output but also in terms of reliability and durability, usually turns out to be significantly worse than expected. There is therefore often merit in erring towards over-sizing prime-movers and procuring any special accessories that make the system more 'fail-safe'.

8.2.6 Efficiency

The efficiency of a pumping system is important because it affects the cost of the pumped water. If a system has to pump a certain volume of water through a given head, an efficient system will require less energy to do this. For a petrol-engine system, less petrol will be needed, and the operating costs will be lower. For a solar pumping system, a smaller PV array will be required, and the capital cost will be less. It wastes money to have under-sized pipework or badly-matched components in a pumping system.

Efficiency is often stressed in books such as this, yet many field installations are found to have appallingly low efficiency, and their owners go on using them, apparently unaware of the losses they are incurring. It appears that users make their choice of pumping system on the grounds of convenience, availability, and initial cost, and never appreciate that one system may be much less efficient than another; few users have the opportunity to compare one pumping system with another.

The challenge to manufacturers and development organizations is to make the benefits of efficiency apparent. Efficiency is especially important for human or animal-powered pumps, when the energy available is limited, and in situations where energy is expensive, in terms of fuel prices or electricity tariffs. Demonstration sites that allow users to test different options and to see the differences in performance assist people to understand the hidden principles of efficiency. In the end, the owners and users have the right to choose what they want, and efficiency will only be one factor in the choice, but decisions can be better if all the factors are understood.

8.2.7 Potential for local manufacture

This is of more immediate interest to policy makers than local users, although the users will benefit from local manufacture in due course.

One of the principal reasons to seek alternatives to petroleum fuelled engines for water pumping is because of the inability of many countries to import sufficient petroleum to meet present, let alone future, needs. The shortage of foreign exchange to import oil equally affects the import of foreign solar pumps or other alternatives. Therefore, any system that lends itself to whole or partial local manufacture is of potential economic importance. However, the benefits of local manufacture do not end with import substitution.

Other important results of local manufacture, or part-manufacture, are:

- The creation of local industrial employment, which also improves the local economy.
- The enhancement of industrial skills.
- Improved local availability of spare parts.
- Improved local expertise in the technology.

In other words, local manufacture can help to overcome many of the constraints mentioned previously in supporting the initial diffusion of a new technology. At the same time it can help to develop the local industrial and manufacturing base. The economy of the country gains twice from local manufacture of irrigation equipment, first from internalizing the manufacture and second from the enhanced agricultural production once the equipment starts to be widely applied.

APPENDIX: CONVERSION OF COMMON UNITS OF MEASUREMENT

To convert			
From:	*To:*	*Multiply by*	*Notes*
Windspeed			
mph	m/s	0.447	miles per hour
km/h	m/s	0.278	
kn or kts	m/s	0.514	knots, nautical miles per hours
Flow			
US gpm	m^3/h	0.227	US gallons per minute
Imp. gpm	m^3/h	0.273	Imperial (British) gallons per minute
l/s	m^3/h	3.6	litres/second
l/s	m^3/d	86.4	
Energy			
kW	W	1,000	kilowatt
MJ	J	1,000,000	megajoule
$m^3.m$	kWh	0.00272	* see note
kWh	$m^3.m$	367 (=1/0.00272)	* see note
$m^3.m$	J	9,800	* see note
kWh	MJ	3.6	kilowatt-hour
Area			
ha	m^2	10,000	hectare
ha	acres	2.471	
m^2	sq. yd	1.196	square yards

*1 $m^3.m$ (sometimes, and perhaps more confusingly, written 1 m^4) is the energy used to lift 1 m^3 of water through 1 m, and the density of water and the acceleration due to gravity are implicit in this quantity. This conversion factor assumes a value of gravity, g, of 9.8 m/s^2. (Although g is often given as 9.81 m/s^2 in books, it actually varies at different places on the globe, being less near the equator. A value of 9.8 m/s^2 is usually sufficiently accurate, and is actually closer to the true value for most developing countries.)

GLOSSARY

aquifer	layer of rock or soil able to hold or transmit water
annuity	cash accrued from a series of constant payments, see Section 8.1.1
bore	internal diameter of a pipe or pump body
borehole	narrow-diameter well drilled for water supply
bucket pump	occasionally-used generic term for piston pump, see Section 6.5; the 'Bucket Pump' is also a specific design of bucket and windlass, see Section 6.3.3
centrifugal pump	a rotating pump that relies on the centrifugal force induced in the water to produce pressure; see Section 6.8.4
CI	Compression Ignition (engines), diesel engines
counterpoise lift	bucket balanced on a counterweighted arm; see Section 6.3.2
CWS	Community Water Supply
DCF	see 'Discounted Cash Flow'
dhab	Bangladeshi name for counterpoise lift
dhone	Bangladeshi name for a see-saw gutter lift, also spelt 'doon'
discount factor	factor relating the present value of a payment to its future value
discounted cash flow	analysis of the future value of series of payments; see Section 8.1.1
diesel	fuel, English word for 'gasoil'
diesel engine	internal combustion engine using the diesel or 'Otto' cycle
doon	see 'dhone'
double-acting pump	reciprocating pump that pumps water on both the forward and return stroke
dragon spine/dragon wheel	see 'water ladder'
drum wheel	see 'tympanum'
FAO	Food and Agricultural Organisation of the United Nations
fathi	efficient form of the tablia; see Section 6.4.3
flash wheels	large, mechanized paddle wheels; see Section 6.6.1
foggara	Arabic name for sloping tunnels used to tap into water table
foot valve	inlet valve at the base of a handpump
full-bore handpump	see 'Deepwell handpumps' in Section 6.5.2
gasoline	American word for 'petrol'
gasoline engine	see 'petrol engine'
gasoil	American word for 'diesel' fuel
gear pump	pump using two meshing, rotating gears to pump fluid
HDP/HDPE	High Density Polyethylene, plastic commonly used for water pipes
helical rotor pump	see 'progressive cavity pump'
HTN	Handpump Technology Network; contact through SKAT
hydram	see 'ram pumps'
IC	Internal Combustion (engines)

impulse pumps	see 'ram pumps'
INGO	International Non-Governmental Organization; see also NGO
IRC	International Reference Centre for Community Water Supply and Sanitation
IRR	Internal Rate of Return; see Section 8.1.3
ITDG	Intermediate Technology Development Group, U.K.
kerosene	American word for 'paraffin'
kerosene engine	see 'paraffin engine'
ladder pumps	see 'water ladder'
LCD	Litres per Capita per Day, estimate of water requirement per person
life cycle costs	total cost of operating equipment over its whole operating life
lobe pump	pump using rotors with shaped meshing lobes
LPCPD	Litres Per Capita Per Day
$m^3.m$	Measure of pump output, equivalent to volume of water × height lifted
mohte	flexible leather or rubber 'buckets', see Section 6.3.3 and Section 7.3.1
Moineaux pump	see 'progressive cavity pump'
Mono pump	see 'progressive cavity pump'
MOSTI	Manually Operated Shallow Tubewell for Irrigation, referring to a No. 6 handpump
Moyno pump	see 'progressive cavity pump'
NGO	Non-Governmental Organization, usually meaning a local or national development organization; see also INGO
No. 6 handpump	a specific design of handpump, developed in Bangladesh
noria	see Section 6.4.1
NPV	Net Present Value, see 8.1.3
NPW	Net Present Worth, see 'NPV'
open-topped handpump	handpump in which piston can be pulled up through the top of the pump, see 'Deepwell handpumps' in Section 6.5.2
OTC	Open-Topped Cylinder, see 'open-topped handpump'
p.c. pump	see 'progressing cavity pump'
paraffin	English word for 'kerosene'
paraffin engine	internal combustion engine fuelled by paraffin/kerosene
paternoster	see 'rope and washer'
peristaltic pump	pump moving water along by trapping it in a section of tube; see Section 6.6.4
Persian Wheel	lifting device with buckets attached to the perimeter of a wheel; see Section 6.4.1
PV	PhotoVoltaic or Present Value, depending on context
petrol	English word for 'gasoline'
petrol engine	an internal combustion engine fuelled by petrol/gasoline
piston pump	a pump using a reciprocating piston and valves
potable (water)	water fit for drinking
progressive/ progressing cavity pump	rotating pump that moves water inside it axially trapped in voids between the rotor and casing; see Section 6.6.3
qanat	Farsi name for sloping tunnels used to tap into water table
rahad	Thai name for the 'water ladder'

ram pumps	impulse pumps relying on water hammer effect to lift part of flow going through them
Rankine engine	internal combustion engine using the rankine cycle; see Section 7.8.4
reciprocating pump	pump in which the main working element moves forwards and backwards; see piston pump
regenerative pump	see Section 6.8.2
reticulation	division into a network, generally meaning the pipework of a water distribution system
rower pump	reciprocating piston pump operated with a rowing action; see Section 7.2.3
sakia	see Section 6.4.3
shadoof	see counterpoise lift
shadow pricing	price reflecting the availability of a resource; see Section 8.1.4
shaduf	see 'counterpoise lift'
SI	Spark Ignition (engines), petrol engines
single-acting pump	reciprocating pump that only pumps when its piston is moving in one direction, not on the return stroke
SKAT	Swiss Centre for Development Cooperation in Technology and Management
snore	a mixture of water and air taken into a pump when the inlet is not fully submerged
steam engine	engines operated by steam; see Sections 7.5.1 and 7.8.4
Stirling engine	engine using the Stirling cycle; see Sections 7.5.2 and 7.8.4
suction pump	see 'Suction handpumps/bucket pumps' in Section 6.5.2
suction valve	see 'footvalve'
tapak-tapak pump	see 'treadle pump'
treadle pump	foot operated piston pump
tubewell	see 'borehole'
turbine pump	centrifugal pump with diffuser around the impeller
tympanum	rotary lifting device composed of scoops; see Section 6.4.3
UN	United Nations Organisation
UNICEF	United Nations Children's Fund
UNDP	United Nations Development Program
valve	unit controlling the flow of water, in pumps usually allowing flow through it in only one direction
vane pump	rotating pump with vanes in its rotor
volute	shape of pump casing; see Section 6.8.2
Water Decade	International Drinking Water Supply and Sanitation Decade, 1981–1990
water hammer	large pressure rise in water pipes when a flow is stopped quickly
water hammer pumps	see 'ram pumps'
water ladder	see Section 6.4.6
WHO	World Health Organisation
WMO	World Meteorological Organisation, part of the UN
Wp	peak watts of a solar module – see 'Photovoltaic properties' in Section 7.8.3

REFERENCES

1. C. Kerr, Ed.; *Community Health and Sanitation*; Intermediate Technology Publications, London, 1990; ISBN 1 85339 018 6.

2. D. Whittington and V. Swarna; R and D on Drinking Water Supply and Sanitation, The Economic Benefits of Potable Water Supply Projects to Households in Developing Countries; Economic Staff Paper, No. 53, January, 1994, Asian Development Bank, Manila.

3. S. Rabindranath; Facing the Challenge— Germany funds IIMI Action Research; *D+C Magazine*, No. 4, 1993.

4. *World Resources—A Guide to the Global Environment (1994–1995), People and the Environment*; Oxford University Press, 1994; ISBN 0195210441.

5. P.S. Stern; *Small-scale Irrigation*; IT Publications, London, 1979.

6. J. N. Pretty; *Regenerating Agriculture—Policies and Practice for Sustainability and Self-Relience*; Earthscan, London, 1995; ISBN 1853831980.

7. *World Development Report—1982*, World Bank/ OUP, Oxford, 1983.

8. G. Leech; *Energy and Food Production*; IIED, London, 1975.

9. D. Hillel; Small-Scale Irrigation for Arid Zones—Principles and Options; Development Series 2; FAO, Rome, 1997.

10. M. Kay and N. Hatcho; *Small-scale Pumped Irrigation: Energy and Cost; Irrigation Water Management, Training Manual*; FAO, Rome, provisional edition, 1992.

11. R. Franceys with J. Pickford and R. Reed; *A Guide to the Development of On-site Sanitation*; WHO, 1992; ISBN 9241544430.

12. S. Arlosoroff, G. Tschannerl, D. Grey, W. Journey, A. Karp, O. Langenegger and R. Roche; *Community Water Supply, The Handpump Option*; IT Intermediate Technology Publications, London and The World Bank, 1998; ISBN 1853393835.

13. D. A. Okun and W. R. Ernst; Community Piped Water Supply Systems in Developing Countries, A Planning Manual; Technical Paper No. 60; The World Bank, Washington, 1987; ISBN 0-8213–0896-3.

14. P. Chatterjee; Water in India: Mismanaging a Vital Resource; *D+C (Development and Co-operation) Journal*, No.2, March/April, 1997.

15. D. E, Walling (Ed.), S. S. D. Foster, P. Wurzel; Challenges in African Hydrology; IAHS Publication No. 144; International Association of Hydrological Sciences, 1984.

16. P. Morgan; *Rural Water Supply and Sanitation, A Text from Zimbabwe's Blair Research Laboratory*; Macmillan, London, 1990; ISBN 0333485696.

17. H. T. Mann and D. Williamson; *Water Treatment and Sanitation, Simple Methods for Rural Areas*; Intermediate Technology Publications, London, 1982; ISBN 090303123X.

18. T. Jordan Jnr.; *A Handbook of Gravity-Flow Water Systems for Small Communities*; Intermediate Technology Publications, London, 1984; ISBN 0946688508.

19. J. V. Meel and P. Smulders; *Wind Pumping, a Handbook*; World Bank Technical Paper Number 101, Industry and Energy Series; The World Bank, Washington, 1989; ISBN 0821312359.

20. C. Brouwer, K. Prins, M. Heibloem; Irrigation Scheduling; Irrigation Water Management Series, Training Manual No. 4; FAO, Rome, 1989.

21. W. B. Snellen; Irrigation Scheme Operation and Maintenance; Irrigation Water Management, Training Manual No. 10; FAO, Rome, 1996.

22. B. E. van den Bosch, J. Hoevenaars, C. Brouwer, N. Hatcho; Canals; Irrigation Water Management, Training Manual No. 7; FAO, 1992.

23. Community Gardens Using Limited Groundwater Resources; Institute of Hydrology/British Geological Survey Pamphlet, 1995.

24. J. Doorendos and W. O. Pruitt; Guidelines for Predicting Crop Water Requirements; Irrigation and Drainage Paper No. 24; FAO, Rome, 1977.

25. WEDC, 1991; Water, Engineering and Development Centre, Loughborough University, UK; *The Worth of Water*, Technical Briefs on Health, Water, and Sanitation; Intermediate Technology Publications, London, 1991; ISBN 1853390690.

26. S. J. Batchelor and J. S. Goodchild; Treadle Pumps—The Experience of Christian Outreach (NGO) in Cambodia; unpublished paper by Christian Outreach, 1994.

27. WHO, 1993; *Guidelines for Drinking Water Quality*, Volume 1, Recommendations; WHO, Geneva, 1993.

28. Quality Control, World Water, Developing World Bulletin, Issue 1, 1992.

29. T. C. Dougherty and A. W. Hall; Environmental Impact Assessment of Irrigation and Drainage Projects; Irrigation and Drainage Paper No. 53; FAO, Rome, 1995; ISBN 9251037310.

30. W. Rybczynki, C. Polpraset and M. McGarry; *Appropriate Technology for Water Supply and Sanitation*; World Bank, 1982.

31. WHO, 1989: Health Guidelines for the Use of Wastewater in Agriculture and Aquaculture; Technical Report Series No. 778; WHO, Geneva, 1989.

32. FAO, 1995: Design and Optimization of Irrigation Distribution Networks; Irrigation and Drainage Paper No. 44; FAO, Rome, 1995; ISBN 9251026661.

33. D. B. Kraatz; Irrigation Canal Lining; Land and Water Development Series No. 1; FAO, Rome, 1977.

34. A. Harvey with A. Brown, P. Hettiarachi and A. Inversin; *Micro-Hydro Design Manual, A Guide to Small-Scale Water Power Schemes*; Intermediate Technology Publications, London, 1993; ISBN 1853391034.

35. C. Bielenberg and H. Allen; *How to Make and Use the Treadle Irrigation Pump*; Intermediate Technology Publications, London, 1995; ISBN 1853393126.

36. A. Molenaar; *Water Lifting Devices for Irrigation*; FAO, Rome, 1956.

37. W. Roberts and S. Singh; *A Text Book of Punjab Agriculture*; Civil and Military Gazette, Lahore, Pakistan, 1951.

38. J. Collett; Hydro Powered Water Lifting Devices for Irrigation; Proceeding of the FAO/DANIDA Workshop on Water Lifting Devices in Asia and the Near East, Bangkok, December 1979; FAO, Rome, 1981.

39. P. L. Fraenkel; *Food from Windmills*; IT Publications, London, 1976.

40. R. Lambert; *How to Make a Rope-and-Washer Pump*; Intermediate Technology Publications, London, 1990; ISBN 1853390224. *There is a video to accompany this book: How to Make a Rope-and-Washer Pump and Micro-scale Irrigation; IT Publications, 1990; ISBN 1853393568.*

41. S. B. Watt; *Chinese Chain and Washer Pumps*; I T Publications, London, 1977.

42. P. D. Dunn; *Appropriate Technology*; Macmillan, London, 1978.

43. T. D. Jeffrey, T. H. Thomas, A. V. Smith, P. B. Glover and P. D. Fountain; *Hydraulic Ram Pumps, A Guide to Ram Pump Water Supply Systems*; Intermediate Technology Publications, London, 1992; ISBN 1853391727.

44. G. Leech; *Energy and Food Production*; IIED, London, 1975.

45. D. B. Kraatz; Socio-Economic Aspects – Cost Comparison and Selection of Water Lifting Devices; Proceedings of the FAO/DANIDA Workshop on Water Lifting Devices in Asia and the Near East, Bangkok, December 1979; FAO, Rome, 1981.

46. Intermediate Technology Development Group; Water for Rural Communities; *Appropriate Technology Journal*, Vol. 9, No. 1; IT Publications, London, 1983.

47. E. H. Hofkes; Manual Pumping of Water for Community Water Supply and Small-Scale Irrigation; Proceedings of the FAO/DANIDA Workshop on Water Lifting Devices in Asia and the Near East, Bangkok, December 1979; FAO, Rome, 1981.

48. P. Morgan; letter in *Appropriate Technology Journal*, Vol. 9, No 1; IT Publications, London, 1983.

49. S. S. Wilson; Pedalling Foot-Power for Pumps; *World Water*, Liverpool; Nov 1983.

50. H. R. Khan; Study of Manual Irrigation Devices in Bangladesh; Proceedings of the Appropriate Technology in Civil

Engineering Conference; Inst. of Civil Engineers, London, 1980.

51. McJunkin; *Handpumps for Use in Drinking Water Supplies in Developing Countries*; IRC, The Hague, 1977.

52. Klassen; The Rower Pump; Proceedings of the FAO/DANIDA Workshop on Water Lifting Devices in Asia and the Near East, Bangkok, December 1979; FAO, Rome, 1981.

53. G. Barnes; The Development of Manual Irrigation Device for Developing Countries; IRRI (International Rice Research Institute), Philippines, 1985.

54. M. Snell; *Appropriate Water Lifting Technologies in West Africa*; FAO, 2004.

55. D. R. Birch and J. R. Rydzewski; *Energy Options for Low Lift Irrigation Pumps in Developing Countries: The Case of Bangladesh and Egypt*; ILO, Geneva, 1989.

56. A. Pearson; Animal Power: Matching Beast and Burden; *Appropriate Technology Journal*, Vol. 18, No. 3; IT Publications, London, December 1991.

57. O. P. Hood; *Certain Pumps and Water Lifts Used in Irrigation*; US Geological Survey, Washington DC, 1988.

58. W. A. M. Jansen; *Performance Tests of Kerosene Pumpsets*; Wind Energy Unit, Colombo, Sri Lanka, 1979.

59. N. Smith; *Affordable Electricity Installation for Low-income Households in Developing Countries*; IT Consultants (ODA), Rugby, UK, 1996.

60. A. R. Inversin; *New Designs for Rural Electrification*; NRECA, Washington, 1995.

61. P. Fraenkel, R. Barlow, F. Crick, A. Derrick and V. Bokalders; *Windpumps, A Guide for Development Workers*; Intermediate Technology Publications, London and the Stockholm Environment Institute, 1993; ISBN 1853391263.

62. R. Gasch, editor; *Windkraftanlagen*; B.G. Teugner, Stuttgart, 1996; ISBN 3-519-26334-3

63. I. Troen and E. Lundtang Peterson; *European Wind Atlas*; EU/Risø National Laboratory, Roskilde, Denmark, 1989; ISBN 87-550-1482-8.

64. *Climatalogical Tables of Observations in India*; Programme for the Development and Utilisation of Windmills in India, National Aeronautical Laboratory, Bangalore; September 1978.

65. E. Lysen; *Introduction to Wind Energy*; CWD 82-1; Consultancy Services Wind Energy Developing Countries, PO Box 85, Amersfoort, The Netherlands, 1983.

66. N. H. Lipman et al., (Editors); , *Wind Energy for the Eighties*; British Wind Energy Association; Peter Perigrinus, Stevenage, UK and New York, 1982.

67. ECDC-TCDC; *Renewable Sources of Energy, Volume III, Wind Energy*; UN Economic and Social Commission for Asia and the Pacific, Bangkok, 1981.

68. R. Barlow, B. McNelis and A. Derrick; *Solar Pumping, An Introduction and Update on the Technology, Performance, Cost, and Economics*; Intermediate Technology Publications, London and The World Bank, Washington, 1993; ISBN 1853391794 (U.K.) 0821321013 (U.S.).

69. IT Power; *Electricity from Sunlight, Photovoltaic Applications for Developing Countries*; Department for International Development, UK; October 1997.

70. IT Power; Concerted Action for the Testing and Cost Reduction of PV Water Pumping Systems; Final Report for European Commission AVICENNE Programme, Contract AVI-CT94-0004; unpublished report, IT Power, UK; April 1997.

71. Halcrow/IT Power; Small-scale Solar Powered Irrigation Pumping Systems: Phase I Project Report and Technical and Economic Review; World Bank, Washington DC, 1981.

72. A. Inversin: *Micro-Hydropower Sourcebook, A Practical Guide to Design and Implementation in Developing Countries*; NRECA International Foundation, Washington DC, 1986.

73. A. Williams; *Pumps as Turbines: A User's Guide*; Intermediate Technology Publications, London, 1995; ISBN 1853392885.

74. J. H. P. M. Tacke, Delft University of Technology; unpublished draft material for E. H. Hofkes and J. T. Visscher, editors; Renewable Energy Resources for Rural Water Supply; IRC Technical Paper Series No. 23; International Water and Sanitation Centre, IRC, The Hague, 1986; ISBN 9066870079.

75. P. Garman; *Water Current Turbines: A Fieldworker's Guide*; Intermediate Technology Publications, London, 1986; ISBN 0946688273.

326

76. D. O. Hall, F. Rosillo-Calle, R. H. Williams and J. Wood, Biomass for Energy: Supply Prospects; in T. B. Johansson, H. Kelly, A. K. N. Reddy and R. H. Williams, editors; *Renewable Energy, Sources for Fuels and Electricity*; Island Press, Washington D.C., 1993; ISBN 155963 134 4.

77. L. Kristoferson, V. Bokalders, M. Newham; *Renewable Energy Technologies: An Overview*; Intermediate Technology Publications, London, 1991.

78. N. V. Ravindranath and D. O. Hall; *Biomass, Energy, and Environment, A Developing Country Perspective from India*; Oxford University Press, 1995; ISBN 0198564368.

79. L. R. Brown; Food or Fuel, Paper No.35; Worldwatch Institute, Washington DC., 1980.

80. D. E. Earl; *Forest Energy and Economic Development*; Oxford University Press, Oxford, 1975.

81. V. and M-S Damour; *Development of Small-scale Gasifiers for Irrigation in India*; Paris, 1984.

82. N. E. Bassam; *Energy Plant Species, the Use and Impact on Environment and Development*; James and James, London, 1998.

83. T. B. Johansson, H. Kelly, A. K. N. Reddy and R. H. Williams; Renewable Fuels and Electricity for a Growing World Economy; in T. B. Johansson, H. Kelly, A. K. N. Reddy and R. H. Williams, editors; *Renewable Energy, Sources for Fuels and Electricity*; Island Press, Washington D.C., 1993; ISBN 155963 134 4.

84. R. Metzler; Small Lister Type Diesel Engines of Indian Origin, Their Long Term Performance on Plant Oil as Fuel and Ways to Improve their Reliability; unpublished paper by FAKT, Germany; October 1995.

85. A. van Buren, editor; *A Chinese Biogas Manual, Popularising Technology in the Countryside*; Intermediate Technology Publications, London, 1979; ISBN 0903031655.

86. D. Fulford; *Running a Biogas Programme: A Handbook*; Intermediate Technology Publications, London, 1988; ISBN 0946688494.

87. P. J. Meynell; *Methane: Planning a Digester*; Prism Press, Dorchester, 1982.

FURTHER INFORMATION

CADDET: http://www.caddet.co.uk/
Information on a variety of small-scale renewable energy technologies

CANMET: CANMET Energy Diversification Research Laboratory: http://cedrl.mets.nrcan.gc.ca/retscreen
Free RETScreen software for comparing renewable energy technologies

DTU: Development Technology Unit, Warwick University, U.K.
http://www.eng.warwick.ac.uk/dtu/
Information on ram pumps

Institute of Hydrology: http://www.nwl.ac.uk/ih
Hydrology prediction data and software for various areas of the world

IT Power: http://www.itpower.co.uk
Authors' company website: water pumping and renewable energy projects

National Renewable Energy Laboratory (NREL): http://www.nrel.gov/text/nrel.htm
US-based institute with renewable energy expertise in developing countries

One World: http://www.oneworld.org/news/by_theme/index.html
News on water topics

SKAT: Swiss Centre for Development Cooperation in Technology and Management; http://

www.skat.ch/default.htm
Information on SKAT's work on handpumps, on the HTN, and publications

Steam and Engine of Australia: http://www.steamengine.com.au
Historical information on the Humphrey engine

Stirling Technology Company: http://www.stirlingtech.com
This company manufactures and markets small Stirling engines

Sunpower: Sunpower Inc.: http://www.sunpower.com
Information on various types of Stirling engines

SWS: SWS Rower Pumps: http://ds.dial.pipex.com/town/avenue/ve01/rower/index.htm#links
Rower pumps

WaterAid: http//www.oneworld.org/wateraid/index.html
General information on water projects

World Bank: http://www.worldbank.org
Information and publications on water supply and many other development topics

World Meteorological Organisation; http://www.wmo.ch
Weather information, including wind and insolation data

INDEX

329

331